LAW *as* POLITICS

D1564329

LAW as POLITICS

Carl Schmitt's Critique of Liberalism

Edited by David Dyzenhaus

Foreword by Ronald Beiner

DUKE UNIVERSITY PRESS

DURHAM AND LONDON

1998

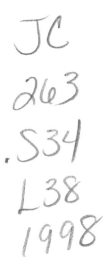

JC
263
.S34
L38
1998

© **1998 DUKE UNIVERSITY PRESS**
All rights reserved | Printed in the United States of
America on acid-free paper ∞ | Typeset in Trump
Mediaeval by Tseng Information Systems, Inc. |
Library of Congress Cataloging-in-Publication Data
appear on the last printed page of this book.

Grateful acknowledgment is made for permis-
sion to reprint the following material in this
volume: | Ernst-Wolfgang Böckenförde, "Der
Begriff des Politischen als Schlüssel zum staats-
rechtlichen Werk Carl Schmitts," in Ernst-Wolfgang
Böckenförde, *Recht; Staat; Freiheit: Studien zur
Rechtsphilosophie, Staatstheorie und Verfassungs-
geschichte.* © Suhrkamp Verlag Frankfurt am Main
1991. | William E. Scheuerman, "Revolutions and
Constitutions: Hannah Arendt's Challenge to Carl
Schmitt." © Rowen & Littlefield Publishers, Inc.,
Lanham, Md., 1998. | Portions of this volume were
previously published in *The Canadian Journal of
Law and Jurisprudence*, vol. 10, no. 1 (1997).

CONTENTS

Foreword

Ronald Beiner

It should come as no surprise that there are radically conflicting conceptions of what it is to practice political philosophy; and the clash between these opposed interpretations of the praxis of theorizing is not only inevitable but also desirable. According to one dominant conception, of which Rawls's *Political Liberalism* is an exemplary instance, we start with an implicit consensus on what we share as members of a liberal political order, and the job of the philosopher is to articulate the basis of this consensus and raise it to theoretical explicitness. According to a different and more radical understanding of political philosophy, this liberal consensus, if such exists, counts for nothing; rather, the philosopher's responsibility is to theorize political order from the ground up, even if it ends up calling into fundamental question the opinions and beliefs that currently sustain social life within a liberal democratic horizon. From this alternative point of view, political philosophy practiced in a Rawlsian mode is a form of theoretical cowardice, perhaps even a betrayal of what properly defines philosophical duty.

There is no question that Carl Schmitt embodies the latter conception of theory in its most uncompromising version. As David Dyzenhaus expresses with beautiful clarity in his introductory chapter, Schmitt raises questions about the ultimate grounding of political and legal order that have dogged modern philosophy and jurisprudence since Hobbes first came to awareness of the obsolescence of pre-modern justifications of political authority. In pursuing this radical inquiry, Schmitt challenges, root-and-branch, all the notions that "we" modern liberals take to be morally authoritative—the meaning of the rule of law, the legitimacy of parliamentary government, the superiority of reason and rational deliberation over sheer will, the reasonableness of political secularity. None of these notions carries any obvious authority for Schmitt; all of them are put to the test.

I don't think anyone can plausibly argue that contemporary liberal democracies are subject to the kind of thoroughgoing crisis of political order that Schmitt encountered in the Weimar Germany of the 1920s and that provoked him, throughout his work, to interrogate liberalism at the level of first principles. On the other hand, neither does it seem that the foundations of liberal politics are so secure, theoretically or politically, that reflection at the level of first principles has been rendered pointless. One can identify both universalistic (philosophical) and particularistic (political) reasons for pursuing the debate with liberalism at the bracing level at which it is pursued by Schmitt. First, as human beings we of course have a universal interest in knowing whether the social order we happen to inhabit actually possesses the kind of normative authority that it claims for itself. The historically established name for pursuit of this human interest is philosophy. Second, as citizens of a liberal regime, we can only vindicate the liberal idea that intellectual openness and freedom of inquiry strengthen rather than subvert a political order by entering into dialogue with those forms of thought that are furthest from the liberal horizon.

If political philosophy involves not only reconfirming the reasonableness of the beliefs to which we are already committed but also challenging those beliefs (Socratically) from a position well outside the boundaries of liberalism, then we can derive immense instruction from the very fine essays that Dyzenhaus has assembled in this volume. Seeing what our liberal world looks like from an illiberal point of view is not only indispensable for intellectual life within a liberal society; it may even do liberal politics some good. As Chantal Mouffe helpfully reminds us at the beginning of her essay, it's no accident that Rawls refers to Schmitt's antiliberalism on the last page of his introduction to the paperback edition of *Political Liberalism*, in the context of restating why the constitutional stability of the liberal polity continues to require liberal political philosophy.

Is a dialogue between Rawls and Schmitt possible? If, as liberals, we know in advance that Rawls must triumph in such a debate, what is the point of pursuing this intellectual contest in the first place? Liberal academics and democratic theorists certainly aren't immersing themselves in the study of Schmitt because they welcome the possibility that he will persuade them to jettison their liberal and democratic commitments.

Rather, they study Schmitt because they know that, philosophically, liberal principles have not (yet) established an unchallengeable claim to normative authority, and because only by engaging in dialogue with a steadfast enemy of liberal dialogue like Schmitt can they vindicate both liberalism and the endless dialogue that is political philosophy.

Acknowledgments

The essays collected here were first published in a special issue of the *Canadian Journal of Law and Jurisprudence.* In putting together that issue, I had considerable help from Heiner Bielefeldt, John P. McCormick, and Bill Scheuerman. My greatest debt though was to Richard Bronaugh, one of the editors of the journal, for his editorial wisdom, patience, and sheer hard work. He also encouraged and assisted in every respect the publication of this book. Publishing with Duke University Press has given me the opportunity to work with another superb editor, Valerie Millholland. Her combination of vision and administrative skills with a tolerance for academic foibles made a complex process seem easy. Finally, I would like to thank Richard Spitz for making the index.

Introduction

Why Carl Schmitt?

David Dyzenhaus

The surge of interest among Anglo-American scholars in Weimar political and legal theory is easily explained. In the developed democracies of the West, the role of the state in public life—indeed, the very future of the state—is in question while in much of the rest of the world new experiments in democracy are taking place under conditions of great instability. The short but vivid experiment in democracy of Weimar attracted the intense attention of a number of brilliant social, legal, and political theorists, many of whom were deeply involved in practical politics. In particular, they worked within that field of German legal and political theory—*Staatslehre*—which is as difficult to translate as its main object of study—the *Rechtsstaat*. "Theory of the state" and "rule of law" are respectively the nearest English equivalents. But they do not go a long way to capture a field devoted to a quest to understand the proper role in public life of the state bound by the rule of law, a field which rejects any strict academic division between legal studies, political, social, and economic theory, and philosophy.

In short, Anglo-American scholars now perceive the need to develop a *Staatslehre*. And so increasing interest in the Weimar practitioners of *Staatslehre* is no surprise.

Among these practitioners, Carl Schmitt gets the most attention and this collection of essays is part of that trend, one which is at the least perplexing, even disturbing when one considers the bare facts of Schmitt's life and theory.

Schmitt was born in 1888 into a Catholic family and, after school, followed a conventional German academic path in law. By the late 1920s he had established a considerable reputation as an innovative scholar of law and political culture, a reputation sealed by the publication in 1928 of a monumental work on the Weimar Constitution and on constitutional theory in general—his *Verfassungslehre*.[1]

One can debate the question of continuities and discontinuities in his work.[2] But it is absolutely clear that by the late 1920s Schmitt had allied himself with the most conservative elements of the German political mainstream and was providing the theoretical basis for a highly centralized dictatorial solution to the problems of Weimar. He argued that the problems of a liberal pluralistic society could be solved only by the elimination of pluralism, including its main political institution—parliamentary democracy.[3]

In place of parliamentary democracy, Schmitt proposed a "truly" democratic leader, one who wins the acclaim of the people through his articulation of a unifying vision of the substantive homogeneity of the people. That leader will create a normal situation out of the chaos of pluralism by making a genuinely political, sovereign decision. Such a decision must distinguish clearly between friend and enemy; it attempts to establish a society composed only of friends, of those who fit the criteria for substantive homogeneity. One can, it seems, know nothing in advance about such criteria other than the fact that the content of the political ideology they prescribe will be antithetical to liberalism. The ultimate test for success of the decision is simply the acclaim of "the people"—*das Volk*.

Schmitt's alliance with German conservatives did not mean support for the most extreme right-wing figures, most notably Hitler. Indeed Schmitt, like the conservative aristocratic politicians whom he advised in the early 1930s, despised the plebeian Nazis. But once the Nazis had seized power, Schmitt quickly joined the Nazi Party and devoted his considerable energies to becoming their official legal theorist, just as Martin Heidegger sought to become the official Nazi philosopher.

Both were ultimately unsuccessful, one suspects not because they became disillusioned with Nazi policies, but because they were both too intellectual for the Nazis, too academic to express properly the visceral basis of Nazi ideology. Once fallen from official favor, both retreated to their academic jobs until the end of the war.

After the war neither would express any regret about their role in supporting Hitler during the period when he consolidated his power, nor any concerns about Nazi atrocities. Schmitt in particular was given to self-pitying denials of any complicity in Nazism, claiming that he had always been a mere academic, involved in the objective legal analysis of his time. Despite the fact that, again like Heidegger, he was not permitted to teach after the war, Schmitt exerted an immense influence on the development of public law and political theory in Germany, mainly through his writings but also through private seminars in which he played the role of *éminence grise*. He died in 1985.

Why then bother with Schmitt, especially if, as is the case with many of those currently engaged with his work, one is deeply committed to the role of the democratic state in public life, including its role in preserving the rights and freedoms for which liberals have traditionally fought? For it is not obvious (*pace* Ernst-Wolfgang Böckenförde) that one can proceed by focusing on the "work" rather than the "person" of Carl Schmitt.[4] If something like the summary version of Schmitt's theory given here is correct, it becomes very difficult to disentangle the trajectory of Schmitt's involvement with the Nazis from his work.

Take for example one of his most notorious essays from the time of his involvement, "Der Führer schutzt das Recht" ("The Führer Guards the Law").[5] In this essay, Schmitt sang praise for Hitler's retrospective validation of the political murders of 1933—where the victims included not only Hitler's rivals within the Nazi leadership but also some of the German conservatives with whom Schmitt was intimate. His praise was based on the fact that Hitler had done everything that Schmitt positively required of a leader. Hitler had made the distinction between friend and enemy, as proved in the murders, had established himself decisively as the supreme source and judge of all right and law, and had done away with the liberal and parliamentary "fictions" of Weimar. Most important of all, he had through his personal representation of the German people as a substantive homogeneous unit, brought about the democratic identity which Schmitt prized above all else. Moreover, there could be no doubt about the popular acclaim, the resounding "yes" that greeted Hitler's vision—he had brought something into being, made a presence of an absence. Schmitt, in short, was committed by his own work to welcoming Hitler's seizure of power, whatever his personal misgivings about Nazi ideology.

I, like those who have contributed to this volume, think that the contemporary interest in Schmitt is fully justified (though I will later suggest that other Weimar legal theorists merit equal attention). In the following section,[6] I will support this contention by showing how the concerns of legal theory are starting to merge with those of a political theory in a way which shows the need for an English *Staatslehre*, one which will have as one of its tasks a response to Schmitt.

States of Emergency

Contemporary debate in legal philosophy is molded by Ronald Dworkin's critique of Anglo-American legal positivism. In particular, Dworkin's work challenges H. L. A. Hart's positivist model of law, a model which divides law into a "core" of positive law—of determinate settled law—and a "penumbra" where the law is uncertain or indeterminate. Hart claimed that in the core the question of what law is is determined as a matter of fact, that is, without resort to moral argument. Questions of law that occur in the penumbra, in contrast, can be settled only by judges making choices which are ultimately determined not by law but by the values which judges happen to hold.[7]

Dworkin's first challenge to Hart advanced the view that in penumbral or "hard" cases judges are under a legal duty to decide the case by resort to principles already immanent in the law. Dworkin's own theory of interpretation holds both that there is in principle one right answer in all such cases and that this answer is fully determined by law.[8] Hart sought to deal with this challenge by claiming that the choice between principles could not be settled by the law but only by a legally unconstrained act of judicial choice or discretion. Put differently, he claimed that the more Dworkin showed that the adjudication of hard cases involves a decision based on legal principles, the better the evidence for the positivist thesis about judicial discretion.[9]

Dworkin's second and later challenge was to Hart's partly implicit claim that a positivist view of legal order as consisting of determinate rules is not threatened by the penumbra of uncertainty. There is supposed to be no threat because the core is in fact much larger than the penumbra and this provides the certainty that makes legal order possible. Dworkin argued there is no core in the positivist sense. What appears to be the core is the product of interpretation in just the way that decisions in the penumbra are. The core is merely an area of provisional agreement as to interpretation.[10]

Dworkin's second challenge makes the first more radical. If there is no clear boundary between core and penumbra so that the core does not so much diminish in size as disappear, then Hart's response to Dworkin's first challenge implodes legal positivism. For if, as Hart indicates, a decision on the basis of an interpretation of legal principles is always ultimately unconstrained by law, and if all questions about what law is are interpretative in this sense, then there is no such thing as law. More precisely, there is no such thing as law in the positivist sense of a set of rules whose content can be determined without resort to moral argument. The problem which positivists acknowledged as occurring only at the margins of legal order now appears throughout.

This conclusion is welcome to those legal and political theorists who argue that it is illusory to believe that law could constrain power. With positivists, such philosophers argue that when the law is indeterminate, legal meaning is always determined by power. But since they also assert that the law is never determinate—all there is is the penumbra—law can never, in their view, operate as a constraint on power itself. Their thesis is the nihilist one that what passes for the content of the law is merely the product of communities powerful enough to have their preferred values imposed as the law.[11]

At its starkest, the choice that confronts legal philosophy today is between two conceptions of legal order and the rule of law. The Dworkinian conception seeks a grounding in a theory about the inherent legitimacy of the law. The positivist conception says that legal order is just the legal instrument of the powerful so that any theory of the inherent legitimacy of the law invites abuse by immoral rulers. It invites, as Jeremy Bentham put it, "obsequious quietism."[12]

Both these conceptions of the rule of law can be seen as a response to a problem about political order whose classical formulation is in Hobbes's *Leviathan*.[13] Hobbes asks a question prompted by the political condition of civil war which prompted his thoughts, a war caused in part by the refusal of one political faction to accept that the king's view of appropriate legal order was right simply because it was the king's view. Hobbes's question is, how is order possible in the first place, given the disintegration of the traditional justifications offered for the legitimacy of supreme power?

Hobbes's question transcends the political turmoil brought about by civil war in England. It addresses what one might think of as the general state of emergency in the political and legal theory of Europe at that time, a time during which the old order is in the process of disintegrating and it is not clear on what basis a new order is to be established. The best-known chapter of *Leviathan*, chapter 13, in which Hobbes describes the perils of the "state of nature," contains his declaration of a state of emergency; and the rest of that work prescribes the measures necessary to preserve order.

Hobbes's answer to the question is that we require a rational justification for political and legal order, one that appeals to reason alone. He argues that reason leads us to accept a positivist theory of law which requires virtually unconditional obedience to a legally unconstrained sovereign. Hobbes's appeal is to the reason of individuals, who, he says, have equal reasoning powers and whose judgments as to what reason requires are each just as good as any other. But this very equality means, he insists, that in general one cannot expect consensus between individuals on any matter where all they have to rely on is their reason. Rather one should expect endless and corrosive dispute.

He makes, however, one important exception to his claim. Individuals can be taken to agree that peace and order, whatever its nature, are preferable to chaos. Thus, each individual should see that it is rational to submit to the judgment of the sovereign, whatever the content of that judgment. Further, the sovereign should express his judgment through a system of positive law, since the determinate content of positive law preempts disputes arising as to what law is, and so preserves the peace. Once order is established in this way, individuals can enjoy their liberty, which is the area of freedom given to them by the silence of the law.

Thus Hobbes is rightly regarded as having provided more than the classical articulation of the problem of order in modernity. As well as founding legal positivism, he also founded the liberal political doctrine which puts the individual at the center of political thought.

But there is a clear tension between his individualism and his political absolutism. The sovereign is legally and politically unconstrained, answerable for his actions not to his subjects but only to Hobbes's laws of nature. These laws are to provide the basis both for the sovereign's judgments and for the legal subjects' obligation of obedience to the sovereign. But the content of these natural laws has to be determined for legal subjects by the sovereign. There is, in short, no place in Hobbes's conception of legal and political order for mechanisms on which legal subjects can rely to enforce the rights which liberals traditionally suppose are inviolable. Indeed, Hobbes's argument for excluding individual rights against the state is that the laws of nature or of morality are always already included or immanent in the positive law enacted by the sovereign.[14]

Since the tension arises because the sovereign can inject whatever content he supposes to be right into the positive law, it can only become more marked once parliamentary democracy becomes the default view of appropriate political order. For the main justification for parliamentary democracy is that it marks the transition in status from subject to citizen. The primacy of individual reason is given institutional expression in a political system which ensures for each individual a role in making the laws to which all are subject. That role is taken to justify requiring obedience to the law. But then individuals are required to submit to the law even when a majority which controls the legislature enacts laws highly oppressive to those particular individuals.

Since contemporary exponents of legal positivism are liberals, their attempt to resolve the tension is to deny that the law is ever in and of itself legitimate. Legitimate law is merely that law which happens to have the right moral content, where the standards of rightness are the standards of liberal morality. Thus their position is the converse of that held by Hobbes, the founder of their doctrine about the nature of law. In their view, the idea of positive law is no longer the solution to the problem of how order is in the first place possible. They hold on to the idea of positive law because that idea seems to them to best explain the nature of law.

Hence Dworkin and contemporary legal positivists share one pivotal assumption: they assume that if the law is to be legitimate, it must meet the standards set by liberalism. And both assume that this liberal morality hovers above the positive law, a by and large universal and eternal set of standards that provide us with the criteria for evaluating particular and changing positive laws. Their conceptions differ only in that Dworkin claims that liberal standards are also already immanent in the law, waiting to be brought to the surface in principled justifications for judicial decisions.

The positivist rejoinder that the immanence of liberal standards depends on contingent facts about the history of particular legal systems may seem realistic in contrast to Dworkin's romantic claim that the positive law always contains at least some core of liberal morality. Dworkin's claim appears as liberal legerdemain to those who put forward the nihilist thesis that what passes for determinate law is just the impositions by the powerful of their preferences. But, while the nihilists join positivists in criticizing Dworkin on this score, they accept that Dworkin's critique of the positivist model of law—the model of core and penumbra—has not been successfully answered.

Dworkin's and the positivists' conceptions of legal order can be seen as representing two paths of development from Hobbes, each of which makes up one pole of the tension in Hobbes's formulation of the problem of order. Against Hobbes, Dworkin claims that there is more to law than positive law, but with Hobbes he claims that sound moral standards are already immanent in the positive law. Against Hobbes, contemporary positivists claim that there is no moral obligation to obey positive law, but with Hobbes they claim that law properly so called is positive law. Nihilists set off one pole against the other to support a thesis that order is just a veneer which attempts to hide general indeterminacy and the struggle of the powerful to control the law.

Well before this position had arisen for Anglo-American legal and political theory, Max Weber had not only set out its basic features, but offered an explanation as to what made it so problematic.[15] In Weber's view, the problem of legal and political order is not stated in Hobbes's question of how order is in the first place possible. Nor can it be dealt with as liberals suggest, whether their suggestions are on positivist or antipositivist lines. Rather the problem is that the order that is possible in modernity cannot resolve the individual's predicament.

In modern capitalism, according to Weber, individuals find themselves in a "disenchanted" world, one stripped of the meaning and significance which unquestioned traditions once imparted. Individuals find themselves forced to create meaning and significance—their "calling" for themselves—but they have no ultimate criteria to judge what is meaningful or significant. Moreover, they undertake this task in the modern economic order, an order which Weber likens to an "iron cage."[16]

We are in the cage not merely because we are compelled to participate in the economic order. The economic order is cagelike because it holds out a promise which it subverts. The economic order is a utilitarian system devoid of any intrinsic meaning, one meant to be instrumental to individual wants. Its promise is then the satisfaction of individual wants. But its logic of instrumental rationality subverts the traditions which are the only solid bases of such wants. And, given facts about economic power, most individuals find themselves unable even to satisfy the wants they happen to have.

Positive law is the most rational way of ordering society under these conditions—it provides the determinate framework of rules which can make life at least predictable. But the rationality of law, like the rationality of the economic order, is purely instrumental. Law has no inherent worth or legitimacy but it must be taken for legitimate by individuals, because there are no ultimate criteria to tell us what legitimacy is.

On Weber's account, then, liberal individualism is a cause of the individual's predicament and not a part of its solution. The liberal positivist claim that law has no inherent value but must be evaluated by the standards of a morality which gives pride of place to the individual can only deepen the sense of frustration of those trapped in the cage.

The only alternatives Weber can see are either an attempt to revive the ideas and ideals that existed before the world was disenchanted or for "entirely new prophets" to arise. Writing before World War I, he said that either would amount to an attempt to revive an idea of duty that "prowls about in our lives like the ghost of dead religious beliefs."[17]

At that time, Weber regarded such a revival as wholly irrational. It involved an appeal to the charismatic form of authority—authority in virtue of special physical or spiritual gifts of the person who claimed authority.[18] However, in the last three years of his life, years which coincided with the birth of the Weimar Republic in a Germany devastated and disillusioned by defeat, he came to believe such an appeal necessary. Without a leader who could provide some vision to inspire a large political following, there would be, he thought, no legitimacy at all to an attempt to reconstruct German society. What was needed was a balance between two ethics—the ethic of responsibility, which takes seriously the consequences of any proposed course of action for the welfare of those who will be subject to it, and the ethic of conviction or of the ultimate values which should guide action.[19]

Correspondingly, he argued that in a modern democratic state the charismatic leader will find his charisma rationalized in that he must seek reelection at some point, and thus become accountable to the electorate. And he pointed out that such a leader would have to stabilize his rule through the mechanisms of a legal order.[20]

Nevertheless, for Weber there are no criteria for success beyond success itself. Although he was himself a liberal,[21] he held that once the people acclaim the leader, his authority is established, no matter the content of the vision which wins their acclaim. And the people's role in democracy, as Weber understood it, is and should be limited to acclaim. Since the essence of politics is conflict, and since the "masses" are capable of acting only in an emotional and dangerous fashion, their role is to be confined to being passive objects rather than political actors.[22]

Weber's death in 1920, a year after he delivered the famous lecture in which he sketched his two ethics, meant that he never developed a proper account of either, let alone of how they might supplement each other as he recommended. But there is every reason to suppose that he took the constitutional structure he argued for in the debates about Germany's constitutional future as the embodiment of both the ethics and the mechanism whereby they might work together. For Weber played an influential role in getting the idea accepted that the parliamentary democracy that was to replace Germany's monarchy should be counter-balanced by a president who would possess the charismatic authority evidenced in his ability to win a popular plebiscitary election.[23]

Moreover, in Weber's plan the president was to be no mere figurehead or symbol for the unity of the German people. Weber argued both in the press and as a member of the constitutional committee that produced the draft of the Weimar Constitution that the president should have the executive powers of a substitute monarch. He should thus have the power to initiate legislation by an appeal over the head of the legislature to the people, the power to appoint the cabinet, power to dissolve parliament, and power to govern alone in a time of crisis, especially when no party could command a parliamentary majority.

These powers would enable the president to lead Germany in accordance with his political vision, a course justified by the legitimacy he enjoyed. His ethic of conviction, expressed in his charismatic vision, would be balanced by his responsibility to parliament—his responsibility to act in accordance with the laws enacted by the legislature. Insofar as he required parliamentary cooperation in order to get his way, he was thus bound by an ethic of responsibility.

As Wolfgang Mommsen has pointed out, Weber in fact saw the relationship between president and parliament as not so much one of counterbalances, but as one in which the president had the upper hand. Parliament's major purpose was not as part of a system of constitutional guarantees on presidential power, but "to perpetually remind him of his responsibilities and to overthrow him if and *when* he fails."[24] But it is difficult to see how Weber thought the relationship could be maintained, at least under conditions of severe political conflict.

The text of the Weimar Constitution modified Weber's proposals by seeking to give primacy to parliament in the relationship. But the powers the president enjoyed, in particular the powers to dissolve parliament, to appoint the cabinet, and to declare a state of emergency, were eventually exploited to subvert and then destroy altogether the place of parliament.

Schmitt and Hans Kelsen, the distinguished Austrian legal positivist, may each be understood as centering their theories of law on one of Weber's two ethics. Kelsen developed a theory of law as a system of positive law which exhaustively contains the political power of the state. His "Pure Theory" of law is one which seeks to show how legal order is a rational order, but only in the sense that it can be conceived without presupposing any substantive ethical or political position.[25] He thus expresses the idea of an ethics of responsibility that somehow floats free from any substantive political aims.

Despite the fact that Kelsen seems committed at times to establishing the *Rechtsstaat* as the legal order of parliamentary democracy, the value neutrality of his Pure Theory always requires him to retreat just before his argument makes a substantive connection between law and political values.[26] His retreat is the result of an avowed relativism about political values, a stance which precludes him from bridging his conceptions of political and legal order by dint of a fully argued commitment to a substantive political theory. Democracy is to be preferred only because it is the expression of a political relativism, itself the product of an epistemological relativism. The result is that in his legal theory the constraints of legality—of the *Rechtsstaat*—become purely formal. Any decision by an official of a legal order is valid as long as that official was authorized to make a decision.

Schmitt, by contrast, argues for substance over form, for an ethic of pure conviction and executive will, unconstrained by any rules. The person who expresses the conviction will indeed be a "new prophet": one who does not so much seek to revive the ghosts of dead religious ideas, but rather to state a new vision that can harness the impulses which cause such ghosts to haunt us. That person will make politics victorious over legalistic rationality. In particular, he will use the technological forces that Weber thought largely constructed the bars of the cage to shatter the cage and construct an idea of the *Volk*, "the people," which can impart meaning to the lives of individuals. And, according to Schmitt, the idea of the *Volk* has substance only when it is understood to refer to an utterly homogeneous group.

In putting forward these ideas, Schmitt joined a larger group of German intellectuals who have aptly been called "reactionary modernists."[27] For them, the loss of the German monarchy introduced the kind of state of emergency into German society that Hobbes had responded to in his day. With Hobbes, they thought that traditional modes of legitimacy could not be revived to deal with the emergency. Unlike Hobbes, they could look back to other centuries in an attempt to find an alternative in a rational grounding for political power. With Weber, they thought that this was a failed attempt. Rationality had created the iron cage. Moreover, they thought that parliamentary democracy was just a cover under which interest groups could capture the state and prey on its subjects. Parliamentary democracy had therefore to be destroyed if the people were to break out of the cage. What was needed was a dictator—a strong man who could rally the people by appeal to the irrational. But the reactionary revolution which would ensue would not be a reaction against all of modernity precisely because it would make use of modern technology.

Schmitt played a special role in a conservative group who wrote while Germany's skies darkened in the late 1920s and early 1930s. While he and his fellow reactionaries constructed hymns to the irrational, they were not able to specify its content. Indeed, that content could not be argued for: the irrational is both beyond and hostile to (rational) argument. Content is revealed by the person with the ability to do so and his ability is gauged by his success. Charismatic authority, to return to Weber's term, is in its nature recognized, not specified by advance criteria.

Schmitt's special role in this group was to argue for the potential within the law to overthrow the bonds of liberal democratic legality. This potential he found in the state-of-emergency provision of the Weimar Constitution—Article 48—read in conjunction with the other executive powers granted to the office of a plebiscitary president, one who acted on commission of the people. On Schmitt's account, the Weimar Constitution is just another liberal attempt to tame and constrain the real irrational sources of political power in chains of legality, but it cannot help but recognize those sources and thus prepares the way for its own destruction. The state-of-emergency provision, in other words, is the constitutional recognition of the general state of emergency in society to which the Weimar Constitution is a necessarily botched and contradictory response.

The situation of Weimar is, of course, much more dramatic than the political situation of England and North America after World War II in which the debates between Hart and Dworkin take place. Nevertheless, there are distinct resonances, once one sees that Hart's penumbra of uncertainty is a kind of mini state of emergency for a positivist theory of law.

It is a state of emergency because, by positivist stipulation, it is not resolvable by law. But it is mini because it is containable: order can be secured as long as the core of law is large enough. But, as we have seen, if the boundary between core and penumbra cannot be sharply drawn, the core seems to disappear; and then for positivists the state of emergency becomes uncontainable and pervasive. Dworkin's principled solution may then seem no solution at all, if, as seems to be the case, there is little consensus as to the principles and their content.

There is no simple way to map the contemporary Anglo-American debate onto one which took place in Germany some sixty years ago. For instance, contemporary positivists will rightly point out that they claim that a positivist account of law is one that denies the legitimacy of law. However, there are strong indications that the debates in contemporary Anglo-American legal theory are fast becoming much more like the debates of Weimar as an essential but hitherto implicit presupposition of contemporary legal positivism and of liberalism comes into view.

This is the presupposition that the problem of how order is in the first place possible has largely been solved. It is this presupposition that makes possible the confidence with which contemporary positivists prescribe that legal subjects should continually question the moral soundness of the law. While the program of contemporary positivism was laid out by Hart in full awareness of the horrors of World War II, he could have that confidence because it seemed that the countries that had largely solved the problem of order—the liberal democracies of the West—had triumphed over those which had failed.

That the presupposition is now both in full view and under attack is due to a new crisis which throws into question the legitimacy of the political and legal orders of the West. On one level, that crisis is one of theory. Debates between communitarians, feminists, democrats, and liberals, which have been the stuff of recent political philosophy, have now become commonplace in legal theory. As a result, legal theory is obliged to respond to radical questions about the legitimacy of law and the nature of legal order.

But as one would expect, the crisis of theory is a manifestation of a crisis in practice. On the one hand, there are the internal challenges to political and legal order by groups that feel both oppressed and unable to satisfy their wants within the constraints of existing order. On the other hand, there is the abyss of civil war into which the West has been forced to look by recent events in Eastern Europe, the former Soviet Union, the Balkans, Africa, and elsewhere.

As I have suggested, this is a crisis for liberalism as well as for legal theory. Writing in 1995, John Rawls, this century's most prominent liberal philosopher, has expressed his "great" puzzlement at the fact that only recently have he and other liberals developed a doctrine of *political liberalism*.[28] But surely liberalism has had to become political because it can no longer be assumed to be the basis of a general political consensus even in the West.

Rawls's understanding of what it takes to be political, however, has much in common with Dworkin's legal theory. Rawls seems to believe that there are values immanent in the political order of the West which merely have to be brought to the surface in order to create the political stability of an "overlapping consensus" about the fundamentals of political order.[29] But the claim of immanence which makes Dworkin's liberal legal theory and Rawls's liberal political philosophy into mirror images must make Rawls vulnerable to the nihilist critique of Dworkin's legal theory. That is, Rawls is attempting to solve the problems of politics merely by stipulating what the fundamental political values are. As I will now show, this turn in political and legal theory neatly illustrates the power of Schmitt's critique of liberalism.

Schmitt and Liberalism

Schmitt presents liberalism as a very supple doctrine. He does not, for example, take it to be committed essentially either to global neutrality between ideologies or to a position that attempts to find some substantive basis for contesting ideologies that assert a global superiority for themselves. He does not claim that liberalism is either more naturally aligned with a positivist view about the nature of law or with a view that claims there is a higher law beyond the positive law to which the positive law is somehow subject. He does not claim that liberalism either presupposes its own truth or makes no claim to truth. And he does not claim that liberalism is either political or antipolitical or apolitical. Rather, what is distinctive about his position is its thesis that liberalism is doomed to shuttle back and forth between these various alternatives.

Further, that liberalism is doomed to this shuttle does not mean for Schmitt that liberalism is doomed. At times, he seems fearful that liberalism will establish itself universally. In part this fear seems to rest on the fact that liberalism quite successfully conceals its politics, which is the politics of getting rid of politics. Liberalism's stance of neutrality, far from being neutral between different conceptions of the good, would undermine all those in conflict with it, thus bringing about its own kind of homogeneity—the homogeneity of a society composed entirely of the market-oriented egoistic and hedonistic human beings—the liberal individuals. However, he predicted that the stance of neutrality would make the liberal state inherently weak and open to conquest because neutrality is a negative value, one which restrains the state. Liberalism is thus incapable of invigorating a conception of the public sphere which can attract the loyalty required to provide a stable basis for a political and legal order.

Under the direction of John Rawls, liberalism today seems driven by the fear that to claim truth for one's position is to invite a clash of truth claims, which can only breed dissent and conflict. Hence liberalism, in seeking to set out the values of the domain of the political, must claim only that these are the values to which it is reasonable to assent. These "freestanding" values together make up an "overlapping consensus" about the basics of political and legal order.[30]

For Rawls, what these values stand free of is particular comprehensive positions or individual conceptions of the good life. While such positions perforce claim truth for themselves if they enter the space of public reason or constitutional discourse, the values which constitute that space claim only reasonableness. But the claim to reasonableness is far from modest. It operates to exclude the truth claims of comprehensive positions from the public and requires them to contest each other only within the sphere which Rawls calls the "social."[31]

Rawls recognizes the effects of relegating comprehensive positions to the sphere of the social. Illiberal groups will find it hard to maintain themselves since their comprehensive positions are perforce undermined by the public culture of political liberalism.[32] And Rawls is clear that if such groups try to gain control over politics they should be "contained."[33] Indeed, he says that in an emergency situation, one in which it looks like containment is not working, political liberalism might have to drop its claim to mere reasonableness and assert its truth in a conflict over political fundamentals.[34] Rawls thus seems to vacillate between a curious "epistemic abstinence" about fundamental political values and a deep practical and epistemological commitment to them.[35]

I suggest that there is more than a passing resemblance between this vacillation and Kelsen's refusal to bridge his conceptions of political and legal order by dint of a fully argued commitment to a substantive political theory. The claim to reasonableness of Rawls's political liberalism and the claim to purity of Kelsen's legal theory aspire to a neutrality that will not alienate otherwise fundamentally divided groups. They both wish to preserve democratic politics by not insisting on the rightness of a set of values. But their epistemic abstinence creates a tension with their commitment to democratic politics.

Indeed, I suggest that Rawls and Kelsen move toward the opposing points of the tension within the liberal idea of the rule of law which Schmitt wishes to highlight. This is the tension existing between a neutrality so neutral that anything goes and a neutrality which is a sham because in effect it privileges a partial liberal understanding of the good.

In Kelsen's positivist conception, laws with any content at all can fit the criteria for the validity of law. Unlike Kelsen, Rawls wishes to privilege certain values as the values of politics. He thus proposes criteria of validity which have more (liberal) substance to them. But since, like Kelsen, he wants truth claims to be checked at the door of politics, he remains evasive about their status in a way which invites the charge of a sham neutrality.

The tension in the liberal conception of the rule of law can be reduced in two different ways. First, Rawls could give up on the justificatory project altogether. But that would take him along the Kelsenian path, where the danger lies not in that it is paved exclusively for either saints or sinners, but in that it cannot discriminate between the two. That is, the tension is reduced at the theoretical level but in a way which leads to the principled defenselessness of liberalism. For the tension is displaced onto a free-for-all of politics, where politics is conceived as a kind of normative vacuum, a space contested by groups making distinctions between friend and enemy, on whatever lines they care. Second, Rawls might develop a full justification for the values of the "political." But that justification would have difficulty avoiding what Rawls wants to avoid—the privileging of any particular views of the good life.

Evaluating Schmitt

Many of the essays in this book fall into a group which in one way or another responds to Schmitt's claim that a vigorous democracy requires a vigorous public sphere, one which provides a positive set of values for citizens while preserving the rights and liberties of the individual.[36] A more or less implicit theme of some of these essays is that liberalism is often conceived in theory and in practice too negatively, as a neutralist doctrine restraining the state. Others suggest that a liberal democracy can successfully internalize Schmitt's friend/enemy distinction by learning to live with the fact of political conflict over fundamentals, as long as some common basis is recognized by the plurality of political groups.

A second group concentrates more on Schmitt's legal theory, on his diagnosis of the problems of legal indeterminacy in liberal democracies, on his sensitivity to different modes of constitutionalism, and on his account of the need for a viable legal order to be able to respond appropriately to political instability.[37]

This second group is distinguished from the first only in that political theory recedes somewhat to bring legal problems to the foreground, just as in the first group political theory is more to the fore with law somewhat in the background. But the fragility of this distinction testifies to the importance of Schmitt's insistence on the political nature of law, even (perhaps especially) when legal theorists claim for themselves the garb of neutrality or value freedom. Put differently, what unites both groups is the sense of a need to work out the politics of a commitment to legalism, of a society's decision to be a *Rechtsstaat.*

In my view, the lesson to be learned from this common enterprise is that Schmitt accurately identified some difficulties liberalism encounters in dealing with important aspects of contemporary society—the idea of a public sphere, constitutionalism and democracy, pluralism, and political conflict over fundamentals. However, the problems that many of the contributors find about Schmitt, in particular his inability to provide alternatives, testifies to the paucity of his own positive thought, even, as I have suggested, to inherent dangers. It is for this last reason that I hope that the interest in Schmitt will broaden to include other Weimar legal theorists, whose positive programs might provide more clues about the solutions to the kinds of problems which make Weimar so interesting to us.[38]

Notes

1 Carl Schmitt, *Verfassungslehre* (Berlin: Duncker & Humblot, 1989).
2 See, for example, John P. McCormick's essay in this volume.
3 In this volume, Dominique Leydet and Chantal Mouffe focus on Schmitt's discussion of pluralism.
4 See Böckenförde's "Concept of the Political" in this volume.
5 Reprinted in Schmitt, *Positionen und Begriffe im Kampf mit Weimar-Genf-Versailles 1929-1939* (Berlin: Duncker & Humblot, 1988), 199-203.
6 This section is adapted from chapter 1 of my *Legality and Legitimacy: Carl Schmitt, Hans Kelsen and Hermann Heller in Weimar* (Oxford: Clarendon Press, 1997).
7 H. L. A. Hart, "Positivism and the Separation of Law and Morals," in H. L. A. Hart, *Essays in Jurisprudence and Philosophy* (Oxford: Clarendon Press, 1961), 62-72.
8 Ronald Dworkin, *Taking Rights Seriously* (London: Duckworth, 1978 [new printing]).
9 Hart, *Essays in Jurisprudence and Philosophy,* 7.

10 Ronald Dworkin, *Law's Empire* (London: Fontana, 1986).

11 The strongest version of this position is to be found in Stanley Fish, *Is There a Text in this Class: The Authority of Interpretative Communities* (Cambridge, Mass.: Harvard University Press, 1980).

12 Jeremy Bentham, *A Fragment on Government* (Cambridge: Cambridge University Press, 1988), 111.

13 Thomas Hobbes, *Leviathan*, C. B. Macpherson, ed. (London: Penguin, 1985).

14 Ibid., chap. 26, 314.

15 See Max Weber, *Economy and Society*, vol. 1, Guenther Roth and Claus Wittich, eds. (Berkeley: University of California Press, 1978), 37. See David Beetham, *Max Weber and the Theory of Modern Politics* (Cambridge: Polity Press, 1985), 265. In the account of the problems which follow from this formulation, I rely heavily on Beetham, ibid., 264–69, as well as Beetham, *The Legitimation of Power* (Atlantic Highlands, N.J.: Humanities Press, 1991), chap. 1. For a particularly rich account of Weber, see David Sciulli, *Theory of Social Constitutionalism: Foundations of a Non-Marxist Critical Theory* (Cambridge: Cambridge University Press, 1992).

16 Max Weber, *The Protestant Ethic and the Spirit of Capitalism*, trans. Talcott Parsons, intro. Anthony Giddens (London: Unwin Hyman, 1989), esp. 181–83.

17 Ibid., 181.

18 See Weber, *Economy and Society*, vol. 1, 241–45, 266–71, and vol. 2, 1127–30.

19 See Weber's lecture "Politics as a Vocation," in H. H. Gerth and C. Wright Mills, *From Max Weber: Essays in Sociology* (London: Kegan Paul, 1947), 77.

20 Weber, *Economy and Society*, vol. 1, 266–71.

21 For an exploration of Weber's liberalism, see David Beetham, "Weber and the Liberal Tradition," in Asher Horowitz and Terry Maley, eds., *The Barbarism of Reason: Max Weber and the Twilight of Enlightenment* (Toronto: University of Toronto Press, 1994), 99.

22 See, for example, "Parlament und Regierung im neugeordneten Deutschland," in Max Weber, *Gesammelte Politische Schriften*, ed. Johannes Winckelmann (Tübingen: J. C. B. Mohr [Paul Siebeck], 1958), 306, 382–406. For discussion, see Beetham, *Max Weber and the Theory of Modern Politics*, chap. 4, and 264–69, at 267.

23 See Wolfgang J. Mommsen, *Max Weber and German Politics: 1890-1920*, trans. Michael S. Steinberg (Chicago: University of Chicago Press, 1990), chap. 9.

24 Mommsen, *Max Weber and German Politics: 1890-1920*, 353, his emphasis. Among Weber scholars, opinion is divided as to just how Weber envisioned the structure of balance between charismatic executive authority and formally rational legal order. Compare Mommsen with Beetham, *Max Weber and the Theory of Modern Politics*. Mommsen's view that Weber intended that charismatic authority should trump legal authority is somewhat tem-

pered in his essay, "The Antinomian Structure of Max Weber's Political Thought," *Current Perspectives in Social Theory* 4 (1983): 289. For a discussion of this issue, which takes as its starting point Weber's attempt to carve out the sphere of the political from the subjectivism of modern culture, see Lawrence A. Scaff, *Fleeing the Iron Cage: Culture, Politics, and Modernity in the Thought of Max Weber* (Berkeley: University of California Press, 1989), chap. 5.

25 See esp. Hans Kelsen, *Introduction to the Problems of Legal Theory*, trans. Bonnie Litchewski Paulson and Stanley Paulson (Oxford: Clarendon Press, 1992, first pub. 1934 as *Reine Rechtslehre: Einleitung in der rechtswissenschaftliche Problematic*).

26 See esp. Hans Kelsen, *Vom Wesen und Wert der Demokratie* (Aalen: Scientia Verlag, 1981).

27 Jeffrey Herf, *Reactionary Modernism: Technology, Culture, and Politics in Weimar and the Third Reich* (New York: Cambridge University Press, 1984). Herf's account includes besides Schmitt, Oswald Spengler, Ernst Jünger, Martin Heidegger, Hans Freyer, and Werner Sombart. For an illuminating account of such issues in regard to Schmitt, see John P. McCormick, *Carl Schmitt's Critique of Liberalism: Against Politics as Technology* (New York: Cambridge University Press, 1997).

28 John Rawls, "Reply to Habermas," *Journal of Philosophy* 92 (1995): 133, n. 1.

29 This idea is developed in John Rawls, *Political Liberalism* (New York: Columbia University Press, 1993).

30 Ibid., 140.

31 Ibid., 220.

32 Ibid., 199–200.

33 Ibid., 37, 54, 60–61.

34 Ibid., 152–56.

35 I owe the term "epistemic abstinence" to Joseph Raz, "Facing Diversity: The Case of Epistemic Abstinence," in Raz, *Ethics in the Public Domain: Essays in the Morality of Law and Politics* (Oxford: Clarendon Press, 1994), 45–81.

36 See the essays by Heiner Bielefeldt, Ernst-Wolfgang Böckenförde, Robert Howse, Ellen Kennedy, Dominique Leydet, Reinhard Mehring, and Chantal Mouffe.

37 See the essays by Renato Cristi, Ingeborg Maus, John P. McCormick, William E. Scheuerman, and Jeffrey Seitzer.

· 38 In my view, Hermann Heller is the most promising candidate in this regard—see my *Legality and Legitimacy: Carl Schmitt, Hans Kelsen and Hermann Heller in Weimar*. But there are of course other candidates. See William E. Scheuerman's treatment of the Frankfurt School lawyers, *Between the Norm and the Exception: The Frankfurt School and the Rule of Law* (Cambridge, Mass.: MIT Press, 1994). For the most comprehensive treatment in English, see Peter Caldwell, *The Theory and Practice of Weimar Constitutionalism* (Durham, N.C.: Duke University Press, 1997). See also the forthcoming book of extracts from the work of Weimar legal theorists, *Weimar: A Jurisprudence of Crisis*, Arthur Jacobson and Bernhard Schlink, eds. (Berkeley: University of California Press, 1999).

PART I

Political Theory and Law

Carl Schmitt's Critique of Liberalism

Systematic Reconstruction and Countercriticism

Heiner Bielefeldt

Preliminary Remarks

Critique of liberalism has a long tradition. However, those launching critical attacks against liberalism frequently turn out to be liberals themselves who are concerned, for instance, about the common equation of liberalism with a bourgeois attitude of "possessive individualism" or with the reduction of liberal politics to an empty proceduralism. The recent debate between liberalism and communitarianism largely amounts to such a kind of liberal self-criticism. Even outspoken communitarian critics, like Sandel,[1] undoubtedly appreciate important achievements of liberalism; often they take these achievements more or less for granted.

Carl Schmitt's critique of liberalism is different. His polemic does not fit into the tradition of liberal self-criticism. As I have tried to demonstrate elsewhere,[2] Schmitt systematically undermines the liberal principle of the rule of law. He wants it to be replaced by an authoritarian version of democracy, a democracy based upon the "substantial homogeneity" of the collective unity of the people rather than one resting upon the principles of a participatory republicanism. Although Schmitt until 1933 opposed the Nazi party, his ardent anti-liberalism entails from the outset the potential for fascism. It is thus more than a pure coincidence that he finally proved able to espouse the political ideology of the Third Reich and to take up for some time the role of a legal adviser to the Nazi regime, without substantially changing his previously developed political concepts.

My response to Schmitt is given from a standpoint which I would like to label Kantian in the broad sense. Kant's philosophy of moral autonomy and republicanism can provide the source of inspiration for a genuinely ethical and political liberalism which is centered around universal human rights and republican commitment within an open civil society.[3] I will first reconstruct the main points of Schmitt's critique of liberalism to which I will subsequently give a Kantian response.

Carl Schmitt's Critique of Liberalism

A typical feature of Carl Schmitt's way of arguing is that he attempts to prove liberalism guilty of conflicting sins. On the one hand, Schmitt charges liberalism with being illusionary: the normative principles of neutrality and the rule of law as well as the liberal project of a constitutional democracy rest, he says, upon contradictory premises and hence finally result in liberal self-deceit. On the other hand, he accuses liberals of being hypocritical: by invoking purportedly universal principles, liberals simply hide their particular purposes and selfish economic goals. Either self-deceit or hypocrisy—this is the Schmittian trap in which he wants to destroy the normative claims of liberalism. This either-or structure occurs in many variations of which I will give three examples, namely: Schmitt's attacks on the claim of neutrality, on the principle of the rule of law, and on the concept of constitutional democracy.

Liberal "Neutrality" as Lack of Substance
According to Schmitt, it is typical of liberals that they pretend to take a "neutral" standpoint vis-à-vis religious, ideological, and political conflicts. This claim of neutrality constitutes a main target of Schmitt's polemic because, he thinks, it simultaneously reveals both the lack of ethical and political substance and the hypocrisy of the liberal bourgeois who pursues his interests without visibly and openly engaging in political conflict.

First, for Schmitt neutrality means lack of substance. Rather than taking a clear ethical and political position, liberals tend to resort to purportedly neutral procedural rules. Even when confronted with the question, "Christ or Barrabas?" they will try to avoid a clear decision and, instead, vote for postponing the question and setting up a committee of inquiry.[4] In the face of existing political conflicts, this claim of neutrality amounts to weakness, evasiveness, and cowardice; it indicates liberalism's lack of ethical and political commitment.

Schmitt considers liberal neutrality to be the final result of a history of increasing "neutralization" in the course of which the original mythological and theological substance of political conflict has been lost.

In the wake of the early modern religious wars, theological questions were gradually replaced by metaphysical questions which themselves later gave way to humanitarian concerns. In the age of liberalism, even humanitarian morality has become a merely private matter. What remains is economic issues which, according to Schmitt, make up the core of modern liberalism.[5]

Liberal neutrality does not mean that liberals abstain from pursuing their purposes politically. The liberal approach to politics, however, is purely instrumental, because it is only for the sake of safeguarding private and economic interests that liberals engage in politics.[6] This instrumental approach to politics is mirrored in the fact that liberals typically hide their particular goals behind allegedly neutral or even universal normative standards. From this perspective, liberal neutrality ultimately amounts to hypocrisy.[7] This charge of hypocrisy is Schmitt's second critique of liberal neutrality; it is the flip side of the charge that liberalism lacks ethical and political substance.

In his famous essay *Der Begriff des Politischen* (*The Concept of the Political*), Schmitt gives a definition of the political which is precisely the opposite of neutrality, because it focuses on the need of drawing a clear line between friend and enemy: "The specific political distinction to which political actions and motives can be reduced is the distinction between *friend* and *enemy*."[8] Schmitt is convinced that the friend-enemy distinction represents an inescapable political reality. At the end of the day, liberals, too, will have to face this reality and thus abandon their claim of neutrality. In any serious political crisis, Schmitt says, liberal neutrality is doomed to break down. The liberal state must do away with the illusion of neutrality and openly declare and defend its particular political goals. Alternatively, the state will fall prey to a strong and determined enemy.[9] In either case, however, the liberal pretense of neutrality will necessarily disappear.

The Liberal Illusion of the "Rule of Law"
For Schmitt the principle of the "rule of law," one which lies at the core of liberal constitutionalism, represents another example of the illusionary or hypocritical character of liberalism. The idea of the rule of law suggests the primacy of abstract normative principles over concrete political positions and decisions. According to Schmitt, however, the opposite is true. Normative principles cannot have an effect on human society unless they are interpreted by particular agents and applied to particular circumstances. Particular perspectives are thus always in-

volved in the implementation of normative principles and undermine their claim to universal validity.[10]

This reality most clearly comes to the fore in the state of emergency which in German is called "state of exception" (*Ausnahmezustand*). Schmitt is fascinated with this situation because the state of exception, in which the entire legal order is at stake, reveals the factual primacy of the "rule of man" over the "rule of law." The state of exception is the breakthrough of political sovereignty in the strong Hobbesian sense, that is, a sovereign decision uninhibited by any normative principles. In the opening sentence of his *Politische Theologie* (*Political Theology*), Schmitt declares, "Sovereign is he who decides on the state of exception."[11]

Schmitt's point is that the state of exception cannot be defined and regulated in conformity to abstract legal principles, because these principles by their very nature are unable to determine in advance the scope of political power that is needed to deal with a unique and unpredictable crisis. Consequently, in such an ultimate situation of crisis the government itself has to decide what amount of power seems appropriate to overcome the crisis. This, he thinks, proves the reality of sovereign power in the strict sense, that is, a supreme political authority operating unconstrained by constitutional requirements: "What characterizes the state of exception is principally unlimited authority, which means the suspension of the entire existing order."[12]

Schmitt emphasizes that, although the state of exception certainly is an unusual case, it is not a marginal case that can be ignored in political and legal debates. On the contrary, the mere *possibility* that such a situation of an utmost crisis can actually occur already reveals the *factual* limitations of legal rationality and liberal constitutionalism in general. With regard to the state of exception, it becomes obvious that the constitutional order as a whole, after all, depends on the political will of a sovereign authority to establish, defend, and—whenever it seems necessary—suspend this order. Liberals, Schmitt says, either forget or conceal this political truth. Again, it is the situation of crisis—that is, the state of exception—which urges liberals to overcome self-deceit as well as hypocrisy and to admit the reality and inevitability of political sovereignty which ultimately prevails over liberal constitutionalism.

The Contradictory Nature of Constitutional Democracy
For Schmitt constitutional democracy is a mere combination of two components which finally do not fit together: the liberal component of

constitutionalism and the political component of democracy. Schmitt's above-mentioned two charges against liberalism—the antagonism between neutrality and substance and the contradiction between constitutionalism and sovereignty—also appear in his attacks on constitutional democracy. As a result, he perceives constitutional democracy to be a self-contradictory and self-undermining project.

First, Schmitt holds that the inherent tension between constitutionalism and democracy represents an example of the general antagonism between substance and neutrality: whereas democracy entails the political substance of a particular people, constitutional procedures are a method of safeguarding private and economic interests of the liberal bourgeois. Second, Schmitt thinks that constitutional democracy is illusionary; in any serious crisis the constitutional principle of the "rule of law" has to give way to unconstrained political sovereignty, a sovereignty which in a democracy is exercized by the collective will of the people.

In his *Verfassungslehre (Constitutional Theory)* Schmitt defines democracy as a particular form of political sovereignty. What ultimately counts in a genuine democracy, he says, is the sovereign authority of the collective unity of the people, a unity facilitated by, and resting on, some sort of "substantial homogeneity."[13] The question of what this substantial homogeneity should consist of is deliberately left open. One may think of common tradition, language, ethnic origin, religion, or ideology. What is crucial for Schmitt, however, is that this substantial homogeneity must be something particular: a medium through which a people can distinguish itself from other peoples and thus find its specific identity. Against normative universalism he emphasizes, "Political democracy cannot rest upon the indistinctiveness of all human beings; instead, it is based upon membership in a particular people. . . ."[14] Democracy in the Schmittian sense ultimately means the unconstrained political expression of a particular people's collective identity.

Unlike democracy, constitutionalism does not epitomize any political substance. Rather, constitutionalism is an instrument of the liberal bourgeoisie to defend its private and economic interests by setting up a bill of individual rights and a separation of powers. Whereas democracy is a particular way of *exercising* political sovereignty, constitutionalism is exactly the opposite, namely, a way of *preventing* political sovereignty. It is the purpose of liberal constitutionalism to "moderate" and "tame" political power by combining and balancing different constitutional institutions—president, parliament, courts—none of which is allowed to exercise sovereign authority in the strict sense. Modern constitutionalism thus ultimately amounts to a new version of the ancient model of a *regimen commixtum*. In keeping with this old tradition of a "mixed government," liberal constitutionalism "rests upon a peculiar method of linking, balancing, and relativizing monarchic, aristocratic, and democratic elements of form and structure."[15] Since it represents a kind of "mixed government," however, constitutional democracy cannot claim to be a pure democracy; it is at best a moderated and half-hearted democracy, inhibited and tamed by a set of constitutional institutions.

Carl Schmitt is convinced that constitutionalism and democracy do not in principle fit together. To be sure, it is quite possible that the members of a democratic polity may decide to establish a constitution, including a bill of rights and a separation of powers. This, however, does not mean that democracy and constitutionalism actually form one whole. Even though the conflict between the two elements may be concealed, the inherent contradiction continues to exist. According to Schmitt, one of the two elements must ultimately prevail: either political democracy or the normative requirements of constitutionalism.

The first possibility, however, necessarily means dismissing the binding force of constitutional principles and norms altogether. In a true Schmittian democracy the constitution is in fact nothing but a superstructure based on the political will of the people whose absolute authority can override all constitutional requirements at any time. Thus Schmitt emphasizes: "In a democracy the people is the sovereign; it can break through the entire system of constitutional norms and decide a court case, like the prince in an absolute monarchy could decide cases. It is supreme judge as well as supreme legislator."[16]

The second possibility means that constitutional constraints inhibit the exercise of democratic authority in a way that will finally destroy the very existence of the state. Constitutional democracy then turns out to be literally a self-undermining project. If the political unity of the people is denied its role of a supreme and unconstrained sovereign authority, it will not be able to defend its particular existence and identity in a serious political crisis.

Again, the political crisis will destroy liberal self-conceit and hypocrisy and reveal the factual nature of the state. In the state of emergency the illusion of the "mixed government" will evaporate: either the state will transform itself into a real body politic centered around political sovereignty in the strict sense, or the different institutions of the liberal "mixed government" will fall apart, thus leaving the state vulnerable to be conquered by a strong and determined enemy.

A Liberal Response to Schmitt

A defense of liberalism against Schmitt's attacks must be a self-critical defense. It would be absurd to deny the fact that within that broad modern movement, which is labeled "liberal" influential "bourgeois" or "technocratic," currents exist which may indeed lack ethical and political substance. It seems also fair to admit that liberals do have problems with the state of emergency and that the concept of constitutional democracy harbors tensions and possible conflicts. And yet in my opinion Schmitt is wrong in alleging that his criticism hits liberalism per se and that a solution to the inherent contradictions of liberalism can only be expected from an anti-liberal standpoint. In order to oppose this claim, I will have to show that the liberal tradition itself includes genuinely ethical and political substance, in the light of which Schmitt's counterposing of neutrality and substance can eventually be overcome. I will further argue that liberal constitutionalism is more than an abstract and empty proceduralism. Liberal constitutionalism epitomizes substantial ethical and political convictions and thus should be able to survive even serious situations of political crisis, such as the state of emergency. Finally, I will explain the thesis that democracy and constitutionalism essentially belong together, thus forming a complex whole rather than a mere combination of contradictory components.

The Political "Substance" Behind the Claim of Neutrality
In order to overcome the Schmittian antagonism of neutrality versus substance, it seems necessary first to point to an ambivalence within the concept of neutrality, an ambivalence which Schmitt seems to ignore completely. In the German political and constitutional debate two different meanings of neutrality are frequently distinguished: *Weltanschauungsneutralität* and *Wertneutralität*.[17] *Weltanschauungsneutralität* means the requirement that the state should remain neutral in questions of religion and *Weltanschauung*. Above all, the state is not permitted to discriminate against people because of their particular religious or nonreligious convictions. Neutrality in this context is the flip side of the liberal principle of nondiscrimination, a principle which itself is based on universal human rights, especially religious liberty and freedom of conscience. Insofar as the liberal requirement of nondiscrimination relates to moral principles such as human rights, however, it proves exactly the opposite of *Wertneutralität* which itself means neutrality toward all ethical and moral values. Hence, *Weltan-*

schauungsneutralität and *Wertneutralität,* after all, turn out to be not only different but even opposite concepts.

Whereas *Wertneutralität* would indeed amount to a complete lack of ethical and political commitment, *Weltanschauungsneutralität* does involve a normative idea, an idea on which liberalism, especially Kantian liberalism, on the whole is based. This underlying normative idea is respect for the dignity of every human being as a morally autonomous subject. It is an old insight, traceable to the Judeo-Christian Bible or ancient Greek philosophy, that human dignity consists in the person's capacity to act as a morally responsible being. Kant gives a new interpretation to this traditional idea by extending the scope of moral responsibility of each individual to the point that this responsibility also includes the "legislative" creation of moral norms. This is the meaning of "moral autonomy" in the Kantian sense. Kant, at the same time, emphasizes that moral autonomy is the opposite of moral "sovereignty," because human responsibility necessarily remains under the spell of an inalienable inner command. The principle of moral self-legislation is a categorical imperative: "Act only according to that maxim by which you can at the same time will that it should become a universal law."[18] Due respect for the law of morality is ultimately synonymous to respecting the dignity of the person as a source of moral self-legislation. Hence it is the one-and-only categorical imperative — i.e., the very principle of moral self-legislation — which can also be formulated in the following way: "Act so that you treat humanity, whether in your own person or in that of another, always as an end and never as a means only."[19] Being both a subject and an object of unconditional moral respect, the individual stands above any market price.[20]

In the realm of politics the inalienable dignity of the person as a morally autonomous subject should be recognized in an order of equal freedom and participation. Kant emphasizes the fundamental significance of freedom as the only "birthright" of every human being, a right which therefore must be equally accorded to everyone. In his *Metaphysics of Morals* he writes: "There is only one innate right. *Freedom* . . . , insofar as it can coexist with the freedom of every other in accordance with a universal law, is the only original right belonging to every man by virtue of his humanity."[21] Modern liberalism differs from premodern political thought in that it requires that freedom must not be confined to a privileged minority but, rather, constitutes a universal claim; freedom and equality therefore necessarily belong together.[22] Further, given that freedom and equality together constitute the basic principle of the entire political and legal order, they must also find expression within the realm of politics itself. Hence the inherent connection of human rights and modern participatory democracy.[23] Together they represent the liberal principle of equal freedom and participation, a principle which finally points to the dignity of every person as a morally autonomous subject.

It is only within this normative framework of equal freedom and participation that the concept of neutrality can make sense. Neutrality is not a principle that stands on its own, as Schmitt seems to assume, and liberal neutrality should by no means provide a pretext for remaining neutral between good and evil, right and wrong, or between justice and injustice. Rather, neutrality serves as an antidote to all sorts of biases and discrimination. *Weltanschauungsneutralität,* for instance, is a way of preventing discrimination based on religion and *Weltanschauung.*

From this perspective, it is clear that neutrality does not mean weakness, as Schmitt alleges. Liberal neutrality can quite well go along with the willingness and readiness to engage in political conflict. Liberalism, especially Kantian liberalism, is after all a fighting political ideology. It fights, first and foremost, all kinds of oppression and discrimination, whether in the domestic realm or in foreign affairs. Rather than being an expression of evasiveness, the principle of neutrality can be used as a critical standard within that liberal fight for political justice. For the principle of neutrality calls for permanent self-critical reflection and public critical debate in order to articulate ever new experiences of oppression and discrimination and to discover potential biases even behind purportedly universal validity claims. This critical and self-critical endeavor in turn is the sine qua non to approaching the ideal of a liberal community in which people respect each other's dignity and freedom on the basis of equality.

Overcoming the Hiatus Between Principles and Practice
Like the liberal claim of neutrality, the principle of the rule of law should not be viewed in isolation. It is not an abstract mechanism that runs itself, but rather is part of that comprehensive liberal idea of political justice which is inherently connected to democracy and human rights. The ethical and political substance of the liberal idea of justice as a whole should be strong enough to enable a liberal state to survive even exceptional situations of crisis, including the state of emergency, without abandoning its liberal constitution.

Schmitt is right in saying that a political crisis can conceivably result in a state of exception, that is, a situation requiring unusual political decisions which themselves do not fit into any given set of legal and constitutional norms. Schmitt, however, goes a step further. He holds that there is an *unbridgeable hiatus* between abstract legal norms on the one hand and the particular situation on the other. In the state of exception, this unbridgeable hiatus between abstract normativism and the particular situation, which under normal circumstances may be concealed, suddenly becomes patent and thus leads to open decisionism. The state of exception, according to Schmitt, reveals the hidden truth that the entire constitutional order ultimately depends on political sovereignty in the strict Hobbesian sense, that is, a sovereignty that stands beyond all constitutional requirements as well as all normative principles. The state of exception thus proves the ficticious character of liberal normativism and constitutionalism in general.

In order to refute Schmitt, one has to show that this purported hiatus, upon which his argument is based, is questionable. What is needed, in other words, is a mediating link between general norms on the one hand and the particular situation on the other, a mediating link through which the Schmittian hiatus can actually be bridged. Such a mediating link can be found in the concept of a *precedent*.[24] A precedent occurs in a particular situation and, at the same time, transcends the very particularity of that situation by pointing to an *implicit* rule. That is why it can claim a certain degree of normative authority, even in the case where an *explicit* legal norm does not exist. The concept of a precedent thus points to a way to overcome Schmittian decisionism, even in the extreme situation of the state of exception.

This is to say that even the state of exception in the strict Schmittian sense—i.e., a situation out of the reach of constitutional normative provisions—should be dealt with in such an attitude as if one were setting up a new precedent. On the one hand, such an exceptional situation cannot be settled by simply resorting to positive legal norms or an established practice. On the other hand, the decision that may be necessary to cope with this new situation of crisis should transcend mere arbitrariness in order to do justice at least to the *normative idea* underlying the rule of law. That is, the decision should be taken as a potential precedent to which one should (theoretically) be able to refer *in every comparable situation.* Unlike bare decisionism, a precedent thus entails an element of reasonability and accountability by means of which the enactment of a precedent goes beyond mere arbitrariness.

Given that the precedent points to an *implicit* (albeit not to an *explicit*) rule, it can, at least indirectly, be connected with the constitutional principle of the rule of law. After all, Schmitt is wrong in assuming that liberal constitutionalism is but an abstract construct detached from the ever-changing concrete circumstances of real life. Instead, by referring to normative principles which themselves derive from people's ethical and political practice, liberal constitutionalism is a way of rendering *explicit* what exists already *implicitly*, that is, the rationality and accountability implied in all normative practice.

The state of exception, admittedly, may reveal the limitations of *explicitly* formulated legal and constitutional rules and thus pose a challenge to constitutionalism. But even such a challenge would not be the end of accountable political practice and its *implicit* normative reasonability. From a liberal point of view, a politically responsible decision in the state of exception would not be an act of sovereignty in the Hobbesian or Schmittian sense, that is, an act of bare decisionism in which the rule of men would openly prevail over, and eventually destroy, the rule of law. On the contrary, for the decision in question to be an expression of political responsibility, such a decision must be bound—at least implicitly—by reasonable principles, even though these principles may not be formally enshrined in legal statutes. At any rate, those taking political decisions in the state of exception will be held accountable for what they are doing before a court.

Constitutional Democracy

Schmitt's criticism of constitutional democracy rests on the assumption that a true democracy must be the unconstrained expression of the collective political will of the people. If this were the case, constitutionalism would indeed be either a mere legal fiction without any binding force or a method of taming and inhibiting a real democracy. Constitutionalism would, at any rate, be an undemocratic superstructure imposed on democracy as an external constraint.

From a Kantian perspective, however, democracy means the opposite of collective decisionism in the Schmittian sense. The Kantian understanding of democracy[25] is inherently and inextricably connected with the "innate right" of freedom and equality, a right which in turn points to the due respect for the equal dignity of every human being. Kant's innate right of freedom and equality is nothing alien to democracy, but rather makes up the inner normative quality of a democratic union of citizens who mutually recognize each other on the basis of equality, by establishing an order of equal freedom and participation.

Being itself an expression of equal freedom and participation, democracy does not have a merely instrumental status on behalf of protecting preexisting liberal rights. Republican commitment and democratic responsibility cannot be confined to safeguarding a given list of individual rights. Rather, democracy includes the very *creation* of individual rights which themselves must be brought about politically and thus remain a part of the political debate. It is no coincidence that Kant, unlike Locke, does not provide a comprehensive list of individual rights, rights which in Locke's view are purported to be *prior* to all political legislation. By contrast, Kant focuses on freedom as the one and only "birthright" of every human being rather than a comprehensive catalog of rights. By doing this he leaves it to the legislator to spell out concretely which individual rights should be recognized and guaranteed.[26]

However, provided that a constitutional bill of rights epitomizes the very principle that underlies democracy as well—i.e., the principle of equal freedom and participation—it cannot be considered to be merely an external imposition on democracy, as Schmitt asserts. Rather, the constitutional guarantee of liberal rights is a way of recognizing and protecting the normative source of liberal democracy itself.[27] Likewise, the individualism inherent in individual human rights cannot be reduced to the selfish goals of the *bourgeois*, as Schmitt does. Individual rights also aim at protecting the freedom of the *citoyen* whose personal integrity must always be respected for a free democratic discourse to be possible. Again, the guarantee of liberal rights ultimately proves helpful for protecting the precondition of free democratic commitment and hence the very source of democracy.

Although the constitutional bill of rights, in principle, cannot remain outside political legislation and political debate, its crucial importance for liberal democracy should be recognized by giving it a status that is indeed beyond the grip of pure majority rule. With regard to the liberal-democratic principle of equal freedom and participation, democracy cannot be equated with majority rule, which itself is but *one* procedural method of taking decisions, within a complex framework of various constitutional institutions and procedures. The establishment of a constitution—including a bill of rights and a separation of powers—can be viewed as an institutional device of maintaining this crucial difference between democratic principles and bare majoritarianism.

From this point of view, constitutionalism proves a genuinely democratic requirement. Far from being an undemocratic constraint, constitutionalism provides the occasion of an institutional *self-control* of a democracy which thereby ought to check itself as to whether or not it operates in accordance with *its own* normative principle: equal freedom and participation. This normative principle, at the same time, supplies the ultimate criterion against which all constitutional institutions and procedures constantly need to be critically checked in order to remain a legitimate expression of liberal democracy.

Notes

1 Michael J. Sandel, *Liberalism and the Limits of Justice* (New York: Cambridge University Press, 1982).

2 See Heiner Bielefeldt, "Deconstruction of the Rule of Law. Carl Schmitt's Philosophy of the Political," *Archiv für Rechts- und Sozialphilosophie* 82 (1996): at 379–96. This article is largely based on the second chapter of my book *Kampf und Entscheidung. Politischer Existentialismus bei Carl Schmitt, Helmuth Plessner und Karl Jaspers* (Würzburg: Königshausen & Neumann, 1994).

3 See Heiner Bielefeldt, "Autonomy and Republicanism. Immanuel Kant's Philosophy of Freedom," in *Political Theory* 25 (1997): 526.

4 See Carl Schmitt, *Politische Theologie. Vier Kapitel zur Lehre von der Souveränität*, 2d enlarged ed. (Berlin: Duncker & Humblot, 1934), at 78.

5 See Carl Schmitt, *Der Begriff des Politischen* (Berlin: Duncker & Humblot, 2d enlarged ed., 1932, together with an introduction and three corrolaries of 1963), at 80 and 88ff.

6 Ibid., at 68–71.

7 See Carl Schmitt, "Staatsethik und pluralistischer Staat," *Kant-Studien* 35 (1930): 28, at 39: "He who invokes humankind is about to cheat."

8 Supra n. 5, at 26.

9 Ibid., at 54: "If a people no longer has the energy or the will to maintain itself in the sphere of the political, the political itself will not vanish from the world. Only a weak people will disappear."

10 This criticism can already be found in one of Schmitt's first publications: *Gesetz und Urteil. Eine Untersuchung zum Problem der Rechtspraxis*, 2d ed. (Munich: C. H. Beck, 1969).

11 Supra n. 4, at 11.

12 Ibid., at 18.

13 See Carl Schmitt, *Verfassungslehre* (Berlin: Dunker & Humblot, 1928), at 228ff.

14 Ibid., at 227.

15 Supra n. 13, at 216.

16 Supra, at 275.

17 See, for example, Hans Buchheim, "Religion und Politik—Einige systema-

tische Überlegungen," in Erhard Forndran, ed., *Religion und Politik in einer säkularisierten Welt* (Baden-Baden: Nomos, 1991), at 65.

18 Immanuel Kant, *Foundation of the Metaphysics of Morals*, R. P. Wolff, ed. (New York: Macmillan, 1969), at 44.

19 Ibid., at 54.

20 Supra n. 18, at 60: "In the realm of ends everything has either a *price* or a *dignity*. Whatever has a price can be replaced by something else as its equivalent; on the other hand, whatever is above all price, and therefore admits of no equivalent, has a dignity."

21 Immanuel Kant, *The Metaphysics of Morals*, M. Gregor, ed. (New York: Cambridge University Press, 1991), at 63.

22 See Ibid., at 63: "This principle of innate freedom already involves the following authorizations, which are not really distinct from it: . . . innate *equality*, that is, independence from being bound by others to more than one can in turn bind them. . . ."

23 It should be noted in passing that Kant himself does not espouse the concept of democracy, but rather speaks of republicanism. Nevertheless, persuasive arguments for a "radically democratic" reconstruction of Kant's political philosophy are given in Ingeborg Maus, *Zur Aufklärung der Demokratietheorie. Rechts- und demokratietheoretische Überlegungen im Anschluss an Kant* (Frankfurt: Suhrkamp, 1992).

24 The concept of a precedent does not explicitly exist in Kant's moral and legal philosophy. As Arendt has argued, however, Kant's *Critique of Judgment* implicitly entails a political philosophy, because it aims at mediating between abstract principles and concrete cases or situations. Exactly this is also the structure of a precedent which, technically speaking, can be viewed as an example of "reflective judgment." See Hannah Arendt, *Lectures on Kant's Political Philosophy*, R. Beiner, ed. (Chicago: University of Chicago Press, 1982).

25 See supra n. 23.

26 Like Locke, Kant assumes that private rights exist also in the state of nature. Kant differs from Locke, however, in justifying these private rights by the very same principle of right that is explicitly realized only in *public* law. The private rights of the state of nature thus are not prepolitical in the sense of being outside of political debate. See Heiner Bielefeldt, *Neuzeitliches Freiheitsrecht und politische Gerechtigkeit. Perspektiven der Gesellschaftsvertragstheorien* (Würzburg: Königshausen & Neumann, 1990), at 116ff.

27 See Jürgen Habermas, *Faktizität und Geltung. Beiträge zur Diskurstheorie des Rechts und des demokratischen Rechtsstaats* (Frankfurt: Suhrkamp, 1992), at 339ff.

The Concept of the Political

A Key to Understanding Carl Schmitt's Constitutional Theory

Ernst-Wolfgang Böckenförde

The focus of this chapter is not on the person, but on the *work* of Carl Schmitt, in particular the significance of Schmitt's concept of the political for an understanding of his legal and constitutional theory. Let me start with a short personal memory.

When I was a third-year law student, I read Schmitt's *Verfassungs-lehre*. I came across the formulations that the state is the political unity of a people[1] and that the rule-of-law component in a constitution is an unpolitical component.[2] I was puzzled by these two remarks. I had learned from Georg Jellinek that the state, from a sociological perspective, is a purposeful corporative unit and, from a legal perspective, represents a territorially based corporation. I had also gathered some knowledge about "organic" state theories, especially that of Otto von Gierke who considers the state an organism and a real corporative personality rather than a mere legal fiction.[3] On the basis of these theories, I felt unable to understand Schmitt's point that the state is the political unity of a people because in those theories the political aspect is largely missing. It was only later that, by reading and studying Schmitt's essay *Der Begriff des Politischen*, I gradually learned to make sense of the above remarks. Thus I have discovered that that essay, and the understanding of the political elaborated in it, contains the key to understanding Schmitt's constitutional theory in general. I will now explain this.

I

Let us start with the general content and the core message of the concept of the political. Given the debate triggered by that essay and in the face of its wide repercussions, one has to rescue Schmitt's core message from an array of misunderstandings. To discuss and refute these

misunderstandings—which partly stem from the intellectual and political situation to which Schmitt addressed his essay and partly reflect a
deliberate refusal of any serious understanding—would require another
chapter. I therefore confine myself to mentioning two common and
influential misunderstandings.

The first misunderstanding relates to the distinction between friend
and enemy which Schmitt develops in that essay. The misunderstanding consists in holding that this distinction serves to turn the domestic
debate *within* the state into a relationship between friend and enemy
and, where possible, to create a corresponding reality. This seems to
thwart any peaceful (albeit perhaps combative) search for compromise
and agreement as well as for shaping the domestic political and social
order. The second misunderstanding takes Schmitt's essay to constitute
a *normative* theory of politics and political action in such a way that
the friend-and-enemy distinction as well as the resulting militant conflict becomes the purpose and substance of politics. This widespread
misunderstanding has largely shaped the debate on Schmitt's concept
of the political. It may be true that Schmitt did not explicitly distance
himself from such an interpretation. Nevertheless, that interpretation
can easily be refuted by reference to Schmitt's text.[4]

The central message as well as the academic significance of Schmitt's
concept of the political can be seen in the fact that it focuses on the
phenomenological criterion not of politics but of "the political" or,
more precisely, the degrees of intensity within the political. To know
and recognize this criterion is a precondition to any meaningful political action. The criterion in question, according to Schmitt, is that the
political, considered and determined as a phenomenon, can possibly
lead to an extreme antagonism between friend and enemy, an antagonism which includes the readiness for conflict, even for armed conflict.
It is from this inherent possibility that the political gets its phenomenological definition. I have elsewhere[5] defined the political as follows: The
political does not consist in a determined sphere of objects, but rather
is a public relationship between people, a relationship marked by a specific degree of association or dissociation which can potentially lead to
the distinction between friend and enemy; the content underlying this
relationship can originate from any sphere or area of human life.

It is from this definition that the second core message of the concept
of the political becomes meaningful—a message formulated mostly implicitly until it was made explicit in the introduction to the new edition

from 1963 of *Der Begriff des Politischen*. This is the assertion that the state is the political unity of a people.

In light of Schmitt's idea of the political, the state as a *political unity* means a pacified unity encompassing the political. While fencing itself off against other external political unities, its domestic distinctions, antagonisms, and conflicts remain *below* the level of friend-enemy groupings. This is to say that all these domestic relationships are embraced by the relative homogeneity of the people held together by some sense of solidarity (i.e., friendship). Domestic conflict can thus be integrated into a peaceful order guaranteed by the state's monopoly of coercive power. This in turn means that, as Schmitt himself pointed out, unlike foreign politics, politics within the state is "political" only in a secondary degree.[6] Domestic politics in its classical sense aims at good order within the community by trying to keep conflicts and debates within the framework of peaceful coexistence. Thus it is the purpose of the state as a political unity to relativize domestic antagonisms, tensions, and conflicts so as to facilitate peaceful debates as well as solutions and ultimately decisions that are in accordance with procedural standards of argumentation and public discourse.

However, against a widespread misunderstanding, I should emphasize that the sphere of domestic politics within a state is by no means completely detached from the concept of the political; nor is the term "political" used with a completely different meaning in such a case. Rather, the above definition of the political holds also for domestic politics, if only in a derivative sense. On the one hand, it is only on a minor scale that the concept of the political applies to domestic politics; on the other hand, this domestic application is logically derived from the criterion of the political in general. The reason for this is as follows. Conflicts about how to shape the order of coexistence also occur within the political unity, even though this unity is shielded from the intensity of a friend-enemy grouping. In such a case people publicly form groups with and against each other. Given that the political does not constitute a closed sphere in itself, this grouping can potentially occur in various spheres of public life, such as in cultural, economic, or foreign policy, and the like. The decisive point is only that this grouping must not reach the intensity of a friend-enemy relationship. Nevertheless, this phenomenon of grouping can be called political in the Schmittian sense because, if reasonable politics and conflict management fails, it possibly can escalate to the ultimate degree of intensity. The "Kulturkampf" in Prussia and in the German Reich during the Bismarck era, for instance, stopped short of the friend-enemy grouping. It even escalated to the point of an existential conflict between the state and the Roman Catholic part of the population. Bismarck was a shrewd enough politician to see that the very existence of the Reich was at stake. Hence he searched for reconciliation with the Catholics, however stubborn they might have appeared to him. Something like this can potentially occur in every sphere of life. Escalating political conflict can arise over questions of university reform, education, or—perhaps in a few years—garbage disposal.

From a logical point of view, it seems appropriate to characterize this as a "second order concept of the political," since it is connected with, rather than completely detached from, the political friend-enemy definition. As Schmitt says, the political is neither thoroughly absent within the established political unity of a state; nor is it confined to the sphere of foreign affairs. Facing the ever-lurking potential of an escalating friend-enemy grouping, it is also present within the state, even though it does not visibly manifest itself in a normal situation.

This is to say that once a political unity has been accomplished it can never be taken for granted but must continuously preserve and reconfirm itself through the actual cooperation of the people in question. The political unity can be jeopardized both from without, that is, by threats and attacks from external enemies, as well as from within. The integration and domestication of the political sphere into the encompassing order of the state can come into question; it can become precarious to the point of concealed or open civil war, which would finally dissolve the state's very unity as a political unity. To overcome such a menace, one has to stabilize the domestic order and preempt existing or looming tensions and conflicts. What is needed above all is to avoid the escalation of conflicts and an intensity of dissociation that could lead to a breakdown of the political solidarity (i.e., political "friendship") that is based on the relative homogeneity of the people. A reasonable policy is thus one that comes about through and is determined by understanding the peculiar quality of the political.

If what I have explained so far is indeed the precise meaning of the definition of the state as a political unity of a people, some consequences for constitutional law can be drawn. Constitutional law then appears as the binding normative order and form determining the existence, maintenance, and capability for action of a political unity in the above sense. It is and must be the specific telos of constitutional law to facilitate, preserve, and support the state as a political order and unity. An interpretation of constitutional law challenging or even undermining such an order would thus be an oxymoron. In this sense constitutional law is a genuinely political law: It deals with politics not only indirectly and incidentally, but immediately addresses the existence, form, and action of the political unity; its object, so to speak, affects the gravitational field of the political itself.[7]

II

In this section, I try to demonstrate how Schmitt's concept of the political and the corresponding characterization of the state as a political unity facilitates an understanding of crucial concepts, statements, and theses within Schmitt's constitutional theory. I also try to show how these concepts, statements, and theses—despite problems of understanding their adequacy and consistency—receive their inner justification and coherence. I do not want to anticipate the discussion of whether the purpose Schmitt pursues by these concepts and statements could also have been achieved (perhaps even better) by different means. I want to show the systematic coherence of his concepts, a coherence which frequently has been denied and yet seems to me is of crucial importance in his constitutional theory.

Ellen Kennedy has pointed to the fact that Schmitt's *Verfassungslehre* and the first version of *Der Begriff des Politischen* were written around the same time. Hence it is not surprising that the features of *Der Begriff des Politischen* are reflected in *Verfassungslehre*, even though Schmitt does not mention this explicitly. The state as political unity of a people, the rule-of-law component as an unpolitical part of the constitution— these theses are indeed put forward in *Verfassungslehre* without any further explanation. And yet, does this very fact not point to the underlying assumption, that is, the general intellectual framework? And is it not possible that this holds not only for Schmitt's *Verfassungslehre* but also for his entire work on constitutional questions?

I will now give seven examples that illuminate the thesis that *Der Begriff des Politischen* entails a key to understanding Schmitt's constitutional theory in general.

1. *The concept of sovereignty and its unavoidability in constitutional law.* The formula is well known: "Sovereign is he who decides on the state of exception."[8] Political unity constitutes and preserves itself by superseding tensions, antagonisms, and conflicting interests; it strives toward unity and community in such a way as to relativize and inte-

grate these conflicts. For this to happen, however, the possibility of a final decision, i.e., a decision beyond further appeal, is needed. Thus sovereignty, which includes this authority of making a final decision, is a necessary authority for the state as a unity of peace.[9] Sovereignty also facilitates a decision on whether the state of exception (translator's note: in German, state of exception—*Ausnahmezustand*—means state of emergency) applies and, if this is the case, how to deal with it. In the concept of sovereignty this authority is formulated as a legal title; that is, the sovereign has a constitutional "right" to take such a decision. This possibility fully manifests itself in the extreme endangering of the political unity, a situation which can neither be defined in advance nor be limited with reference to specific cases, because in such an extreme situation the very existence of the political unity is in jeopardy. In this conference the "right to rescue,"[10] which means the same phenomenon, has already been mentioned. Schmitt holds that sovereignty can neither be limited by legal means nor be given up, unless the state itself as a self-preserving political unity ceases to exist.[11] Whether there are actual limits on power or some political obligations which—as such or in particular situations—hinder the full elaboration of sovereignty is a different question. Limits of such a kind always exist and depend on the development of political conflict as well as on changes in power relations. Such factual limitations, however, do not put into question sovereignty as understood from a legal perspective. And even if sovereignty is legally abolished, given up, or integrated in such a way that its authority of final decision gets lost, this would not be the end of sovereignty as such; rather, it would mean the transition of sovereignty to another, more encompassing political unity which itself would then claim and, if the need arises, invoke this right of sovereignty.[12] A previously independent political unity would thus become a dependent unity, the political authority of which would be limited to deciding merely internal conflicts under the umbrella of another political unity.[13]

2. *The relationship between state and constitution.* It is a premise of Schmitt's political thought that it is not the constitution which forms the state but, rather, the state which facilitates setting up a constitution. This premise necessarily follows from the concept of the state as a political unity. As a political unity—i.e., a unity of power and peace, vested with a monopoly of coercive power in domestic affairs— the state is something *factually* given; it is given first as a concentration of power. In addition to this—and this seems especially important to me—the relative homogeneity of the people is also factually given

rather than a normative postulate or something produced by compliance with the constitution. This relative homogeneity constitutes the basis and precondition of the unity of peace as well as the application of monopolized state power which itself, first of all, must be accepted by the citizens. The legal constitution—as well as the obedience to, and application of, its normative understanding—does not constitute the state; it is much more the case that the state, as a political unity, is the presupposition of constitutional validity. This is not to deny that the state by means of its legal constitution receives a fixed form, a more precisely determined regulation of governmental activities, and hence a higher degree of stability. The very existence and substance of the state, however, does not derive from its constitution.[14]

3. *The constitution and its elements.* The constitution is not a contract, but a decision. More precisely, it is a decision about the type and form of the political unity.[15] As Schmitt explains in *Verfassungslehre*, a constitutional contract is possible only between existing political unities which thereby establish a confederation or federation of states.[16] The main example of this is a federal contract of the kind concluded by the German Confederation, the North German Confederation, the Swiss Confederation, or by the Act of Confederation between the states of New England. *Within* the state, however, the basic form and order cannot rest on a contract, because in such a case the principle and guarantee of unity—and hence the state as a political unity—would cease to exist. If one is to maintain the political and legal meaning, constitution by contract would be possible only as a contract between independent and autonomous political forces within the state. If this were the case, however, the principle and guarantee of state unity would be highly problematic. The question is how, under these circumstances, constitutional amendments and changes, and decisions on constitutional debates are conceivable—unless one assumes the relative tranquillity of a *"juste milieu"* or of the "halcyonic days," a situation which would facilitate permanent and harmless compromises.[17]

Given the concept of the state as a political unity, Schmitt's distinction between political and unpolitical elements of the constitution, a distinction frequently criticized and not easily understandable, can make sense and receive its intrinsic rationale. This holds also for the characterization of the rule-of-law as an unpolitical component of the constitution. To be sure, prima facie the critical question arises whether the rule-of-law component does not represent a part of the political order of the commonwealth. Yet the political in the Schmittian sense is what underlies, facilitates, and shapes the political unity as unity: a degree of intensity of that association which supersedes conflicts and antagonisms in such a way as to provide both form and organization and furnish and maintain a working political order. This includes the legitimation of state activities, a legitimation which in a democracy originates from the people. Those elements of a constitution, however, which affect the state unity in a hindering, balancing, liberating, and perhaps pluralizing way—i.e., basic rights, separation of powers, and the accommodation of an autonomous realm of economic and commercial activities—cannot be called political in the Schmittian sense, because they relativize and limit the political unity of the state on behalf of unpolitical and liberty-serving goals of the individual.

From this perspective, it is no leap but just a logical step to asserting the priority of the political element within the constitution over the principle of the rule of law. Those regulations which establish the state's organs, shape the state's activities, and set up the procedures necessary for facilitating and preserving the political unity's activity, preservation, and defense, prevail over those elements which limit state activities on behalf of private and societal freedom. For such private and societal freedom does not constitute anything politically; it does not create the political association. Instead, liberalization and individualization, originating from the respective elements of the constitution, amount to a weakening of the political unity and its underlying homogeneity rather than to a necessary and integrating part of the political unity.[18] Differently put, the constitutional guarantee of the rule of law must be added to an existing political unity and form. It cannot exist independently of such a political unity; nor can it achieve efficacy by claiming a general priority over the political unity. Thus it is only the existing and working political unity which makes it possible to guarantee individual rights and liberties; it is the political unity which protects and maintains them in the face of human endangerment and violation.[19]

4. Constitutional jurisprudence and the "Guardian of the Constitution." From the perspective of the concept of the political, we can make sense of Schmitt's general thesis that a genuine constitutional jurisdiction is a political jurisdiction.[20] Recall that constitutional law, with respect to its content, is political law. It is political law not only in the sense that law always has to deal with politics by regulating and shaping coexistence within a political unity; but also, it is political in the sense of defining the conditions, procedures, authorizations, and limits of state activities as well as the options and authorizations for maintaining and protecting the political unity of the state.[21] Accordingly, constitutional law, in its very content and telos, refers to the political from which in turn it receives its own definition. It is with regard to this political definition that constitutional law must be interpreted and applied; moreover, this interpretation and application itself is part of specifically political conduct.

Consequently, constitutional jurisdiction cannot be a pacified realm detached from political dissociation and the corresponding dangers, an idea suggested by the concept of a jurisprudence obedient to determinate laws which themselves are enacted in the course of political debate. Such an unpolitical jurisprudence deals with laws only after they have undergone the process of political will-formation and decision. Given the result of that decision, these laws are generally detached from (potentially) political dissociation and are to be interpreted and applied with regard to their determinate content. Being obedient only to the law and, beside that, fully independent, the judge himself does not become a political actor.[22] Constitutional jurisdiction, by contrast, has to decide over the content and interpretation of constitutional law, i.e., that law which determines and procedurally regulates the political unity and its capability of action. It therefore necessarily falls into the gravitational field of the political, in which associations and dissociations are potentially present which can ignite into conflict. If constitutional jurisdiction takes on its task in an appropriately teleological way, it is inevitably "political" jurisdiction, which—to avoid a misunderstanding—does not mean that it is bare party politics.

For Schmitt, a court operating in accordance with the standards of ordinary jurisdiction cannot serve as the guardian of the constitution.[23] Why not? Again *Der Begriff des Politischen* gives a hint. A court, as it has developed in the history of European constitutionalism, is—in its task, function, and the self-understanding of its actors—detached from the gravitational field of politics. It works only on request (no judge without plaintiff); it is bound by the claims brought forward (*ne ultra petita*); and it operates in obedience to norms which are not to be created by the judge but are, as a rule, given in legally defined statutes. The court has to apply law without being required or permitted to pursue more general political goals or purposes. The guardian of the constitution, by contrast, must act as a political organ.[24] Given that the constitution shapes the legal form of the political unity, the guardian of the constitution is at the same time the guardian of the political unity itself. This derives also from Schmitt's understanding of the relationship between state and constitution.[25]

Incidentally, the question may arise as to what degree during the Weimar Republic Carl Schmitt and Rudolf Smend might have agreed on this point. If one carefully reads Smend's *Verfassung und Verfassungsrecht* one will notice that constitutional jurisdiction is never mentioned in that book. The constitution does not appear as a part of the legal system upheld by jurisprudence and jurisdiction; it rather regulates the process of integration in which the state receives life and reality. The legal function and the legal system, including jurisdiction, are consciously separated from the system of state power, because they pursue an idea of value that differs from the political integration brought about by the state.[26] Also what Smend writes about the peculiar goals of constitutional interpretation, that is, maximization of integration and flexible adjustment of the constitution itself,[27] does not refer to a court. That process of integration which is undertaken by the state and whose order also forms a part of the constitution is not to be guaranteed by a court.

5. Independence and relative separation of the political sphere from private and societal spheres. If I understand Schmitt's theory of the state correctly, a bright line running through his work is the thesis that, for preserving the political unity, the political sphere must be concentrated with the state and its organs; hence the state must hold the monopoly of the political. This becomes manifest in three aspects.

First, basic liberties constituting an autonomous realm not regulated by the state belong only to the private, unpolitical sphere. Their spilling over into the political sphere must be rejected in order to avoid the decomposition of the political sphere, a decomposition by which state organs would become instruments of private and societal self-manifestation.

The place basic liberties occupy within the general structure of *Verfassungslehre* confirms this theory.[28] Basic liberties in the sense of prepolitical and transpolitical human rights are confined to the individualistic rights of freedom in the strict understanding, i.e., the rights of the isolated individual which define and protect his or her private sphere. Among these rights are the rights of faith and conscience, personal freedom, inviolability of the private home, secrecy of the mail, and private property. The next group of rights which combine the rights of one individual with those of another—freedom of opinion, expression, and the press, freedom of assembly and association—harbor a certain ambivalence in that their social character marks the transition to the political sphere. According to Schmitt, these rights must be considered as genuine basic rights "insofar [as] the individual does not leave the merely societal realm and free competition and free debate between individuals are to be acknowledged."[29] However, these rights can easily lose their "unpolitical character"(!) and then cease to be individual rights of freedom guaranteed as prepolitical freedom in accordance with the principles of constitutional distribution of rights.[30]

Clearly separated from these rights are the rights of political participation. They do not belong to the individual as a prepolitical subject of private interests, but address him or her as a member of the political people, that is, as a *citoyen*.[31] Hence Schmitt's clear critique of the secret ballot which destroys the public character of political legitimacy in a democracy because it summons the individual as a private person (*homme*) rather than as a member and part of the political people (*citoyen*); it thereby harbors—and this is the half-explicit crucial point in the critique—the danger of decomposition of the political unity which itself thus remains unprotected against its being overwhelmed by private and societal interests.[32]

Second, the state cannot be prevented from intervening in those spheres of basic liberties which may become politically relevant by immediately affecting fundamental preconditions of the political unity, such as a relative homogeneity of the people. From my first reading of *Verfassungslehre* I still remember the following remark: "The political problem of cinema movies influencing the masses is so important that no state can leave that powerful psycho-technical machine without control. The state must neutralize it politically. Given that the political is inevitable, neutrality means that the state must employ cinema movies to serve the political order, even if the state may lack the courage needed to openly use them as a means of integration on behalf of a socio-psychological homogeneity."[33]

The concrete context of this remark is the justification of a caveat on behalf of possible censorship of cinema movies, a caveat enshrined in the Weimar Constitution (Article 118, Sec. 2) and actually implemented in a law of 1920. In Schmitt's essays from 1932 and 1933, the years of the Weimar Republic's final crisis, his statements are even more outspoken. The background might be the practical experience of mass manipulation by the new media. Schmitt now writes that, however liberal a state might be, it can never afford leaving those new means of mass manipulation and of building a public collective opinion to another institution.[34] Schmitt implicitly (though not explicitly) holds that otherwise the state would surrender itself and cease to exist as a political unity. One could be tempted to apply this insight to contemporary media like television; but this would be another article.[35]

A second remark can be found in a contribution to the *Handbuch der Staatsrechts*. (Schmitt was always proud of that remark and of the fact that Rudolf Smend had immediately noticed and appreciated it.) In his article Schmitt categorizes Article 135 of the Weimar Constitution as freedom of religion and—in opposition to Anschütz—not as freedom of an antireligious conviction.[36] The state, concerned with the relative homogeneity of the people as the precondition of its own existence, cannot remain completely neutral—in the sense of agnosticism—with regard to religion or nonreligion.

Third, economic and social interest groups must be confined to their specific realm and prevented from taking control over political functions of the state which itself must be shielded against political pluralism. For Schmitt, political representation of organized interest groups is impossible. Political influence of interest groups leads to a weakening or questioning of the state as a political unity—unless and until these groups take direct political responsibility as bearers of political decisions.[37] A *stato corporativo* would have been conceivable for Schmitt. Such a state rests on the constitutional recognition of guilds, unions, or other organized groups as bearers of political decision and political responsibility. What Schmitt had to criticize and actually did criticize was the occupation of the political by indirect powers, be it socioeconomic or religious and denominational powers, which for instrumental purposes extend their grip to political functions of the state without being held accountable for political decisions.[38] Hence his principled opposition to every kind of *potestas indirecta*, including that of the church.[39]

6. The necessity of a "pouvoir neutre" within the state. For the political unity of the state to be preserved and realized, an encompassing point of reference is needed which itself must be willing and able to achieve agreement and integration of conflicting and antagonistic interests. This is the task and role of a *pouvoir neutre*.[40] It is needed in order to avoid the escalation of conflicting interests and other potential antagonisms to a friend-enemy grouping and hence a threat to the political unity itself. In establishing the state order as a unity of power and peace, one does not abandon once and for all the possibility of political dissociation; depending on various circumstances, its poisonous potential can always reemerge. To prevent this, one needs a policy of order and agreement on an encompassing scale. Such a policy, however, cannot be conducted by political forces that are tied to particular (though legally permissible) antagonistic interests.

In his book *Der Hüter der Verfassung* Schmitt looks for such a *pouvoir neutre*, which he finally finds (within the Weimar state) in the public service and in the Reich's president.[41] Whether this assessment still holds for the final phase of the Weimar Republic is a *quaestio facti* (question of fact). What I am interested in here is the *quaestio iuris* (question of law), namely, the inevitability of such a *pouvoir neutre*—whatever its actual constitutional location—for the maintenance and capability of action of any state order.

7. *Carl Schmitt's concept of representation.* Although Schmitt's concept of representation is difficult to understand and would require another chapter, I will not skip the problem here. In Schmitt's work, representation always relates to the political unity of the people, i.e., the state; it does not mean representation of the society vis-à-vis the state or representation of interests within the society. Moreover, the subject of representation is not the people *in* the state but, rather, the politically united and organized people which is the state itself.[42] Obviously, this derives from the idea that only the state as such, that is, the political unity, is capable of representation and that any other representation than that of the state would necessarily dissolve the political unity.

It is possible that the concept of representation—which, as far as I can see, Schmitt for the last time mentioned in *Verfassungslehre*—did not find a definitive theoretical formulation. One can follow various stages within the development of this concept, with different nuances and different formulations. The concept occurs first in *Romischer Katholizismus und politische Form*, later in a lengthy footnote in *Die geistesgeschichtliche Lage*, finally and in detail in *Verfassungslehre* (here also within a debate with Rudolf Smend).[43] (Leibholz's habilitation thesis on representation appeared only in 1929 and thus was not yet available when Schmitt wrote his *Verfassungslehre*.)

One has to take into account that representation of societal interests and groups constitutes a problem for the concept of representation, as it is elaborated in *Verfassungslehre*; representation of interest groups is not even considered. Another problem is democratic representation by which the citizens are represented in terms of what they have in common in order to achieve political unity.[44] Representation is conceived of in a rather static way; it means representation of something invisible and yet real, which thereby is made visible.[45] Representation thus appears like a picture of something already present rather than a process of actively bringing about unity and a conscience of commonality.[46]

On the other hand, in a chapter of *Verfassungslehre* one also finds the insight that the political unity of the people is not naturally given but rather is the object of political efforts: "Every political unity must in some sense be integrated, as it is not given by nature but rests on human decision."[47] This statement comes close to Smend's doctrine of integration from which it differs, however, in that integration in the Schmittian sense always derives from decision. Schmitt further writes: "Representation brings about unity, yet what it brings about is always the unity of a people in its political state."[48] Here the stress very much lies on active conduct, which means that representation, properly speaking, is reserved for government agents since only they can be active. To put it more precisely, it is government in the strict sense, not administration, because representation is reserved for those who epitomize and concretize the spiritual principle of political existence.[49] In this context, Schmitt cites Lorenz von Stein. But he also mentions the nineteenth-century dualism of two representations, a representation of the people vis-à-vis the monarch who himself was to represent the state as a whole, especially in foreign affairs and international diplomacy.[50] Does this mean that the former was no representation at all, not even an element of representation? Another question is how to conceive of *democratic* representation. This question occurs because representation, as a constitutional concept, always refers to the state unity as an entirety. If this is the case, however, one has to wonder how representation of the people within the state or within parliament is conceivable. It seems to me that in this regard many questions remain open and await an answer which I cannot provide here.

III

The purpose of this chapter was to display Carl Schmitt's Constitutional Theory, not to argue critically about it. I have tried to analyze this work and — against the common charge of occasionalism[51] — to demonstrate its logical consistency from a systematic point, a point that seems indeed fundamental to me. The question of whether the basic concepts, distinctions, and assertions of Schmitt's theory are appropriate for an understanding of the reality of state, state life, state existence, and state order so far has only been raised and not yet answered. It seems to me that this question should be debated on the basis of a systematic analysis of Schmitt's work. Let me conclude by hinting at two aspects which I consider crucial for such a debate. The first aspect concerns the question of whether Schmitt's criterion of the political and his concept of the state as a political unity are right. The second aspect concerns the importance of liberty—individual as well as political liberty—for the unity and order of the state. Is Schmitt's definition appropriate or is it not—especially in view of the establishment and development of a relative homogeneity and solidarity of a people as the basis of the state's unity and capability of action?

Notes

This chapter is reprinted from Ernst-Wolfgang Böckenförde, *Recht, Staat, und Freiheit: Studien zur Rechtsphilosophie, Staatstheorie und Verfassungsgeschichte* (Frankfurt: Suhrkamp, 1991), by permission of the author and Suhrkamp. Translated by Heiner Bielefeldt. The original title is "Der Begriff des Politischen als Schlüssel zum staatsrechtlichen Werk Carl Schmitts."

1 Carl Schmitt, *Verfassungslehre* (Berlin, 1928), at 2, 125 *passim*.
2 Ibid., at 200.
3 Otto von Gierke, *Das Wesen der menschlichen Verbände. Rektoratsrede* (Berlin, 1902), at 8ff.
4 Carl Schmitt, *Der Begriff des Politischen. Text von 1932 mit einem Vorwort und drei Corrolarien* (Munich, 1963) (hereafter *Der Begriff*), at 34–35: "War is by no means the goal or purpose or even content of politics. Being a real possibility, however, war is an ever existing presupposition which in a peculiar way determines human action and thought thereby yielding a specifically political behavior." This statement, though abbreviated and slightly different, can also be found in the third edition from 1933, at 17.
5 Ernst-Wolfgang Böckenförde, "Staat-Gesellschaft-Kirche," in *Christlicher Glaube in moderner Gesellschaft*, vol. 15 (Freiburg, 1982), at 82.
6 Schmitt, *Der Begriff*, supra n. 4, at 30f. See also the introduction of the 1963 edition, ibid., at 10f.
7 See Ernst-Wolfgang Böckenförde, "Die Eigenart des Staatsrechts und der Staatsrechtswissenschaft," in *Recht und Staat im sozialen Wandel. Festschrift H.U. Skupin* (Berlin, 1983), at 317 and at 330ff.
8 Carl Schmitt, *Politische Theologie*, 2d ed. (1934), at 11.
9 Ibid., at 20. Hence Schmitt writes that sovereignty, defined legally, does not mean a monopoly of coercion or power but a monopoly of decision. See also H. Heller, *Die Souveränität* (1927), in *Gesammelte Schriften*, vol. 2 (Tübingen, 1971), at 120ff. and 185ff.).
10 See the paper by E. R. Huber in H. Quaritsch, ed., *Complexio Oppositorum. Über Carl Schmitt* (Berlin, 1988), at 33ff.

11 Schmitt, *Der Begriff*, supra n. 4, at 39; see also Heller, supra n. 9, at 185ff. This is the starting point of Schmitt's theory of confederation which rests on the assumption that, due to the homogeneity within the confederation, an existential conflict between the federal and the state level does not occur; hence the question of sovereignty can be left undecided. See *Verfassungslehre*, supra n. 1, at 370ff.

12 Schmitt, *Der Begriff*, supra n. 4, at 51–54. Loss of sovereignty would be synonymous to loss of final political decision. In regard to such a case, Schmitt writes: "If a people lacks the force or will to maintain itself within the sphere of the political, the political does not thereby disappear. What disappears is merely a weak people" [scil.: as a political unity]. Ibid., at 54.

13 The classical legal concept for such a case is protectorate; the political concept is hegemony.

14 The relationship between state and constitution is already implied in the concept of constitution in that this concept means the decision about the way and form of the political unity whose very existence is thus presupposed. See *Verfassungslehre*, supra n. 1, at § 3 I, at 21f. This does not preclude the possibility that in a particular historic and political situation the act of constitution-giving coincides with setting up the political unity of the state. An example is the situation of state secession. However, this is not necessarily the case, and it was not the case with the establishment of the great paradigmatic constitutions, such as the French Constitution of 1791 or that of the United States in 1787.

15 Ibid., at § 3, 20 and 21–23.

16 Ibid., at § 7 II, 62ff.

17 Hence Schmitt's constant criticism of the constitutional dualism as it is typical of the constitutional monarchy. This criticism can already be found in *Verfassungslehre*, supra n. 1, at § 6 II 5, 53ff. It is much harsher in his *Staatsgefüge und Zusammenbruch des Zweiten Reiches* (Hamburg, 1934) where Schmitt takes the constitutional conflict of Prussia as an example to demonstrate that a constitutional monarchy is a permanent compromise between opposite principles of political legitimacy. For a different opinion, see E. R. Huber, *Deutsche Verfassungsgeschichte seit 1789*, vol. 3 (Stuttgart: W. Kohlhammer, 1963), at 1–20. Important in this connection is Rainer Wahl's argument that a constitutional review and constitutional monarchy could not fit together. See Rainer Wahl, "Der Vorrang der Verfassung," *Der Staat* 20 (1981): at 485ff.

18 This is not in contradiction to Schmitt's thesis in *Legalität und Legitimität* (Munich, 1932), at 87f. that, in the face of the crisis of the Weimar Republic, the second main part of the Weimar Constitution should be preserved and purged of the contradictions and fictions of a merely technical and functional system of legality to which the first part had developed. Given that the second part of the constitution contained not only liberal basic rights (in the

sense of private and societal rights) but also "orders of community life," that part of the constitution could become effective only within the framework of a working "political" order whose restoration Schmitt therefore demands.

19 It is the common conviction of political philosophers as different as Thomas Hobbes and Immanuel Kant that the state and the concentration of sovereign power established by the state are necessary to protect the individual against the dangers and threats by their fellow people. See Thomas Hobbes, *Elementa philosophica de cive* (Oxford: Clarendon Press, 1983), at chaps. 5 and 6–7; Thomas Hobbes, *Leviathan* (New York: Cambridge University Press, 1991), at chap. 17; Immanuel Kant, *Metaphysik der Sitten* (New York: Cambridge University Press, 1991), at pt. I, § 44; Immanuel Kant, *Ideen zu einer allgemeinen Geschichte in weltbürgerlicher Absicht*, vol. 9, Weischedel, ed. (Hamburg, 1954), at 40f.

20 Carl Schmitt, "Das Reichsgericht als Hüter der Verfassung" (Berlin, 1929), in *Verfassungsrechtliche Aufsätze* (Berlin, 1958), at 73ff. and 97ff. (hereafter *Reichsgericht*). Carl Schmitt, *Der Hüter der Verfassung* (Tübingen, 1931), at 26–34 (hereafter *Hüter*). By constitutional jurisdiction Schmitt means juridical decisions of constitutional conflicts in the original sense, that is, conflicts which concern the gravitational field of the political, such as the struggle for, as well as the maintenance, stabilization, and questioning of, political power and its execution.

21 Böckenförde, supra n. 7, at 320f.

22 Within the framework of the political system, the judge is called upon to interpret and apply laws independently of a possible former political struggle over their content. Rather than "making politics with different means," he has simply to refer to the context of the existing legal order. Exactly this is the "political" character of his task and role. See Niklas Luhmann, "Funktionen der Rechtsprechung im politischen System," in *Dritte Gewalt heute? Schriften der Evangelischen Akademie Hessen Nassau*, vol. 4 (1969), at 9f.; Ernst-Wolfgang Böckenförde, *Verfassungsfragen der Richterwahl* (Berlin, 1974), at 89ff.

23 Schmitt, *Hüter*, supra n. 20, at 48ff.; Schmitt, *Reichsgericht*, supra n. 20, at 97ff., including the postscript at 108.

24 *Hüter*, supra n. 20, at 132ff.

25 Ibid., at 2.

26 Rudolf Smend, *Verfassung und Verfassungsrecht* (Berlin, 1928), at 98 and 152f.

27 Ibid., at 78ff. and 137ff.

28 See *Verfassungslehre*, supra n. 1, at 163–70, esp. the schematic overview at 170.

29 Ibid., at 165.

30 Ibid.

31 Ibid., at 168ff.

32 This criticism first appears in *Die geistesgeschichtliche Lage des heutigen*

Parlamentarismus, 2d ed. (Munich, 1926), at 22f. (hereafter *Geistesgeschicht-liche Lage*). In a succinct and straightforward way it is repeated in the article "Der bürgerliche Rechtsstaat," *Abendland* (1928): 202, as well as in *Verfas-sungslehre,* supra n. 1, at 245f. The critique voiced in *Die geistesgeschicht-liche Lage* has explicitly been approved by Smend, supra n. 26, at 37, n. 4.

33 *Verfassungslehre,* supra n. 1, at 168.

34 Carl Schmitt, "Weiterentwicklung des totalen Staates in Deutschland," (1932–33), republished in his *Verfassungsrechtliche Aufsätze* (Berlin, 1958), at 360; see also *Machtposition des modernen Staates* (1933), at 368f.

35 See the impressively sober and well-balanced analysis by K. Eichenberger, "Beziehungen zwischen Massenmedien und Demokratie," *Festschrift Leo Schürmann* (Freiburg/Switzerland, 1978), at 405ff.

36 Carl Schmitt, "Inhalt und Bedeutung des zweiten Hauptteils der Reichs-verfassung," *Handbuch des Staatsrechts,* vol. 2 (1932), at 584; G. Anschütz, *Die Verfassung des deutschen Reiches vom 11. August 1919,* 14th ed. (1933), remark 4 with n. 2 referring to Art. 135.

37 See *Der Begriff,* supra n. 4, at 40–45; also Carl Schmitt, *Staatsethik und pluralistischer Staat* (Berlin, 1930); Carl Schmitt, *Positionen und Begriffe* (Berlin, 1940), at 133ff. and esp. at 136–42.

38 Schmitt, *Hüter,* supra n. 20, at 71: "Pluralism, however, means a majority of organized social power, running across different areas of the state as well as across the boundaries of countries or municipalities. This social power, although lacking the quality of a state, nevertheless manipulates the will-formation of the state."

39 Carl Schmitt, *Der Leviathan in der Staatslehre des Thomas Hobbes* (Berlin, 1938), at 117: "It is essential for an indirect power that it blurs the rela-tionship between command and political danger, power and responsibility, protection and obedience. Being unaccountable in its indirect and yet effec-tive exercise of power, it takes all the advantages of political power and avoids all its dangers."

40 *Hüter,* supra n. 20, at 114f., 132ff.

41 Ibid., at 149ff. and 156ff.

42 *Verfassungslehre,* supra n. 1, at 212 and 210.

43 *Römischer Katholizismus und politische Form,* 2d ed. (Berlin, 1925), at 25ff. (referring to personal dignity and representation of a spiritual principle); *Die geistesgeschichtliche Lage,* supra n. 32, at nn. 3–43 (applying representation to the political realm); *Verfassungslehre,* supra n. 1, at 204–16 (development of representation as a constitutional concept).

44 See Ernst-Wolfgang Böckenförde, *Demokratie und Repräsentation* (Han-nover, 1983), at 21–26.

45 *Verfassungslehre,* supra n. 1, at 209: "Representation means to render some-thing invisible publicly visible and hence present." See also Böckenförde, *Demokratie und Repräsentation,* at 207.

46 On the process of representation, see M. Draht, "Die Entwicklung der Volks-repräsentation," (1954), in H. V. Rausch, ed., *Zur Theorie und Geschichte der Repräsentation und der Repräsentativverfassung* (Darmstadt, 1995), at 260ff. (esp. at 275ff. and 292ff.).

47 *Verfassungslehre*, supra n. 1, at 207.

48 Ibid., at 214.

49 Ibid., at 212.

50 Ibid., at 210f.

51 Translator's note: Böckenförde here alludes to an article by Karl Löwith who accuses Schmitt of propagating a radical political decisionism (= occasional-ism) by which the very continuity of time and experience is dissolved. See Karl Löwith, "Der okkasionelle Dezisionismus von C. Schmitt," in *Gesam-melte Abhandlungen. Zur Kritik der geschichtlichen Existenz* (Stuttgart: Kohlhammer, 1960), at 93–126.

From Legitimacy to Dictatorship—and Back Again

Leo Strauss's Critique of the Anti-Liberalism

of Carl Schmitt

Robert Howse

Introduction

The encounter between Carl Schmitt and Leo Strauss remains a source of fascination and polemics for the friends and enemies of both thinkers. According to Stephen Holmes, both Schmitt and Strauss belong to a single tradition of anti-liberalism, whose ultimate practical implication is suggested by Schmitt's fate as a Nazi apologist.[1] Indeed, Holmes places much emphasis on Strauss's criticism of Schmitt for failing to develop a critique of liberalism that goes beyond the horizon of liberalism itself and interprets this criticism of Schmitt as a call for a form of anti-liberalism more extreme and virulent than that propounded by Schmitt on the very eve of his membership in the Nazi party.[2]

Friends of Schmitt, or those who wish to revive his thought on the Right, have used his exchange with Strauss to a quite different effect. Drawing on the prestige of Strauss in America, and his international reputation as a Jewish thinker, it is possible to display Strauss's clear sympathy with elements of Schmitt's thought as an indication that the "last word" or deepest teaching of the latter cannot be fascism. Thus, Heinrich Meier, one of the leading apologists for Schmitt in Germany today, focuses on a quite different dimension of Strauss's critique of the *Concept of the Political*—in particular, on Strauss's supposition that Schmitt's ultimate concern in facing off with liberalism is to vindicate or restore the seriousness of life as against liberalism's reduction of the human drama to mere economics and entertainment.[3] Meier argues that the ultimate *dis*agreement between Strauss and Schmitt is as to whether the seriousness of life finds its vindication in theology (Schmitt) or Socratic philosophy (Strauss). Understood in this way, the deepest intent of neither thinker is to justify fascism or virulent *political* anti-liberalism.

Meier's efforts on behalf of Schmitt appear to dovetail in some measure with recent attempts by friends of Strauss[4] to save him from Holmes's charge of anti-liberalism. Thus, Peter Berkowitz—in a penetrating review of Holmes's book in the *Yale Law Journal*[5]—questions Holmes's reading of many of the passages in Strauss's work that he uses to justify placing Strauss squarely in the anti-liberal tradition. Berkowitz shows persuasively that Holmes ignores the context of many of these passages, as well as many other statements of Strauss where he indicates his sympathy for liberal democracy, and his clear preference for the liberal regime over the alternatives available in our times. Likewise, in an essay entitled "Leo Strauss's Liberal Politics," Nasser Behnegar seeks to respond to Holmes, among others, by attempting to show that, even if he rejected liberal theoretical principles in favor of classic natural right, Strauss was able to see important affinities between the demands of classic natural right and modern liberal democracy. These affinities are visible in liberalism's openness to individual excellence, its protection of the freedom to philosophize and its opposition to and constraints on arbitrary and immoderate, i.e., tyrannical, power.[6]

A debate about Strauss's relationship to liberalism also exists among French post-Marxist thinkers of a progressive or liberal persuasion. Claude Lefort sees Strauss's thought as of great importance in the recovery of a solid normative ground from which to diagnose the excesses of twentieth-century totalitarianism.[7] Luc Ferry and Alain Renaut, by contrast, argue that Strauss's rejection of modern subjective freedom in the name of a fixed hierarchical conception of the human good places his thought in implacable opposition to the very idea of human rights, which for Ferry and Renaut must be at the core of any plausible contemporary liberal democratic, or liberal republican, theory.[8]

Although they have made a prima facie case that there are ways of reading Strauss compatible with some dimensions of liberalism, those who would establish Strauss's credentials as a friend of liberalism have as yet failed to provide an adequate explanation for his sympathetic engagement with the thought of Schmitt and especially an explanation of what Strauss meant by his call for a "horizon beyond liberalism." Moreover, on the basis of Strauss's own observation that even Schmitt's anti-liberalism shares important premises or assumptions with liberalism, one might attribute statements of Strauss that have affinities with liberal thought to a shortfall in Strauss's aspiration to work pure, as it were, his *own* anti-liberalism, and to a self-consciousness of his inability to find a self-standing anti-liberal viewpoint.

There is an important reason why Strauss's call for a "horizon ·beyond liberalism" cannot easily be dismissed as an early, perhaps naive, position of a thinker who had not yet seen the worst consequences of twentieth-century anti-liberalism. The reason is that, in his intellectual autobiography, "Preface to the English Translation of *Spinoza's Critique of Religion*"[9] published in the 1960s, Strauss refers to his comments on the *Concept of the Political* not indeed as an example of his early, surpassed thought, but rather as "the first expression" of a "change in orientation," i.e., toward the recovery of ancient and medieval philosophy, that would mark his mature thought.[10] (And in fact Strauss had his comments on the *Concept of the Political* reprinted at the end of the English Spinoza volume.)

In this chapter, I intend to contribute to the debate on Strauss's relationship to liberalism, through reinterpreting his engagement with Carl Schmitt in a manner that, I hope, will serve to clarify what Strauss meant by a "horizon beyond liberalism." I shall argue, *contra* Holmes, that in calling for a "horizon beyond liberalism" Strauss was not seeking a more virulently anti-liberal position than Schmitt. Instead, he was grasping for a perspective from which one could, dispassionately and with philosophic clarity, assess the claims both of liberals and their enemies. Strauss achieved this perspective through the tentative and experimental adoption of the position of classic natural right. The ultimate result of the adoption of this perspective is neither liberalism nor anti-liberalism but a recognition of the limits of both, limits that relate to their common distant origins in the philosophic revolution of early modernity. Strauss's "horizon beyond liberalism"—classic natural right—provides a response to Schmitt's decisionism while taking seriously many of decisionism's own premises concerning the limits of the rule of law. At the same time, the classic perspective shows the inadequacy of positivistic and relativistic strains of liberal legal and political theory to provide a convincing response to Schmittian decisionism.

In addition to clarifying Strauss's relation to liberalism and its enemies, a consideration of Strauss's engagement with Schmitt can also contribute to our understanding of the controversies surrounding the intent of Schmitt himself. Once Strauss had found the "horizon beyond liberalism" that he called for in his comments on Schmitt, the result was a much less sympathetic assessment of Schmitt's ultimate intent. This is reflected most clearly perhaps in the chapter on classic natural right in *Natural Right and History*, where in the course of elaborating on the classic perspective, Strauss had occasion to revisit many of Schmitt's arguments in light of classical principles, albeit without naming him. This reassessment was based in part on a recognition of the Machiavellian character of decisionism—a recognition not present in Strauss's "Notes on the *Concept of the Political*." In 1932, Strauss took at face value Schmitt's declared debt to Hobbes, in part because Strauss had not yet discovered that Machiavelli, not Hobbes, was the deepest source of modernity. Unlike Hobbes, who oriented himself by the exception in order to produce a societal order that would, as far as possible, secure against the exception, Machiavelli, like Schmitt, admired and embraced the exception. Schmitt's last word is not theology or any transcendent basis for human seriousness—his last word is the eternal relation of protection and obedience, the unconstrained rule of the strong over the weak as the one authentic form of order implied in the universality of man's animal striving. This striving leads the strong to seek domination and the weak protection; the strong to acquire and the weak to try to hold on to what they possess. Whether man's animal striving is viewed as good or evil depends on whether one adopts the perspective of the higher group of ruling men or the lower group of men who must be ruled. But Schmitt deviates from Machiavelli in a crucial respect— he admires the resolve and honesty of overt and self-confident dictatorship, not domination as such. He seeks, therefore, not a combination of the lion and the fox, but rather a Cesare with the soul of Luther. Thus, when in *Political Theology* Schmitt refers to the "exacting moral decision" as "the core of the political idea,"[11] this does not refer to the aspiration to ground decisionism in a higher morality—what is morally exacting is the requirement to decide "out of nothingness." Moral exactness means nothing more or less than the courage and honesty to affirm one's own will to power as the only ground of the decision.

In *Natural Right and History*, Strauss invokes the perspective of classic natural right not to complete the anti-liberal thrust of Schmitt's thought but to oppose it. Strauss now argues, not that decisionism is inadequate because it remains within certain premises of liberal relativism, but that, because of its complex relationship to decisionism, liberal relativism is inadequate as a basis for opposing "fanatical obscurantism," i.e., fascism. He presents the perspective of classic natural right as providing a theoretically rich set of resources for addressing the claims of decisionism in a manner that does not say farewell to the rule of law. But Strauss's concluding remarks in his presentation of the classic perspective leave open whether the results of the experimental adoption of this perspective point ultimately to the definitive choice of classic natural right over liberalism, or rather to the rediscovery, not only of the premoderns, but also of forgotten or suppressed dimensions of the liberal tradition, dimensions concealed or obscured by the predominance of relativistic and positivistic forms of liberalism in Strauss's and Schmitt's own time.

The Character of Schmitt's Anti-Liberalism: An Interpretation of *Political Theology* and *The Concept of the Political*

Political Theology and *The Concept of the Political* set out the most crucial dimensions of Schmitt's anti-liberalism in relatively brief, if sometimes cryptic, form. Both these works interweave a set of bold, incisive, and arresting claims with often rambling and pedantic discussions of scholarly literature in the fields of law, philosophy, and social science. While, as is obvious and often noted by Schmitt himself, his thought and the categories he employs are themselves "polemical," in these works at least, Schmitt seems consciously to choose the pose of jurist and professor. Schmitt's discussions of the literature, along with his collections of unoriginal and often inconsistent criticisms of liberalism,[12] can easily detain and distract a reader, especially one who is a scholar or a dogmatic liberal, or both. In fact, access to the argument of both these works depends on connecting the bold, incisive, and arresting claims that are dotted throughout (even if sometimes these very claims are buried in quotations from other authors that Schmitt explicitly endorses).

The first chapter of *Political Theology* opens with what seems almost to be an internal critique of liberal legalism. Liberal legalism, in understanding sovereignty in terms of a system of general legal norms, cannot account for the exception, the situation of dire emergency where the very existence of the (liberal) state is at stake. The preservation of the state in these circumstances may require the suspension of the entire legal order, and yet—by definition—the state, and thus the sovereign, must subsist regardless of this suspension. Although Schmitt recognizes the attempts by liberal states to deal with this problem through constitutionally stipulating by whom, and under what circumstances, emergency powers may be exercised, all these attempts are inadequate and merely conceal the fundamental nature of the exception. How can one adequately anticipate in advance, and thereby adequately stipulate in law, the range of situations where the existence of the state may require the exercise of unlimited power? An emergency is an emergency. And if we accept the premise that genuinely *unlimited* power may be necessary to the existence of the state, does this not also entail accepting that such power is, by definition, also power to suspend any prior legal strictures that purport to limit the exercise of emergency power itself?

Schmitt thus moves swiftly from the proposition that emergency powers may be required to preserve the liberal state in a crisis to the proposition that *unlimited* powers are required. This implies at least the possibility that if power is limited in *any* way under a state of emergency this may lead to the downfall of the state. But one could object: as an empirical matter, can it be shown that there is any likelihood that circumscribed emergency powers will be inadequate to deal with a crisis of the liberal state? Thus, a liberal constitutionalist might simply say that circumscribed emergency powers trade off the small risk that such powers may be insufficient to save the liberal state against the larger risk to liberal constitutionalism of giving anyone truly unlimited power.

Schmitt's concession to this objection marks a decisive shift in his argument. "If measures undertaken in an exception could be circumscribed by mutual control, by imposing a time limit, or finally, as in liberal constitutional procedure governing a state of siege, the question of sovereignty would then be considered less significant but would certainly not be eliminated." Schmitt now goes on to reproach, not the liberal state, but liberal *jurisprudence* for its avoidance of the problem of the exception.[13] But as Schmitt himself notes, liberal jurisprudence has what seems like a fully internally consistent answer to this reproach, namely that legal science is by its nature concerned with the general and normative, not with the exceptional and anomalous.[14] In responding to this answer, Schmitt begins by turning on its head the emphasis on systemic unity in Hans Kelsen's liberal jurisprudence: the exception cannot be ignored because it "confounds the unity and order of the rationalist scheme." But of course, as Schmitt suggests in citing Gerhard Anschütz's remark "here is where public law stops," liberal jurisprudence may understand the exception, the anomaly, as the limiting case of an internally unified system. Thus, rather than confounding the scheme, the exception may be viewed as simply setting the bounds of it—the idea of a *bounded* rational order is not alien to neo-Kantianism.

This is the point at which the normative ground of Schmitt's position begins to open, and he no longer presents himself as concerned with the demands of liberal jurisprudence but rather with those of "a philosophy of concrete life." "The exception is more interesting than the rule. . . . In the exception the power of real life breaks through the crust of a mechanism that has become torpid by repetition."[15]

This rearticulation of the significance of the exception prepares the way for the radicalization of Schmitt's encounter with liberal legalism in chapter 2 of *Political Theology*. In chapter 2 the issue is shifted from the requirements for the preservation of an existing state or order to the manner in which a new order is created. We may suspect that where "real life breaks through" is in the establishment or founding of a new order, not in the various police and military decrees and actions required to deal with a crisis in the existing order. The pride of place given to the exception therefore shifts focus from the conservative, and putatively legitimate, task of defending an existing regime during a crisis that threatens it, to the revolutionary, and less obviously legitimate, undertaking of creating or founding a new order.

Schmitt refers to Kelsen's conception of the state as a legal order characterized by "a system of ascriptions to a last point of ascription and to a last basic norm."[16] This last basic norm, the *Grundnorm*, cannot by definition be derived from the system itself, yet it is on the *Grundnorm* that the coherence of the entire system ultimately rests. And if, as Kelsen wishes to do, one severs law from morality,[17] it is almost inevitable that one views the *Grundnorm* as a decision or command that has no justification outside itself. The foundation or *Grundnorm* must either be "a further tautological circumscription of the 'unity' or a brutal sociopolitical reality."[18]

The final step in Schmitt's radicalization of the problem of the exception occurs toward the end of chapter 2, following a long and rather arid discussion of the use of the concept of form in various sociological and political theories. Drawing on Max Weber's notion of the requirement of a trained bureaucracy or professional class to interpret and apply legal norms, Schmitt argues that legal norms never permit automatic or immediate application. They entail a decision by individual persons in particular cases, a decision which almost by definition cannot be fully determined by the norm. This insight is the basis of the much more radical claim that "the decision emanates from nothingness."[19]

The underdetermined character of legal norms from the perspective of the correct decision of individual cases is, Schmitt implies, inseparable from radical indeterminacy. Such a move from the claim of underdeterminedness to that of radical indeterminacy is possible precisely on the basis of what we have identified as the previous basic step in Schmitt's argument, the recognition of the fundamental ungroundedness of the *Grundnorm*, already implicit in the separation of law and morality in Kelsen's positivist version of liberal legalism. There are no foundational normative sources of legal order to which the decision maker can draw on to overcome the underdetermined character of the legal norm itself in the hard case.[20] The ultimate implication is that, even in the case of the liberal state, the machine does not run itself. Normatively ungrounded personal decisions, previously identified with the exception, in fact permeate even the liberal legal order. This reveals the precise ground of Schmitt's attack on liberal legalism—the attack is not based on the notion of the weakness or incapacity for decision of a liberal order, much less its inability to act decisively during a crisis, but rather on liberal *jurisprudence* or *ideology*, which hides or obscures the decisionist character of all rule.[21] Ironically, positivist liberal jurisprudence, when examined carefully, actually reveals what it seeks to hide—we need only consider Kelsen's *Grundnorm*, the sources of which are shrouded in mystery or obscurity but which actually turns out to be a foundationless foundation.

For Schmitt, the supposed Catholic conservative, laying bare the groundlessness of the city of man might logically imply a return to the City of God, to the divine order as the basis for conscience or normative constraints in the exercise of power. It is precisely this expectation that is raised by the title of the next chapter, "Political Theology." But the fundamental claim that emerges out of this chapter, a claim that is prepared by Schmitt's discussion of the interpenetration of theological and political ideas in the historical development of the West, is that "conceptions of transcendence will no longer be credible to most educated people. . . ."[22] The restoration of the dignity and self-respect of decisionist command, the restoration of open and unapologetically personalistic domination cannot occur on the basis of a transcendent concept of legitimacy, such as the divine right of kings. It must occur on the ground of immanent legitimacy, on the ground of democracy. By referring to dictatorship as the solution of a Catholic philosopher of the state (Donoso Cortes) to this dilemma Schmitt can hardly be said to have obviated the crucial question that an orthodox Catholic might ask: why should dignity and self-respect be attached to personalistic rule *if* it lacks a credible transcendent normative basis? Thus the final chapter of *Political Theology* entails a confrontation of Schmitt's decisionism and orthodox Catholicism. This confrontation, often ignored by interpreters who assume Schmitt's "last word" is his attack on *liberalism,* brings into sharp relief the radical, nihilistic character of Schmitt's decisionism.

Thus, in the final chapter, it is all too easy to be detained by Schmitt's rather blunt and old-hat attack on liberals and particularly anarchists for their assumptions about man's natural goodness (an attack already made in much more pointed fashion, for example, by Nietzsche and by Dostoyevsky in his *Devils*). In fact, the core of the final chapter is Schmitt's rather more subtle, if decisive disagreement with certain thinkers in the Catholic tradition who view man's "evil" in terms that Schmitt finds too simplistic or too absolute. Schmitt thus cites his agreement with the Abbé Gaduel who "voiced misgivings about [Cortes's] exaggeration of the natural evil and unworthiness of man."[23]

In what respect does Schmitt find Cortes's view exaggerated? Cortes's view "was indeed more horrible than anything that had ever been alleged by an absolutist philosophy of the state in justifying authoritarian rule." The meaning of this statement is elucidated by Schmitt's observation that to Cortes "the stupidity of the masses was just as apparent . . . as was the silly vanity of the leaders."[24] Precisely if the leaders are as evil as the masses, an absolutist philosophy of the state can hardly stand (except, as in Hobbes, under the guise of the rule of a sovereign who is an *artificial* person). If all men are equally evil in their striving for power, in their "will to power," then the rule of some men over others is as little justified as in the anarchist hypothesis of all men's equal natural goodness.

The exaggerated or undifferentiated account of evil in Cortes and other conservatives like Maistre may be related to a defect in their thought to which Schmitt points us—they were incapable of "organic" thinking, that is unable to comprehend the "mutual penetration of opposites."[25] One may say that the mutual penetration of opposites that Cortes and Maistre needed to grasp was that man's evil, his greediness and striving for power, is connected to the goodness or at least superiority of a certain class of men.[26] For man's evil implies his need of dominion, and this implies the possibility of a class of men strong and resolute enough to dominate, and therefore not simply evil, i.e., a class of men in which desire cannot be understood simply as weakness. In the absence of such a complex understanding of "evil," the ultimate confrontation between the decisionism of Cortes and Maistre and the anarchism of Bakunin risks being a standoff between two oversimplified views of man's nature. The aporia of anarchism—good man and corrupt government—is matched by the aporia of the decisionism of Cortes and Maistre—evil man and good government. If decisionism is ultimately to win, it must find a basis beyond good and evil, or at least beyond the simplistic opposition of good and evil. And this basis must also solve the further difficulty that, while the decision that emanates from dictatorship is "an absolute decision created out of nothingness," at the same time dictatorship itself must somehow be sanctioned by "the will of the people."[27]

In *Concept of the Political*, Schmitt offers a reformulation of decisionism that attempts to solve these difficulties. He proposes the friend/enemy distinction as the core of the political. The distinction of friend and enemy denotes the utmost degree of intensity of a union or separation, of an association or disassociation. It can exist theoretically and practically, without having simultaneously to draw open all those moral, aesthetic, economic, or other distinctions. . . . Only the actual participants can correctly recognize, understand, and judge the concrete situation and settle the extreme case of conflict. Each participant is in a position to judge whether the adversary intends to negate his opponent's way of life and therefore must be repulsed or fought in order to preserve one's own form of existence.[28]

Who is a friend and who is an enemy is completely mutable, dependent on a concrete situation, and cannot be traced to any subsisting opposition whether moral, aesthetic, economic, or religious. Thus, the friend/enemy distinction provides a democratic criterion for the decision—preserving the collective existence or way of life of an entire people—but at the same time a criterion beyond discussion, because it does not refer to any normative benchmarks beyond the concrete situation in which the decision about the enemy is taken. The decision becomes both (democratically) justified and beyond any normative reference frame that would usually be implicit in the idea of justification.

Schmitt emphasizes that the friend/enemy decision does not simply apply to the case of hostilities or actual war, but to the possibility of war. While some of Schmitt's apologists invoke this fact to show the nonbellicose nature of his concept of politics,[29] the radical implication of Schmitt's move is to allow the possibility of war to determine the whole content of politics, even under conditions of peace, thereby eroding any possible moral meaning in the distinction between the requirements of normal politics and those of an extreme situation such as an emergency. The decision concerning the enemy determines the meaning of all the concepts within normal politics—the meaning of these concepts is always polemical.[30] Moreover, the power to decide concerning the enemy extends to the power to declare as (internal) enemy and treat accordingly any internal force or group that questions the primary decision concerning the enemy.[31] Thus, the friend/enemy distinction implies a form of sovereignty that is absolute and fatal to pluralism.

Schmitt goes on to explore two other senses in which the friend/enemy distinction implies absolute or unlimited power. First of all, because the decision about the enemy is always existential and concrete, it precludes the idea of a war fought from justice, i.e., in the name of a universal principle. Here Schmitt turns on its head the apparent liberal pacificist idea that no cause however just can vindicate the command to surrender one's life in battle. The implication is that, if all war is radically unjust, then the just war tradition cannot be invoked to distinguish in justice the limited, defensive war from an aggressive, expansionist war employing genocide. Schmitt turns pacificism against the natural law, just war tradition in order to remove *any* moral constraint from the conduct of war—thus we see how little his approach is really nonbellicose.

Second, Schmitt claims that liberalism (or the concrete "enemy" that hides behind the ideology of liberalism) seeks a final war to end all wars, a war in the name of a universal humanitarian ideology that would replace the political itself, the opposition of peoples and nations, with a world state. "What remains is neither politics nor state, but culture, civilization, economics, morality, law, art, entertainment, etc."[32] The implication of Schmitt's characterization of the humanitarian cause of a war to end all wars is that a people that wishes to preserve its own way of life against *this* enemy, cannot simply withdraw within its borders and wage *defensive and limited war.* The imperialistic project to end the friend/enemy distinction itself, at least in the immediate term, has the effect of intensifying the distinction even beyond its traditional meaning. The defense of the way of life of a people may imply not only a war unconstrained as to means, but also unconstrained as to its geographical scope. Purely defensive war—war to protect the integrity of one's own borders—would seem precluded by the very absolutist and universalist terms in which the enemy has cast the struggle: ". . . a war between the major powers today may easily turn into a world war."[33]

Yet this intellectual preparative for total war embroils Schmitt in a crucial difficulty. If the political is itself something unsuppressible, then he who seeks a war to end the possibility of war is not a worthy or meaningful adversary, since his defeat is *certain.* If liberal internationalism is to be a worthy enemy, then in principle it must be capable of victory. But victory, in eliminating the very basis for the friend/enemy distinction, would necessarily destroy any ground for the political. The problem of the political would disappear. And since the situation of friend and enemy is always concrete and existential, what objection can Schmitt make to the disappearance of the very possibility of this situation?

One prong of Schmitt's response to this difficulty is to admit that the struggle to destroy the political, to end all wars *may* succeed. The other prong is to argue that this success may be only temporary, that the power of some men over others will always reassert itself and therewith the potential of a friend/enemy grouping—but this second part of the response seems to depend, as Schmitt at first admits, on pure conjectures or an anthropological confession of faith that itself cannot be derived from the friend/enemy distinction.

This leads into the final and most fundamental part of the argument of *Concept of the Political*—the part of the argument that reveals the fact or hypothesis about the nature of political things that is more fundamental than the friend/enemy distinction itself. This is the hypothesis of man's dangerousness, the basis for the "eternal relation of protection and obedience."[34] It is in light of this relation that the friend/enemy distinction takes on its meaning as the core of the political.

Schmitt almost immediately moves the discussion from the issue of whether man is "by nature evil or by nature good" to the meaning of "evil."[35] What is called "evil" may manifest itself either in qualities such as "corruption, weakness, cowardice, stupidity, or also as brutality, sensuality, vitality, irrationality, and so on." One might say that the first set of qualities is contemptible while the second is, at least from Schmitt's perspective, admirable. While he also describes a set of qualities associated with goodness (including reasonableness but also "the capacity of being manipulated"), Schmitt goes on to clarify only the implication of the dual character of "evil." Having alluded to a variety of fables or stories describing animal behavior, and particularly the relationship of predator to prey, of strong to weak, Schmitt identifies evil with the various "drives" not of men as such but rather of "subjects," those who are ruled. Schmitt cites with unqualified approval ("it is unnecessary to differ from") a statement of Dilthey paraphrasing Machiavelli's understanding of human nature: "animality, drives, passions are the kernels of human nature—above all love and fear." Moreover, "from this principal feature of human nature [Machiavelli] derives the fundamental law of all political life."[36] This analysis results in the reformulation of "evil" as "dangerousness." This dangerousness manifests itself, however, in qualities among the weak, the mass of men, that can be considered "evil" in a more precise sense, in the sense of a lack or shortcoming that is not admirable. Such men are "evil" in that if they are not restrained or dominated, their natural drives slide "from passion into evil."[37] But if such men are not to destroy each other then one must presuppose the existence of other men who are able to rule. This might seem to require a modification of Machiavellianism in favor of a theory that finds "good" as well as "evil" in men's natures, i.e., qualities such as reasonableness and the ability to be guided or directed by reason. But this would only be true if men's drives as Machiavelli had described them (at least, according to Dilthey's summary) did not also generate in some class of men the qualities required to dominate—and as Schmitt's own references to the animal world suggest, it is precisely the other side as it were of man's animal drives, his passions, that leads to the will to dominate—"brutality," "vitality," etc.

Thus, Machiavellian premises are sufficient to generate that which is truly fundamental to the political and in light of which the friend/enemy distinction must be understood—the eternal relation of domination and obedience. And by using the word eternal here Schmitt clearly intends a contrast with all other political truths, including the friend/enemy distinction itself, which acquire their meaning *entirely* situationally and historically.[38] It is true that Schmitt asserts that he does not want "to decide the question of the nature of man."[39] In fact, by endorsing Dilthey's paraphrase of Machiavelli, he does settle this very question—if not metaphysically then at least politically.

But, even if Machiavelli's teaching is an adequate account of human nature for political purposes, it remains to understand in the name of what concrete political situation, in the name of what concrete antagonism between friend and enemy, this teaching must now be recalled. Schmitt supplies the following answer by reference to the revival of Machiavelli in German thought in the nineteenth century: "When it became important for the German people to defend themselves against an expanding enemy armed with a humanitarian ideology, Machiavelli was rehabilitated by Fichte and Hegel."[40] And has Schmitt not already characterized the forces that defeated Germany in 1918 as "an expanding enemy armed with a humanitarian ideology," an ideology whose universalist ambition implies precisely that a war against the enemy who hides behind that ideology will take on the most intense and brutal character?

There is, however, in Schmitt's intellectual climate, a difficulty in directly invoking Machiavelli. Machiavelli met a certain "misfortune":

"the political adversaries of a clear political theory will . . . easily refute political phenomena and truths in the name of some autonomous discipline as amoral, uneconomical, unscientific. . . ."[41] Learning from Machiavelli's "misfortune," Schmitt puts Machiavelli's teaching in the form of legal scholarship, which at times appears to be a learned internal critique of an "autonomous discipline," i.e., juridical science. And he attributes much of Machiavelli's teaching to Hobbes, a "systematic" thinker[42] whose "mathematical relativism"[43] is in one sense an advantage—he cannot be dismissed as "unscientific."

Thus, immediately after his discussion of Machiavelli, Schmitt attributes to Hobbes the view that "the rule of a higher order" means "that certain men of this higher order rule over men of a lower order."[44] But, of course, Hobbes had in fact premised his theory on the natural equality of *all* men, and therefore had to conceive of the sovereign as an *artificial* person whose commands take the form of laws or universal prescriptions equally binding on all citizens.

Once the fundamental political situation has been described as the rule of the higher order of men over the lower, Schmitt can speak not of the antagonism between *peoples* but between the higher men of each nation, for example, "the fanatical hatred of Napoleon by the German barons Stein and Kleist."[45] The friend/enemy distinction mediates between decisionism and democracy. The higher men determine the antagonisms that justify obedience from the lower men as protection against the "enemy." Thus if there were no longer nation-states potentially antagonistic to one another, man's nature would remain dangerous, but the immanent, democratic basis for the obedience that curbs that dangerousness (i.e., protection against an enemy people) would disappear. The implication, if one connects Schmitt's discussion of "evil" in *Political Theology* to that which we have just discussed, is that either men would have to find new gods, i.e., return from democratic immanence to theocratic transcendence as a basis for obedience, or the Hobbesian state of nature would become a reality. This is what Schmitt means by "optimistic or pessimistic conjectures": in fact, both conjectures presuppose, in the end, man's dangerousness but differ on whether there can again be a satisfactory *transpolitical*, i.e., non-Machiavellian, basis for dealing with it.

Strauss's "Notes on *The Concept of the Political*"

Many of the subtle features of Schmitt's thought are identified by
Strauss in his "Notes," which appeared in 1932 following the publication of *The Concept of the Political*. Strauss observes, for example,
that Schmitt's attack on liberalism is not that it is in fact unpolitical
or suppresses the political, but that it hides or denies its own political character. He recognizes in Schmitt's attack a moral judgment in
favor of "sincerity." Strauss also notes that, unlike Hobbes, who emphasizes the state of exception, the state of nature in order to negate
Schmitt admires or affirms man's dangerousness: "expressed appropriately," Strauss writes, "that affirmation is the affirmation of power as
the power that forms states, of *virtu* in Machiavelli's sense."[46]

Why, then, does Strauss not recognize the position underlying
Schmitt's amoralism as Machiavellianism? Strauss is struck by "the
resolution with which Schmitt refuses to come on as a belligerent
against the pacifists."[47] However, given what Schmitt had said about
"Machiavelli's misfortune," it is (as we have argued above) understandable that Schmitt should present himself not as a latter-day Machiavelli
but as a latter-day Hobbes, i.e., the disciple of a thinker who could not
be characterized as "unscientific," but rather (in Hobbes's own description) as the first scientific student of politics.

Strauss does recognize in his "Notes" that Schmitt is an inconsistent
Hobbesian. But these inconsistencies—for example, Schmitt appears to
identify the primary conflict as that between peoples not individuals
and rejects Hobbes's view that the state can demand only conditional
obedience from its subjects—do not point back from Hobbes to Machiavelli. Instead, for Strauss, they point to the problem of any critique of
liberalism that attempts to remain within the horizon of Hobbes.[48] The
moral intention in light of which Schmitt inconsistently follows the apparently "scientific" amoral teaching of Hobbes is, Strauss believes, the
restoration of the seriousness of life as against liberalism's attempted
reduction of the drama of life to mere entertainment.[49] Strauss perceived that there was a moral intention behind Schmitt's own apparent
scientism—what he failed to see was that the moral intention was the
moralization of the will to power itself, a moralization beyond conjectures about good and evil in the sense that its *basis* is a fact and not
even a purely human fact. That fact is the naturalness of man's animal
striving, of his passions.[50] The "morally exacting decision" is the decision that is taken with the honest and courageous self-consciousness

that it is taken out of nothingness, its sole ground and basis the will to power of he who decides.

As Strauss would later note in the preface to the American edition of his book on Hobbes, in the 1930s he was still under the belief that Hobbes, not Machiavelli, was the founder of modern political philosophy, primarily due to a misunderstanding of Machiavelli.[51] Strauss had accepted Machiavelli's own self-presentation of his thought in the *Discourses* as the revival of the *virtu* of the ancient republican founders, and not as something fundamentally new.[52] It is therefore not surprising that, in 1932, Strauss was unable to move from an appreciation of Schmitt's differences with Hobbes to an appreciation of his Machiavellianism—at the time, Machiavelli was for Strauss merely a transitional figure between scholastic and genuinely modern political philosophy, and perhaps not even a philosopher, but primarily an ideologist or political historian.[53]

And only an appreciation of Schmitt's Machiavellianism leads one to an understanding of his modification of Machiavelli. Machiavelli does not explicitly praise sincerity in the exercise of power—the prince must be a fox as well as a lion.[54] A consistent Machiavellianism would not teach the superiority of domination by open force of will to domination by stealth. Thus, unlike Schmitt, a consistent Machiavellian would have no ground for finding fault with liberalism which seeks (according to Schmitt) to dominate by stealth or fraud. Schmitt adds to Machiavellianism a secularized Christian dimension—the demand of probity, of intellectual and moral (not just physical) courage. (The core of *Political Theology* is not a return to the City of God but, it should be recalled, the ultimate translation of transcendent categories into immanent, or purely human ones, in accordance with the requirements of the democratic age.)

In light of the demand for probity in the decision, how then should we assess Schmitt's own apparent concealment of his Machiavellianism behind the image of the "systematic" thinker Hobbes? Schmitt might respond in truly Machiavellian fashion that the ultimate danger that the liberal enemy poses justifies, if only temporarily, the use of his own tools or weapons. But then one would have to ask whether the masses are indeed supposed to understand the friend/enemy distinction in the same way as the higher men, i.e., whether they are supposed to discern that its ultimate basis is not the romantic ideal of the nation, the dignity of a people and its way of life, but the rule of the stronger or higher men over the masses. But this narrows rather than contradicts the notion of probity. Probity entails that the higher men be true to themselves, that they have confidence in their own will to power. Schmitt sought not to revive popular self-confidence in the German nation, but rather the self-confidence of Germany's leaders—another reason why *Concept of the Political* contains so little of the typical rhetoric of bellicose nationalism. But, finally we must ask, of what value is *this* task if patriotism itself turns out to be of secondary or derivative importance?[55]

In any case, there *is* no transcendent morality that vindicates human seriousness behind the thought of Schmitt, struggling to escape from his apparent Hobbesian scientism. The morally exacting decision *is* the test and proof of human seriousness not the means to its restoration. Schmitt was not waiting for a god, but rather a führer who would combine animal vitality with Christian probity.

From Dictatorship Back to Legitimacy: Strauss's Reformulation and Critique of Decisionism in Light of the Classic Perspective

For Strauss, the discovery of a "horizon beyond liberalism" entailed the recovery of the classic perspective on politics: if an adequate ground for a morality that would vindicate the seriousness of life could not be won on modern (i.e., Hobbesian) premises, then one had to find a perspective from which those premises themselves might be put in question. This would require, at least as a preliminary step, a return to that way of thinking which *could* not have been influenced by those premises, i.e., premodern thinking.[56]

A reading of Strauss's most concentrated and synoptic presentation of the classical position—the chapter on classic natural right in *Natural Right and History*—might lead one to the conclusion that Strauss did in fact find in the classic teaching a solid normative basis for decisionism, a basis in a morality that vindicated seriousness as human excellence.[57] Consider the following statements that Strauss attributes to the perspective of classic natural right, all of which seem entirely in the spirit of Schmittian decisionism, and many of which seem almost identical to explicit claims of Schmitt: ". . . even despotic rule is not per se against nature";[58] "While some men are corrupted by wielding power others are improved by it";[59] "No law, and hence no constitution, can be the fundamental political fact, because all laws depend on human beings";[60] "Let us call an extreme situation a situation in which the very existence or independence of a society is at stake";[61] ". . . societies are not only threatened from without. Considerations that apply to foreign enemies may well apply to subversive elements within society";[62] "it is not possible to define precisely what constitutes an extreme situation in contradistinction to a normal situation. Every dangerous external or internal enemy is inventive to the extent that he is capable of transforming what, on the basis of previous experience, could reasonably be regarded as a normal situation into an extreme situation."[63]

Yet far from being a mere affirmation of these Schmittian claims in the name of classic natural right, Strauss's chapter is largely devoted to showing why these claims do not imply saying farewell to the rule of law, or to the idea of legitimacy. Only when understood on the basis of a positivist or relativist view of law and legitimacy do these claims point the way to decisionism. Thus, Strauss's discussion of the classics is preceded in *Natural Right and History* by a critique of positivism and relativism, in the form which originated in Max Weber and culminated in the neo-Kantian juridical science of Kelsen.[64]

In *Natural Right and History*, as in his "Notes on *The Concept of the Political*," Strauss again raises the dependency of decisionism on relativist and positivist premises—but this time not to show the inadequacy of Schmittian anti-liberalism but rather the inadequacy of contemporary social science and jurisprudence (dominated by relativism and positivism) to respond to the claims of that anti-liberalism. As Behnegar puts it: ". . . the connection Strauss emphasizes between relativism and National Socialism is not so much that relativism leads one to embrace such movements but that it disarms any principled opposition to them."[65] *Natural Right and History* shows how radical historicism (having been unwittingly prepared by the simplification of natural right in early modern political philosophy) first surfaced, not in the thought of Hegel and Marx, but of "eminent conservatives" and culminated in "fanatical obscurantism," fascism.

In *Natural Right and History*, Strauss fails to cite Schmitt by name. But his concern with the decisionist thought that accompanies fascism is central to this work. Writing in the early 1950s for a largely American audience, Strauss has virtually not a critical word to say about Marx or communism, but, as noted, identifies "eminent conservatives" as the originating intellectual source of the totalitarianism of the Right. The answer as to why in the 1950s Strauss was concerned both by decisionism and the "Weimarization" of American social science and jurisprudence that rendered social science and jurisprudence incapable

of adequate response to decisionism, can be found in the most fundamental political phenomenon at the time of his writing *Natural Right
and History:* McCarthyism. In 1954 (a year after the publication of *Natural Right and History* and at the height of McCarthyite terror), breaking
a silence in his postwar writings on specific contemporary political
personalities and disputes, Strauss referred to "men like Senator Joseph
McCarthy" as among the principal causes of the "contemporary dangers
to intellectual freedom," the other being the dogmatism of academic
liberalism and "scientific" social science, i.e., the dogmatic positivism
and relativism incapable of principled opposition to "men like Senator
Joseph McCarthy."[66]

Precisely in light of the presence of an external "enemy" of unprecedented brutality and dangerousness, McCarthy had sought to loosen or
at least indirectly undermine the legal constraints of American constitutionalism. And based upon the threat from the external enemy,
McCarthy sought (in Schmittian fashion) to consolidate his power by
the identification of internal enemies, those who were "unAmerican,"
the outsiders within.[67] Anyone who did not agree with the correctness of McCarthy's friend/enemy distinction could himself be declared
an internal enemy—a perfect illustration of the strategy described by
Schmitt as the decisionist response to "pluralism."[68]

According to the classic perspective as articulated by Strauss, the
legitimation of the exercise of power must begin with the recognition
of man's natural sociability. What is meant by natural sociability here is
not akin to what Schmitt describes as the anarchist premise of man's
natural goodness or even less to altruism. Man is naturally sociable because those excellences of which he is capable by nature, and on which
his fulfillment or flourishing as a human being depend, can only arise in
society and must depend on the support of society. "He is so constituted
that he cannot live, or cannot live well, except by living with others."[69]
At the same time this sociability is not purely instrumental—for every
truly "human" act, every act that is oriented toward the distinctively
human excellences, implies the communicative, noninstrumental use
of speech (i.e., its use not merely to persuade others to provide for one's
own private pleasure).

Man's rationality implies freedom—"a latitude of alternatives such as
no other earthly being has."[70] But because this rationality is mediated
through speech, it implies the recognition of others or otherness as intrinsic to human flourishing. Inasmuch as rationality is central to and
the natural basis for human freedom, it equally implies a natural sense

of constraint, a constraint based on recognition of the claims of others and otherness.

Society ultimately justifies itself, and justifies both freedom and constraint, by facilitating "the pursuit of excellence."[71] But society, if it is to balance freedom and constraint so as to maximize the pursuit of excellence, must be based on trust between its members. The classics therefore preferred small, closed societies to the world state or empire, because such societies permitted the kind of trust necessary to permit that combination of freedom and constraint best suited to the flourishing of human excellence. But the classics rejected, at the same time, the premise of nationalism, i.e., that there is an essentialist basis for the division of humanity into different groups: "there is an element of choice and even of arbitrariness involved in the 'settling together' of these particular human beings to the exclusion of others."[72] Thus, the classics' defense of the closed society points to the limits as well as the necessity of the closed society. Classic natural right provides a basis in justice for patriotism, but not for bellicose nationalism or the absolutization of the difference between peoples into an existential conflict of the greatest human intensity.[73]

If freedom and constraint are inseparable, so then are freedom and coercion. "Man is so built that he cannot achieve the perfection of his humanity except by keeping down his lower impulses."[74] Here, the perspective of the classics according to Strauss clearly contrasts with Schmitt's Machiavellian account of man's "dangerousness." The need for constraint, or obedience, is not simply based on the potentially "evil" nature of the impulses of the lower men, but also and above all on the need for, or directedness toward, excellence of *all* men or almost all men.

From the classic perspective, the superiority of the ruler to those ruled is based on the notion that "serious concern for the perfection of the community requires a higher degree of virtue than serious concern for the perfection of an individual."[75] Rule or domination is only admirable in its own right when it is ultimately directed to the perfection of the community.

The elitist or anti-egalitarian dimension of the classic natural right teaching is premised not on the distinction between weak and strong, but rather on the notion that not all human beings have an equal capacity for "progress toward perfection. . . ."[76] If human perfection requires society, and all societies are necessarily closed societies, each society will embody a choice for some forms of human excellence over others.[77] In the light of this choice, greater or lesser dignity or praise will attach to individual citizens depending on the extent to which they embody the forms of human excellence that are privileged. This is the paradox of freedom—man has enormous latitude concerning the possibilities of human flourishing that he may pursue, but to realize these possibilities he must live in a closed society, which necessarily privileges some over others. Thus, the defense by a community of its way of life against a threat to that way of life has a ground in natural justice. But this very ground suggests that the identification of the preservation of any particular society's way of life with the survival of the political, or of human seriousness or excellence generally, is a distortion. Indeed the existence of multiple closed societies is primarily to be wished for on the grounds of preserving the range of human possibilities, which never gets full play within any single closed society.[78]

Having presented the classic perspective as grounding the legitimacy of coercion on the orientation of human society toward excellence, Strauss now introduces a qualification to this claim. Many societies, or regimes, are legitimate even if they vary greatly among themselves in the extent to which they are directed to human excellence.[79] This introduces the distinction between the just and noble. "A very imperfect regime may supply the only just solution to the problem of a given community; but, since such a regime cannot be effectively directed towards man's full perfection, it can never be noble."[80]

The distinction between the just and noble reveals the twofold root of natural right. Society should naturally be oriented toward human perfection, but society requires order; the demands of social support for human perfection need not always coincide with the requirement of order. In some cultural, economic and geographical conditions, order can only be maintained by severely circumscribing that freedom required for man's perfection. Thus, at the limit the classic perspective gives to Schmitt the possibility that the rule of a society might entirely be oriented toward order, or the suppression or control of man's "dangerousness." But this limiting case does not require the abandonment of human excellence or perfection as a standard of legitimacy. It is always a question, a matter for *discussion,* whether in a given case too much has been conceded, in the circumstances, to the demand for order.[81]

Yet Strauss now goes on to articulate the classic identification of the best regime with the *absolute* rule of the wise, an articulation that seems consistent with decisionism, not discussion. However, the classic perspective introduces explicitly a premise in the defense of absolute rule that is not present in decisionism, and points to a crucial difficulty in decisionism—the premise that those who rule absolutely will be wise.

As Stephen Holmes notes in a criticism of Schmitt's decisionism, at a certain level the problem of the "exception" only leads to an acceptance of the conferral of extraordinary powers on a dictator or a particular group of men, if we assume that the dictator or the particular group of men will be able to decide *correctly* the exception, i.e., to correctly identify the enemy and the measures needed to defend the way of the life of their own people against that enemy. But, as Holmes suggests, Schmitt "completely neglects the distinction between intelligent and stupid decisions. Yet sovereigns have been known to destroy themselves by foolish choices."[82]

As Strauss indicates, the classic understanding of wisdom itself may imply the view that such wisdom as would *guarantee* the correct decision is unavailable to human beings: "There is no guaranty that the quest for adequate articulation [of the whole] will ever lead beyond an understanding of the fundamental alternatives or that philosophy will ever go beyond the stage of discussion or disputation and will ever reach the stage of decision."[83] Strauss notes that if the wise were to rule, they would depend on consent of the unwise: "the few wise cannot rule the many unwise by force."[84] Schmitt had, of course, admitted that, at least in his own times, dictatorship could only be established on the basis of the will of the people. But what guarantee is there that the people will say yea to someone who will correctly rather than foolishly decide the exception, who will correctly rather than foolishly identify the enemy and the means required to defeat him?

Indeed Strauss suggests, "What is more likely to happen is that an unwise man, appealing to the natural right of wisdom and catering to the lowest desires of the many, will persuade the multitude of his right: the prospects for tyranny are brighter than those for rule of the wise. This being the case, the natural right of the wise must be questioned, and the indispensable requirement for wisdom must be qualified by the requirement for consent."[85] And indeed this follows as well from what Strauss already suggested concerning the classic view of philosophy, or the quest for wisdom: the few wise may doubt the possibility that the quest for adequate articulation of the whole can "ever reach the stage of decision."[86] Therefore the life of the wise will be characterized by inquiry and discussion rather than decision. The many are unlikely to be able to consent to the absolute rule of the wise because the genuinely wise are unlikely to present themselves as candidates for the position.

The solution to the difficulty that Strauss attributes to the classics is something akin to democratic constitutionalism—"that a wise legislator frame a code which the citizen body, duly persuaded, freely adopts."[87] This assumes that democratic constitutionalism provides a moment or an environment that can engage the genuinely as opposed to the spuriously wise, and where at the same time the people can recognize the genuinely wise. Somehow, while philosophy may not lead to the point of decision, it can inform the process of creating general rules for a society. "Persuasion" is the characteristic element of democratic constitutionalism. It is this element, the "discussion" for which Schmitt has such contempt, that is able to bridge wisdom and consent.

This view of constitutional formation as exhibiting superior rationality to normal political operations must be contrasted with Kelsen's understanding of the *Grundnorm* as the arbitrary starting point of a system that is internally rational once it gets going. It can also be contrasted with Schmitt's related claim in *Political Theology* that in the moment of founding, the character of the decision—i.e., as a decision out of nothingness—is clearly revealed.

Having returned to the legitimacy of legality from absolutism by way of a reflection on the inexorability of democracy, Strauss now revisits and reformulates some of the key claims of decisionism.

First of all, he admits that "the administration of the law must be intrusted to a type of man who is most likely to administer it equitably, i.e., to 'complete' the law according to the requirements of circumstances which the legislator could not have foreseen."[88] As against Schmitt, Strauss suggests that the adaptation of the law to the "requirements of circumstances" does not imply its radical indeterminacy. Even if the administrator is not wise, he may nevertheless be capable of understanding the "spirit" of the law, or the spirit of the wise legislator. By referring to the task of the administrator as completion of the law, Strauss implies that the normative reference point for the administrator is the spirit of the legislator, i.e., what the legislator would have done when confronted with the circumstances in question. Conceding that this cannot be known with "exactness" does not entail the conclusion that the adaptation of the law to unanticipated circumstances must be a decision out of nothingness.

What is crucial is the attitude and disposition of the administrator.

One could say that the administrator must be sufficiently liberated from a simplistic identification of justice with the letter of the law to be able to adapt the law intelligently, while at the same time sufficiently public-spirited to resist using his power to adapt the law for corrupt or extra-constitutional purposes. The elitism of the classics here seems based on the view that, in the context of the ancient city, the appropriate attitude and disposition would be most likely found among the urban gentry.

Thus, the answer of the classics to the problem of the exception, at least as posed by Schmitt to liberal constitutionalism, hinges on the importance of character and education in the case of those who decide the exception. The classic perspective is in agreement with Schmitt that there are no higher order *rules* that can adequately determine or constrain the decision of the exception, either legal or moral. Yet, contrary to Schmitt's secularized Christian categories, nothing can really come out of nothing. So if the decision on the exception is undetermined or underdetermined by rules, the content of the decision must be accounted for by something. For the classics, this something resides in the *character* of he who decides. If the exception can never be decided according to rules, there is no reason why the spirit of the constitution or the law generally cannot, through education, be assimilated into the moral and intellectual dispositions and competences of those who decide.[89]

This answer to Schmitt's problem of the exception is, however, only tentative or incomplete. It is not Strauss's last word, because it does not adequately address a situation where what is called for is not "completion" of the law, but rather the suspension of the entire legal order under conditions of emergency. Strauss's full answer, or the answer he attributes to classic natural right, entails a radicalization of the problem of the exception even beyond that undertaken by Schmitt.

Such a radicalization is implied by the very orientation of classic natural right toward human perfection or excellence as the legitimate end of politics. This orientation issues in a view of justice as giving to each person what is required to realize fully her own excellences, what is required for her perfection as a human being. Yet the classics admit that individual natures differ, and the closer one remains to the Socratic-Platonic natural right teaching, the further one is from the view that any set of general rules is up to the task of determining what is good for each individual in society. The deepest implication of the classic natural right teaching would therefore seem, at first glance, to be not the rule of law but individualized education and therapy for each citizen—a kind of anarchism that would differ only from a sort of Marcusean Marxist utopia in the emphasis on the naturalness of constraint as an ingredient in human perfection.

But again, every society also requires general rules of "citizen-morality"—the basic rules of conduct without which people cannot live together in trust. Natural right in its purest or most radical form, allocating to each what is good for him or her, potentially puts in question any set of hard-and-fast general rules needed for basic social order. Therefore, unless it is to become "dynamite," natural right must be diluted "in order to become compatible with the requirements of the city."[90] At the same time, and now Strauss returns to the problem posed by the fact of every social order being a closed social order, the possibility of war means that even the general rules may have to be suspended, or at least not applied to the enemy. So even these rules cannot take on the character of absolute commandments. In a sense, therefore, the classic natural right teaching is in agreement with Schmitt that the political is coeval with the friend/enemy distinction, for only this distinction seems capable of explaining or legitimizing the application of rules within society that are not applied to others on the outside. But classic natural right lays bare the problematic character of the friend/enemy distinction from the perspective of pure natural right. It points to the *limits* of politics, to the tension between the demands of politics and the unqualified good for man.

The implication of these limits, is not, however, the abandonment of natural right as a standard, or its self-destruction under the weight of its own internal tensions. What is required is the kind of statecraft that can distinguish those circumstances or those contexts where political life can afford to orient itself toward the cultivation of human excellence and those where "public safety is the highest law."[91] Turning Schmitt's rhetoric on its head, Strauss's classical perspective accepts the critical importance to statecraft of correctly identifying the exception but for the opposite reason—i.e., so that one reduces to the essential *minimum* those cases where public safety is the highest law and where the decision must forget the concern with those principles of justice that point to human perfection.

What is crucial to the perspective of classic natural right is the recognition that more is at stake in the decision of the exception than the adaptation or suspension of the normal rules required for social order in the name of the preservation of that social order against an "enemy," external or internal. The fate of human excellence in that society is also at stake. Thus one cannot leave matters by saying that the problem of statecraft can be solved through the education of a political class able, in the name of the spirit of the rules, to decide the exception in order to preserve the rules.

This leads to the following final and most comprehensive formulation of the classic perspective on the problem of the exception: The variability of the demands of that justice which men can practice was recognized not only by Aristotle but by Plato as well. Both avoided the Scylla of "absolutism" and the Charybdis of "relativism" by holding a view which one may venture to express as follows:

> There is a universally valid hierarchy of ends, but there are no universally valid rules of action. . . . [W]hen deciding what ought to be done, i.e., what ought to be done by this individual (or this individual group) here and now, one has to consider not only which of the various competing objectives is higher in rank but also which is most urgent in the circumstances. What is most urgent is legitimately preferred to what is less urgent, and the most urgent is in many cases lower in rank than the less urgent. But one cannot make a universal rule that urgency is a higher consideration than rank. For it is our duty to make the highest activity, as much as we can, the most urgent or the most needful thing. And the maximum of effort which can be expected necessarily varies from individual to individual. The only universally valid standard is the hierarchy of ends.[92]

Strauss admits that no adequate legal expression is possible of the difference between Machiavellianism, which denies natural right or legitimacy, and the classic perspective, which admits that natural right is infinitely variable in the manner just described. But this difference *can* be expressed in terms of the character of the one who decides. The classic perspective supports the disposition to deviate from the strict principles of justice only reluctantly or hesitantly. Schmitt, like Machiavelli, actually contemplates the decision of the exception with admiration, and even goes further than Machiavelli, it will be recalled, in moralizing the capacity to decide the exception with sincerity as a secular equivalent of Christian probity. The disposition toward the exception implied by the classic natural right teaching, by contrast, is unmistakably similar to the hesitant and uncomfortable liberal disposition toward the exception that is held in contempt by Schmitt.[93] Moreover, classic natural right, in affirming a hierarchy of ends but not of decision-rules, leaves both a *bench-mark* and an *unclosable* space for discussion about whether any given decision appropriately balances, in light of the hierarchy of ends, the requirements of urgency with the strict requirements of justice. Once the norm is itself seen as more flexible and contextual than a set of rules, the recognition of the exception clears the path not for the destruction of the norm, but the strict justification of the exception.

Conclusion: Liberalism and the Horizon beyond Liberalism

These last observations raise the issue of the ultimate relationship of the classic perspective to liberalism. Clearly, on the basis of taking seriously those premises that render decisionism plausible, the classic perspective as employed by Strauss ends up vindicating the rule of law and a certain form of democratic constitutionalism. At the same time, essential to the classic perspective is the orientation of politics toward human perfection or excellence, an orientation that justifies the existence of closed societies but qualifies the friend/enemy distinction implied by that existence. Because the classic perspective understands human excellence in terms of a hierarchy of ends or goods, it seems squarely in tension with the egalitarian dimension of liberalism, at least that version of liberalism that requires that the state be neutral as between competing conceptions of the good.[94]

Strauss goes on in subsequent chapters of *Natural Right and History* to argue that the founders of liberalism created natural public law on the basis of a simplification or oversimplification of natural right. By viewing the principles of justice as simply pertaining to those rules required for social peace, or trust, and divorcing natural right from perfection, Hobbes and Locke sought to normalize the exception on the very basis of the Machiavellian principle that the public safety is the highest law. By simplifying the problem of the exception, the founders of modern public law in fact prepared the way for the fateful confrontation between left-wing anarchism and Schmittian decisionism. On the basis of Rousseau's critique of the state of nature teaching of Hobbes and Locke, it became questionable whether, if perfection is forgotten and the only solid ground of public law is self-preservation, men can be bound by natural right to any social order at all; and since the self-preservation of the individual is in any case problematic as a justification for a collective order that must reckon with the possibility of war, the principle that public safety is the highest law would become the principle that there is no law that constrains what a people or its leaders may do to preserve their *collective* existence. And instead of rising to these challenges, liberalism tended simply to incorporate their skeptical or even nihilistic dimensions within itself, becoming relativistic and positivistic in orientation, and rejecting the idea of natural right altogether.

But none of these reflections, either individually or together, suffice to show that Strauss's deepest intent is to revive classic natural right as a positive doctrine of public law. Indeed, the self-consciously incomplete character of classic natural right as a *teaching*, its incapability of generating rules for action, would preclude such a possibility.[95] At the same time, even the tentative adoption of the classic perspective yields a powerful internal critique of decisionism. And, on the basis of the recovery of the full dimensions of the *problem* of natural right through the tentative adoption of the classic perspective, i.e., the questioning of the simplification of the problem of justice beginning with Machiavelli, one must reassess the resources of the *liberal* tradition to address the problem in its full complexity and richness.

Strauss himself interprets the turn of liberalism from natural right not as inevitable but as a choice: "When liberals became impatient of the absolute limits to diversity or individuality that are imposed even by the most liberal version of natural right, they had to make a choice between natural right and the uninhibited cultivation of individuality."[96] But the classic perspective itself does not solve the tension between individuality and natural right—there is a hierarchy of ends, but general rules cannot determine or prescribe what is required for the perfection, for the excellence of soul, of each individual. And Strauss ends the chapter on classic natural right by concluding that by at least one thinker, indeed a pivotal thinker in the liberal tradition (Montesquieu), the tension was understood much in the same way as it was by the classics. Indeed, he suggests that what Montesquieu teaches "is nearer in spirit to the classics" than the teaching of St. Thomas. Since Thomism was *the* natural right alternative to liberalism in Strauss's own time,[97] a reengagement of liberals with the idea of natural right would depend not only on tracing the incapacity of relativistic and positivistic liberalism to respond to the main threat to liberty (McCarthyite decisionism), but also on clearly distinguishing the Platonic-Aristotelian-Stoic perspective on natural right from the conservative natural law teaching of the Thomists. There are logical points of affinity and fruitful engagement between liberalism and the classic perspective, which have been obscured by the fall of liberalism into relativist dogmatism and the fall of the classic perspective into Thomistic natural law dogmatism.

While the classic perspective (Plato-Aristotle-the Stoics) insists that law cannot close the gap between the norm and decision, Thomism attempts to solve this incompleteness by reference to theology, or the theologization of the political. The opposition to hierarchy that motivates in part the modern simplification of natural right can in fact be traced to an agreement with the classics that "natural right should be kept independent of theology and its controversies."[98] Yet, of course, the contingent hierarchy of ends postulated by the classic perspective leaves a space for democratic deliberation that is closed by the Thomistic hierarchy of rules and decisions based ultimately in divine authority, or revelation. The implication of the classic perspective is that there is no *decision* not open to revision, i.e., before which a normative question mark may not, in future, be put.

There is thus room for disagreement with Ferry and Renaut,[99] and certainly with Holmes, when they suggest that the hierarchical dimension in Strauss's recovery of the ancient perspective is *simply* inconsistent with or opposed to liberalism. Liberals who are democrats, and particularly social democrats, cannot do without a contingent hierarchy of ends. For if human flourishing requires a claim on social resources that goes beyond the requirements of mere survival, then such a claim must be stated in terms of an account of the good. And if one is to accept the scarcity of social resources on which one can call—in other words, if one is not to slide into a particularly discredited form of Marxism—then such claims must imply some kind of priority setting, the assertion that some goods are in principle more important, or more decisive, for human flourishing than others. To use a Benthamite image, if society cannot sustain the resources to support excellence at both poetry and pushpin, then the case for poetry depends on an implicitly hierarchical account of the good that puts it above pushpin in the hierarchy of publicly recognized ends.

Of course, it is a vitally important question whether and how such an implicit appeal to hierarchy can be reconciled with the central liberal idea of the equal moral worth of persons, a question that haunts, for instance, the recent work of Martha Nussbaum that defends a transhistorical account of the good in social democratic terms.[100] In part, the answer may lie precisely in the democratic space created by the refusal in the classic perspective to close the gap between norm and decision. In this space, any claim that a particular law or decision adequately reflects the hierarchy of human good is subject to the contingency of context, and to the critical power of Socratic skepticism.[101]

Notes

My main debt is to David Dyzenhaus, with whom I have carried on a discussion for several years about the relationship of Strauss to Schmitt's antiliberalism, and to the students in our seminar "Liberalism and its Enemies" for their many insightful reactions to some of my initial thoughts on the Strauss-Schmitt dialogue. Peter Berkowitz has been an invaluable source of encouragement and advice. I am grateful to Nasser Behnegar, Peter Berkowitz, and Steven B. Smith for very helpful comments on earlier versions of this essay. Any mistakes and omissions are my responsibility. Dan Markel provided excellent editorial assistance.

1 S. Holmes, *The Anatomy of Anti-Liberalism* (Chicago: University of Chicago Press, 1993).

2 Holmes, ibid., at 60: "For Strauss, then, Schmitt fails to be anti-liberal enough." See L. Strauss, "Notes on Carl Schmitt, *The Concept of the Political*," in G. Schwab, ed., *The Concept of the Political*, trans. H. Lomax (Chicago: University of Chicago Press, 1996) (hereafter *Concept of the Political*). All further references to *Concept of the Political* and to Strauss's "Notes" are to this edition; however, there are problems with the translation of the latter that I will occasionally correct in my citations.

3 H. Meier, *Carl Schmitt and Leo Strauss: The Hidden Dialogue*, trans. H. Lomax (Chicago: University of Chicago Press, 1995) (hereafter *Carl Schmitt and Leo Strauss*).

4 I use this expression to indicate that these scholars are sympathetic to Strauss, but without necessarily being Straussians.

5 "Liberal Zealotry," 103 *Yale L.J.* 1994, 1363.

6 N. Behnegar, "The Liberal Politics of Leo Strauss," in M. Palmer and T. L. Pangle, eds., *Political Philosophy and the Human Soul: Essays in Memory of Allan Bloom* (Lanham, Md.: Rowman and Littlefield, 1995), at 259ff.

7 C. Lefort, "Droits de l'homme et politique," 7 *Libre* (1980): 28.

8 L. Ferry and A. Renaut, *Philosophie politique III: des droits de l'homme à l'idée républicaine* (Paris: Quadrige/PUF, 1996), particularly chapter 1, "Le droit naturel antique contre les droits de l'homme." This reading of Strauss is based on a very serious and thoughtful engagement with Strauss's writings by Luc Ferry in the first volume of *Philosophie politique, le droit: la nouvelle querelle des anciens et des modernes* (Paris: Quadrige/PUF, 1996). This work has the advantage of stating a position like that of Holmes, but without the potshots and unfair polemics that often distract from Holmes's serious intent.

9 In L. Strauss, *Spinoza's Critique of Religion*, trans. E. Sinclair (New York: Schocken, 1965), at 1-34.

10 Ibid., at 31.

11 C. Schmitt, *Political Theology: Four Chapters on the Concept of Sovereignty*,

trans. G. Schwab (Cambridge, Mass.: MIT Press, 1985) (hereafter *Political Theology*), at 65–66. All further references are to this edition.

12 Most of Schmitt's criticisms are really just versions of attacks on liberalism by earlier thinkers such as Rousseau and Nietzsche, particularly liberalism's attempt to reduce politics to economics, the predation of the state by private interest groups, and the attempt to make man, or understand man as, undangerous. Many of these criticisms were, as well, part of the "conservative ideology" of Schmitt's time—the discourse of a whole range of academics including Oswald Spengler and Ernst Junger, which as Bourdieu suggests, nourished Heidegger just as it was nourished by him. P. Bourdieu, *The Political Ontology of Martin Heidegger* (Stanford, Calif.: Stanford University Press, 1991), chap. 2, esp. at 13–15.

13 *Political Theology*, supra n. 11, at 13–15. It should be noted that Harvey Mansfield, one of Strauss's best students, has in a recent study brought to light the complexity and subtlety with which the liberal tradition and its progenitors dealt with the problem of the exception through the articulation of the notion of executive power. See H. C. Mansfield Jr., *Taming the Prince: The Ambivalence of the Modern Executive Power* (New York: Free Press, 1989). This work is an illustration of the premise, developed in the conclusion to this article, that Strauss's articulation of the classic perspective may be a basis for recovering overlooked resources in the modern liberal tradition.

14 Ibid.

15 Ibid., at 15.

16 Supra n. 13, at 19.

17 See, for example, H. Kelsen, "Law and Morality," in O. Weinberger, ed., *Essays in Legal and Moral Philosophy*, trans. P. Heath (Dordrecht and Boston: D. Reidel, 1976), at 83: "Now not only is the methodological purity of legal science endangered by failure to observe the boundary separating it from natural science; it is still further endangered by the fact that it is not divided, or not clearly enough divided, from ethics—that no sharp distinction is made between law and morality."

18 *Political Theology*, supra n. 11, at 20. Strauss, near the beginning of *Natural Right and History* (Chicago: University of Chicago Press, 1965), at 4, n. 2, cites a passage in the 1925 German edition of Kelsen's *General Theory of Law and State* in which Kelsen himself comes very close to drawing the decisionist implication of the groundlessness of the *Grundnorm:* Kelsen states that a dictatorship is just as much a legal order as any other form of human ordering—to deny to the will or command of the despot the character of legal order is to engage in naive natural-right thinking (naturrechtliche Naivität). H. Kelsen, *Allgemeine Staatslehre* (Berlin: 1925), at 335–6. Strauss notes that, although Kelsen had this passage removed from the postwar English translation of this work, insight into the ultimate fate of legal posi-

tivism in Germany had not in fact opened up Kelsen to reconsideration of the natural right tradition.

19 *Political Theology*, at 31–32.

20 One can understand Ronald Dworkin's nonpositivistic jurisprudence as precisely a response to this problem with positivism as a liberal legal theory—if one can always revert to the moral sources of legal norms in applying them to cases which the norms themselves on their face underdetermine, then one can in principle solve the indeterminacy problem. The response, of course, is that reversion to the moral sources is merely reversion to the personal will or outlook of the decision maker. And see D. Dyzenhaus, "'Now the Machine Runs Itself': Carl Schmitt on Hobbes and Kelsen," 16 *Cardozo L. Rev.* 1994, 1.

21 See D. Dyzenhaus, *Legality and Legitimacy: Carl Schmitt, Hans Kelsen, and Herman Heller in Weimar* (Oxford: Clarendon Press, 1997); see also W. Scheuerman, "Carl Schmitt's Critique of Liberal Constitutionalism," *Review of Politics* 58 (1996): 299, at 306–7.

22 *Political Theology*, supra n. 11, at 50.

23 Ibid., at 57–58.

24 Supra n. 13, at 58.

25 Ibid., at 61.

26 The entire criticism here of the simplistic view of man as "fallen" shows the inaccuracy in Meier's interpretation that for Schmitt, "in light of the truth of original sin, . . . everything that anthropology can bring to light remains secondary." *Carl Schmitt and Leo Strauss*, supra n. 3, at 69.

27 *Political Theology*, supra n. 11, at 66.

28 *Concept of the Political*, supra n. 2, at 26–27.

29 See, for example, the translator George Schwab's remarks in the introduction to the English edition of *Concept of the Political*.

30 *Concept of the Political*, supra n. 2, at 30–31.

31 Ibid., at 43.

32 Supra n. 2, at 53.

33 Ibid., at 54.

34 Ibid., at 52.

35 Ibid., at 58.

36 Ibid., at 59.

37 Ibid.

38 See for example, ibid., at 31–32.

39 Ibid., at 65.

40 Ibid., at 66.

41 Ibid., at 65–66.

42 Ibid., at 65.

43 *Political Theology*, supra n. 11, at 34.

44 *Concept of the Political*, supra n. 2, at 67.

45 Ibid.

46 Ibid., at 97.

47 Ibid.

48 Ibid., at 107.

49 Ibid., at 100–1.

50 Here there are unmistakable parallels to Nietzsche. For an interpretation of Nietzsche that wrestles with the paradoxical project of a moral standard beyond good and evil, see P. Berkowitz, *Nietzsche: The Ethics of an Immoralist* (Cambridge, Mass.: Harvard University Press, 1995).

51 L. Strauss, *The Political Philosophy of Hobbes: Its Basis and its Genesis* (Chicago: University of Chicago Press, 1952), at xiv–xvii.

52 Ibid., at xvi.

53 Strauss's mature reflections on Machiavelli are to be found in his *Thoughts on Machiavelli* (Chicago: University of Chicago Press, 1958).

54 See N. Machiavelli, *The Prince*, trans. M. Musa (New York: St. Martin's Press, 1964), chap. XVIII.

55 Indeed, Strauss himself, after publishing his "Notes," had begun to suspect that the friend/enemy distinction, the animosity between peoples was secondary in Schmitt's thought to the eternal relation of protection and obedience. As Strauss suggested in a letter to Schmitt dated September 4, 1932, the ultimate basis of Schmitt's politics is the need for dominion "but dominion can be established, that is, men can be unified, only in a unity against— against other men." See "Letter Two," in *Carl Schmitt and Leo Strauss*, supra n. 3, at 125.

56 See his "Preface to the English Translation" in *Spinoza's Critique of Religion*, supra n. 9, at 31.

57 L. Strauss, *Natural Right and History* (Chicago: University of Chicago Press, 1965). By classic natural right, Strauss means a teaching which appears to have several variants—Socratic-Platonic, Aristotelian, Stoic, and Thomistic. However, Strauss clearly associates the key concepts of classic natural right with features that are common to the Socratic-Platonic, Aristotelian, and (pre-Christian) Stoic variants. As will be noted in the conclusion to this article, the Thomistic variant constitutes in fact a very different kind of teaching.

58 Ibid., at 133.

59 Ibid.

60 Ibid., at 136.

61 Ibid., at 160.

62 Ibid.

63 Ibid., at 161.

64 On this aspect of Strauss's thought the work of Nasser Behnegar is particularly illuminating. See his "The Liberal Politics of Leo Strauss," supra n. 6, particularly at 253–55, and N. Behnegar, "Leo Strauss's Confrontation with Max Weber," *Review of Politics* 59 (1997): 97.

65 N. Behnegar, "The Liberal Politics of Leo Strauss," supra n. 6, at 253.

66 L. Strauss, "On a Forgotten Kind of Writing," in *What is Political Philosophy? And Other Studies* (Chicago: University of Chicago Press, 1959), at 223. Here I do not wish to suggest that Strauss, in the 1950s, viewed Schmitt himself as his main philosophical or intellectual adversary—what Strauss was concerned with was the political outlook of right-wing nihilism, whose philosophically most important representative was Heidegger. Yet, as Bourdieu notes, precisely the apparent a- or anti-political vocabulary and manner of expression of Heidegger, his avoidance of the "naively political" and the "crude language of politics," tends to exclude or impede a satisfactory open debate about the political meaning of nihilism. Bourdieu, *The Political Ontology of Martin Heidegger*, supra n. 12, at 36–37. Here Schmitt holds the advantage over Heidegger of not avoiding the "crude language of politics." The closeness of Schmitt's analysis of the political to Heidegger's analytic of Dasein is discussed in K. Löwith, "The Occasional Decisionism of Carl Schmitt," in R. Wolin, ed., *Martin Heidegger and European Nihilism* (New York: Columbia University Press, 1995), at 137–69. See particularly the postscript to this essay, where Löwith elaborates on the "political decisionism" of Heidegger. I am grateful to Steven B. Smith for reminding me of these matters and Rosemary Coombe for letting me know the importance of Bourdieu's work here.

67 On McCarthyism, see, among other works, E. Schrecker, *The Age of McCarthyism: A Brief History with Documents* (New York: St. Martin's Press, 1994); T. Reeves, ed., *McCarthyism* (Hinsdale, Ill.: Dryden Press, 1973), esp. the introduction by Reeves; R. S. Feuerlicht, *Joe McCarthy and McCarthyism: the Hate that Haunts America* (New York: McGraw-Hill, 1972).

68 See *Concept of the Political*, supra n. 2, at 43.

69 *Natural Right and History*, supra n. 57, at 129.

70 Ibid., at 130.

71 Ibid., at 131.

72 Ibid., at 132.

73 In recent work, the young Italian social democratic philosopher Maurizio Viroli has sought to distinguish patriotism from nationalism, and defend a kind of patriotism based on a rational understanding of the goodness or soundness of the goals or ends which one's own society is seeking to procure. Strauss would hardly be surprised that Viroli resorts to the natural right teaching of Cicero to support his approach. See M. Viroli, *For Love of Country: An Essay on Patriotism and Nationalism* (Oxford: Clarendon Press, 1995).

74 *Natural Right and History*, supra n. 57, at 132.

75 Ibid., at 133.

76 Ibid., at 134.

77 Ibid., at 136–37.
78 Ibid., at 132. I have made an argument for multiculturalism based on this observation. See R. Howse, "Terms of Engagement: Liberalism and the Good of Multicultural Communities," McGill Legal Theory Workshop, Faculty of Law, McGill University, 1996.
79 *Natural Right and History,* supra n. 57, at 139–40.
80 Ibid., at 140.
81 Thus, the classic perspective implies that, although both freedom and constraint have a basis in natural right, there is no contextless legal standard for balancing them. In the light of current debates about liberalism, this would place the classic perspective in fundamental opposition to the project of Rawls, for instance, to freeze the contours of freedom in a concept of "public reason" placed beyond revisability in normal democratic debate. Classic natural right, although often identified with a kind of rigid universalism, may be more contextually sensitive (without thereby becoming relativistic) than certain strands in contemporary liberal theory. See on Rawls's political liberalism, D. Dyzenhaus, "Liberalism After the Fall: Schmitt, Rawls and the Problem of Justification," *Philosophy and Social Criticism* 22 (1996): 9.
82 S. Holmes, *The Anatomy of Anti-Liberalism,* supra n. 1, at 47.
83 *Natural Right and History,* supra n. 57, at 125.
84 Ibid., at 141.
85 Ibid.
86 Ibid., at 125.
87 Ibid., at 141.
88 Ibid., at 141–42.
89 This is akin to the model of legal education or formation that has been recently articulated by Dean Anthony Kronman, in contrast to the scientistic or technocratic orientation of legal education implied by the notion of jurisprudence as technical skill in the application of an internally coherent system of *rules*. See A. Kronman, *The Lost Lawyer: Failing Ideals of the Legal Profession* (Cambridge, Mass.: Belknap Press, 1993). See also *Natural Right and History,* supra n. 57, at 152.
90 Strauss, *Natural Right and History,* at 152. "This dilution of natural right can be assisted through the instruction of rhetoricians/politicians by philosophers, the latter motivated by the need to acquire political friends who protect them against popular persecution." See also R. Howse, "Between the Lines: Exotericism, Esotericism and the Philosophical Rhetoric of Leo Strauss," in *Philosophy and Rhetoric* (forthcoming).
91 Ibid., at 160.
92 Ibid., at 162–63.
93 See particularly *Concept of the Political,* supra n. 2, at 12.
94 But of course there are important perfectionist accounts of liberalism that deny the idea of state neutrality toward the good, for example, Joseph Raz,

The Morality of Freedom (Oxford: Clarendon Press, 1989). Strauss was well aware of the perfectionist dimension in the thought of J. S. Mill, who looms large in Strauss's essay "Liberal Education and Responsibility," in *Liberalism: Ancient and Modern* (Chicago: University of Chicago Press, 1995). In another essay in the same collection, "The Liberalism of Classical Political Philosophy," Strauss describes the kind of liberalism that "forgets quality, excellence, and virtue" as "perverted liberalism" (at 64).

95 The best account of the tentative and experimental nature of Strauss's adoption of the classic perspective is to be found in his review article, "On a New Interpretation of Plato's Political Philosophy," *Social Research* 326 (1946); where Strauss provides a scathing critique of another scholar's effort to revive Platonism as a doctrine that would solve contemporary theoretical and practical controversies. In the review article, Strauss describes the kind of return to the classic perspective that *he* is advocating in liberal terms as the attempt to free one's mind from modern preconceptions or prejudices so that one can judge objectively the strength of the attack on modern rationalism by nihilism. "Adherents of the modern principles who lack the ability to take a critical distance from the modern principles, to look at those principles not from their habitual point of view but from the point of view of their opponents, have already admitted defeat: they show by their action that theirs is a dogmatic adherence to an established position. Thus the only answer to the attack on the modern principles which is legitimate on the basis of those principles themselves [i.e., the freedom to doubt or question any dogmatic position] is predetermined by the nature of the modern principles. They were evolved in opposition to, and by way of transformation of, the principles of classical philosophy. . . . Therefore a free examination of the modern principles is necessarily based on their conscientious confrontation with those of classical philosophy" (at 326–27).

96 *Natural Right and History*, supra n. 57, at 5.

97 Ibid., at 7.

98 Ibid., at 164.

99 *Philosophie politique III*, supra n. 8.

100 See M. Nussbaum, "Non-Relative Virtues: An Aristotelian Approach," in M. Nussbaum and A. Sen, eds., *The Quality of Life* (Oxford: Clarendon Press, 1993), at 242–69.

101 See the idea of liberalism's fall into democracy developed in Dyzenhaus, "Liberalism After the Fall," supra n. 81.

Hostis Not Inimicus

Toward a Theory of the Public
in the Work of Carl Schmitt

Ellen Kennedy

*Der Krieg ist durchaus nicht Ziel und Zweck oder gar Inhalt der Politik, wohl aber ist
er die als reale Möglichkeit immer vorhandene* Voraussetzung, *die das menschliche
Handeln und Denken in eigenartiger Weise bestimmt und dadurch ein spezifisch
politisches Verhalten bewirkt.*[1]

In an early review of the *Verfassungslehre* (1928), Margit Kraft-Fuchs
criticizes Carl Schmitt's argument as circular and illogical. While claiming to establish an entirely new constitutional theory, not a general
theory of the state, Schmitt in fact relies on a tautology and derives "an
is from an ought."[2] Quoting Schmitt's argument in *Der Wert des Staates
und die Bedeutung des Einzelnen* (1914) that "The mere actuality of
power at no point provides a justification unless it assumes a norm by
reference to which its claim is legitimated," Kraft-Fuchs concludes that
it is "astonishing he has forgotten this basic logical insight between
1914 and 1928."[3]

The tautology in question—the state is political unity is the state—
was posed by Schmitt a year before the *Verfassungslehre* was published.

The Critique of Liberalism

Delivered originally as a lecture at the Hochschule für Politik in Berlin
(May 1927), *Der Begriff des Politischen* was written in the context of
Weimar's dual crises: in the international arena as a consequence of
defeat in World War I and the Versailles Treaty; and domestically as the
constitutional crisis of a contested regime. Schmitt pays little attention
to the second of these here, probably because he was also writing a
major work on the Weimar Constitution as an example of the liberal
Rechtsstaat at this time. While much of *Der Begriff des Politischen* is

polemical, aimed at deconstructing the liberal hegemony of the Western Allies over defeated Germany, the *Verfassungslehre* assumes that, despite its contradictions and confusions, the Weimar Constitution contains a coherent core. Schmitt is constructively critical in that work, writing with the explicit assumption that because it is the valid constitution of Germany, a way must be found to make it into an effective instrument of government.

Both crises—the internal challenges to the Weimar Republic and Germany's weakness internationally—were the result of defeat in 1918. Here and in Schmitt's other works in the 1920s the results of Allied victory appear as more than just defeat in war. The Versailles Treaty of 1919 and the Weimar Constitution of 1919 are artifacts of a thoroughgoing metaphysical transformation: the destruction of the German Empire and the breakup of the Austro-Hungarian Empire establishes liberalism as the predominant political system in Europe. It is, he comments, "an astonishingly consequential system."[4] The Bolshevik Revolution poses the only significant challenge to liberalism, because communism alone among nineteenth-century ideologies meets liberalism on its own conceptual territory with the instruments of class warfare.[5]

Recent scholarship has discovered Schmitt's early work as an important source for understanding the development of his later thought, and I have suggested elsewhere that the dilemma "romanticism vs. politics" was the major question for his generation.[6] The question appears throughout his later works. Beginning with a scathing attack on romanticism that equates liberalism with "occasionalism" and indecision (*Politische Romantik* 1919), Schmitt consistently identifies liberalism as an "unserious" culture. While his antiliberal polemic conjures up a world of folly, self-deception, and idle dreams, the culture that would support Schmitt's concept of the political remains vague.

Der Begriff des Politischen (1927 and 1932) and the *Verfassungslehre* do, however, elaborate a theory of political realism that culminates in a conception of the public in an age of mass democracy. Each works via a critique of liberal culture, defining a political culture as what liberalism is not.

Liberalism as Hegemonic Discourse
Contemporary liberalism appears in *Der Begriff des Politischen* as the substance of international treaties, as the rhetoric of a mass psychology, as a hegemonic discourse. Liberalism is the prose of Schmitt's world. Its interpretation proceeds by analogies which make possible "the mar-

velous conformation of resemblances across space" whose immense power enables it to reveal similarities that are not visible, "substantial ones between things themselves."[7] Before the twentieth century the French aristocracy in the decade before 1789 provides the most catastrophic example of liberal pathos: the ancien régime "noticed nothing of the Revolution; how strange, the security and incomprehension with which the privileged spoke about the goodness, sweetness and innocence of the people, even in 1793—'spectacle ridicule et terrible'," Schmitt remarks with Tocqueville.[8]

The language of liberalism has changed, but its function remains the same. Like the romantic idealization of primitive man (or of the child) by Rousseau in the *Discourse on Inequality* or *Emile* and his demonization of "civilization," contemporary liberal thought is based on a dualism. "Humanity" is to it what "natural man" was for Rousseau; it is a polemical word that negates its opposite. Humanity as such cannot make war, at least not on this planet Schmitt remarks, because it includes every concrete entity which could otherwise be friend or enemy. "Humanity" enjoys a power of suggestion that works in combination with related notions from liberal ideology which shield people from pessimism about the political sphere. "Justice," "freedom," "peace," "progress," and "civilization" all evoke a world from which the issues of life and death have vanished. As in a massive advertising campaign, the political world appears sanitized and tamed because the characters who inhabit it have been transformed into seekers after peace and cooperation—from groups with interests into "humanity."[9]

The fulcrum of the liberal movement was and is private property. It is the center of liberal political theory, a keystone for the assembly of a coherent and systematic worldview. Economics predominates, while the political is disqualified as simple "violence" which could be eradicated through the processes of liberal organizations and the concept of humanity. All law becomes civil law, focused on the institution of property. Even Locke's theory of individual rights begins with the assertion that every man has a "property" in himself. The constitution of the Federal Republic of Germany constructs basic human rights in terms of "inviolable" human dignity, a term borrowed from the law of property. There is, finally, an ethical pathos in liberalism which, combined with an insistence on "objectivity" or neutrality, transforms all political concepts: war becomes competition or discussion; the state becomes society which is redefined further as humanity or even the economic system of production and consumption; will becomes the ideal of progress; the people or nation become a cultural public (listeners or viewers, museum visitors, tourists, sports fans, and so forth) or "consumers"; government and power wander away from the original meaning of the public and become either "advertising" or "control."[10]

The cultures of liberalism and the political are mutually exclusive. Excepting liberalism, there are no political theories which deny that man is problematic and dangerously dynamic in his passions and interests. Liberalism does not reject the state, but transforms it into "the rule of law" and as a consequence dissolves the political into ethics and economics. The state and its structures serve the individual, first in the ideology of rights (especially human rights) and, second, by orienting the public toward issues of private morality and economics to the exclusion of political thinking. In Schmitt's work, the worlds of liberalism and the political stand in stark contrast to each other:

LIBERALISM	THE POLITICAL
1. Individualism	1. Political unity
2. Ethics, economy, culture	2. Friend/enemy distinction
3. Private	3. Public
4. State = security of property	4. State = existential decisions about defense

Of all liberalism's nineteenth-century opponents, Schmitt concludes in *Der Begriff des Politischen*, Karl Marx's critique was the most powerful, because it alone followed liberalism into its own territory, the world of individualism and private property. Marxism's ideological power lay in its simplification of history into class struggle, and that again into the clash of bourgeoisie and proletariat. With the triumph of bolshevism in Russia and Lenin's revisions of Marx, the ideas of militant socialism found their constitution in the antiliberal form of the political.[11]

The Political and the Private in German Jurisprudence
It is hardly surprising that the relationship of the state (and thus the law) to politics became one of the main themes in German jurisprudence during the Weimar Republic. The first German Republic came into existence under circumstances of contested legitimacy. The product of military defeat and revolution, Weimar never really gained the confidence of important groups in German society. Much of the civil service and armed forces regarded the new constitution with suspicion, and extremist political parties on the left and right openly called for its

subversion. While Communists called it the tool of industrialists, many of them (and reactionary groups such as the East Prussian landowners) thought of Weimar as a virtual dictatorship of the lower classes.[12]

Within that broad context a set of rather narrow issues in administrative law played a crucial role in the development of Germany's political culture. This shaped Schmitt's theory of the public and its culture.

Well before the First World War the definition of political status had begun to vex administrative lawyers in France and Germany. The questions were simple. Which activities of the state are "political" and which are administrative? How are "political" activities in society to be defined? The answers, however, were not simple. For Weimar's pluralistic structure of parties, classes, and interest groups, the issue of the definition of politics was particularly important and, as in England, the legal question arose first with regard to the churches. Before 1906 the churches were governed by an 1850 Prussian law which treated all church and religious activities as public and subject to state regulation. When a lower court decision[13] redefined them as private, new legislation was passed in 1908 which stated that "every association which aims to influence public matters is a political association."[14] While "political" literally meant attempting to preserve, change, or otherwise influence institutions of the state, or the functioning of its subsidiary agencies, the new law could produce strange results. For example, mortuaries performing cremations became "political" associations because the disposal of corpses was regulated by the state.[15] While this example illustrates a bizarre enlargement of what counts as political, Schmitt emphasizes a contrary aspect of the courts' practice under the new law. Case law on political association, he comments, marks "a decisive stage" in creating certain substantive areas as interest and influence spheres for particular groups and organizations. "In the language of the 19th century, 'society' faces the 'state' independently."[16] The logical deduction from that dualism is that everything "social" is "unpolitical"—either a naive mistake, Schmitt remarks, or a very useful tactic in domestic politics.[17]

The classic form of the issue arose in nineteenth-century France, but it was not an exclusively French constitutional problem. Italy adopted French practice in 1889 ignoring, Rudolf Smend commented, its casuistry.[18] There the definition of political power became more closely associated with power in exceptional circumstances, and Italian law specifically recognized "riots and plagues" as instances where governmental (political) power was required and imminently justified. The

English constitution, too, recognized prerogative power and insulated it from judicial and legislative review. In the United States, the Supreme Court exempted "political questions" from its review, using the formal criterion of "separation of powers" and not defining a principle or giving a catalog of such acts.[19]

The foreign practice regarding political powers, Rudolf Smend argued in 1923, was an unsatisfactory example for Germany. When Smend wrote, the issue was not just one of association law—important as that was to become in the course of the Republic—but of executive power, too. The new Republic's constitution provided for emergency government in Article 48, and its provisions were broadly used by Friedrich Ebert during 1919–25.[20] He used the Reichswehr, or army, to suppress civil disturbances including strikes, rebellion, and *putsch* attempts by right- and left-wing extremists, and also to take away local government by a Communist regime in Saxony. The political turmoil of those years included separatist movements in the Rheinland and Pfalz, conflicts between the central government in Berlin and Bavaria, the Great Inflation, a series of foreign policy crises and assassinations (including that of the Foreign Minister Walter Rathenau in 1922).

Article 48 gave the Reichspräsident freedom to rule without regard for the Reichstag and allowed him to suspend certain basic rights, including those of free speech, press, assembly, and privacy of the post and household. During Ebert's presidency, Article 48 was used in a "commissarial" fashion, to restore order and preserve the constitution. But its practice remained controversial throughout the 1920s and legislation to define it more specifically was never enacted.[21]

The Staatsgerichtshof did not consider the issue of Article 48 until it arose over Chancellor van Papen's action against Prussia in the last year of the Republic, but it had heard a case on the distinction between political and administrative acts in 1925 which left their definition unresolved.[22] The results in both cases seem to confirm the view that courts, even the highest courts, cannot effectively adjudicate fundamental "political" questions. The basic issue of political acts remained a topic in German political science and legal theory throughout the Republic.[23]

Despite these controversies, German public law retained a relatively unproblematic concept of the political. What the state does, or what is done with reference to it, is political (this was the theory behind the 1908 revision of the Prussian Vereinsgesetz); everything else is by definition "unpolitical." The long debate among administrative lawyers and constitutional lawyers over the issue of political versus administrative acts should in the view of some jurists, including Schmitt and Smend, have forced a fundamental rethinking of the distinction. Instead the lines of debate were drawn more sharply, dividing the participants into two opposing camps.

The first, represented by Richard Thoma, Gerhard Anschütz, Hugo Krabbe, and Hans Kelsen, defined the state in terms of positive law and institutions, and most of them were at least "Vernunftrepublikaner" (republicans in virtue of reason rather than personal conviction) in Thomas Mann's phrase. But their work largely ignored the insights of sociology and political science into modern government and society, focusing instead on the formal study of laws, the state, and constitutions. Kelsen's Pure Theory of law went further, making the expurgation of all historical and political aspects from the constitution into a first principle of jurisprudence. His idea of a "Justizstaat"[24] was normative positivism. Essentially liberal in political intent, Kelsen's positivism developed the concept of the rule of law to a near caricature. The claims of the Staatsgerichtshof to exercise constitutional jurisdiction and to review ordinary laws echoed much that was asserted in Weimar Germany within liberal circles about the need for an unpolitical decision maker.

A second school of jurists, including Schmitt, Rudolf Smend, Heinrich Triepel, Erich Kaufmann, and Hermann Heller, thought reliance on formal definitions and distinctions was the root of the confusion in German law. They argued that such reliance excluded the social, metajurisprudential, and political content of legal concepts and that reliance on logical analysis alone actually increased uncertainty in the law. The question of what is political, or of government versus administrative acts, cannot, Smend argued, be resolved unless the constitution is construed as the governmental task of creating and maintaining unity.[25] In a similar vein, Heller asserted that politics is the art of creating "unity from diversity"; the state's purpose cannot be excluded from legal interpretation. "All the problems which have always been the most important in thinking about the state," Heller wrote, "questions about the character, the reality and the unity of the state, its goals and their justification, analysis of the relationship between power and right, the problem of the state as such and of its relationship to society are excluded from the theory of the state as 'metajurisprudential.'"[26] For Gustav Radbruch, an SDP (Social Democratic Party) member of the Reichstag and Minister of Justice in the early years of the Republic (1921–22 and 1923), the dominant method of "Begriffsjurisprudenz" (analytical jurisprudence) was inappropriate; the object of law is "empirical" he argued; it is "a cultural science, but its method has become an abstract science of norms."[27]

The critics of legal positivism were divided in their opinions of the Republic and in their party-political allegiances. All of them agreed that constitutional law in a democratic regime required more than a study of formal law, but none took Schmitt's conceptually radical approach.

Rather than divorcing the questions of politics and the state, Schmitt's argument incorporated their historical evolution in relation to each other. Against attempts by political theorists to describe the state analogously as an organism (Spann), a machine (Montesquieu), a person or an institution (Hobbes), a society or a community (Gierke), a factory (Weber), a beehive, or even a simple "process," Schmitt defines the state as a status: the political unity of a people living in a closed territory. While accepting the essence of Max Weber's definition,[28] Schmitt goes further than Weber in making a theory of the state dependent on a concept of the political.

Rejecting attempts to derive a conception of the political from a theory of the state, Schmitt reverses the equation, making the political primary and the state dependent upon it: "the concept of the state assumes a concept of the political."[29] The discussion transforms the state as a public-law concept into a question about the essence (Wesen) of "the political" which emphasizes its precedence over the legal or formal. The grounds for its preeminent position are existential: the political is the field on which issues of life and death are met for the public; security within and security outside its territory are the chief purpose of the state.

The Public and the Political

Liberal jurisprudence set the principle of "is/ought" above the data of empirical politics in a manner, Schmitt argued, that rendered it fruitless. If "the link between de facto and de jure power is the fundamental problem of sovereignty," then maintaining a categorical separation of the normative from the empirical world ends in an antipolitical theory.[30] Kelsen (and nineteenth-century *Begriffsjurisprudenz* before him) assumed the fundamental unity of the legal system. In *Politische Theologie* Schmitt again reverses the liberal focus. The first question of a constitutional theory must be the political question of unity and not the question of the logical unity of the law.

The Criterion of the Political
The distinction of friend and enemy appears in *Der Begriff des Politischen* as a phenomenal criterion, not of politics, but of an aggregate condition, "the political." Knowledge of it is, as Ernst-Wolfgang Böckenförde argues, the postulate of sound political judgment and action.[31]

Der Begriff des Politischen asserts that human existence can be divided into logically coherent categories. These are exhaustive of "existence" and they are empirically given. Schmitt's language moves from "categories" to "life-spheres," using these almost interchangeably. Three substantive life-spheres are immediately identified: the moral, the aesthetic, and the economic, each of which has distinctive criteria. Let us assume, he argues, that the ultimate criteria of these are the distinctions good or evil (moral), beautiful or ugly (aesthetics), and profitable or unprofitable (economics). Is there a specifically political distinction?[32]

All political motives and actions lead back to the distinction of friend or enemy. It is relatively independent of the other criteria, not in the sense of being "a new substantive sphere," but because it is not based on them and cannot be derived from them. The political enemy is not necessarily ugly or evil; it is not necessarily unprofitable to trade with him. "The distinction of friend and enemy signifies the outer limits of an association or dissociation; it can exist theoretically without applying any moral, aesthetic and economic distinctions simultaneously."[33] Because the political is entirely independent of the other spheres and their criteria, the good, the beautiful and the profitable are not necessarily "friends" any more than their obverse is necessarily the "enemy."

The distinction friend/enemy is not a definition of politics or its content, but an objective criterion which measures the intensity of association or dissociation. As such the political delimits a sphere of conflict and potential conflict, but it has no substance. It can be about anything over which people disagree so strongly that war over it is possible. The enemy is "the other" whose essence lies precisely in the existential recognition that it would be possible to kill him. In a sovereign state the political in this primary sense disappears from society. But if the monopoly on the use of violence breaks down, and the authority of the state begins to disintegrate, the political reappears as civil war. It is always possible in relations between states.[34]

Schmitt's argument is not a normative recommendation nor does he argue that political existence is "nothing but bloody war." Every polity does not constantly face the question about how to distinguish between a friend or an enemy. By contrast to contemporaries such as Ernst Jünger, or even Erich Kaufmann,[35] Schmitt neither idealizes war nor does he regard struggle as a virtue. The central elements of the argument — friend, enemy, war — are defined in terms of physical killing: "War is just the extreme realization of enmity. It need not be a common occurrence, nor something normal, neither must it be an ideal or something to be longed for; but it must persist as a real possibility, if the concept of an enemy is to retain meaning."[36] In this primary sense of an existential decision about friends and enemies, the political appears instead as the exception.

The Concept of the Public

The most important aspect of Schmitt's argument for a theory of the state is that the friend/enemy distinction is not a private matter. The "enemy" does not refer to a person's (or a group's) opponent: it is always a public question because it challenges the existence of the political unity of the people. The enemy is *hostis* not *inimicus* and must be understood as a real threat to the continued existence of a concrete people. There is ample room in this conception for a variety of private competitions in every other sphere of life. But in the political sphere, there are no private enemies. "The public" appears here as different from the liberal idea of it and different, too, from contemporary theories of mass society.

In the history of political thought the idea belongs to a larger theory of education and enlightenment. "The public" for liberal philosophers was essentially "public opinion," the expression of liberal rationality for Jeremy Bentham and the keystone of a series of freedoms and parliamentary institutions for nineteenth-century thinkers. In *Geistesgeschichtliche Lage des heutigen Parlamentarismus* (*The Crisis of Parliamentary Democracy*) Schmitt argued that "openness" and "discussion" define liberal political theory. Belief in those justifies all other aspects of representative government: "Openness and discussion are the two principles on which constitutional thought and parliamentarism depend in a thoroughly logical and comprehensive system." Quoting the French historian Alphonse Lamartaine, Schmitt writes: "All progress, including social progress, is realized 'through representative institutions, that is, regulated liberty — through public discussion, that is, reason.' "[37]

Three objections to that concept of the public are raised in *Geistesgeschichtliche Lage des heutigen Parlamentarismus*. It remains an individualist theory. Freedom of opinion is always the individual's opinion, "a freedom for private people" within a competitive system. For John

Stuart Mill (as for the earlier generation of Utilitarians) public opinion happens in a "marketplace of ideas" from which individuals select what appears right or true to them. Moreover, that private person's freedom appears unrealistic to Schmitt; force and intrigue are absent, all choices are utterly free. "Where the public can exercise pressure—through a single individual casting a vote, for example—here, at the transition of the private into the public, the contradictory demand for a secret ballot appears."[38] The liberal public is, finally, a concept that contradicts that of the political. There are no enemies (or friends), only opponents in a discussion.

If a liberal public is rational and individual, the alternative conception in contemporary thought was neither. Research into "crowd psychology" had presented a very different social reality than that of classical liberalism by the time Schmitt wrote *Der Begriff des Politischen*. Attention to the behavior of people in groups encouraged social science to focus on mass society as a profoundly irrational phenomenon. In *Psychologie des Foules* (1895) Gustave Le Bon had asserted that "The substitution of the unconscious action of crowds for the conscious activity of individuals is one of the principal characteristics of the present age." Liberal philosophers such as Locke and Bentham and the men of the Enlightenment had presented the individual as a rational, perfectible being, but Le Bon emphasized the way "unconscious qualities obtain the upper hand." In a crowd the individual loses his inhibitions, experiencing a feeling of power he would not have normally. There is a "contagion" among the members of a crowd resulting from their high level of "suggestibility," a phenomenon Le Bon compares to that of the hypnotized individual. In a crowd "the individual differs essentially from himself" and is capable of great heroism or barbarity.[39]

The First World War and the revolutions which followed further stimulated the study of crowd psychology. Sigmund Freud's *Massenpsychologie und Ich-Analyse* (1921) accepted much of Le Bon's argument, while noting that a crowd intensifies affect and inhibits intellect.[40] In Freud's argument, irrational characteristics of the mind enable the psychology of the crowd through suggestion and libido. These bind the individual to the leader and the crowd, allowing the primitive to emerge within civilization.[41]

The work of "elite theorists" such as Gaetano Mosca, Vilfredo Pareto, and Robert Michels developed the argument that crowds subordinate reason to the irrational influence of the leader and the group. They all stressed the weakness of rationality in politics, arguing that subconscious suggestion dominates politics in mass society. Rousseau saw democracy as a means of human perfection in which governed and governing are identical. When Max Weber redefined it as a method of leadership selection, this "demystified" democracy. For the elite theorists, democracy as an ideal and as a method were equally misleading myths that clothed the structures of power with comforting notions of participation. The people never rule, these sociologists argued; elites rule.

For this second way of thinking about it, then, "the public" was at best something to be led by better, more rational men and at worst a primal horde without civilized inhibitions.[42]

Schmitt's "public" is neither. It is something less, certainly, than the liberal idealization of reason transcending power and interest. It remains a rational construct in public law. But it is something more than the elitists' "crowd," although Schmitt's public is still a group moved by the primal instinct of self-preservation. Both the (liberal) public and the crowd are too vague to convey Schmitt's intentions. "Volk" (people) or 'öffentliche Meinung" (public opinion) are used in the *Verfassungslehre*. These are both concepts from public law where "Öffentlichkeit" had no existence but "Volk" did.[43] Schmitt's use of people rather than public suggests an actor in historical terms such as Europe had seen many times in the century since the French Revolution, an actor different from the private person, and different too from the reasoning, discussing public of the liberal philosophers. In constitutional terms, the "people" exist as an aggregate before and above it, as the active element (voters) and as "public opinion."

In the context of Schmitt's constitutional theory, then, *Der Begriff des Politischen* suggests two aspects of the public: the people as a political agent and the people as beings whose lives are at stake in the primary meaning of the political. The constitutional implications of this are brought out more clearly in the *Verfassungslehre* but they are implicit here too where the distinction *hostis/inimicus* underlines the public nature of "enemy." Schmitt uses Plato's *Republic* to illustrate this. In that text, Socrates distinguishes between war and faction, arguing that their differentiae are "the friendly and kindred on the one hand and the alien and foreign on the other. Now that term employed for the hostility of the friendly is faction, and that for the alien is war."[44] The rest of this conversation in the dialogue is a discussion of why the Greeks can only make war against barbarians, not against each other. Even when divided by enmity, the Greeks "are still by nature friends."

That sense of the public is constitutive: "the political unity of the people."[45] As a really existing entity, the people is finally the subject (in both senses) of politics: its real initiator (the constitutional people) but also its object (the people of a state's foreign policy).

Finally, *Der Begriff des Politischen* suggests Schmitt's awareness of political facts used by the elite theorists and crowd psychology, but this theme works its way through the text more as an intrigue than a statement. There is only one reference to that literature (Pareto) and no discussion of the political movements of the day.[46] The underlying urgency of the text, however, conveys a sense of the political as irrational and unpredictable. While the elite theorists saw only the fact of the crowd, Schmitt sees it as something that can be transformed into the Volk of public law while recognizing (as they did) its volatility.

Notes

I am grateful to Karol Soltan and Jack Knight for comments on an earlier version of this paper and to my colleagues at The International Summer School in Political Science and International Relations in Mierki, Poland, for a stimulating and supportive environment.

1　The English translation of the epigraph quote is: "War is neither the aim nor the purpose nor even the very content of politics. But as an ever present possibility it is the leading *presupposition* which determines in a characteristic way human action and thinking and thereby creates a specifically political behavior." Carl Schmitt, *The Concept of the Political*, trans. and intro. George Schwab (Chicago: University of Chicago Press, 1996), at 34.

2　Margarit Kraft-Fuchs, "Prinzipielle Bemerkungen zu Carl Schmitt's Verfassungslehre," *Zeitschrift für öffentliches Recht* 9 (1930): 511.

3　Ibid., at 512–14. Carl Schmitt, *Der Wert des Staates und die Bedeutung des Einzelnen* (Tübingen: Hellerauer Verlag/Jakob Hegner, 1914).

4　Carl Schmitt, *Der Begriff des Politischen* (Berlin: Duncker & Humblot, 1979), at 70. *Politische Theologie* (Berlin: Duncker & Humblot, 1990, first pub. 1922) develops a method Schmitt calls "radical conceptualization" to uncover "the ultimate, radical structure" of an intellectual world. Such an approach assumes that a conceptual construction can be compared to the social structure of a given period, so that its analysis explains why certain ideas appear as "self-evident" in a given historical period. "Metaphysics is the most intense and clearest expression of an epoch." Ibid., at 58–60.

5　It is remarkable that there is no mention in *Der Begriff des Politischen* of fascism despite the attention Schmitt gave it in *Die geistesgeschichtliche Lage des heutigen Parlamentarismus* (Munich, 1923) as an ideology of equal rank to communism. Mussolini had been in power for nearly five years when Schmitt wrote *Der Begriff des Politischen*, and Schmitt's admiration for him extended in the book on parliamentarism to comparing Mussolini with Machiavelli: "Just as in the 16th century, an Italian has once again given expression to the principle of political realism." The reference is to Mussolini's October 1922 speech in Naples. Schmitt, *The Crisis of Parliamentary Democracy*, trans. and intro. Ellen Kennedy (Cambridge, Mass.: MIT Press, 1985), at 76.

6 Ellen Kennedy, "Carl Schmitt und Hugo Ball: Ein Beitrag zum Thema 'Politischer Expressionismus,'" *Zeitschrift für Politik* 35 (1988): 143; and Ellen Kennedy, "Politischer Expressionismus: Die kulturkritischen und metaphysischen Ursprünge des Begriffs des Politischen von Carl Schmitt," in Helmut Quaritsch, ed., *Complexio Oppositorum. über Carl Schmitt* (Berlin: Duncker & Humblot, 1988), 233. For a review of more recent literature see Reinhard Mehring, "Vom Umgang mit Carl Schmitt. Zur neueren Literatur," *Geschichte und Gesellschaft* 19 (1993): 388; and Herfried Münkler, "Carl Schmitt in der Diskussion," *Neue Politische Literatur* 35 (1990): 289.

7 Michel Foucault, *The Order of Things. An Archeology of the Human Sciences* (London: Tavistock, 1970), at 21.

8 Schmitt, *Der Begriff des Politischen*, supra n. 4, at 68.

9 Ibid., at 54–55.

10 Ibid., at 71. All translations are my own.

11 Ibid., at 73.

12 "It cannot be emphasized too strongly that this was not a 'loyal opposition,' that is, one which was prepared to operate within the existing constitutional framework and to abide by its rules. . . . [T]here existed a sizeable number of people on the Right of the political spectrum who did not consider a parliamentary Republic to be the appropriate political system for Germany or 'fulfillment' of Versailles the correct diplomacy. Their number was swelled by men and women from a very different social and ideological background on the extreme Left, whose proposals for the economic organization of the country could not be accommodated within the Weimar structure." Volker Berghahn, *Modern Germany. Society, Economy and Politics in the Twentieth Century* (Cambridge: Cambridge University Press, 1982), at 74.

13 Urteil des Kammergerichts vom 12. Februar 1906 (Johow Bd. 31, 32–34), quoted in Schmitt, *Der Begriff des Politischen*, supra n. 4, at 22.

14 Deutschen Reichsvereinsgesetz vom 19. April 1908, par. 3, sect. 1. In ibid., at 22–23. Schmitt refers *inter alia* to H. Geffcken, "Öffentliche Angelegenheit, politischer Gegenstand und politischer Verein nach preussischem Recht," in *Festschrift für Ernst Friedberg* (1908), at 287ff.; Jeze, *Les principles généraux du droit administratif* (1925); and R. Alibert, *Le contrôle juridictionnel de l'administration* (1926).

15 Rudolf Smend, "Die politische Gewalt im Verfassungsstaat und das Problem

der Staatsform" (1923) in Smend, *Staatsrechtliche Abhandlungen* (Duncker & Humblot: Berlin, 1968), at 82; Smend refers to the decision of the Preuss. Oberverwaltungsgesicht, 39, 444.

16 Schmitt, *Der Begriff des Politischen*, supra n. 4, at 22.

17 V. Pareto, *Traité de sociologie generale* (French ed., 1917 and 1919), I. at 450ff. and II. at 785ff.). Quoted by Schmitt, ibid., at 22.

18 Smend, supra n. 15, at 72.

19 Ibid., at 75–76 relies on J. P. Thayer, *Cases on Constitutional Law* (1895) for his discussion of the issue. Among the examples given from American practice are dictatorial power in the South during Reconstruction; international relations; and expulsions from the United States. The Nixon Administration's claim of "executive privilege" is a landmark in the history of these changing concepts of political or executive powers.

20 Article 48, par. 2, was used 135 times between October 20, 1919, and April 29, 1925. Fritz Poetzsch, "Vom Staatsleben unter der Weimarer Verfassung," *Jahrbuch des öffentlichen Rechts* 21 (1933–34): at 141ff. See Berghahn, "War and Civil War 1914–1923," supra n. 12, at 38–67 for an overview of emergency powers.

21 Contrary to the final sentence of the Article. Under President von Hindenburg, Article 48 became a corrosive agent in the disintegration of the liberal Rechtsstaat. In the context of a "fragmented party democracy" Article 48 grew into a "sovereign dictatorship" before Weimar finally gave way to the Third Reich. The use of emergency powers came before the Staatsgerichtshof in *Preussen contra Reich* (1930) but the issue was implicit in much French and German jurisprudence throughout the 1920s. The terms "commissarial" and "sovereign" dictatorship are Schmitt's: *Die Diktatur. Von den Anfängen des modernen Souveränitätsgedanken bis zum proletarischen Klassenkampf* (Berlin: Duncker & Humblot, 1921 and 1927). See also M. Rainer Lepsius, "From Fragmented Party Democracy to Government by Emergency Decree and National Socialist Takeover: Germany," in Juan Linz and Alfred Stephen, eds., *The Breakdown of Democratic Regimes: Europe* (Baltimore, Md.: Johns Hopkins University Press, 1970).

22 Reichsgericht für Zivilsachen (RGZ) 112, supplement, at 5 (21 Nov. 1925).

23 It made its way into contemporary social science with Karl Mannheim's discussion of it in *Ideologie und Utopie* (1929) as "the orientation point for politics."

24 The phrase is Schmitt's, coined in his debate with Kelsen over "Who should be defender of the constitution?" Schmitt, *Der Hüter der Verfassung* (Tübingen: J. C. B. Mohr [Paul Siebeck], 1931), at 13.

25 Smend's conception of government as the process of integrating all social, economic, and political factors became the basis of his *Verfassung und Verfassungsrecht* (Munich, 1928). It was the first political theory based on "integration" and was resoundingly rejected when it appeared. The reviews

were so scathing that Smend never published another book, writing only articles for the rest of his life.

26 Hermann Heller, "Die Krisis der Staatslehre," in *Gesammelte Schriften* vol. 2 (Tübingen: J. C. B. Mohr [Paul Siebeck], 1992, first pub. 1926), at 10.

27 Gustav Radbruch, *Grundzüge der Rechtsphilosophie* (Leipzig, 1914), at 186.

28 Schmitt rejects Weber's conception of politics as an effort to gain power or the "leadership of or influence over a political organization: today, the state." Max Weber, *Politics as a Vocation. From Max Weber: Essays in Sociology*, trans. and intro. H. H. Gerth and C. Wright Mills (London: Routledge & Kegan Paul, 1974), at 77.

29 Schmitt, *Der Begriff des Politischen*, supra n. 4, at 20.

30 Schmitt, *Politische Theorie*, supra n. 4, at 27.

31 Ernst-Wolfgang Böckenförde, "Der Begriff des Politischen als Schlüssel zum Staatsrechtlichen Werk Carl Schmitts," in *Complexio Oppositorum über Carl Schmitt*, supra n. 6, at 284.

32 Schmitt, *Der Begriff des Politischen*, supra n. 4, at 26.

33 Schmitt, ibid., at 27.

34 Schmitt, *Der Begriff des Politischen*, supra n. 4, at 34.

35 Among the enormous amount of literature of the period glorifying war, see, for example, Ernst Jünger's novel, *Im Stahlgewitter* (Berlin, 1920); Erich Kaufmann's treatise on international law, *Das Wesen des Völkerrechts und die clausula rebus sic stantibus* (Tübingen, 1911). "The monstrous development of military technology today . . . has made everything which had been heroic and admirable about it, personal courage and the thrill of battle, utterly meaningless." Schmitt, ibid., at 74–75.

36 Schmitt, ibid., at 33.

37 Carl Schmitt, *The Crisis of Parliamentary Democracy*, trans. Ellen Kennedy (Cambridge, Mass.: MIT Press, 1985, first pub. 1926), at 49. Schmitt quotes from *Histoire de la révolution de 1848*.

38 Ibid., at 39.

39 "The individual forming part of a psychological crowd . . . is no longer conscious of his acts. In his case . . . certain faculties are destroyed, others may be brought to a high degree of exultation." Among Le Bon's examples of such behavior are the Crusades, juries, parliamentary assemblies, and men of the French Revolutionary Convention. Gustave Le Bon, *The Man and His Works* (Indianapolis: Liberty Press, 1979), at 57–65. This edition is a reprint of the 1896 translation.

40 Sigmund Freud, *Group Psychology and the Analysis of the Ego*, The Pelican Freud Library, vol. 12, *Civilization, Society and Religion* (Harmondsworth: Penguin, 1987), at 116.

41 Ibid., at 124. Freud refers to mass belief in the "fantastic promises" of Wilson's 14 Points and the bonding of First World War soldiers to each other and to their military commanders. Primal society was "a horde ruled over

despotically by a powerful male. . . . The group appears to us as a revival of the primal horde." Ibid., at 154–55.

42 Crowd theory became the basis of "mass society" theories of modern politics. These were considerably later than Schmitt's text, and they include: William Kornhauser, *The Politics of Mass Society* (New York: Free Press, 1959); Joseph Schumpeter, *Capitalism, Socialism and Democracy* (New York: Harper, 1947); C. Wright Mills, *The Power Elite* (New York: Oxford University Press, 1956). An interesting, little-known study of the psychology of mass politics (especially political movements) is Richard Behrendt, *Politischer Aktivismus* (Hirschfeld Verlag, 1932).

43 As a substantive, "Öffentlichkeit" (the public in German) almost never appears in Schmitt's writing, except when he is referring to liberal theories. Where *Der Begriff des Politischen* refers to the public quality of the political, Schmitt uses the adjectival form of the word. "Volk" is sometimes rendered as nation into English. They are distinguished in the *Verfassungslehre:* "In contrast to the general concept 'people,' 'nation' refers to an individual people characterized by its political consciousness." *Verfassungslehre* (Berlin: Duncker & Humblot, 1989, first pub. 1928), at 231. The Weimar Constitution begins: "The German people [das deutsche Volk] has given itself this constitution"—not 'the public.'"

44 *The Republic*, Book V, 470. I do not know if Schmitt also knew Cicero's comments on *hostis:* "A further point is that the name given to someone who ought properly to have been called a foe (*perduellis*) is in fact a *hostis*. I notice that the grimness of the fact is lessened by the gentleness of the word. For *hostis* meant to our forefathers he whom we now call a stranger. . . . What greater courteousness could there be than to call him against whom you are waging war by so tender a name?" *On Duties* (Cambridge: Cambridge University Press, 1996), at 16.

45 Schmitt, supra n. 43, at 5.

46 These are discussed in *The Crisis of Parliamentary Democracy* where Schmitt's fascination with communism and fascism is apparent.

Pluralism and the Crisis of Parliamentary Democracy

Dominique Leydet

Carl Schmitt levels two kinds of criticism against liberal parliamentarism. First, Schmitt seeks to refute the liberal conception of politics (which assumes the possibility of rational will formation) on the basis of his own existential view of the political (which employs the distinction between friend and foe).[1] Second, Schmitt attempts to show why and how the evolution of our political system, specifically the development of mass democracy, has made parliament an obsolete institution. This approach is both more dangerous and plausible, because it does not presuppose an acceptance of Schmitt's own controversial conception of politics and relies on observations about the parliamentary system that are shared and deplored equally by many liberals. In *The Crisis of Parliamentary Democracy*,[2] Schmitt does not confront directly what he considers to be fundamental principles of the parliamentary system—rational and public discussion—but rather shows that since these principles are unrealizable given the changes which the system has undergone, parliamentary institutions remain an empty shell, devoid of any justification and credibility.

Schmitt also pursues this second strategy in writings such as *Der Hüter der Verfassung* (*The Guardian of the Constitution*),[3] although here the focus is changed from the question of legitimacy to the problems raised by pluralism. This concept is defined by Schmitt as a situation in which the state has become dependent upon, or subordinate to, the various social and economic associations that make up contemporary industrial societies.[4] The state thus appears as nothing more than the aggregate of compromises between heterogeneous groups, as the sum total of their agreements. In such a situation, not only are the integrity and unity of the state undermined, but parliament, according to

Schmitt, loses its ability to rationally mediate and integrate divergent interests. It is in this context that parliamentarism is the object of Schmitt's criticism. Here again it is not its underlying principles we see him criticize, but the impossibility of their realization.

Schmitt's arguments, especially in writings such as *Der Hüter der Verfassung*, are directed primarily toward the specific situation of Weimar Germany. Yet his criticism of pluralism and the resulting inadequacy of the parliamentary system is clearly of a more general nature.[5] He sees pluralism as the consequence of historical factors common to most industrial states and related to the transformation of the nineteenth-century neutral state toward the "total state."

Distinctions between varieties of pluralist states can be one of degree only, and the polarized pluralism[6] which characterized Weimar Germany represented simply its fullest realization. In other words, Weimar displayed an extreme situation in which a decision could not be eluded: either the state itself collapsed because of centripetal pressures, or its unity was reaffirmed through an authoritarian presidential rule, based not on parliamentary support but on plebiscitary acclamation.[7] What Germany's predicament shows clearly for Schmitt is that liberal parliamentarism is not the way of the future.

Schmitt's analysis of pluralism thus leads to a dire dilemma: either the state enjoys undisputed supremacy over associations, meaning that the state has the authority to determine the common will, independently of associational claims, or it is subordinate to associations, in which case such decisions will be the result of compromises between opposing interests. In other words, either the common will is arbitrarily determined by the state, embodied in a strong executive, or it is reduced to whatever uneasy agreements are reached between particular interests. Even in this latter case, the common will remains devoid of any principled rationality.[8] Excluded here is the possibility that the common will could be formed by conciliating the diverse interests present in contemporary society, and at the same time ensure the integrity of the state and reflect the common good.

This third alternative brings us back to liberal parliamentarism. It is here that Schmitt's criticism of parliament in a context of pluralism is significant. Schmitt's main argument is premised on his assumption that what makes parliament into an institution that allows for rational political decision making is the process of public deliberation and consensus formation. In order to reach the conclusion that parliament cannot mitigate the problems of pluralism, he must simply demonstrate that the evolution of political parties from loose associations to bureau-cratized organizations has made a farce of deliberation.

The strength of Schmitt's argument turns on the undeniable fact that strict enforcement of party discipline makes it difficult, if not impossible, for real public deliberation to occur in parliament. Excluding a fundamental change in the way the political game is played, the only viable strategy, therefore, must be to reexamine the central premise of his argument. The question is whether his strict definition of public deliberation must be met in order to make parliament an institution which fosters the rational formulation of common interests. This exercise might prove helpful in light of the importance attached to the deliberative model in current theories of democracy. More specifically, it might indicate how the concept of public discussion must be reformulated in order to remain relevant to contemporary politics.

The following discussion is divided into two parts. First, I will examine Schmitt's historical analysis of why parliamentarism could only work in the context of the nineteenth-century neutral state and how the development of pluralism and the "total state" transformed parliament into a "showplace for pluralist interests." Schmitt's analysis of the ways in which pluralism produces an inherently unstable situation that leads to extreme fragmentation will also be discussed. Second, I will sketch an alternative description of how the parliamentary game might work in a way that encourages the formulation of principled compromises between the divergent interests that make up heterogeneous societies.

I

Schmitt's arguments are premised on his supposition that the effectiveness of parliament during the first three quarters of the nineteenth century was based on the dualism of constitutional monarchy and its associated series of tensions between prince and people, state and society, government and parliament, executive and legislative powers.[9] This dualism was implied in the view that the constitution was a pact between prince and people, wherein parliament stood as the representative of society and of the people itself. Since the representative assembly was the stage upon which society appeared before the state, parliament could plausibly be seen to stand for society's interests against those of the Crown. This meant essentially that parliament's job was to defend society's autonomy against executive power, thus minimizing the intervention of the state in social and economic matters.

For Schmitt, this goes a long way to explain how the dual system encouraged a noninterventionist or neutral state. According to this analysis, most economic and social questions were resolved through the free workings of the market and the free competition of ideas which formed public opinion and determined the common will. Both society and parliament were understood by most nineteenth-century liberals to be coterminous with the bourgeoisie, whose members shared basic assumptions about the market, society, and the state. The existence of such shared understandings[10] was an essential precondition for the open, rational discussion of policies that were carried out in nineteenth-century parliaments.

The distinction between state and society, and the concomitant state neutrality, allowed for the existence of a plurality of social forces in a way that did not threaten the state's integrity. According to Schmitt, the state was strong enough to confront, on its own terms, these social forces. Thus, it could play the role of a standard in reference to which the various currents that ran through society could be validated and integrated. On the other hand, the state's neutral stance toward religion and the economy meant that those different domains enjoyed a significant degree of autonomy.[11]

It is the final victory of parliament over the Crown which, paradoxically, sealed parliament's own fate by undermining the dualism which was its own condition of possibility. Shorn of its role as the counterweight of the Crown, parliament could no longer stand as the representative both of society and of the people. Although Schmitt does not make this point here, one can see how democratic demands for the expansion of the suffrage, and the final success of these demands, could fit in this account. What Schmitt does emphasize is that the separation of state and society is now replaced by their fusion, meaning that potentially all social and economic questions that were not the object of state intervention become political. This spells the end of the neutral state and heralds the turn toward the "total state," in which the totality of life is opened to state intervention. If the fusion of state and society entails that society, and all the diverse groups that compose it are potentially the object of state action, it also implies the converse: that the state becomes the focus of those groups' claims and pressures. In this context, the state is to be equated with the self-organization of society, meaning that the various social forces will come to constitute the state, primarily through the action of political parties.

Since the state has become fused with society, political parties become completely determined by various social and economic interests. Instead of being the loose associations of individuals sharing similar opinions on a given issue, as was presupposed by liberal theories and constitutions, most major parties have become stable organizations with their own bureaucracy. They may even be seen as part of a whole social power complex which, through its various organizations, ministers to all the needs (spiritual, social, and economic) of a given segment of the population. Such political parties thus realize the conditions of the total state, though limited to the segment of the population which they control.[12]

Political parties, representing different and often opposed social and economic interests, invest parliament. Yet they also rob it of its ability to function as spelled out in classical parliamentary theory. Since parties enforce discipline, there can be no public deliberation. Representatives are not free to change their minds upon hearing what they might consider to be a better argument. They are but party delegates, and through their parties, representatives of interests to which they must remain faithful. Moreover, the basic homogeneity that existed in the nineteenth-century parliament has disappeared, and with it those shared understandings that made up the unquestioned common basis of discussion. Because of the distance between the various parties, there can be no common deliberation. Publicly, parties express opposing demands, while in secret negotiations, they jockey for possible advantages that may be won through the state's actions. Far from being the scene upon which divergent interests may be expressed, mediated, and integrated into a common will, the representative assembly is nothing but "the showplace for pluralist interests."

This is how the legislative state, that is, the state dominated by the legislative power, becomes in fact subordinate to the groups which control parliament. This is what Schmitt calls a situation of pluralism, closely tied to the evolution away from the *status mixtus* of constitutional monarchy, characterized by a balance between the legislative and the executive states, toward parliamentary supremacy.

Pluralism so defined necessarily constitutes a threat to the state's integrity and unity. It can only be inherently unstable, so that the difference between, for example, England and Germany is simply a question of where each falls on the slippery slope that leads to complete fragmentation. In "Staatsethik und pluralistischer Staat,"[13] Schmitt distinguishes between three possible versions of the pluralist state, representing three distinct points on that slope. He points out that in conditions of pluralism, the unity of the state can only last as long as the various parties share certain premises. Unity, then, rests primarily upon the constitution, which spells out common principles.

Such a constitutional ethic produces a more or less stable and effective unity, depending on the constitution's clarity, authority, and substantial character. Thus, a constitution that clearly expresses a substantial consensus on fundamentals between the parties would indicate a condition of stable unity. On the other hand, if the consensus is a weak one, and the constitution merely states the rules of the game by which the parties agree to abide, then the parties' commitment to those rules creates a situation, characterized by Schmitt, as an ethic of *fair play*. Yet this situation is an inherently unstable one, which eventually leads to the pluralistic dissolution of the state, where the state is reduced to an "aggregate of the changing agreements made between heterogeneous groups." This is followed by a further step in the process of fragmentation, governed by what Schmitt calls the ethic of *pacta sunt servanda*, which is incompatible with state unity.

The main difference between the ethics of *fair play* and *pacta sunt servanda* is that in the former the unity of the state is presupposed in the rules which govern the pluralist game. However, in the latter case, the various social groups, as the contracting parties, are themselves the seats of authority and make up the rules as they go, in a process of mutual accommodation. In such a context, what is left of unity is no more than the result of a temporary and tenuous alliance between competing social forces. The result is little more than a truce, implying the possibility of war. In fact, the ethic of the *pacta sunt servanda* is an ethic of civil war. In a situation of extreme fragmentation, when the state cannot secure the normal situation in which ethical and legal norms alone are possible, there is, for Schmitt, a clear duty to reestablish the state's unity against centripetal forces.

What should be stressed is that, for Schmitt, the difference between a country enjoying the stability afforded by an effective constitutional ethic, and the same country sliding into the *pacta sunt servanda* version of the pluralist state, cannot be explained on the basis of differences between the political institutions themselves. This can be illustrated by considering the case of England, as a more stable version of the pluralist state. The point here is that, for Schmitt, this stability is not due, in any essential way, to some feature of the English parliamentary system, but rather to the resilience and strength of the English sense of national unity. There can be no working (viz., stable) pluralist political system.

Evidence of this can be found in a few remarks that Schmitt makes about the English parliamentary system in the *Verfassungslehre*. In the section concerning the evolution of the parliamentary system, Schmitt writes that even "friendly compromises and the loyal alternating rule of the two parties can only take place if they do not try to eliminate or annihilate each other but seek to abide by rules of fair play."[14] This remains possible only as long as the opposition between parties is not so radical as to endanger the framework of national and social unity. However, as soon as "religious, class or national differences become decisive inside parliament, this prior condition is not met anymore."[15]

In England the ethic of fair play prevailed until the appearance of the Labour Party, which introduced a new social element and, potentially, "a real class opposition."[16] In fact, the new party had already upset the bipartisan political system, demonstrated in the 1923 elections which led to the development of a three-party system. The 1924 elections, won handsomely by the Conservative Party, can be explained, according to Schmitt, "through the necessity in which one found oneself, confronted with a socialist conception of class, to express clearly the fundamental prior condition of English parliamentarism, that is political unity on a national basis."[17]

Two points can be made here. First, the development and success of the Labour Party shows, for Schmitt, that fundamentally the same forces are at work inside England as they are in the rest of Europe, and that they put a stress on the parliamentary system. Second, the fact that the English state has resisted these centripetal forces more successfully than the German Republic is not the result of any particular virtue inherent in the English political system. Rather, it depends upon the stronger sense of unity felt by the people of England, a feeling confirmed and reasserted by the results of the October 1924 elections. In fact, the only specific institutional feature which has helped to resist the divisive tendencies represented by Labour has nothing to do with parliament itself, and everything to do with the *first past the post* electoral system.[18] As opposed to proportional representation, which Schmitt severely criticizes in *Der Hüter der Verfassung*,[19] the *first past the post* system allows significant distortions between the number of votes expressed and the seats won by a given party. This constitutes a bulwark against third parties.

Schmitt notes that the 1924 elections have not eliminated Labour's hold on a significant part of the electorate. The social divisions which explain Labour's continued existence remain a source of instability. The question of whether English national unity can resist the divisiveness of class remains open.

What is at stake here is the unity of the people when confronted with possibilities of division along religious, national, and especially class lines. The question is, What should be done to effectively alleviate class divisions, so that they do not threaten state stability? In his 1928 article, "Politische Demokratie und soziale Homogenität," Hermann Heller presented an analysis of the difficulties facing parliamentary democracy that was in many ways similar to Schmitt's analysis. He too emphasizes the importance of a shared basis of discussion as a necessary condition of parliamentarism and considers the radical nature of the opposition between left-wing and right-wing parties as a grave threat. For Heller, the crux of the issue is the problem of what he calls social homogeneity, that is "the social-psychological state in which the inevitably present antitheses and conflicts of interest appear constrained by a consciousness and sense of the We, by a community will which brings itself into being."[20] For Heller, social homogeneity has very concrete conditions of possibility, notably conditions of relative economic equality. Political democracy may survive class divisions only if radical economic changes provide a greater degree of economic and social equality between classes.

To put it mildly, this is not the approach favored by Schmitt. In "Staatsethik und pluralistischer Staat," he briefly delineates the various possible types of unity.[21] There can be unity from above, through command and power, unity from below, through the "substantial homogeneity of a people," or unity through continuous compromises between social groups, meaning unity through consensus making. Here Schmitt insists on the importance of power as the means to produce consensus. The crucial issue is who will control the processes through which consensus is achieved. In stark contrast to the British pluralists, Schmitt affirms that these means must belong to the state, as the embodiment of the political union of a people. To deprive the state of those means, and allow the various social groups to dispose of them, would result in the ethic of *pacta sunt servanda*.

For Schmitt, when the "substantial homogeneity of the people" is endangered by divisions in society, the state must reassert its unity by identifying a public enemy. Once the fundamental distinction between friend and foe is made, remaining tensions in society lose their force and the integrity of the state is safeguarded. In other words, existing social divisions are not to be alleviated through economic changes, but rather disqualified through a decision by the ruling elite. The authoritarian character of this rule is reconciled with democratic principle through the use of plebiscitary elections. In Weimar Germany, the illustration of extreme pluralism, this implies that power must be wrested away from parliament and transferred to the executive, that is, to the directly elected president, who will dictate the common will. Schmitt's way out of what he calls the "ethic of civil war" is not to address, head on, the underlying issues and try to construct a viable peace. It reads very much like a declaration of war.

II

Schmitt's solution amounts to the following: given conditions of pluralism, the only way to maintain the unity and integrity of the state, subject to ever-increasing centripetal pressures, is to strengthen the state's hand by establishing an authoritarian government with democratic legitimacy. The only alternative to this is a process by which the common will is reduced to a series of compromises negotiated between various interest groups. Schmitt denies that these compromises amount to anything more than the results of unprincipled bargains struck by rival interest groups. The parliamentary system cannot offer anything better.

Schmitt's main argument is straightforward. The development of an interventionist state, most striking in economic matters, has greatly increased the number of issues which directly touch the interests of various social groups. These groups, in turn, have organized themselves into political parties that, far from being loose associations of individuals sharing similar ideas, are stable and bureaucratized organizations. These parties are permanent representatives of the interests of particular segments of the electorate, and elected members are expected to vote along party lines.

The first consequence of this development is that discussion disappears from parliament. Because of party discipline, the force of a given party on a particular issue corresponds simply to its numerical strength in parliament. As Schmitt notes, no public parliamentary debate can influence a delegate who is voting according to the position of his party, which is itself determined strictly by the interests it serves. Even discussions inside parliamentary committees are really nothing more than business negotiations.

In such circumstances, the public character of parliamentary debate also disappears. The plenary session of parliament is not the place where decisions are made rationally as a result of public discussion. Parliament becomes an authority which reaches decisions through bargaining and makes known the result of such horse trading by staging formal votes. The various speeches that precede the vote are nothing but staged-managed remnants of a bygone era.[22]

Before considering Schmitt's conception of public deliberation, I must object to two assumptions that are central to his argument. First, in the context of the interventionist state, political parties are simply the mouthpieces of different social groups and interests. This robs parties of the ability to mediate between different sectional interests, for this ability presupposes some degree of distance between political parties and interests. This is a significant point. If political parties, and their parliamentary wing, were wholly directed by the interests and social forces which they purport to represent, parliament would be no more than a corporatist assembly. The problem with corporatist representation, as Hans Kelsen showed in his *Vom Wesen und Wert der Demokratie* (*The Nature and Value of Democracy*) is that an assembly, constituted along professional lines, does not have the means to integrate clashing interests.[23] In fact, members of a corporatist assembly are like the delegates of the ancien régime's Estates-General who, as representatives of their estate in a given region, were only carriers of particular grievances. As such they lacked the legitimacy to articulate a position on issues for which they had received no mandate. In this context, the king was the only true representative of the whole realm and was thus empowered to determine autocratically the common will.

This is precisely why Schmitt characterizes the parties as delegates of interests or social forces, stripped of all autonomy. We are presented here with another difficult dilemma: either parties are loose associations, as in the early nineteenth century, or they are politically organized social and economic forces. The first option is obviously unrealistic, the second one distinctly undesirable. Two arguments can be made to extricate ourselves from this apparent dilemma. One is to simply deny Schmitt's empirical assertion that political parties are identical to certain social forces. This poses no great difficulty, since it seems as much an overstatement as Schmitt's thesis that the contemporary state and society have merged. The fact is that parties which were closely associated with certain social forces always maintained a degree of autonomy. A notable example of this is the Labour Party, which traditionally was closely linked to trade unions, while still maintaining a significant freedom of movement.

The second argument starts from Kelsen's characterization of that which distinguishes the modern representative system from a corporatist assembly. The modern system, writes Kelsen, "considers each voter, not only as a member of a particular profession, but as a member of the state as a whole and . . . consequently supposes the elector to be interested, not only in professional questions, but in principle in all those issues that may become the object of state regulation."[24] In principle then, what gives political parties the room to maneuver and allows them to integrate different interests and reach compromises is, first, the varied nature of the questions that they have to address, some of which raise issues quite foreign to the concerns of their electoral basis. This gives them a flexibility that interest groups do not have.[25] Second, the elections themselves give political parties the legitimacy to act on this flexibility in a way which may not always please their backers but is key to their relative autonomy.

Schmitt's second assumption is that rational public discussion is the only process by which parliament can mediate and integrate divergent interests. This focus imposes an overly narrow view of how the machinery of parliament might encourage compromises. This point does not concern the question of how parliament may foster principled agreements but of how the parliamentary game, as such, imposes constraints which constitute the basic framework in which the more demanding conditions of rational discussion become realizable. In making this point, I will once again borrow from Hans Kelsen's own defense of parliamentary democracy and, more particularly, his analysis of the majority principle.

In *Vom Wesen und Wert der Demokratie*, Kelsen starts by criticizing two extreme views of the majority principle which can be stated in the form of a false alternative. Either the majority is assumed also to represent the minority, which entails that its will is equivalent to that of the entire group, or alternatively the majority dominates the minority.[26] Kelsen makes the point that the true nature of minority-majority relations is not one of domination, but of reciprocal influence, since numerical inequality between majority and minority is tempered by their respective political and social importance. The majority has no real interest in using its superior strength to constantly and completely dominate the minority, because the latter would lose all incentive to persist in playing the parliamentary game. If the minority were to quit altogether, the majority would not be a majority any longer, but would appear despotic and consequently lose the legitimate basis of its power.

It is this need of the majority to keep the game going which ensures, for Kelsen, the possibility for the minority to exercise some influence upon policy making. This also explains why the majority principle implies a certain guarantee of minority rights.[27]

This shows how playing the parliamentary game imposes certain constraints on the majority which serve to discourage extremism and favors a coming together, of sorts, between minority and majority. Kelsen's point is that the majority principle will have integrating effects on the parties themselves. In this case, it is not the quality of public discussion which is the issue, but rather the fact that participating in the game, even if it is mostly staged, imposes constraints on partisan behavior.

Obviously, Kelsen's description only holds as long as the various players are committed to the game. As Schmitt argued, it is quite possible to imagine that a party gaining a majority of seats could use its democratic legitimacy to close the door behind itself.[28] Moreover, the majority principle can only operate in the way described by Kelsen if there is a working majority, of sorts. But the point here is not that the parliamentary machinery can function effectively even in conditions of polarized pluralism, where there is a breakdown of the political system, but rather to show how the parliamentary system builds upon such existing commitments and thus promotes compromise.

Still, we must agree with Schmitt that the notion of rational public discussion is central to any account of parliamentary institutions, for it is in reference to this idea that the rational character of collective decision making in representative democracy is usually justified. Therefore, to demonstrate that deliberation has definitely disappeared from parliaments, given fundamental conditions of contemporary politics, certainly constitutes a serious challenge to our commitment to this form of government. We can respond by showing that the classical idea of public deliberation is not the only way to think through the rationality of the democratic political process. Here, I will simply indicate how it might be possible to reformulate the notion of rational public discussion in a way that avoids such pitfalls, while still ensuring the principled character of political decisions.

In *The Crisis of Parliamentary Democracy*, Schmitt states that the specificity of parliamentary rule rests on a particular kind of public discussion which he defines as "an exchange of opinion that is governed by the purpose of persuading one's opponent through argument of the truth or justice of something, or allowing oneself to be persuaded of something as true and just."[29] This rational exchange must be the determining factor in political decisions, if it is to be meaningful: "Parliament is in any case only 'true' as long as public discussion is taken seriously and implemented."[30] Schmitt's definition thus implies two conditions that may prove unnecessarily strict given our objective. The first one concerns the link between deliberation and decision, the second one the understanding of impartiality. In the following, I will examine each condition in turn.

The first condition is that decisions must be the product of the exchange of arguments through which one attempts to convince the adversary of the truth of one's own position. This definition of public deliberation is in itself noncontroversial and resembles an understanding of deliberation commonly found in contemporary political theory.[31] If public deliberation is a process of collective will formation, then the collective decision must be the result of an exchange of arguments, and deliberation must precede decision. But is this the only way to conceive of the discursive rationality of parliamentary debates?

To answer yes may be to fall into Schmitt's trap, for it seems that, given the fundamental conditions of politics in the democratic context, the deliberative model cannot be realized or even approached. As we have seen, Schmitt insists mainly upon party discipline to guarantee that parliament's vote will not be the result of public deliberation. Yet, another factor should be stressed here. As Schmitt remarked, and as contemporary critics like Habermas have insisted, public speeches made in parliament are directed much less to the political adversary than to the electorate.[32] For the opposition, the goal is to embarrass the government as much as possible, to convince the electors of its incompetence, and to express alternative policies that might prove popular. On the government's side, the point is to defend legislative proposals and, more generally, to defend and extol the government's record. Again, in all of this the main interlocutor is not one's political adversary but the body of the electorate.

This is a feature of our political system that is not about to change, because it is not a reflection of party discipline, which could be relaxed, but is fundamental to the workings of contemporary politics. The extension of the suffrage has changed parties into vote-seeking organizations[33] and has made the general electorate into the first interlocutor of political parties. This means that substantially weakening party discipline would not be enough to change the fact that during parliamentary debates, representatives of the different parties would keep talking past each other with their eyes on their respective constituencies. This fact implies that the positions of the parties on a given legislative issue are determined by the competition for the electorate's favor, rather than by the exchange of arguments within parliament. Political decisions, translated in the final vote on a legislation, are thus not the result of public deliberation but of party strategy.

If the reality of politics makes deliberation unrealizable in the strict sense of the term, that is, as a collective process of will formation, this does not necessarily render meaningless parliamentary exchange of rational arguments. What it means is that we should understand its significance differently. One possibility would be to consider such exchange as what Bernard Manin has called the "épreuve de la discussion publique."[34] According to Manin, it is a mistake to consider representative government as an indirect form of people's self-government. This entails that the function of public discussion is to generate a decision. Rather, we should conceive of representative democracy as a system whereby "everything that concerns government is submitted to public judgement."[35]

Manin sees "public judgement" as consisting of two allied processes. First, the people become the judge of policies, inasmuch as it is "through their retrospective appreciation of the government's relatively autonomous initiatives that they control the conduct of public affairs." Here, Manin is simply focusing on elections as the main way for citizens to have an impact on politics, by using the electoral process as the occasion for a retrospective judgment on the government's performance.[36] Second, and more important for our purposes, Manin notes that parliament, as the "discussing authority" (*instance discutante*) also plays the role of a judge, in that all proposals must be submitted for its approval, even though they may not all emanate from it.

I want to use this concept as a point of departure and expand on it. The idea of public judgment seems to be an improvement over the concept of deliberation, because it does not presuppose a real exchange between participants—be it between MPs belonging to different parties, or even between electors and candidates. In the following, I would like to reformulate the concept of public judgment in a way that helps us better understand the significance of the public exchange of arguments inside parliament. What I will argue is that if today's parliament is not a deliberative body in the strict sense of the word, it is the arena in which government policies are to be justified before the public.

In other words, debates do not have to be deliberative in nature to be worthwhile. Parliamentary debates on proposed legislation can be considered as a kind of public screening which must precede enactment. Such screening makes possible the public disclosure of potential sources of injustice and/or injudicious spending of public monies. In responding to the opposition, the government party must justify its choices and clarify its purposes. Although today, such questioning of government policy is far from limited to parliament (in that the media and interest groups play a role that is equally important, if not more important, in conducting that test and shaping its outcome), it is still true that parliamentary debates serve as a focus around which this public testing takes place. It is inside parliament that the government has to disclose the content of its proposed policies, and it is on the basis of this disclosure, relayed by the media, that public discussion takes place. The opposition party sometimes takes the lead in this and sometimes simply uses arguments first formulated by outside players. This public testing can result in the amendment or even the withdrawal of certain projects. If the government decides that a given policy is too important to its program to be abandoned, though it has provoked substantial opposition, then it must accept the political costs of such a decision and its possible effect on the next electoral results.

This suggests that it would be more useful to think of the public expression of arguments in parliament not as a process of collective deliberation per se, but as a key moment in the process of public justification of government policies, on the basis of which the electorate can perform its own function as judge. Can this process be called a discussion? Between opposing parties, there is an exchange of arguments of sorts, in the sense that, for instance, the majority party has to answer claims made by the opposition and vice versa. Yet it is not a discussion in a substantial sense, since the participants direct their arguments mainly to a third party that is not present. Could we not say then, as Bernard Manin sometimes does, that the discussion takes place between the candidates and the electorate? This seems to be misleading since the notion of discussion implies that interlocutors are participants in the same fashion, which of course does not hold here. Thus the exercise of public justification can only be called a discussion in a weak sense. A question remains, however, concerning the quality of the arguments made to justify or criticize government policies. In other words, what makes an argument into a good reason?

This question brings us back to the second condition implied in Schmitt's definition of deliberation, concerning the notion of impartiality or disinterestedness. This concept can be used in two different ways to characterize rational discussion. First, it can refer to the quality of the arguments themselves, meaning that the reasons given to support a position should be general or impersonal and refer, for instance, to principles of justice. Second, impartiality may refer to the disinterestedness of the participants. Are they moved by selfish interests or by the sincere desire to find the best solution to a given problem? Those two versions of impartiality are present in Schmitt's conception of deliberation. This is clearly shown by the way in which he distinguishes between rational discussion and deal making. This distinction is an important one that remains central to current democratic theory. It allows us to differentiate between principled and unprincipled compromises, between a decision that can be publicly justified and one that cannot. The question is not whether we should dispense with this distinction, but rather whether we formulate it in the way chosen by Schmitt. We can accept as uncontroversial that, in a rational discussion, arguments should be impartial. But the requirement that participants should be disinterested seems exaggerated. In fact, as Moritz Julius Bonn remarked,[37] even in the heyday of nineteenth-century parliamentarism, it is very difficult to believe that representatives in parliamentary debates always fulfilled this strict requirement and that their "rational" discussions were so clearly different from negotiation. In the following, I want to examine whether this requirement of disinterestedness does not impose an unnecessarily strict condition on the concept of rational discussion.

Schmitt's definition of deliberation presupposes that the shared objective of participants is not to win but to find the true answer to a given policy issue. This implies the independence from partisan links and "freedom from selfish interests."[38] But today, adds Schmitt, very few would consider such disinterestedness to be at all possible. This skepticism forms part of the crisis of parliamentarism.[39] Bargaining is defined by Schmitt as entailing partiality, as being governed by the will to win: "By contrast conduct that is not concerned with discovering what is rationally correct, but with calculating particular interests and the chances of winning and with carrying these through according to one's own interests is also directed by all sorts of speeches and declarations. But these are not discussions in the specific sense. . . . Openness is just as inappropriate in this kind of deliberation as it is reasonable in a real discussion."[40]

The problem is that if we consider disinterestedness as what distinguishes discussion from mere deal making, this clearly imposes a condition that may well prove to be impossible to satisfy, even in the best of possible political worlds. To avoid this trap, we will follow Jon Elster, who understands argumentation in a way that allows for the strategic use of impartial arguments.

In "Argumenter et négocier dans deux Assemblées constituantes,"[41] Elster notes that it is often in the interest of participants in a debate to invoke the impartial equivalent of their selfish interest. Instead of justifying their support of a given policy by admitting point-blank that it falls within their own best interests, it may often be advantageous to justify the same policy by the use of general principles and by referring to the common good. This may be so because there is a social norm which discourages individuals from expressing positions that cannot be justified as advantageous to the collectivity. Alternatively, an individual may in fact convince neutral parties to support her position by invoking general reasons.

That participants in a public debate may hide their selfish interest behind appeals to the common good is well known. The question is whether the obligation to do so has any substantial effect. Does the need to give a principled justification of one's position on a given issue impose any real constraint on its content? If not, then saying that participants in a political debate must make use of principled justification would be no more than asking politicians to change their rhetoric. Constant references to the common good may make political speeches sound grand, but need not alter the reality of politics as a contest between competing particular interests. Elster's point is to indicate how the use of general reasons does impose certain constraints. The thrust of his argument is that it is not to the advantage of a participant wishing to disguise his selfish interest to choose an impartial argument which perfectly coincides with it, for then his real intention would become transparent, greatly undermining his credibility. The optimal impartial equivalent to a selfish interest is not its perfect equivalent. It must be an "argument which is sufficiently different from their selfish interest to be accepted by others, but not so distanced that they would not get any benefit from its acceptance."[42]

If this is true, then it shows that rational discussion, even when loaded with the strategic use of impartial arguments, still ensures fairer results than negotiation: "argumentation, especially in the context of public debates, will prevent the powerful from using their negotiating power to its fullest. The optimal impartial equivalent will be the one that compensates their selfish interest with the consideration of the interests of the weaker."[43]

Elster's point is plausible, although its practical significance cannot be easily ascertained. What it indicates is the value of the constraints that the exercise of public justification imposes on participants. It also shows that it is not necessary to appeal to the existence of disinterested motives in order to distinguish, in a significant way, between rational discussion and deal making. The use of impartial arguments as opposed to the use of promises or threats would be enough to characterize rational argumentation as essentially different from negotiation.

Can we claim to have shown that rational, public discussion is still possible within our contemporary parliamentary system? And does this amount to a successful response to Schmitt's criticism of parliament as an obsolete institution? It is clear that the proposed description implies a substantial weakening of the original idea of parliament as a public arena for rational discussion. We have had to accept that the ties between deliberation and political decision are not as tight as we might hope. In fact, we have had to acknowledge that contemporary parliamentary debates can be considered discussions only in a weak sense. We have also had to let go of the idea that the substantial rationality of discussion depends on the disinterestedness of its participants. What we are left with is that, first, parliamentary debates serve as a public test for policies. Second, this exercise in public justification and criticism must rest on the use of impartial arguments.

The crucial question is whether or not what remains ensures that the end result of the political process is more than unprincipled compromises between divergent interests. Here, we can only answer this question tentatively. To the extent that parliamentary debates involve a public screening of policy, which can result in certain options being abandoned or modified because they would prove unacceptable to public judgment, we can say that these debates impose significant constraints on participants. Although the decision to choose a particular policy option may not have been reached in a principled way, the test of public discussion demands that it be justified on the basis of certain shared principles.

This result would surely not satisfy Schmitt. His criticism of parliamentary democracy is premised upon a conception of collective rationality which is extremely demanding, and to which there seems to be no other alternative than an irrational, existential conception of politics. For those of us with the goal of seeing how our societies could be made more rational, Schmitt's alternative is not acceptable. But what it tells us is that there is not much to gain from clinging to an overly idealistic conception of collective rationality. What we must do is reflect upon the means that could help us achieve our more modest objective, and this we can only do by gaining a better understanding of the meaning and significance of our political institutions.

Notes

1 See Carl Schmitt, *The Concept of the Political*, trans. George Schwab (New Brunswick, N.J.: Rutgers University Press, 1976).

2 Carl Schmitt, *Die geistesgeschichtliche Lage des heutigen Parlamentarismus*, 7th ed. (Berlin: Duncker & Humblot, 1991); Carl Schmitt, *The Crisis of Parliamentary Democracy*, trans. Ellen Kennedy (Cambridge, Mass.: MIT Press, 1985).

3 Carl Schmitt, *Der Hüter der Verfassung*, 2d ed. (Berlin: Duncker & Humblot, 1931).

4 In "Staatsethik und pluralistischer Staat," *Kant-Studien* 35 (1930): 28, at 31, Schmitt writes that "Der Staat erscheint tatsächlich in weitem Masse von den verschiedenen sozialen Gruppen abhängig, bald als ein Opfer, bald als Ergebnis ihrer Abmachungen." In *Der Hüter der Verfassung*, ibid., at 71, Schmitt defines pluralism in the following way: "Pluralismus dagegen bezeichnet eine Mehrheit festorganisierter, durch den Staat . . . sozialer Machtkomplexe, die sich als solche der staatlichen Willensbildung bemächtigen, ohne aufzuhören, nur soziale (nicht-staatliche) Gebilde zu sein." Schmitt's definition here is clearly polemical. Pluralism entails, by definition, a situation in which social forces *overtake* the state.

5 In "Staatsethik und pluralistischer Staat," ibid., Schmitt writes, for instance, that "Vor allem entspricht die pluralistische Auffassung dem empirisch wirklichen Zustand, wie man ihn heute in den meisten industriellen Staaten beobachten kann."

6 I use the notion of polarized pluralism as defined by Giovanni Sartori in his book *Parties and Party Systems: A Framework for Analysis*, vol. 1 (Cambridge: Cambridge University Press, 1976), at 132ff. Sartori identifies two defining characteristics: first, the presence of antisystem parties which undermine the legitimacy of the ruling regime; second, the "existence of bilateral oppositions," which are mutually exclusive, so ideologically distinct as to be unable to join in their opposition. This precludes the formation of a viable alternative to government parties. In his book, Sartori uses Weimar Germany as an illustration of polarized pluralism.

7 Schmitt describes this alternative in supra n. 3, at 147–49.

8 The distinction I make here between principled and unprincipled compromises mirrors the distinction made by Jon Elster between the thin theory and broad theory of collective rationality. The former only requires formal

consistency and goes no further than the aggregation of preferences, while the latter implies a normative requirement, that is that rational discussion be conducted in reference to the common good, which may entail the transformation of preferences. See Jon Elster, *Sour Grapes: Studies in the Subversion of Rationality* (Cambridge: Cambridge University Press, 1983), at 26–43. As Bernard Manin notes, it is clear that "lorsque les fondateurs du gouvernement représentatif réfléchissaient sur le type d'échange auquel ce régime devait conférer un rôle crucial, ils avaient manifestement à l'esprit une communication faisant appel à la raison en un sens particulier et éminent." Bernard Manin, *Les Principes du Gouvernement Représentatif* (Paris: Calmann-Lévy, 1995), at 254, n. 8.

9 For this section see supra n. 7, at 73–91.

10 Carl Schmitt, *Verfassungslehre* (Berlin: Duncker & Humblot, 1989). All references are taken from the French translation: *Théorie de la Constitution*, trans. Lilyane Deroche (Paris: Presses Universitaires de France, 1993).

11 Supra n. 7, at 73.

12 In his reply to Schmitt, Hans Kelsen correctly notes that the ideas of the total state and pluralism are contradictory. "Wie kann dieser Zustand sozusagen einen Gipfelpunkt des 'Pluralismus' und zugleich eine 'Wendung zum totalen Staat' darstellen, wenn Pluralismus nur möglich ist, sofern die staatliche Willensbildung aus einer sozialen, nicht-staatlichen Sphäre her beeinflusst wird, in deren Aufhebung und Verstaatlichung gerade die 'Wendung zum totalen Staat' besteht?" Furthermore, as Kelsen notes, Schmitt's claim that the contemporary state and society have merged is a crude overstatement. See Hans Kelsen, "Wer soll der Hüter der Verfassung sein?" (1931–32) in *Die Justiz*, at 603–5.

13 "Staatsethik und pluralistischer Staat," supra n. 4, at 41.

14 *Théorie de la Constitution*, supra n. 10, at 473.

15 Ibid.

16 Ibid., at 470. According to Schmitt, although the constitution of an Irish nationalist party, for the first time, did politically express a true heterogeneity, it did not have lasting consequences for two reasons. First, it did not have the strength to break the bipartisan system. Second, the creation of a free Irish state diffused the problem.

17 *Théorie de la Constitution*, supra n. 10, at 470.

18 Ibid.

19 Supra n. 7, at 85–87.

20 Hermann Heller, "Politische Demokratie und soziale Homogenität," in Arthur Jacobson and Bernhard Schlinck, eds. and trans. David Dyzenhaus, *Weimar: The Jurisprudence of Crisis* (Berkeley: University of California Press, 1998). Originally in *Gesammelte Schriften*, vol. 2 (Leiden: A. W. Sijthoff, 1971), at 428.

21 "Staatsethik und pluralistischer Staat," supra n. 4, at 35.
22 These two consequences are spelled out by Schmitt in Carl Schmitt, *Théorie de la Constitution*, supra n. 10, at 466.
23 Hans Kelsen, *Vom Wesen und Wert der Demokratie* (Tübingen: J. C. B. Mohr, 1929). All references to this work are taken from the French translation: *La Démocratie: Sa Nature, Sa Valeur*, trans. C. Eisenmann (Paris: Economica, 1988), at 54.
24 *La Démocratie: Sa nature, sa valeur*, supra n. 23, at 55.
25 See Joshua Cohen, "Deliberation and Democratic Legitimacy," in Alan Hamlin and Philip Pettit, eds., *The Good Polity* (Oxford: Blackwell, 1989), at 31–32.
26 It is worthwhile to note that Schmitt himself resorts to this alternative. He posits that the will of the majority is equivalent to that of the whole group as a fundamental axiom of democratic theory. Unless one accepts this axiom, the majority principle then appears as the principle of majority domination. See, for example, supra n. 7, at 145.
27 Proportional representation is the best electoral system, according to Kelsen, precisely because it allows even minority interests to be represented in Parliament and be subjected to the integrative effect of the majority principle. See *La Démocratie: Sa nature, sa valeur*, supra n. 23, at 60–63. Concerning minority rights, it is difficult to see how the majority principle could, in itself, provide a satisfactory guarantee. See Peter Koller, "Zu einigen Problemen der Rechtfertigung der Demokratie" in Werner Krawietz, Ernst Topitsch, and Peter Koller, eds., *Ideologiekritik und Demokratiekritik bei Hans Kelsen* (Berlin: Duncker & Humblot, 1982), at 324–25.
28 See Carl Schmitt, *Legalität und Legitimität* (Munich: Duncker & Humblot, 1932).
29 *The Crisis of Parliamentary Democracy*, supra n. 2, at 5.
30 Ibid., at 4.
31 See, for example, supra n. 24, at 22–23.
32 See *The Crisis of Parliamentary Democracy*, supra n. 2, at 6 and Jürgen Habermas, *L'Espace Public* (Paris: Payot, 1988), at 215.
33 See supra n. 6, at 21.
34 Manin, supra n. 8, at 234ff. For a similar understanding of deliberation, see Cass Sunstein, "Beyond the Republican Revival," 97 *Yale L.J.* 1988, 1539.
35 Manin, supra n. 8, at 245.
36 Of course, it is not at all clear that such retrospective judgment is what actually motivates the electors' choice.
37 See Ellen Kennedy's introduction to *The Crisis of Parliamentary Democracy*, supra n. 2.
38 Ibid., at 5.
39 Ibid., at 6.

40 Ibid., at 5–6.
41 Jon Elster, "Argumenter et négocier dans deux Assemblées constituantes," *Revue Française de Science Politique* 44 (1994): 187. See esp. section 6, 241ff.
42 Ibid., at 241.
43 Ibid., at 248.

Liberalism as a "Metaphysical System"

The Methodological Structure of Carl Schmitt's

Critique of Political Rationalism

Reinhard Mehring

It is a commonplace that liberalism appears to be in crisis. While the tragedy of German liberalism consists above all in its collapse into National Socialist dictatorship, at present one often speaks of liberalism's final victory. There is no alternative, it appears, to the constitutional state. Liberal constitutional principles have been so fulfilled that no political goals and lessons seem left beyond their global self-affirmation.

Once victory is achieved, there is nothing more to fight about. Corresponding to the triumph of constitutional principles, we find a decline of the liberal parties. Within the landscape of the German Federal parties, the Free Democrats, who for years were, in any case, merely a coalition party which assisted either the Christian or Social Democrats to govern, find themselves threatened with complete removal from state legislatures, with increased uselessness, and with being voted out of existence.[1] All of the major parties make use of liberal rhetoric. Starting in the 1980s, the alternative party of the Greens, working from an ecological, futuristic platform, adopted a liberal political profile and established themselves on both a state and national level as Germany's third strongest party. Despite persistent, major problems of development and social integration since reunification, there is presently no substantial opposition in Germany to the reigning system. Even the Party of Democratic Socialism (the PDS), successor to the official state party of old East Germany (the SED), can only mobilize potential support by breaking with the old regime. As an alternative to the system, "socialism" has largely played itself out, even among the utopians and sentimentalists. In Germany, every significant political entity is committed to the idea of a constitutional state; and a consensus has emerged that the liberal political program is in trouble as a result of that idea's triumph.

In the course of reaching such (rather superficial) conclusions, we might distinguish an original liberal political "idea" from its immanent reality, the liberal program from the system as such. In doing so, we would be following an idealizing and abstracting hermeneutic method that Carl Schmitt used with great clarity and precision in his critique of liberalism. Schmitt defined the concrete liberal situation as a deviation from the ideas and "principles" which he had derived by a process of abstraction. What interested him was thus not the liberal worldview as such (what H. Heller has termed a "complex of ideas"),[2] but the political idea of liberalism as it emerged through its actual institutionalization. In formulating his critique, Schmitt asserted that he had detected a crisis in parliamentary culture and in the general parliamentary structure of the Weimar Constitution. He discovered a powerful "tension" between liberalism and democracy at work in the Weimar system, and, basing his arguments on a radically anti-liberal concept of democracy, took liberalism to task for failing to implement institutionally its core political idea.

In his critical response to a debate initiated by Ellen Kennedy[3] concerning Schmitt's influence on the Frankfurt School, Jürgen Habermas has concisely analyzed the systemic implications of Schmitt's critique of liberalism.[4] Habermas values, above all, a certain topical realism in Schmitt's exploration of the constitutional state's "normative foundations." He agrees with Schmitt's principle-oriented critical argument to the effect that "we can only understand the function and sense of parliamentary procedures in the light of such presumptions of rationality [as Schmitt's 'principles of parliamentarism']." At the same time, Habermas criticizes Schmitt's "idealist intensification and his ridicule" of these presumptions. It is not necessary to believe "in the foundational power of ideas in order to ascribe considerable, real importance to that legitimating power at work in the self-understanding of an established practice. We can comprehend the interest in parliamentary government's intellectual-historical origins in this more trivial sense as well." In any event, it is not the method which focuses on principles but the "separation of democracy and liberalism" that Habermas calls the "truly problematic aspect" of Schmitt's thought: Schmitt limits "the process of public discussion to the role of parliamentary legislation and severs it from democratic decision-making in general."[5]

Ulrich Preuss has also responded to Kennedy from the perspective of constitutional law, pointing out that in Schmitt's constitutional theory "the principles of liberalism are opposed to those of democracy."[6] Preuss thus understands Schmitt's distinction between legality and legitimacy as a strict contradiction. In my view, this is not entirely accurate. Schmitt does not deny parliamentarism the possibility of democratic legitimacy; he simply confirms its breakdown in Weimar's "legislative state." In other words, legality and legitimacy are not in systemic, but rather in historical, opposition. In the beginning, according to Schmitt, parliamentarism had the full benefit of the legitimacy accompanying historical faith in its principles. As he explains in "Legalität und Legitimität,"[7] the "parliamentary legislative state" only lost its legitimacy in Weimar's intellectual-historical situation, as an accompaniment to loss of faith in itself. It did so by granting constitutional approval to the advent of "three extraordinary legislators," thereby opening the possibility of a "legal revolution."[8] By "legislators" Schmitt means legal possibilities for legislation going beyond normal parliamentary procedure. It thus diminishes Schmitt's argument to understand his critique of liberalism as emerging from an anti-liberal interpretation of the notion of democracy. Rather, his notion of democracy results from an analysis of liberalism's self-annulling transformation into democracy.

In the following discussion, I will focus on the basic approach Schmitt takes in his critique of liberalism without any intention of developing the sort of democratic counterargument one might, for instance, extrapolate from Habermas. In order to systemically scrutinize the principles behind Schmitt's claims, thus relating them to the theory of democracy, it is necessary to first trace out his complex argumentation. The critique, especially its expression in the essay of 1923 entitled *Die geistesgeschichtliche Lage des heutigen Parlamentarismus* (The Intellectual-Historical Situation of Contemporary Parliamentarism),[9] is among the most well-known elements of Schmitt's constitutional theory; nevertheless, the historical nature of most of the research thus far has widely impeded an adequate exploration of his methodology and its systemic implications.[10]

Starting, then, with a review of the critique centered primarily around Schmitt's argumentative approach, I shall subsequently evaluate the latter's implications before adding some words on the evolution of liberalism's meaning. As I am concerned above all with the appearance of this approach within Schmitt's anti-liberalism, I shall not discuss its historical-political context. Hence I do not discuss either Schmitt's ideal-typical definition of liberalism nor his constitutional-historical interpretation of the collapse of the National Liberal movement in the 1848 revolution. Likewise, I shall neither locate Schmitt's ideas within the wider anti-liberal tradition, nor describe in detail the implications of his method for constitutional theory and for critiques of parliamentarism, pluralism, and the party system.

With the last qualifying sentence, I do not wish to suggest that Schmitt's conceptual apparatus—e.g., his criticism of the "political-party state"—is no longer relevant. But in making use of it, one appropriates the apparatus, not its situation-bound analysis and polemical stance.[11] Within our present historical-political situation, and that of constitutional law, Schmitt's analysis, conceptual structures, and theories can no longer be uncritically assimilated. On the other hand, in limiting my focus to Schmitt's basic method, I shall be clarifying a theoretical claim that still possesses systemic importance, even though I shall attempt no "topicalization" of Schmitt in relation to contemporary debates. All of these qualifications are necessary so that, facing the complexity of Schmitt's thematic concerns, we can formulate a specific conclusion to a circumscribed problem. The conclusion will be that Schmitt is offering a historicist deconstruction, in which liberalism is seen as based on postulates of historical reason that have been exhausted. In my view, this approach to liberalism is implausible.

I

Schmitt's critique of liberalism is omnipresent in his oeuvre; equally so is his avoidance of any detailed description of the liberal complex of ideas. As a jurist less interested in political ideas than in their institutional consequences, he viewed liberalism as an embodiment of the Weimar Constitution with which he had to grapple. In this regard, his initial concern was the institution of parliamentarism. The *Verfassungslehre* (1928) then expanded his critique to a general critique of the "constitutional bourgeois *Rechtsstaat*"; Schmitt here understood modern constitutional ideas as "components of the constitutional state" that in themselves lacked any formal principle which could structure a state: Considered in itself, the constitutional-state component, with its principles of (1) basic rights (as a principle of distribution) and (2) separation of powers (as a principle of organization), contains no state-form; it merely involves a series of state limits and controls, a system of guarantees of civic freedom and the relativization of state power. In this system, the state that is meant to be controlled is assumed as a given.

A state can clearly be modified and tempered by principles of civic freedom; these cannot in themselves establish a political form.[12]

Schmitt is always careful to distinguish historically as well as systemically between state and constitution.[13] He understands "representation" and "identity" as the state's formal principles, discussed in a "theory of monarchy" and a "theory of democracy." Within the theory of monarchy, he designates the parliamentary system as an "aristocratic element," thus already contesting its democratic legitimacy in a certain respect. As the quotation above indicates, within the constitutional-state components Schmitt distinguishes the "distribution principle" of basic rights from the "organizational principle" of separation of powers. Before explicating these two "principles of the bourgeois *Rechtsstaat*," he inserts a section titled "The Constitutional State's Concept of Law." This section examines the "so-called formal concept of law" as the theoretical postulate for the concept of the bourgeois *Rechtsstaat*; it distinguishes this concept from a "political concept of law" that Schmitt adheres to in his subsequent theoretical analysis.

This preeminence of legal over constitutional principle is of central importance.[14] Through the 1930s, in the cause of restoring the sovereignty and supremacy of the (führer) state, Schmitt stresses the political function of the law as an instrument of measures taken by the state; he speaks formulaically of the law as "the will and plan of the Führer"[15] — which he then modifies in speaking of law as the "unity of order and orientation."[16]

Setting aside its political-constitutional consequences, let us note that this legal-theoretical analysis and critique of a shift in the law's form and function was a formidable scholarly achievement. It was taken up directly by a number of Schmitt's contemporaries,[17] and in postwar Germany led to a discussion, revived by Ernst Forsthoff,[18] concerning "exceptional legal measures." Here I do not wish to evaluate these influences and echoes, but rather Schmitt's sociological theory of legal validity.

According to this theory, which has clear consequences for political order, the "postulate of the generality of law" only makes sense under two conditions: that, on the one hand, of a politically "normal" situation; and that, on the other hand, of a shattering, in states of emergency, of the historical faith in generally shared ideas.[19] In this context, I would like to pass over both Schmitt's alternate model of the "exceptional state" and his criticism of the political-polemical underpinnings to liberalism's "formal" concept of law: that is, his "positioning" of the liberal emphasis on the rule of law within the context of the nineteenth-century battles over the incorporation of sovereignty into the constitutional system.

The core of Schmitt's criticism is not simply the political rhetoric of liberalism's demand for the supremacy of law; he is stressing a different kind of presumptiveness than that of political expedience and the law's dependence on effective implementation for its claims to validity. In other words, it is true that Schmitt repeatedly uncovers the political stakes at play in *Rechtsstaat* rhetoric and takes part in the politically significant battle over the notion of a constitutional state with several articles favorable to National Socialism.[20] But he does not take liberalism seriously only as a political movement. Above all, his approach has maintained its interest because of his understanding of liberalism as the "metaphysical system" of a "relative rationality."

Schmitt articulates his critique of liberalism as a "metaphysical system" most elaborately in *Die geistesgeschichtliche Lage des heutigen Parlamentarismus.*[21] Our glance at the *Verfassungslehre* has pointed to the "formal" concept of law as a necessary postulate for the validity of parliamentary principles: the legal cohesion of state power is only possible when "formal" law stands as an effective instrument at the disposal of the parliamentary legislative state. For its part, this concept of law is based on a specific notion of rationality: the liberal "metaphysics" of "relative rationalism,"[22] which also determines the "principles of parliamentarism"—"discussion" and "publicity."[23]

Schmitt describes parliamentarism in terms of a "faith" in an arrival at "truth and justice" through public discussion in parliament.[24] Where he sees the orientation of parliamentary discourse toward justice as possibly grounded in the functionality of parliamentary legislative procedure, he sees the orientation toward truth as moving beyond such strategic, functional "justice." Rather, it is concerned with the process of public discussion itself. It is not the result of parliamentary deliberation that really represents truth; rather, it is the process. Faith in the truth of parliamentarism is the truth of the faith that, in its procedural principles, parliamentarism is an exemplary way of limiting state power through the constitution—one capable of preserving might through right. In this sense, Schmitt considers "liberalism as a consistent, comprehensive metaphysical system."[25] What it values as true is parliament's exemplary claim to be the site for a rational articulation of public opinion. This truth is the faith in liberalism's "relative rationalism."

In this regard, parliamentarism is not simply a mirror, but also a medium, for the sensible articulation of interests. Separation of powers —the "organizational principle" of the "bourgeois *Rechtsstaat*"—is merely an institutional consequence of this "relative rationalism"; it involves the institutionalization of the "eternal dialogue" between the powers.[26]

The principles of parliamentarism thus extend their domain beyond that of governmental form, involving the entire organization of the state: the separation of powers allows their "balancing" in eternal dialogue. The explication of parliamentary principles hence leads us toward the doctrine of "balancing" through the division of power. Imputing to such division a sense of "balance" between equipoised political forces is, for Schmitt, one distinguishing characteristic of liberal metaphysics.

To be sure, this sense of balancing was aimed at dividing parliamentary forces into a multiplicity; most of all it affirmed, however, a distinction between the powers of parliament and government. As Schmitt depicts it, the "relative rationalism" of classical liberalism affirmed the distinction between parliamentary and governmental powers by dint of their particular instruments—parliament-enacted law and executive decree. According to this view the "parliamentary concept of law" still affirmed the functional difference between law and decree. Within the metaphysical system of "relative rationalism," then, "rule of law" did not signify any "direct constitutional enactment,"[27] no rule directly "through the law" but a binding of executive action to the "warrant" of a law. Classical liberalism was concerned simply with a sensible balance of power, the primacy of "truth and justice" in parliamentary procedure, and a linkage of might with right that appeared to be a "victory of right over might."

Keeping in mind our focus on the argumentative method, let us note that it would be an error to endow at this point the hermeneutic abstraction of Schmitt's parliamentary principles with a specific political position. The driving force behind Schmitt's method is—in Max Weber's sense—interpretation of value,[28] applied to the ultimate intellectual principles of liberal political thought. No particular stake regarding these principles is yet at work here, and we must distinguish methodologically between their abstraction by Schmitt, on the one hand, and his intellectual-historical developmental outline of their self-annulment (the decline of liberal faith in its own principles), on the other. Only with the latter in mind, can we infer an anti-liberal stance on his part.

Let us consider the developmental outline more closely. Schmitt is offering, as an accompaniment to his hermeneutic critique of contemporary parliamentarism in light of its originary values, an inner history and dialectic of the self-annulment of liberalism's ideal premises. He thereby ascertains the self-transcendence of "relative rationalism" as an "absolute rationalism"—in turn transformed into a set of "irrational theories of direct application of force." That Schmitt places himself on the terrain of this new "irrationalism" is already apparent in the categories proposed in his *Verfassungslehre.*

Here Schmitt makes an antiliberal and irrationalist exposition of "democratic legitimacy" into the basis of a "positive" constitutional definition: a constitution is the same as a "total decision about the type and form" of existence, the political unity of a people (*Volk*). The people is its own sovereign, existing free unto itself as a "nation" due to the strength of its political "will," "the originary ground of all political events."[29] Decision means distinction. The elementary decision concerning a people's political constitution brings with it a distinction of friend from foe. In his *Begriff des Politischen,* Schmitt links a people's will to political existence with the readiness for an "assertion, true to one's being, of one's own form of existence in opposition to the enemy."[30]

Liberalism, in contrast, is a "negation of the political." For Schmitt, there is "no liberal politics per se, but only a liberal critique of politics";[31] and the "systematics of liberal thought" is aimed at the "dissolution" of all political phenomena into the "polarity of ethics and economy."[32] Ascribing economic motives to the ethical rhetoric of liberal politics, he considers, for instance, the policies of the "Western hemisphere" concerning foreign affairs and international law as "economic imperialism" garnished with the rhetoric of "humanity."[33] For Schmitt, liberalism is anything but unpolitical in its intent and effect; it simply uses a rhetoric of ethics to cover up the placing of economic interests at the center of political concern. Such a strategy cannot address, however, the actual human duty of political activity: for Schmitt, politics constitutes, preeminently, an elementary decision over one's own way of being; self-determination carrying with it both responsibility and danger.

A look at the interconnected texts *Der Begriff des Politischen* and the *Verfassungslehre* thus shows that, from the perspective of political self-determination and formation of being, Schmitt declared the liberal understanding of politics to be fundamentally inadequate.[34] Since his diagnosis of the functional weaknesses and structural problems of the Weimar Republic emerges from a diagnosis of the self-annulment of liberalism into a new "democratic" irrationalism, a closer look at the latter, dialectic schema is necessary for an adequate grasp of his methodology and way of arguing. I would like to now consider the schema by way of a return to *Die geistesgeschichtliche Lage des heutigen Parlamentarismus*.

In this essay, Schmitt offers a unique exposition. In the preface and opening chapter, we find the description of a contemporary "contradiction" between parliamentarism and democracy, with parliamentarism decayed—in face of an irrationally grounded democratic legitimacy—into a mere, multiple-party–dominated "facade," lacking precisely the legitimacy of democratic "identification."[35] With the emergence in this historical moment of the difference between parliamentarism and democracy, the nature of parliamentarism has taken on a historical perspective, and a hermeneutics of its original ideas and principles has become possible. Hence the basis for an understanding of a historical movement is retrospection.

Toward the end of the first chapter, titled "Democracy and Parliamentarism," Schmitt states the following: "The evolution taking place between 1815 and 1918 can be described as the evolution of a concept of legitimacy: from dynastic to democratic legitimacy."[36] What now follows is—considered closely—not in fact an overview of the bourgeois century's constitutional movement as a battle between dynastic and democratic legitimacy; rather, what we find is Schmitt's outline of the dialectical transition from a rationalist to an irrationalist interpretation of democratic legitimacy.

Schmitt formally characterizes democracy as a striving to realize identity through an "identification" of the ruled with their rulers. He comments: "There always remains a distance between real equality and the results of identification. . . . Everything depends upon the manner in which the will is formed. The age-old dialectic contained in the doctrine of popular will has not yet been resolved: a minority can possess the true will of the people; the people can be fooled; indeed techniques of propaganda and the manipulation of public opinion are long-standing."[37]

Consequently, the central concern of political analysis is not to maintain identity, but the critical scrutiny of techniques of identity. Practically, what thus emerges is "the question of who disposes of the means of forming the people's will." In this context, Schmitt observes that it is "apparently the fate of democracy to transcend itself in the problem of the formation of will." He offers a diagnosis of the "suspension of democracy in the name of a true democracy that still needs to be created" most immediately as an annulment of the "relative rationalism" of power-balancing in favor of the "absolute rationalism," founded in a philosophy of history, of an enlightened dictatorship.[38]

Within such a transformation of "relative" into "absolute" rationalism, Schmitt already stresses the political function and role of the philosophy of history in his look at "dictatorship in Marxist thought"—a special point of interest for him since his early writing on dictatorship.[39] Transformations into enlightened dictatorships are merely the politically most explosive response to classical liberalism. Another response is the shift of classical liberalism into the German "organic liberalism" of the period prior to the revolution of March, 1848. Both responses are permeated with Hegel's historical thought: Schmitt both acknowledges Hegel's importance for the period prior to the revolution of March 1848 and critically scrutinizes the Marxist appropriation of his philosophy of history.[40] The peaking of "historical construction" on the "dialectical highpoint of the tension between bourgeoisie and proletariat," with its emphasis on the critical moment of decision over a positively unformed future, finds its "evidence" in the basis laid by Hegel's "absolute rationalism."[41] However, the dialectical peaking of world history in the critical moment of present-day decision is transformed, along with the myth of class struggle and decisive battle, into an irrationalist "theory of immediate use of force and direct action." According to this schema, Hegel's philosophy not only marks the transition from a "relative" to an "absolute" rationalism, but simultaneously the self-transcendence of political rationalism into a new irrationalism.

In the fourth chapter of his text—"Irrationalist Theories of Direct Use of Force"—Schmitt for the most part examines Georges Sorel's "theory of direct concrete life" in connection with the anarchist tradition. According to Schmitt, this theory is irrationalist because it does not attach its historical "evidence" to the rationalist construction of a necessary historical process, but to the assertion of a creative "capacity," in the context of the direct action of the general strike, "for acting and heroism."[42] The theory constitutes a "philosophy of concrete life" because, as with Bergson, it celebrates action as the enthusiastic outbreak of creative energies. Schmitt rests his case, in contrast, on Mussolini's "national myth," asserting the myth of the nation to be a "stronger myth" than that of the general strike.[43] This is intended as a political possibility: doubtless, Schmitt considers Italian fascism—the "foundation of a new authority, a new feeling for order, discipline, and hierarchy"—as preferable to communism. Nevertheless, at the same time he emphasizes the "hypothetical danger of such irrationalities": the danger of "polytheism."[44] With these words, he expresses his reservations regarding the metaphysics of political irrationalism.

Our concern here is not to establish the relation of Schmitt's "political theology"[45] to the political and religious resonances of the "national myth," nor to gain an overview of the nineteenth-century constitutional struggles, but to examine the dialectical shift of political rationalism into a new irrationalism. Claiming to confirm a historical change in the "metaphysical" postulates of politics, Schmitt in turn sees the political consequences as affecting the history of metaphysics. He clarifies this process, above all, in relation to the myth of decisive battle: that irrationalist overturning of the absolute rationalism of history's construction. As the above-cited title indicates, his term for this perceived mutual interaction of political ideas and metaphysical postulates is "political theology." He signifies it methodologically as "sociology of concepts."

The method of sociology of concepts emerges from politics, political order, and the idea of a political subject; it ascribes to politics a "metaphysical rule," by which Schmitt in the first instance only intends to signify an ideal-typical hypothesis for grasping and representing forms of political order: The precondition for this type of sociology of juridical concepts is thus a radical conceptuality, i.e., a consistency which is driven to the point of metaphysics and theology. The political image of the world possessed by a specific age has the same structure as that which is readily intelligible in the form of its political organization.[46] This method—first formulated in the memorial volume for Max Weber[47]—is clearly one influenced by Weber's notion of the "ideal type."

It is clear that Schmitt, basing his arguments on the juridical application of relative constancies of order, has a tendency to pass off ideal-typical constructions as "real types," and to accept that there are principles which mark off epochs;[48] within the realms of constitutional and political history he thereby not only grants ideal-typical constructions the real-typical sense involved in grasping historical tendencies and forms of order—a procedure typifying the constitutional-historical perspective, as opposed to ordinary history;[49] he also uses such constructions as a means for representing metaphysical differences.

In the present context, one can only assert that this hermeneutics of metaphysical substances attached to the various political complexes of ideas serves to contour metaphysical differences for a practical purpose.[50] Schmitt is here taking up the cause of a Christian myth whose dogmatic content is scarcely describable—as indicated, for instance, in his talk of "polytheism" as a "hypothetical danger."[51] We frequently find such practical focus among social scientists. Even Max Weber's typology of ultimate stances toward the world—with its narrow political-economic focus on the economic ethic of the world religions—was not only an analytic method of "value-interpretation" (termed "social philosophy" by Weber), but was also honed from the perspective of an "ethics of responsibility": as a cultivated man installed—in Weber's famous phrase—in a "God-estranged, prophetless age," he considered this the only honorable perspective.[52] In any case, Schmitt's lasting metaphysical hostility to liberalism's "metaphysical system"—which knows no sin and no decision—here interests us strictly as a hermeneutics of liberal principles, formulated for the sake of analyzing the crisis of liberalism in Weimar.

What, in this specific context, are the results of this approach? Let us consider one example. In its implications for constitutional theory, the most significant exposition of Schmitt's methodology is his essay "Legalität und Legitimität" (1932). If we read the text as a further development of the diagnosis and response offered in *Geistesgeschichtliche Lage*, its constitutional-theoretical implications become clear.[53] In Schmitt's view, the above-mentioned inauguration—alongside and against itself—of three extraordinary, democratic legislators by the "legality-system" of the liberal "legislative state," brings about a structural problem in the Weimar Constitution. Since it contains, in self-negating and suicidal fashion, the tension between liberalism and democracy within itself, it is destined—according to both Schmitt's constitutional-political prognosis and warning on the one hand and his own choice on the other—to founder on the rocks of this triadic alliance. Read in connection with *Die Geistesgeschichtliche Lage*, Schmitt's analysis of the Weimar Constitution's structural problems yields the thesis that the collapse of faith in liberalism was accompanied by a loss in an awareness of principle: not following through on the principles of liberalism opened the constitutional-legal path for an anti-liberal understanding of democratic legitimacy.

From the perspective of constitutional politics, these structural inconsistencies amounted to openings through which a politically virulent "anti-" and "second-constitution" could unfold. Schmitt discovers the legal result of the movements and battles typifying such politics in the compromise character of constitutions; he considers the self-annulment of these compromises in looming political decisions as unavoidable. In this respect, his attitude toward the regulatory force of constitutions, and of their compromises, is ambivalent. He thinks of constitutions as the product of the compromises resulting from constitutional battles; at the same time, he holds that the power of such compromises to constitute an order is limited to being procrastinating and "dilatory." Constitutions cannot hold up political movements, but through their compromises they simply advance legal positions for further battle.[54]

This, then, is the method and underlying thesis of Schmitt's critique of liberalism. Schmitt's hermeneutics of the principles of liberalism (based on the classical liberal texts) uncovers the "metaphysical" postulate of a "relative rationalism" as the basis for the credibility of the constitutional state's concept of law, as well as for the ideas and institutions of the liberal constitutional state. According to Schmitt, the loss of such postulates of faith—a loss which is not independent of their political success—signifies a collapse in the awareness of political principles. The power of maintaining the organizational structure falls with the awareness of principles, and that both creates incoherence in the constitutional-political institutionalization and self-assertion of liberalism and leads to the downfall of liberal politics in general. Schmitt sees the source of such incoherence in the lack of self-awareness.

Schmitt's hermeneutics of political principles is, however, not meant to recover originary ideas and ideals. He is not a disappointed liberal who has betrayed his own idealizations in favor of a false reality. On the contrary, his hermeneutics, with its focus on "metaphysical implications" and the presuppositions of political ideas, also points to the irrevocability of their historical collapse. This applies most immediately to political ideas. Schmitt does not deny the possibility of a functional continuation of discredited ideas as a "facade." For this reason, he would have been able to concede the validity of Rudolf Smend's lapidary insistence that "here ideology can decay and integration remain."[55]

Schmitt's analysis of a constitution's structural problems and the accompanying constitutional-political implications thus ought not to be interpreted as a prophecy of doom, grounded in a philosophy of history. Schmitt simply ascertains tendencies, not inevitable developments. In any event his hermeneutics do not seem to discern the possibility of a change in the significance of institutions: at least in regard to parliamentarism, such a new "foundation" is not, for Schmitt (in contrast with Max Weber and others), in sight. He also leans toward the idealistic conviction that the decline of ideas and legitimations is followed by a decline of institutional functionality. And as indicated, he recognizes only a hermeneutic return to originary foundations. We here have an entire catalog of theses and questions regarding the systemic meaning of Schmitt's critique of liberalism.

II

Schmitt was not interested in contributing to the intellectual history of liberalism. He was interested in offering a hermeneutic critique of the relationship of present-day liberalism to its original "principles." Returning to these principles, he constructed a path leading to self-transcendence in an irrationalist "myth"—what I suggest may be termed a historicist deconstruction.[56]

Schmitt sharply sketches originary ideas, concepts, and principles with a view to placing them in context, and he describes their history as a change in meaning which results in specific structural and functional problems. A critical view of the present situation thus determines the perspectivist orientation: the idealizing abstraction and hermeneutics of original principles is for the sake of a constitutional diagnosis. In presenting his constitutional-political verdict as diagnostic, Schmitt immunizes it against objections. His procedure can be termed historicist because it constructs a historical context—a history of the interpretation of "democratic legitimacy"—in terms of an irreversible dialectical sequence.[57] Schmitt's historicism is hence not concerned with events, but with ideas and principles, with intellectual history, from whose perspective he considers institutional history and the tracing of epochal orders.

Hermeneutic procedures tend to become histories of a decline from originary conclusions, insights, questions—we need only think of Heidegger's destruction of the West's "forgetting of Being." What is problematic here is less the hermeneutic method itself—less the return to (abstractly and selectively understood) originary ideas—than the idealistic assumption of a lasting, exclusive influence of these ideas that disregards the possibility of a change in their foundations and motivations and of recreating institutions through new principles and sources. While Schmitt repeatedly presents a diagnosis of the "shift in sense and meaning" of ideas and institutions, this never leads him to grant them a second historical chance.[58]

Schmitt, then, writes history as the history of the decline of ideas into institutions. We have seen that in his constitutional-political approach to the historical dynamic he never maintains a strict historical logic—and in this respect breaks with the rationalism of "historical construction"; nevertheless, it is impossible to overlook his dramatizing of historical tendencies into a history of decline. This presents us with a first apparent objection to Schmitt's critique of liberalism: that the historical exposition of a hermeneutics grounded in a history of ideas provides no argument. The maintenance of liberal institutions is possible even when their originary assumptions are no longer held by anyone. To once again cite Smend: "here ideology can decay and integration remain." It is the case that Schmitt was not claiming to have once and for all done away with the future possibilities of liberalism through a hermeneutic critique of its developmental history; he had no interest in such predictions. His historical construction was simply meant to assert the crisis of liberalism's contemporary institutions, insofar as they were not consistently representing their original political ideas.

But considered more closely, it is clear that Schmitt was not arguing only at the level of the historical contingency of ideas and institutions, but was concerned more fundamentally with the historical contingency of metaphysical postulates. The institutions and ideas of liberalism, he insists, might still be entirely functional and defensible; the metaphysical postulates of "relative rationalism" are, however, irrevocable. Following Böckenförde, we might now revive, say, the linkage of normality and normativity as a basis for understanding the German Federal Republic's normal situation;[59] we would then be confirming, in constitutional-theoretical terms, the generality of law—both freedom guaranteeing and calculable—as the political order's normal situation. Nevertheless, says Schmitt, the idealistic faith in the legal form of freedom, as it was developed in the eighteenth century up to Kant, is no longer defensible in its original sense.[60] Schmitt's historicism thus centers primarily around the assertion of the irreversible historical contingency of metaphysics: its contingency on intellectual history by which is meant a history of metaphysics. Following the argument of *Die Geistesgeschichtliche Lage*, at the core of all "metaphysics" are an epoch's postulates and definition of rationality, understood practically as its idea of freedom. The history of metaphysics would then be equivalent to the history of human self-understanding and of the understanding of freedom.

In this sense metaphysics is irreducible.[61] The strong claim to the irreversible historical contingency of metaphysics will not be examined here. It is relevant for an understanding of Schmitt's critique of liberalism only insofar as (1) it links the differentiation of principles, ideas, and institutions to a differentiation of rationality postulates, thus (2) grasping "faith" in specific political principles as evidence of a specific concept of rationality, and (3) drawing a connection between the

146 Political Theory and Law

historical contingency of metaphysical postulates and the history of
political institutions. As human structures, institutions can always be
founded and maintained anew. In this sense the constitutional state
will always remain a political possibility and opportunity. Nonetheless
the hopes and expectations originally placed in these institutions are
tied in with human historical and practical self-understanding (to thus
define metaphysics) in such a manner that the constitutional state does
not always realize the same conception of freedom. Schmitt's reasoning is thus to the effect that the institutions of liberalism can certainly
persist (as an enduring possibility), and that the possibility of new ideas
and principles confirming these institutions can also not be excluded,
but that the practical understanding of the institutions changes irreversibly along with human historical self-understanding. A comparison
of Kant's sense of freedom with Max Weber's would appear to make this
glaringly obvious.[62] Up to this point, the hermeneutic approach manifested in Schmitt's critique of liberalism strikes me as both plausible
and sensible.

Now, as indicated, Schmitt's assertion of a connection between
an awareness of principles and an institutional awareness is in fact
stronger. He argues not only for a linkage between the historical contingency of political ideas and the history of the self-understanding of
corresponding institutions, but also claims that there is a strict correspondence between a lack of awareness of principles and structural
problems in institutions. Since an institution's structural system depends on the manifestation of that awareness, the collapse of the institution has its source in the incoherent execution of the principles. The
intent behind Schmitt's argument is heuristic; he presents it strikingly
by examining the self-annulment of liberalism and parliamentarism in
Weimar, not only in regard to the constitution's structural problems,
but also in regard to the diminished sense of constitutionality dominant in politics. Schmitt's thesis must be rejected, however, insofar as it
claims to be an argument based on principle.

Political and constitutional incoherence stems most immediately and
frequently from strategic compromises with competing forces. Beyond
this, we certainly find examples of the inadequate structural implementation and preservation of specific constitutional ideas and principles
emphasized by Schmitt. Political accomplishments are often con-
demned wholesale for these reasons. German liberalism, for instance,
is said to have revealed itself in Weimar as incapable of mastering the
Wilhelmian heritage (and Wilhelmian debt) through a carefully imple-

mented development of parliamentary structures. This opinion is about as correct as its negation. If, however, strictly speaking, the historical contingency of a political complex of ideas concerns only the historical contingency of human self-understanding and of the understanding of freedom, then there is no irreversible historical contingency of a political awareness of principles; and it does not follow that there must be a necessary incoherence of constitutional-political consciousness. True, as a constitutional-legal diagnosis, the assertion of such a connection seems largely accurate. Here as well, Schmitt is simply offering a heuristic thesis; but his assertion does not address the problem of whether there is any irreversible historical presumptiveness to the connection.

Our discussion of Schmitt's critique of liberalism can thus be summarized as follows. The assertion of a connection between an awareness of principles and an awareness of constitutional politics hits the mark. Political institutions are based on political ideas, and their maintenance is dependent on an awareness by the appropriate agents of their political meaning. Since human self-understanding is irreversibly rooted in history, expectations regarding institutions change. This does not necessarily involve a change in awareness of principles, leading to an institutional concern about the coherent implementation and preservation of fundamental ideas. Institutions can be tended to like rituals, without one having to share their original metaphysical implications.

Institutions—including liberal institutions—are created by human beings, founded on ideas, and consciously borne, maintained, and changed by people who believe in the ideas; from the vantage of the sociology of authority, Max Weber here speaks of "motives for obedience." They can also be founded and maintained, even if only in a purely strategic fashion, when these motives have changed. Admittedly the historically justified point is often made that Wcimar's democracy foundered because there were too few democrats; nevertheless its preservation would have been possible if "rational republicans" had maintained control of political events. No historical considerations can, then, negate the possibility of liberalism's endurance in principle. However trivial the point appears, it must be directly articulated in face of Schmitt's vehemently argued, and ubiquitously proclaimed, rhetoric of life and death. As a matter of principle, we must reject his claim to a historical refutation of the possibility of liberalism and parliamentarism— cultivated, for instance, in his constant talk of the "posthumous" character of the Weimar Constitution.[63]

The authentic challenge Schmitt poses in his critique of liberalism lies in his assertion of the irreversible historical contingency of the rational assumptions of all political principles and ideas, institutions and policies. In contrast to Hans Kelsen[64] or Gustav Radbruch,[65] Schmitt understands the "worldview" of democratic "relativism" as such a postulate and not simply as a theoretical and practical position, which makes his concept—here I can only assert this—systemically more fruitful.

As we saw at the outset, Habermas has recognized this; true, he speaks of (intersubjective) "presumptions of rationality," not of historical postulates of rationality. In doing so, he passes over (in his brief remarks) the problem of accessibility that Schmitt wishes to underscore: are the historical postulates of rationality of liberalism irreversible and irrevocable? Or do they in a sense invite reflection over their content, encouraging an awareness that their institutional nurture is possible?

As indicated, Schmitt does not insist on the inaccessibility of hermeneutic horizons. To the contrary, he explicitly assumes the possibility of an adequate relationship between concepts and postulates of order. "Metaphysics" he declares, is "the most intense and most lucid expression of an epoch."[66] If the principles at work in an epoch's postulates of rationality are accessible to both self-description and historical consideration, they can also be consciously cultivated: this includes parliamentarism as a "facade." In 1926 Schmitt writes: What has been offered in recent years in defense of parliamentarism only adds up, in the end, to the fact that the parliament presently functions well, or at least tolerably, as a useful, even indispensable instrument of social technique. To make the point once again: that is an entirely plausible way of seeing things. But a concern with the deeper foundations will surely also be necessary.[67]

Let me offer a few remarks linked to a liberal hope for preserving the "facade." The hope is that within the medium of the constitutional state, we will see a civilizing of politics: a process steered by constitutional political forms, in their turn increasing the opposition's sensitivity to a constitutional perspective on politics. The constitutional state's functionality involves, then, not only the basic duty of legislation and forming government within the political system; it is not limited to "integration" of the opposition through attaching it to civic structures; rather, it is meant to lead to a change in the understanding of politics. I should like here to speak of an inversion of political orientation through its direction toward constitutional state structures.

In political practice, the constitutional structuring of maxims for political action can turn against the intentions of politicians. What then follows is a derivation of political meaning from political paths and structures. This is not always an advantage: forming policies under the particular time pressure of looming elections and referendums is a well-known problem for democracies, and the "care for the future, for our descendants," which Max Weber[68] understood to be the heart of any ethically responsible politics, is scarcely possible in the daily play of power. But if democracy is organized irresponsibility, at least it allows citizens their share of irresponsibility. The constitutional state is a moderating form of political conduct—we might call it the state-form of conciliation. It prefers to regulate conflicts through negotiation, since it subsumes political truth claims to adherence to constitutional forms and it approaches decisions in terms of a strict balancing of interests. Because of its mode of decision making, it excludes fundamentalisms. Hobbes already defined this process: *Autoritas, non veritas facit legem.*[69]

Within the constitutional state, political decisions have no particular claims to truth—they are only valid thanks to the authority of those bodies making the decisions. The notion of "truth" is politically superfluous, insofar as it must always be linked to questions involving the strategic correctness of the instrumental rationality of decisions. This logical consistency is never entirely calculable and thus can only be asserted, political decisions requiring not truth, but authority. Their *authority* refers first of all to the way in which the decisions have been made—their legitimacy and conformity to legal procedures. It refers hence to their binding force, the authority of decisions thus being a result of the authority of the institutions behind them. It is apparent that democracies do not exclude all dogmatic worldviews, but only those which make undemocratic political demands.

These brief remarks can only touch on the liberal hopes tied up with the constitutional state. These hopes were of course not unknown to Schmitt. In talking of parliamentarism, he refers to the "cunning of the ideas and institutions"[70] involved in being the "stage for a transformative process" that turns the "party-egoism" of practical interest into a "unified state-will." Schmitt, however, in conformity with his theory of sovereignty, considers this process of parliamentary transformation only from the "decisionistic" perspective of government. As a result of his focus on the misuse of constitutional forms by extremist parties, he does not explicate the more fundamental principle discussed in these pages: that of the constitutional state's moderating of politics through the inversion of its orientation.

In any event, as indicated, the constitutional state is not only an instrument of power, but also a medium for peace and conciliation. Speaking against Schmitt in 1961, Dolf Sternberger referred to peace as "the ground and mark and norm of political activity—all these at once";[71] from this he coined the term "constitutional patriotism," by which he meant a loyal identification with the political constitution as a form of general public consensus regarding one's political identity.[72]

Sternberger's term deserves a detailed discussion. Here we have focused on only one "mark" of the constitutional state: its ability to use the political system to see through conflicts, diminishing their vehemence and placing them back on common ground. This ground is the fundamental recognition which even one's political opponents experience in the constitutional state through their acceptance of forms and rules. The liberal case for the constitutional state resides beyond exaggerated expectations about the power to create community and consensus and about the rational orientation and regulatory capacity of the political system; the case rests on the moderating power of its institutions. The source of Schmitt's desire to find alternatives to the liberal constitutional state, his exaggerated expectations regarding the existential status of political entities, must be discussed elsewhere.

Notes

This essay was translated by Dr. Joel Golb.

1 See Patrick Bahners, "Alle Mann nach vorn. Der Parteitag der FDP," *Frankfurter Allgemeine Zeitung* (December 6, 1995): 27.

2 Hermann Heller, *Die politischen Ideenkreise der Gegenwart* (Breslau, 1926).

3 Ellen Kennedy, "Carl Schmitt und die 'Frankfurter Schule.' Deutsche Liberalismuskritik im 20. Jahrhundert," *Geschichte und Gesellschaft* 12 (1986): 380; concerning this debate, see Reinhard Mehring, "Vom Umgang mit Carl Schmitt," *Geschichte und Gesellschaft* 19 (1993): at 394ff.; a reprise of the debate contributing nothing essentially new is to be found in Hartmuth Becker, *Die Parlamentarismuskritik bei Carl Schmitt und Jürgen Habermas* (Berlin, 1994).

4 Jürgen Habermas, "Die Schrecken der Autonomie. Carl Schmitt auf Englisch," in Jürgen Habermas, *Eine Art Schadensabwicklung* (Frankfurt, 1987), at 101–14; see more recently, Jürgen Habermas, "Carl Schmitt in der politischen Geistesgeschichte," in Jürgen Habermas, *Die Normalität einer Bonner Republik* (Frankfurt, 1995), at 112–22.

5 Ibid., at 112–13. See further, Jürgen Habermas, *Faktizität und Geltung. Beiträge zur Diskurstheorie des Rechts und des demokratischen Rechtsstaats* (Frankfurt, 1992); see Jürgen Habermas, "Über den internen Zusammenhang

von Rechtsstaat und Demokratie," in Ulrich K. Preuss, ed., *Zum Begriff der Verfassung. Die Ordnung des Politischen* (Frankfurt, 1994), at 83–94.

6 Urich Preuss, "Carl Schmitt und die Frankfurter Schule: Deutsche Liberalismuskritik im 20. Jahrhundert. Anmerkungen zu einem Aufsatz von Ellen Kennedy," *Geschichte und Gesellschaft* 13 (1987): at 400–418, 410.

7 Carl Schmitt, "Legalität und Legitimität," (Munich, 1932) in Carl Schmitt, *Verfassungsrechtliche Aufsätze* (Berlin, 1958), at 263–350.

8 See Ernst Rudolf Huber, *Deutsche Verfassungsgeschichte seit 1789* VII (Stuttgart, 1984), at 1264; Heinrich August Winckler, *Weimar* (Munich, 1993), at 55ff., 595ff.; see also Carl Schmitt, "Das Problem der Legalität," in *Verfassungsrechtliche Aufsätze*, at 430–9; "Interview mit Dieter Groh/Klaus Figge," in Piet Tommissen, ed., *Over en in Zake Carl Schmitt* (Brussels, 1975), at 89–109.

9 Carl Schmitt, *Die geistesgeschichtliche Lage des heutigen Parlamentarismus* (Munich, 1923).

10 See the observations of Karl Dietrich Bracher, *Die nationalsozialistische Machtergreifung* (Cologne, 1962) at 18, 271; see also Karl Dietrich Bracher, *Das deutsche Dilemma* (Munich, 1971), at 34ff.; Karl Dietrich Bracher, *Zeitgeschichtliche Kontroversen*, 2d ed. (Munich, 1976) at 28, 46; Kurt Sontheimer, *Antidemokratisches Denken in der Weimarer Republik*, 2d ed. (Munich, 1983); Kurt Sontheimer, *Neue Politische Literatur* 3 (1958): at 757–70; Klaus Hansen and Hans Lietzmann, eds., *Carl Schmitt und die Liberalismuskritik* (Opladen, 1988) is of little value; on the wider theoretical context of Schmitt's critique of liberalism, see Hans Boldt, "Parlamentarismustheorie. Bemerkungen zu ihrer Geschichte in Deutschland," *Der Staat* 19 (1980): at 385–412; Helmut Quaritsch, "Zur Entstehung der Theorie des Pluralismus," *Der Staat* 19 (1980): at 29–56; Christoph Gusy, "Die Lehre vom Parteienstaat in der Weimarer Republik," *Der Staat* 32 (1993): at 57–86; more generally, Kurt Kluxen, *Geschichte und Problematik des Parlamentarismus* (Frankfurt, 1983); James J. Sheehan, *German Liberalism in the Nineteenth Century* (Chicago, 1978); Dieter Langewiesche, *Liberalismus in Deutschland* (Frankfurt, 1988).

11 On the "situation-bound" significance of Schmitt's ideas, see Ernst Rudolf Huber, "'Positionen und Begriffe'. Eine Auseinandersetzung mit Carl Schmitt," *Zeitschrift für die gesammten Staatswissenschaften* 101 (1941): 1, at 2–4.

12 Carl Schmitt, *Verfassungslehre* (Munich, 1928), at 200.

13 Reinhard Mehring, *Carl Schmitt zur Einführung* (Hamburg, 1992).

14 Until now scant attention has been paid to the split in Schmitt's analysis of the disintegration of the "bourgeois *Rechtsstaat*," between a focus on the disintegration of the organizational principle, on the one hand, and his legal-theoretical focus on the fundamental distinction between law and means, on the other. The legal-theoretical perspective is more essential. Since the

distinction between law and means evaporates, we also find, according to Schmitt, a breakdown of the constitutional state's organized separation of powers. As a consequence, the Reichspräsident granted "power of rule by decree as the delegate of the law" and becomes a supreme legislator and dictator, uniting legislative and executive authority in his one role. This is a process that Schmitt in no way approves from the perspective of legal theory: see Carl Schmitt, *Der Hüter der Verfassung* (Tübingen, 1931), at 125f.; "Legalität und Legitimität," supra n. 7, at 327f. As Schmitt puts it, "from the perspective of constitutional theory, the real basis of this political confusion, and of this confusion in constitutional law, lies in the debasement of the concept of law" (ibid., at 331). Schmitt sees the source of the breakdown of the distinction between law and means in the absence of a "normal" situation—that is, in the collapse of the relation of normality and normativity accompanying Weimar's state of emergency.

15 E.g., Carl Schmitt, "Der Weg des deutschen Juristen," *Deutsche Juristen-Zeitung* 39 (1934): at 695; "Die Rechtswissenschaft im Führerstaat," *Zeitschrift der Akademie für Deutsches Recht* 2 (1935): at 439; "Aufgabe und Notwendigkeit des deutschen Rechtsstandes," *Deutsches Recht* 6 (1936): at 184. On Schmitt's role in National Socialism, see Andreas Koenen, *Der Fall Carl Schmitt. Sein Aufstieg zum 'Kronjuristen des Dritten Reiches'* (Darmstadt, 1995).

16 Carl Schmitt, *Der Nomos der Erde* (Cologne, 1950), at 13ff.; see *Völkerrechtliche Grossraumordnung* (Berlin: New Impression, 1991), at 81.

17 See, e.g., Franz Neumann, "Der Funktionswandel des Gesetzes im Recht der bürgerlichen Gesellschaft," in Franz Neumann, *Demokratischer und autoritärer Staat. Studien zur Politischen Theorie* (Frankfurt, 1967), at 31–81.

18 See Ernst Forsthoff, *Rechtsstaat im Wandel. Verfassungsrechtliche Abhandlungen 1954-1973* (Munich, 1976), at 105ff.; also noteworthy is Ernst-Wolfgang Böckenförde, *Gesetz und gesetzgebende Gewalt von den Anfängen der deutschen Staatsrechtslehre bis zur Höhe des staatsrechtlichen Positivismus* (Berlin, 1958); in taking issue with such literature (see the last-cited work for additional references), Hasso Hofmann insists upon a "postulate of the generality of law," *Die Allgemeinheit des Gesetzes* (Göttingen: Chr. Starck, 1987), at 9–48; on developments in the debate over constitutional theory after Schmitt, see Reinhard Mehring, "Carl Schmitt und die Verfassungslehre unserer Tage," *Archiv des öffentlichen Rechts* 120 (1995): at 177–204.

19 See Carl Schmitt, "Nationalsozialistisches Rechtsdenken," *Deutsches Recht* 4 (1934): at 225, "Today we are experiencing the bankruptcy of idées générales."

20 Carl Schmitt, "Was bedeutet der Streit um den 'Rechtsstaat'?" *ZgStW* 95 (1935): at 189–201; Carl Schmitt, "Der Rechtsstaat," in Carl Schmitt, *Nationalsozialistisches Handbuch für Recht und Gesetzgebung* (Munich, 1935),

at 24–31; see Carl Hermann Ule, "Carl Schmitt, der Rechtsstaat und die Verwaltungsgerichtsbarkeit," *Verwaltungs-Archiv* 81 (1991): 1.

21 In order to locate Schmitt's essay in relation to other critiques of parliamentarism of the time, it is above all worth comparing it with Rudolf Smend, "Die Verschiebung der konstitutionellen Ordnung durch die Verhältniswahl," (1919) in Rudolf Smend, *Staatsrechtliche Abhandlungen und andere Aufsätze* (Berlin, 1955), at 60–67.

22 Schmitt's sense of a link between legal form and the type of rationality characterizing an epoch may have been influenced by Max Weber's sociology of law, which emphasizes the "formal qualities of modern law." See Max Weber, *Wirtschaft und Gesellschaft,* 5th ed. (Tübingen, 1980), at 387–513.

23 *Verfassungslehre* (supra n. 12, at 307ff.) here speaks of "ideal foundations."

24 Supra n. 9, at 6, 9, 11.

25 Ibid., at 45.

26 Schmitt's (previously developed) critique of romanticism informs his critique of liberalism, insofar as he understands parliamentarism as an institution for romantic dialogue. Despite this juxtaposition of critiques, Schmitt still distinguishes (in ibid., at 58ff.) classical liberalism from the "organic" liberalism of the period in Germany before the revolution of March, 1848. But in contrast to Huber or Böckenförde, he has no particular historical interest in German liberalism, deeming it already politically exhausted in that period.

27 Carl Schmitt, "Rechtsstaatlicher Verfassungsvollzug," in *Verfassungsrechtliche Aufsätze aus den Jahren 1924-1954* (Berlin, 1958), at 452–88.

28 Max Weber, *Gesammelte Aufsätze zur Wissenschaftslehre,* 7th ed. (Tübingen, 1978), at 510ff.

29 Supra n. 12, at 79ff.

30 Carl Schmitt, *Der Begriff des Politischen. Text von 1932 mit einem Vorwort und drei Corollarien* (Berlin, 1963), at 50.

31 Ibid., at 69.

32 Ibid., at 70f., 76f.

33 Among many articles, see Carl Schmitt, "Völkerrechtliche Formen des modernen Imperialismus," in Carl Schmitt, *Positionen und Begriffe im Kampf mit Weimar-Genf-Versailles* (Hamburg, 1940), at 162–80; see Huber, supra n. 11, at 25ff.

34 See Ernst-Wolfgang Böckenförde, "Der Begriff des Politischen als Schlüssel zum staatsrechtlichen Werk Carl Schmitts," in Ernst-Wolfgang Böckenförde, *Recht, Staat, Freiheit. Studien zur Rechtsphilosophie, Staatstheorie und Verfassungstheorie* (Frankfurt, 1991), at 344–66. (This essay appears in translation in this volume, ed.)

35 Supra n. 9, at 29, 62.

36 Ibid., at 39.

37 Ibid., at 35ff.

38 Ibid., at 37.

39 Carl Schmitt, "Diktatur und Belagerungszustand," *Zeitschrift für die gesamte Strafrechtswissenschaft* 38 (1916): at 138–62; Carl Schmitt, *Die Diktatur* (Munich, 1921).

40 An exploration of Schmitt's sketchy remarks (supra n. 9, at 58ff.) is found in Ernst-Wolfgang Böckenförde, *Die deutsche verfassungsgeschichtliche Forschung im 19. Jahrhundert* (Berlin, 1961). During the National Socialist period, an engagement with "organic" liberalism was particularly manifest in the work and influence of Gierke. See, e.g., Reinhard Höhn, *Otto von Gierkes Staatslehre und unsere Zeit* (Hamburg, 1936); Schmitt consistently traced a line from Gierke to Gierke's student Hugo Preuss and on to Rudolf Smend, criticizing this strand of comradely liberalism more vehemently than the liberal legal positivism of Laband. See Carl Schmitt, *Hugo Preuss. Sein Staatsbegriff und seine Stellung in der deutschen Staatslehre* (Tübingen, 1930); Reinhard Mehring, "Geist gegen Gesetz. Carl Schmitts Destruktion des positiven Rechtsdenkens," in Bernd Wacker, ed., *Die eigentlich katholische Verschärfung . . . Konfession, Theologie und Politik im Werk Carl Schmitts* (Munich, 1994), at 229–45.

41 A lecture which Schmitt gave in 1932 on the 100th anniversary of Hegel's death has now been published from Schmitt's literary remains; Piet Tommissen, ed., *Schmittiana-IV* (Berlin, 1994). The lecture focuses on Hegel's dialectical position using the tools of the *Der Begriff des Politischen*.

42 Supra n. 9, at 80.

43 Ibid., at 88.

44 Ibid., at 89.

45 Carl Schmitt, *Politische Theologie. Vier Kapitel zur Lehre von der Souveränität*, 3d ed. (Berlin, 1979).

46 Ibid., at 59–60; see the distinctions drawn by Ernst-Wolfgang Böckenförde in "Politische Theorie und politische Theologie. Bemerkungen zu ihrem gegenseitigen Verhältnis," in Ernst-Wolfgang Böckenförde, *Kirchlicher Auftrag und politisches Handeln* (Freiburg, 1989), at 146–58.

47 Carl Schmitt, *Hauptprobleme der Soziologie. Erinnerungsgabe für Max Weber* (Munich, 1923).

48 Schmitt thus refers in his postwar diary (*Glossarium. Aufzeichnungen der Jahre 1947-1951* [Berlin, 1991], at 107, entry of 2.3.1948) to the "conceptual realism" of his essay "Legalität und Legitimität" as constituting an adequate insight into the "model-character of German developments 1929–33."

49 See Ernst Rudolf Huber, "Vom Sinn verfassungsgeschichtlicher Forschung und Lehre," in Ernst Rudolf Huber, *Bewahrung und Wandlung* (Berlin, 1975), at 11–17; see also Ernst-Wolfgang Böckenförde, "Zum Verhältnis von Geschichtswissenschaft und Rechtswissenschaft," in *Theorie der Geschichtswissenschaft und Praxis des Geschichtsunterrichts* (Stuttgart: Werner Conze, 1972), at 38–44.

50 For a development of this argument, see Reinhard Mehring, *Pathetisches Denken. Carl Schmitts Denkweg am Leitfaden Hegels* (Berlin, 1989).

51 For an attempt to clarify the dogmatic content of Schmitt's confession and Christianity, see Bernd Wacker, ed., *Die eigentlich katholische Verschärfung* . . . (Munich, 1994). The need for a detailed examination of Schmitt's confessional stance is not recognized in Heinrich Meier, *Die Lehre Carl Schmitts* (Stuttgart, 1994).

52 Supra n. 28, at 150f.

53 Gerhard Leibholz already noted this connection in *Die Auflösung der liberalen Demokratie in Deutschland und das autoritäre Staatsbild* (Munich, 1933).

54 Schmitt contests, in a fundamental way, the theory of "constitution as contract" (supra n. 12, at 61ff.; *Der Hüter der Verfassung*, supra n. 14, at 52ff., 60ff.), as it was inherited from the "constitutional monarchy, German style." He understands this theory as veiling the subject of sovereignty and legitimacy, which unveils itself in emergencies. The Prussian constitutional struggle between 1862 and 1868 was decisive for Schmitt's view of "constitutional monarchy": it made clear that the latter actually was already equal to a "parliamentary legislative state" (supra n. 7, at 274. (In 1931 [in *Der Hüter der Verfassung*, supra n. 14, at 135] Schmitt still maintains the distinction between "parliamentary" and "constitutional" monarchy.) The memory of this struggle certainly plays a role in Schmitt's granting the *Reichspräsident* in 1931 the right to "emergency decrees applying to the finance laws," in spite of legal-theoretical reservations (ibid., at 128ff.; see 28f., 123ff.).

The question of the political significance of constitutional compromises was taken up after Schmitt, most significantly in a debate between Ernst Rudolf Huber and Ernst-Wolfgang Böckenförde concerning the position of the Bismarkian Reich's constitution in relation to German constitutional history. Huber emphasized the inherent legitimacy of the monarch's regulative power within that constitution, while Böckenförde emphasized (like Schmitt) the transitory character of the Second Reich. Huber's critique of Schmitt's view of "constitutional monarchy" was made explicit in *Heer und Staat in der deutschen Geschichte* (Hamburg, 1938), at 224ff., 232f., 236, 239. It was directed at Schmitt's *Staatsgefüge und Zusammenbruch des Zweiten Reiches* (Hamburg, 1934), commenting in particular on the settlement of the constitutional conflict through the 1866 "indemnity bill." The latter controversy is documented in Ernst-Wolfgang Böckenförde, ed., *Moderne deutsche Verfassungsgeschichte 1815–1914*, 2d ed. (Königstein, 1981).

55 Rudolf Smend, "Verfassung und Verfassungsrecht" (1928), in Rudolf Smend, ed., *Staatsrechtliche Abhandlungen* (Berlin, 1955), at 153.

56 See Reinhard Mehring, *Carl Schmitt zur Einführung*, supra n. 13, at 72ff.

57 Karl Popper, *Das Elend des Historizmus*, 5th ed. (Tübingen, 1979) in contrast, describes historicism as a process of predicting the future through

the social-scientific assertion of certain developmental laws, whose possibility Popper denies. Arthur Danto, *Analytische Philosophie der Geschichte* (Frankfurt, 1980), endows the philosophical-historical tradition—to a large extent erroneously—with a similar futuristic sense. In fact, far more characteristic for that tradition, as for Schmitt, is the "sense of a historical ending" (phrase from K. Löwith), of a closure of history in the present.

58 Jürgen Habermas's reference to Europe's "second chance" (Jürgen Habermas, *Vergangenheit als Zukunft* [Zürich, 1990], at 97ff.) marks a break with a historico-philosophical idealism that is heavily in debt to Hegel.

59 In opposing Schmitt's thesis of the primacy of the political "normal situation" over questions of legal validity, Jürgen Habermas now stresses the priority of the postulate of an "ethical-political self-understanding" of the normative basis of a republic over its political normalization; see his latest collection of political essays, Jürgen Habermas, *Die Normalität einer Berliner Republik* (Frankfurt, 1995).

60 Contrast Ernst-Wolfgang Böckenförde, "Freiheit und Recht, Freiheit und Staat," in supra n. 34, at 42–57.

61 Schmitt nowhere explicated his concept of Metaphysik more clearly than in *Geistesgeschichtliche Lage.* On metaphysics in the above sense, see Hans-Georg Gadamer, "Hermeneutik als praktische Philosophie," in Hans-Georg Gadamer, *Vernunft im Zeitalter der Wissenschaft* (Frankfurt, 1976), at 78–109; Dieter Henrich, "Was ist Metaphysik—was Moderne? Zwölf Thesen gegen Jürgen Habermas," in *Konzepte* (Frankfurt, 1987), 11–43.

62 Max Weber saw in parliamentary democracy little more than a "future abode of servitude" that at least left open the question of how "in face of the dominance of the trend towards bureaucratization it still will be possible to save some scrap of freedom of action that is in some sense 'individual'"; Max Weber, "Parlament und Regierung im neugeordneten Deutschland," in Max Weber, *Gesammelte Politische Schriften*, 4th ed. (Tübingen, 1980), at 333.

63 See Carl Schmitt, *Staatsgefüge und Zusammenbruch des Zweiten Reiches* (Hamburg, 1934), at 43: "The Weimar constitution offered an answer to a defunct question, one that the authentic present no longer asks. The victory of liberal democracy announced by the Weimar constitution was merely posthumous. It was futile, directed towards a past, without a present or future, the victory that a ghost carries away from the shadow of his opponent."

64 Kelsen's chief state- and political-theoretical writings of the interwar period usually conclude with identical expositions treating the relation between "state-form and worldview," and with expressions of fidelity to a "critical-relativistic" worldview as a prerequisite for a "democratic" position; see Hans Kelsen, *Sozialismus und Staat. Eine Untersuchung der politischen Theorie des Marxismus*, 3d ed. (Vienna, 1965), at 160ff.; *Allgemeine Staatslehre* (Berlin, 1925), at 368ff.; *Vom Wesen und Wert der Demokratie* (Tübin-

gen, 1929), at 98ff.; *Staatsform und Weltanschauung* (Tübingen, 1933), at 28ff. It is not clear whether Kelsen is arguing as a democrat for "relativism" or as a relativist for democracy (i.e., whether the worldview determines the state-form or vice versa). "Relativism" is here a blanket term for a "worldview of critique and positivism," its stance emerging from "mutable and ever-changing experience." In democracy Kelsen sees "simply a form, simply a method, for producing social order"; he disputes the conceptual certainty of fixed systems of value and designates the assertion of such certainties as "metaphysics." He thus distinguishes between "worldview" and "metaphysics" and so understands his relativism as a postmetaphysical worldview. But, in contrast to Schmitt, Kelsen does not understand the state's legal form as the historical outcome of a rational process; he thus does not adequately discuss the rational form of his own concept of law.

65 Already in 1914, Gustav Radbruch—not least under Max Weber's influence—proposed a "legal-philosophical relativism"; *Grundzüge der Rechtsphilosophie* (Leipzig, 1914), at 24ff. In apparent agreement with Kelsen, he writes the following in the foreword to the book's revised edition (1928, 6th ed. [Stuttgart, 1963]): "For relativism is the conceptual postulate of democracy: it declines to identify with a specific political position, being ready, on the contrary, to grant state power to any political position that can form a majority, since it is not aware of any unambiguous criterion for evaluating the correctness of political views" (84). In its rejection of relativism in regard to practice, however, Radbruch's approach is very different than Kelsen's: "The method I have described here can be called relativism, because its chief task is to ascertain the correctness of every value judgment only in relation to a specified supreme value judgment, only in the framework of a specified sense of values and worldview, and not to ascertain the correctness of the value judgment, the sense of values and the worldview, themselves. Relativism, however, belongs to the realm of theoretical and not practical reason. It signifies an abandonment of a scientific grounding of final positions—not abandonment of the positions themselves" (102ff.). Radbruch here justly evokes Max Weber. With Kelsen as his starting point, he summarizes his position in 1934 with the maxim: "Relativism is general tolerance—only not tolerance of intolerance"; Gustav Radbruch, "Der Relativismus in der Rechtsphilosophie," in *Der Mensch im Recht* (Göttingen, 1957), at 86.

66 Supra n. 45, at 60.

67 Supra n. 9, at 12f.

68 Supra n. 62, at 12; see, e.g., at 176f., 440, 549.

69 See Hermann Lübbe, "Carl Schmitt liberal rezipiert," in Helmut Quaritsch, ed., *Complexio Oppositorum. Über Carl Schmitt* (Berlin, 1988), at 427–40.

70 *Der Hüter der Verfassung*, supra n. 14, at 88.

71 Dolf Sternberger, "Begriff des Politischen. Heidelberger Antrittsrede 1960,"

in his *Staatsfreundschaft. Schriften IV* (Frankfurt, 1980), at 293–312, specifically 304f.; see Reinhard Mehring, "Bürgerliche statt demokratischer Legitimität. Dolf Sternbergers Auseinandersetzung um den Begriff des Politischen," in Andreas Göbel, Dirk van Laak, and Ingeborg Villinger, eds., *Metamorphosen des Politischen* (Berlin, 1995), at 233–46.

72 Dolf Sternberger, *Verfassungspatriotismus* (Frankfurt, 1990).

Carl Schmitt and the Paradox
of Liberal Democracy

Chantal Mouffe

In his introduction to the paperback edition of *Political Liberalism*, John Rawls, referring to Carl Schmitt's critique of parliamentary democracy, suggests that the fall of Weimar's constitutional regime was in part due to the fact that German elites no longer believed in the possibility of a decent liberal parliamentary regime. This should, in his view, make us realize the importance of providing convincing arguments in favor of a just and well-ordered constitutional democracy. "Debates about general philosophical questions," he says, "cannot be the daily stuff of politics, but that does not make these questions without significance, since what we think their answers are will shape the underlying attitudes of the public culture and the conduct of politics."[1]

I agree with Rawls on the practical role that political philosophy can play in shaping the public culture of democratic political identities and in contributing to their creation. But I consider that, in order to put forward a conception of the liberal democratic society able to win the active allegiance of its citizens, political theorists must be willing to engage in the arguments of those who have challenged the fundamental tenets of liberalism. This means confronting some disturbing questions, usually avoided by liberals and democrats alike.

My intention in this chapter is to contribute to such a project by scrutinizing Carl Schmitt's critique of liberal democracy. Indeed, I am convinced that a confrontation with his thought will allow us to ac-knowledge—and therefore be in a better position to try to negotiate—an important paradox inscribed in the very nature of liberal democracy. To bring to the fore the pertinence and actuality of Schmitt's critique, I will organize my argument around two topics which are currently central in political theory: the boundaries of citizenship and the nature of a liberal democratic consensus.[2]

Democracy, Homogeneity and the Boundaries of Citizenship

The boundaries of citizenship have lately excited much discussion. Several authors have recently argued that in an age of globalization, citizenship cannot be confined within the boundaries of nation-states; it must become transnational. David Held, for instance, advocates the advent of a "cosmopolitan citizenship" and asserts the need for a cosmopolitan democratic law to which citizens whose rights have been violated by their own states could appeal.[3] Richard Falk, for his part, envisages the development of "citizen pilgrims" whose loyalties would belong to an invisible political community, one which consisted of their hopes and dreams.[4]

Other theorists however, particularly those who are committed to a civic republican conception of citizenship, are deeply suspicious about such prospects, which they view as endangering democratic forms of government. They assert that the nation-state is the necessary locus for citizenship and that there is something inherently contradictory in the very idea of cosmopolitan citizenship. I see this debate as a typical example of the problems arising from the conflict between democratic and liberal requirements. Schmitt, I submit, can help us to clarify what is at stake in this issue by making us aware of the tension existing between democracy and liberalism.

As a starting point, let us take his thesis that "homogeneity" is a condition of the possibility of democracy. In the preface to the second edition of *The Crisis of Parliamentary Democracy* in 1926, he declares "Every actual democracy rests on the principle that not only are equals equal but unequals will not be treated equally. Democracy requires, therefore, first homogeneity and second—if the need arises—elimination or eradication of heterogeneity."[5] I do not want to deny that, given the later political evolution of its author, this assertion has a chilling effect. However, I consider that it would be shortsighted to dismiss for that reason Schmitt's claim about the necessity of homogeneity in a democracy. It is my contention that, interpreted in a particular way, this provocative thesis may force us to come to terms with an aspect of democratic politics that liberalism tends to evacuate.

The first thing to do is to grasp what Schmitt means by "homogeneity." He affirms that homogeneity is inscribed at the very core of the democratic conception of equality, insofar as it must be a *substantive* equality. His argument is that democracy requires a conception of equality as substance and cannot satisfy itself with an abstract conception like the liberal one since "equality is only interesting and invaluable politically so long as it has substance, and for that reason at least the possibility and the risk of inequality."[6] In order to be treated as equals, citizens must, he says, partake of a common substance.

As a consequence, he rejects the idea that the general equality of mankind could serve as a basis for a state or any form of government. Such an idea of human equality—which comes from liberal individualism—is, says Schmitt, a nonpolitical form of equality because it lacks the correlate of a possible inequality from which every equality receives its specific meaning. It does not provide any criteria for establishing political institutions. According to him, "The equality of all persons as persons is not democracy but a certain kind of liberalism, not a state form but an individualistic-humanitarian ethic and *Weltanschauung.* Modern mass democracy rests on the confused combination of both."[7]

Schmitt asserts that there is an insuperable opposition between liberal individualism with its moral discourse centered around the individual and the democratic ideal which is essentially political and aims at creating an identity based on homogeneity. He claims that liberalism negates democracy and democracy negates liberalism and that parliamentary democracy, since it consists in the articulation between democracy and liberalism, is therefore a nonviable regime.

In his view, when we speak of equality we need to distinguish between two very different ideas: the liberal one and the democratic one. The liberal conception of equality postulates that every person is, as a person, inherently equal to every other person. The democratic conception, however, requires the possibility of distinguishing who belongs to the "demos" and who is excluded, and for that reason the democratic conception cannot exist without the necessary correlate of inequality. Despite liberal claims, a democracy of mankind, if it was ever possible, would be a pure abstraction because equality can only exist through its specific meanings in particular spheres, i.e., as political equality, economic equality, and so forth. But those specific equalities always entail, as their very condition of possibility, some form of inequality. This is why he concludes that an absolute human equality would be a practically meaningless, indifferent equality.

Schmitt makes an important point when he stresses that the democratic concept of equality is a *political* one which therefore entails the possibility of a *distinction.* He is right to say that a political democracy cannot be based on the distinctionlessness of all mankind and that it must be rooted in a specific people. It is worth indicating here that, contrary to several tendentious interpretations, Schmitt never postulated that this belonging to a people could only be envisaged in racial terms. On the contrary, he insisted on the multiplicity of ways in which the homogeneity constitutive of a demos could be manifested. He says for instance that the substance of equality "can be found in certain physical and moral qualities, for example, in civic virtue, in *arete*, the classical democracy of *vertus* (*vertu*)."[8] Examining this question from an historical angle, he also points out that "[i]n the democracy of English sects during the seventeenth century equality was based on a consensus of religious convictions. Since the nineteenth century it has existed above all in membership in a particular nation, in national homogeneity."[9]

It is clear that what is important for Schmitt is not the nature of the similarity on which homogeneity is based. What matters is the possibility of tracing a line of demarcation between those who belong to the demos—and therefore have equal rights—and those who, in the political domain, cannot have the same rights because they are not part of the demos. Such a democratic equality—expressed today through citizenship—is for him the ground of all the other forms of equality. It is through their belonging to the demos that democratic citizens are granted equal rights and not because they participate in an abstract idea of humanity. This is why he declares that the central concept of democracy is not "humanity" but the concept of the 'people' and that there can never be a democracy of mankind. Democracy can only exist for a people. As he puts it: "In the domain of the political, people do not face each other as abstractions but as politically interested and politically determined persons, as citizens, governors or governed, politically allied or opponents—in any case, therefore in political categories. In the sphere of the political, one cannot abstract out what is political, leaving only universal human equality."[10]

In order to illustrate his point, Schmitt indicates that, even in modern democratic states where universal human equality has been established, there is a category of people who are excluded as foreigners or aliens and that there is therefore no absolute equality. He also shows how the correlate of the equality among the citizenry found in those states is a much stronger emphasis on national homogeneity and on the line of demarcation between those who belong to the state and those who remain outside it. This is, he notes, to be expected and, if this were not the case and a state attempted to realize the universal equality of individuals in the political realm without concern for national or any other form of homogeneity, the consequence would be a complete devaluation of political equality and of politics itself. To be sure, this would in no way mean the disappearance of substantive inequalities, but says Schmitt, "they would shift in another sphere, perhaps separated from the political and concentrated in the economic, leaving this area to take on a new, disproportionately decisive importance. Under the conditions of superficial political equality, another sphere in which substantial inequalities prevail (today for example the economic sphere) will dominate politics."[11]

It seems to me that, unpleasant as they are to liberal ears, those arguments need to be considered carefully. They carry an important warning for those who believe that the process of globalization is laying the basis for worldwide democratization and cosmopolitan citizenship. They also provide important insights for understanding the current dominance of economics over politics. We should indeed be aware that without a demos to which they belong, those cosmopolitan citizen pilgrims would in fact have lost the possibility of exercising their democratic rights of lawmaking. They would be left, at best, with their liberal right of appealing to transnational courts to defend their individual rights when those have been violated. In all probability, such a cosmopolitan democracy, if it were ever to be realized, would not be more than an empty name disguising the actual disappearance of democratic forms of government and indicating the triumph of the liberal form of governmental rationality that Foucault called "governmentality."

The Democratic Logic of Inclusion-Exclusion

True, by reading him in that way, I am doing violence to Schmitt's questioning since his main concern is not democratic participation but *political unity*. He considers that such a unity is crucial because without it the state cannot exist. But his reflections are relevant for the issue of democracy since he considers that in a democratic state, it is through their participation in this unity that the citizens can be treated as equals and exercise their democratic rights. Democracy, according to Schmitt, consists fundamentally in the identity between rulers and ruled. It is linked to the fundamental principle of the unity of the demos and the sovereignty of its will. But for the people to rule it is necessary to determine who belongs to the people. Without any criterion to determine who are the bearers of democratic rights, the will of the people cannot take shape.

It could, of course, be objected that this is a view of democracy which is at odds with the liberal democratic one. Some would certainly claim that this should not be called democracy but populism. To be sure, Schmitt is no democrat in the liberal understanding of the term, and he had only contempt for the constraints imposed by liberal institutions on the democratic will of the people. But the issue that he raises is a crucial one, even for those who advocate liberal democratic forms. The logic of democracy does indeed imply a moment of closure which is required by the very process of constituting the "people." This cannot be avoided, even in a liberal democratic model; it can only be negotiated differently. But this can only be done if this closure and the paradox that it implies are acknowledged.

By stressing that the identity of a democratic political community hinges on the possibility of drawing a frontier between "us" and "them," Schmitt highlights the fact that democracy always entails relations of inclusion/exclusion. This is a vital insight that democrats would be ill-advised to dismiss simply because they dislike its author. One of the main problems with liberalism—and one that can endanger democracy—is precisely its incapacity to conceptualize such a frontier. As Schmitt indicates, the central concept of liberal discourse is "humanity," which, as he rightly points out, is not a political concept and does not correspond to any political entity. The central question of the political constitution of "the people" is something that liberal theory is unable to tackle adequately because the necessity of drawing a "frontier" is in contradiction with its universalistic rhetoric. Against the liberal emphasis on "humanity," it is important to stress that the key concepts in conceptualizing democracy are the "demos" and the "people."

Contrary to those who believe in a necessary harmony between liberalism and democracy, Schmitt makes us see the way in which they conflict and the dangers that the dominance of the liberal logic can bring to the exercise of democracy. There is an evident opposition between the liberal grammar of equality which postulates universality and reference to humanity and the practice of democratic equality, which requires the political moment of discrimination between us and them. However, I think that Schmitt is wrong to present this conflict as a contradiction that is bound to lead liberal democracy to self-destruction. We can completely accept his insight without agreeing with the conclusions that he draws. What I propose is to acknowledge the crucial difference between the liberal and the democratic conceptions of equality, while envisaging their articulation and its consequences in another way. Indeed, such an articulation can be seen as the locus of a *tension* that institutes a very important dynamic, one constitutive of the specificity of liberal democracy as a new political form of society. The democratic logic of constituting the people and inscribing rights and equality into practices is necessary to subvert the tendency toward abstract universalism inherent in liberal discourse. But the articulation with the liberal logic allows one to constantly challenge, through the reference to humanity and the polemical use of human rights, the forms of exclusion that are necessarily inscribed in the political practice of instituting rights and of defining "the people" who are going to rule.[12] Notwithstanding the ultimate contradictory nature of the two logics, their articulation has therefore very positive consequences and there is no reason to share Schmitt's pessimistic verdict concerning liberal democracy. However, we should not be too sanguine about its prospects either. No final resolution or equilibrium is ever possible between those two conflicting logics and there can only be temporary, pragmatic, unstable, and precarious negotiations of their tension. Liberal democratic politics consists in fact in the constant process of negotiation and renegotiation—through different hegemonic articulations—of this constitutive paradox.

Deliberative Democracy and Its Shortcomings

Schmitt's reflections on the necessary moment of closure which the democratic logic entails has important consequences for another debate, the one about the nature of the consensus that can obtain in a liberal democratic society. Several issues are at stake in that debate, and I will examine them in turn.

One of the implications of the argument presented above is the impossibility of establishing a rational consensus without exclusion. This raises several problems for the model of democratic politics which has been receiving quite a lot of attention recently under the name of "deliberative democracy." No doubt, the aim of the theorists who advocate the different versions of such a model is commendable. Against the interest-based conception of democracy, inspired by economics, and sceptical about the virtues of political participation, these theorists want to introduce questions of morality and justice into politics and envisage democratic citizenship in a different way. However, by proposing to view reason and rational argumentation, instead of interest and aggregation of preferences, as the central issue of politics, they simply replace the economic model with a moral one which, albeit in a different way, also misses the specificity of the political. In their attempt to overcome the

limitations of interest-group pluralism, deliberative democrats provide
a telling illustration of Schmitt's point: "In a very systematic fashion liberal thought evades or ignores state and politics and moves instead in a
typical always recurring polarity of two heterogeneous spheres, namely
ethics and economics, intellect and trade, education and property."[13]

Since I cannot examine here all the different versions of deliberative
democracy, I will concentrate on the model developed by Habermas and
his followers. To be sure, there are several differences among the advocates of this new paradigm. But there is enough convergence among
them to affirm that none can deal adequately with the paradox of democratic politics.[14]

According to Seyla Benhabib, the main challenge confronting democracy is how to reconcile rationality with legitimacy. Or to put it
differently, the crucial question that democracy needs to address is, how
can the articulation of the common good be made compatible with the
sovereignty of the people? She presents the answer offered by the deliberative model in the following way: "legitimacy and rationality can be
attained with regard to collective decision-making processes in a polity
if and only if the institutions of this polity and their interlocking relationship are so arranged that what is considered in the common interest
of all results from processes of collective deliberation conducted rationally and fairly among free and equal individuals."[15]

The basis of legitimacy in democratic institutions derives in this view
from the fact that the instances which claim obligatory power do so on
the presumption that their decisions represent an *impartial standpoint*
which is *equally in the interests of all.* In order for this presumption to
be fulfilled those decisions must be the result of appropriate public processes of deliberation which follow the procedures of the Habermasian
discourse model. The basic idea behind this model is the following:

> [O]nly those norms, i.e., general rules of action and institutional
> arrangements, can be said to be valid which would be agreed to by
> all those affected by their consequences, if such agreement were
> reached as a consequence of a process of deliberation which has the
> following features:
>> a. participation in such deliberation is governed by the norms
>> of equality and symmetry; all have the same chance to initiate
>> speech acts, to question, interrogate, and to open debate;
>> b. all have the right to question the assigned topics of conversa-
>> tion;

c. all have the right to initiate reflexive arguments about the very rules of the discourse procedure and the way in which they are applied or carried out. There is no *prima facie* rule limiting the agenda or the conversation, nor the identity of the participants, as long as each excluded person or group can justifiably show that they are relevantly affected by the proposed norm under question.[16]

Let us examine this model of deliberative democracy closely. In their attempt to ground legitimacy on *rationality*, deliberative theorists have to distinguish between mere agreement and rational consensus. This is why they assert that the process of public discussion must realize the conditions of ideal discourse. And that requires living up to the values of fair procedure—impartiality, equality, openness, lack of coercion, and unanimity. The combination of these values in the discussion guarantees that its outcome will be legitimate since it will produce generalizable interests on which all participants can agree.

Habermasians do not deny that there will, of course, be obstacles to the realization of the ideal discourse, but these obstacles are conceived as *empirical* ones. They are due to the fact that it is unlikely, given the practical and empirical limitation of social life, that we will ever be completely able to leave aside all our particular interests in order to coincide with our universal rational self. This is why the ideal speech situation is presented as a regulative idea.

However, if we accept Schmitt's insight about the relations of inclusion/exclusion which are necessarily inscribed in the political constitution of 'the people'—which is required by the exercise of democracy—we have to acknowledge that the obstacles to the realization of the ideal speech situation—and to the consensus without exclusion that it would bring about—are inscribed in the democratic logic itself. Indeed the free and unconstrained public deliberation of all on matters of common concern goes against the democratic requisite of drawing a frontier between 'us' and 'them'. We could say—using this time a Derridean terminology—that the very conditions of possibility of the exercise of democracy constitute at the same time the conditions of impossibility of democratic legitimacy as envisaged by deliberative democracy. Consensus in a liberal democratic society is—and will always be—the expression of a hegemony and the crystallization of relations of power. The frontier that it establishes between what is and what is not legitimate is a political one and for that reason it should remain contestable.

To deny the existence of such a moment of closure or to present the frontier as dictated by rationality or morality is to naturalize what should be perceived as a contingent and temporary hegemonic articulation of the people through a particular regime of inclusion/exclusion. The result of such an operation is to reify the identity of the people by reducing it to one of its many possible forms of identification.

Pluralism and Its Limits

Because it postulates the availability of a consensus without exclusion, the model of deliberative democracy is unable to envisage liberal democratic pluralism in an adequate way. Indeed, one could indicate how, in both Rawls and Habermas—to take the best-known representatives of that trend—the very condition for the creation of consensus is the elimination of pluralism from the public sphere.[17] Hence the incapacity of deliberative democracy to provide a convincing refutation of Schmitt's critique of liberal pluralism. It is this critique that I will now examine in order to see how it could be answered.

Schmitt's best-known thesis is certainly that the criterion of the political is the friend/enemy distinction. Indeed, for him the political "can be understood only in the context of the ever present possibility of the friend-and-enemy grouping."[18] Because of the way this thesis is generally interpreted, he is often taken to task for having neglected the "friend" side of his friend and enemy opposition. However, we can find in his remarks on homogeneity many indications of how this grouping should be envisaged and this has important implications for his critique of pluralism.

Let us return to the idea that democracy requires political equality which stems from participation in a common substance—which, as we have seen, is what Schmitt means by the need for homogeneity. So far, I have stressed the necessity to draw a frontier between the us and the them. But we can also examine this question by focusing on the us and the nature of the bond that unites its components. Clearly, to assert that the condition of a possibility of an us is the existence of a them does not exhaust the matter. There can be different forms of unity established among the components of the us. To be sure, this is not what Schmitt believes since, in his view, unity can only exist as identity. But this is precisely where the problem lies with his conception. It is useful therefore to examine both the strengths and the weaknesses of his argument.

By asserting the need for homogeneity in a democracy, Schmitt is telling us something about the kind of bond that is needed for a democratic political community to exist. In other words, he is analyzing the nature of the friendship which defines the us in a democracy. This for him is, of course, a way of taking issue with liberalism for not recognizing the need for such a form of homogeneity and for advocating pluralism. If we take his target to be the liberal model of interest-group pluralism which postulates that agreement on mere procedures can assure the cohesion of a liberal society, he is no doubt right. The liberal vision of a pluralist society is certainly inadequate. Pluralism for liberals is not an axiological principle. It is limited to the representation in the public realm of the diversity of interests which already exists in society. In such a view, politics is reduced to a mere process of negotiation among interests whose articulation is anterior to political action. There is no place in such a model for a common identity of democratic citizens; citizenship is reduced to a legal status and the moment of the political constitution of the people is foreclosed. Schmitt's critique of that type of liberalism is convincing. And it is interesting to point out that it chimes both with Rawls's rejection in *Political Liberalism* of the modus-vivendi model of constitutional democracy because that model is very unstable and always revocable. It also chimes with Rawls's declaration that the unity the model creates is insufficient.

Once we have discarded the view that grounds unity in a mere convergence of interests and a neutral set of procedures, how, then, should we envisage the unity of a pluralist society? Is there no other type of unity compatible with the pluralism advocated by liberal societies? On this issue, Schmitt's answer is of course unequivocal: there is no place for pluralism inside a democratic political community. Democracy requires the existence of a homogeneous demos and this precludes any possibility of pluralism. This is why there is, in his view, an insurmountable contradiction between liberal pluralism and democracy. For him, the only possible and legitimate pluralism is a pluralism of states. Rejecting the liberal idea of a world state, he affirms that the political world is a pluriverse not a universe. In his view, "[t]he political entity cannot by its very nature be universal in the sense of embracing all of humanity and the entire world."[19]

In *The Concept of the Political*, taking as his target the kind of pluralism advocated by the pluralist school of Laski and Cole, Schmitt argues that the state cannot be considered as one more association among others, which would be at the same level as a church or a trade union. Against liberal theory, which aims to transform the state into a voluntary association through the theory of the social contract, he urges us to acknowledge that the political entity is something different and more decisive. For him, to deny this is to deny the political: "Only as long as the essence of the political is not comprehended or not taken into consideration is it possible to place a political association pluralistically on the same level with religious, cultural, economic, or other associations and permit it to compete with these."[20]

A few years later in an important article, "Staatsethik und pluralistischer Staat" (Ethics of the State and the Pluralist State), discussing again Laski and Cole, he notes that the actuality of their pluralist theory comes from the fact that it corresponds to the empirical conditions existing in most industrial societies. The current situation is one in which "the state appears as dependent on the diverse social groups, sometimes as their victim, sometimes as the result of their conventions: as a compromise among groups which possess social and economic power, an agglomerate of heterogeneous factors, of parties, interests groups, enterprises, trade-unions, churches, etc."[21] The state is therefore weakened and becomes some kind of clearing office, a referee between competing factions. Reduced to a purely instrumental function, it cannot be the object of loyalty and it loses its ethical role and its capacity for representing the political unity of a people. While deploring such a situation, Schmitt nonetheless admits that, as far as their empirical diagnosis is concerned, the pluralists have a point. The interest of their theory lies, in his view, in their ability "to take account of the concrete empirical power of social groups and of the empirical situation determined by the belonging of individuals to numerous social groups."[22]

Schmitt, it must be said, does not always see the existence of parties as being absolutely incompatible with the existence of an ethical state. In the same article, he even seems willing to admit the possibility of at least some form of pluralism that does not negate the unity of the state. But he quickly rejects this idea, declaring that it will inevitably lead to the type of pluralism that will dissolve the political unity. He says:

> When the state transforms itself in a pluralist state with parties, the unity of the state cannot survive beyond the moment when two or several parties are united by the acknowledgment of common premises. The unity then lies principally on the Constitution recognized by all the parties: in effect the Constitution, which is the common foundation, requires respect without conditions. The ethic of the state becomes then an ethic of the Constitution.

The substance, the univocity and the authority of the Constitution might in fact secure a very efficient unity. But it is also possible that the Constitution would dissolve itself by being reduced to the rule of the game and its ethic to a pure ethic of fair play; in the end, as pluralism destroys the unity of the political totality, the unity is finally reduced to a set of fluctuating agreements among heterogeneous groups. In such a case, the ethic of the Constitution dissolves even more and it becomes the ethic that can be reduced to the slogan: *Pacta sunt servanda.*[23]

Schmitt's False Dilemma

I think that Schmitt is right to stress the deficiencies of the kind of pluralism that negates the specificity of the political association, and I concur with his assertion that it is necessary to *politically* constitute the people. But I do not believe that this must commit us to denying the possibility of any form of pluralism within the political association. To be sure, liberal theory has so far been unable to give a convincing solution to this problem. This does not mean, however, that it is insoluble. In fact, Schmitt presents us with the following false dilemma. We can have unity of the people which requires expelling every division and antagonism outside the demos to the realm it needs to oppose in order to establish its unity. Alternatively, we consider some forms of division legitimate inside the demos and this will inexorably lead to the kind of pluralism which negates political unity and the very existence of the people. As Jean-François Kervégan points out, "For Schmitt . . . either the state imposes its order and its rationality on a civil society characterized by pluralism, competition and disorder, or, as it is the case in liberal democracy, social pluralism will empty the political entity of its meaning and bring it back to its other, the state of nature."[24]

What leads Schmitt to formulate such a dilemma is the way he envisages political unity. The unity of the state must, for him, be a concrete unity, already given and therefore stable. This is also true of the manner in which he envisages the identity of the people; it must also exist as a given. Because of that, his distinction between us and them is not really politically constructed; it is merely a recognition of already existing borders. While rejecting the pluralist conception, Schmitt is nevertheless unable to situate himself on a completely different terrain because he retains a view of political and social identities as empirically given. His position is, in fact, ultimately contradictory. On the one hand, he seems to seriously consider the possibility that pluralism could bring about the dissolution of the unity of the state. If that dissolution is, however, a distinctive *political* possibility, it entails also that the existence of such a unity is itself a contingent fact which requires a political construction. On the other hand, however, the unity is presented as a *fact* whose obviousness could ignore the political conditions of its production. It is only as a result of this sleight of hand that the alternative can seem as inexorable as Schmitt wants it to be.

What Schmitt fears most is the loss of common premises and the consequent destruction of the political unity which he sees as inherent in the pluralism that accompanies mass democracy. There is certainly a danger of this happening, and his warning should be taken seriously. But this is not a reason to reject all forms of pluralism. I propose to refuse Schmitt's dilemma, while acknowledging his point for the need of some form of homogeneity in a democracy. The problem we have to face becomes then how to imagine in a different way what Schmitt refers to as homogeneity.

In order to stress the differences with his conception, I will refer to this problem as the problem of commonality. How can we envisage a form of commonality strong enough to institute a demos but nevertheless compatible with certain forms of pluralism: religious, moral, and cultural pluralism as well as a pluralism of political parties? This is the challenge that engaging with Schmitt's critique forces us to confront. It is indeed a crucial one, since what is at stake is the very formulation of a pluralistic view of democratic citizenship.

I obviously do not pretend to provide a solution within the limits of this article, but I would like to suggest some lines of reflection. To offer a different—resolutely non-Schmittian—answer to the question of the compatibility of pluralism and liberal democracy requires, in my view, putting into question any idea of 'the people' as already given with a substantive identity. What we need to do is precisely that which Schmitt does not do. Once we have recognized that the unity of the people is the result of a political construction, we need to explore all the logical possibilities that a political articulation entails. Once the identity of the people—or rather its multiple possible identities—is envisaged as a political articulation, it is important to stress that, for it to be really a *political* articulation, and not merely the acknowledgment of empirical differences, such an identity of the people must be seen as the *result* of the political process of hegemonic articulation.

Democratic politics does not consist in the moment when a fully constituted people exercises its rule. The moment of rule cannot be dissociated from the very struggle about the definition of the people, about the constitution of its identity. Such an identity, however, can never be fully constituted and it can only exist through multiple and competing forms of *identifications*. Liberal democracy is precisely the recognition of this constitutive gap between the people and its various identifications. Hence the importance of leaving this space of contestation forever open, instead of trying to fill this gap through the establishment of a supposedly "rational" consensus.

To conceive liberal democratic politics in such a way is to acknowledge Schmitt's insight about the distinction between us and them, because this struggle about the constitution of the people always takes place within a conflictual field and implies the existence of competing forces. Indeed, there is no hegemonic articulation without the determination of a frontier, the definition of a them. But in the case of liberal democratic politics this frontier is an internal one and the them is not a permanent outsider. We can begin to realize therefore why such a regime requires pluralism. Without a plurality of competing forces who attempt to define the common good and aim at fixing the identity of the community, the political articulation of the demos could not take place. We would be in the field either of the aggregation of interests, or of a process of deliberation which evacuates the moment of decision. That is, as Schmitt pointed out, to place oneself in the field of economics or of ethics but not in the field of politics.

Nevertheless, by envisaging unity only under the mode of substantive homogeneity and by denying the possibility of pluralism within the political association, Schmitt was unable to grasp that there is another alternative open to liberals, one that could render viable the articulation between liberalism and democracy. What he could not conceptualize, because of the limits of his problematic, he deemed to be impossible. Since his objective was to attack liberalism, such a move is not surprising, but it certainly indicates the limits of his theoretical reflection.

Despite those shortcomings, Schmitt's questioning of liberalism is a very powerful one. It reveals several weaknesses of liberal democracy and brings to the fore its blind spot. Those deficiencies cannot be ignored. To elaborate a view of the democratic society which is both convincing and worthy of allegiance, these weaknesses have to be addressed. Schmitt is an adversary from whom we can learn because we can draw on his insights. Turning them against him, we should use them to formulate a better understanding of liberal democracy, one that acknowledges its paradoxical nature. Only by coming to terms with the double movement of inclusion/exclusion that democratic politics entails, can we deal with the challenge that the process of globalization confronts us with today.

Notes

1 John Rawls, *Political Liberalism* (New York: Columbia University Press, 1996), at lxi.
2 I would have thought that everybody was able to understand that it was possible to use, so to speak, Schmitt against Schmitt, i.e., to use the insights of his critique of liberalism in order to consolidate liberalism—while recognizing that this was, of course, not his aim. However, it does not seem to be the case since Bill Scheuerman in his book *Between the Norm and the Exception* (Cambridge, Mass.: MIT Press, 1994), at 8, criticizes me for presenting Schmitt as a theorist of radical pluralist democracy!
3 David Held, *Democracy and the Global Order* (Cambridge, Mass.: Polity Press, 1995).
4 Richard Falk, *On Human Governance* (Cambridge, Mass.: Polity Press, 1995), chap. 7.
5 Carl Schmitt, *The Crisis of Parliamentary Democracy* (Cambridge, Mass.: MIT Press, 1985), at 9.
6 Ibid., at 9.
7 Ibid., at 13.
8 Ibid., at 9.
9 Ibid.
10 Ibid., at 11.
11 Ibid., at 12.
12 I have made a similar argument concerning the tension that exists between the articulation of the liberal logic of difference and the democratic logic on equivalence in my discussion of Schmitt in *The Return of the Political* (London: Verso, 1993), chaps. 7 and 8.
13 Carl Schmitt, *The Concept of the Political* (New Brunswick, N.J.: Rutgers University Press, 1976), at 70.
14 For a critique of the Rawlsian model and its incapacity to acknowledge the *political* nature of the discrimination that it establishes between "simple" and "reasonable pluralism," see my article "Democracy and Pluralism: A Critique of the Rationalist Approach," 16 *Cardozo L. Rev.* 1995, 1533.
15 Seyla Benhabib, "Deliberative Rationality and Models of Democratic Legitimacy," *Constellations* 1 (1994): 30.
16 Ibid., at 31.
17 This, of course, takes place in a different way in both authors. Rawls rele-

gates pluralism to the private sphere, while Habermas screens it out, so to speak, from the public sphere through the procedures of argumentation. However, in both cases the result is the elimination of pluralism from the public sphere.

18 Schmitt, supra n. 13, at 35.
19 Ibid., at 53.
20 Ibid., at 45.
21 Carl Schmitt, "Staatsethik und pluralistischer Staat," *Kant-Studien* 35 (1930): 1, at 31.
22 Ibid., at 34.
23 Ibid., at 41.
24 Jean-François Kervégan, *Hegel, Carl Schmitt: Le Politique entre Spéculation et Positivité* (Paris: Presses Universitaires de France, 1992), at 259.

PART II

Legal Theory and Politics

Carl Schmitt on Sovereignty
and Constituent Power

Renato Cristi

Schmitt's *Verfassungslehre* stands as perhaps the most systematic and least circumstantial of his works. While his production is marked, on the whole, by an extraordinary sensitivity toward his own concrete situation, leading at one point to an unbounded and shameless opportunism, this particular work seems to rise above the political fray, reflecting possibly the mood of 1928, which marks the halcyon days of the Weimar Republic. Recently, Ernst-Wolfgang Böckenförde has tried to shake off the *Verfassungslehre* from its composed academic bearing by relating its argument to the polemical friend/enemy theory developed by Schmitt in his *Der Begriff des Politischen* (1927) and Schmitt's characterization of the state as the political unity of a nation. Beyond this, Böckenförde has connected the *Verfassungslehre* to the eminently partisan notion of sovereignty put forth by Schmitt in his *Politische Theologie* (1922), where he flaunts his allegiance to the Catholic counterrevolution.

One of the arguments presented by Böckenförde in support of his thesis has Schmitt's definition of sovereignty and the state as its locus. According to Schmitt's *Politische Theologie*, the state has "the monopoly of the ultimate decision."[1] This means that the essence of sovereignty, which he defines "not as the monopoly of domination or coercion, but as the monopoly of decision,"[2] is the ability to lift its subject above the legally constituted order. The decision Schmitt has in mind is an absolute decision, a decision "created out of nothingness."[3] The whole system of legality is thus relativized by a power that stands outside and above it.

I do not wish to dispute Böckenförde's contention that sovereignty is the key notion of Schmitt's conception of public law. My concern is that an important shift marks Schmitt's work during these years, a shift that determines a difference between the conception of sovereignty he held in 1922 and the one he held in 1928 when he published *Verfassungslehre*. In another place I have examined this shift with respect to the notions of liberalism and democracy.[4] Here I would like to extend my thesis to this aspect of Schmitt's work.

The first section of this essay examines the uninhibited view of sovereignty Schmitt develops in his *Politische Theologie*, a view which identifies it with the monarchical principle. In the second section, I compare this radical view to the apparently more balanced conception offered in his *Verfassungslehre*. Sovereignty is here redefined by superseding its identification with the monarchical principle. As a result, both monarchy and democracy can be interpreted as political forms that convey constituent activity. Schmitt, however, does not directly discuss the issue of sovereignty in this context. He tries to circumvent it because the constitutional theory of liberalism, the theory that defines the Weimar Constitution, avoids the issue of politics in general and sovereignty in particular. "It is characteristic of liberal constitutionalism to ignore the sovereign, whether this sovereign be the monarch or the people."[5] The ideal liberal constitution is defined exclusively in terms of the rule of law. Sovereignty, an essentially political notion, ought not, therefore, be given any recognition in a liberal constitution. In this section I show how Schmitt surmounts this liberal view by invoking the notion of constituent power, or *pouvoir constituant*. The third section discusses Schmitt's employment of constituent power as a surrogate for sovereignty. Sovereignty attains visibility only during exceptional situations. According to Schmitt, the destruction of the German Imperial Constitution in 1918 and the genesis of the Weimar Constitution in 1919—events where the *pouvoir constituant* of the people was determinant—expose the notion of sovereignty. Finally, the fourth section examines both the subject and the activity of constituent power to confirm its conceptual kinship with sovereignty. By refusing to develop a political theological interpretation of democracy and adopting a view on representation similar to that of Sieyès, Schmitt intends to take away from the *pouvoir constituant* of the people the fruits of sovereignty.

I

In his *Politische Theologie*, Schmitt attempts to define the notion of sovereignty. He observes that sovereignty no longer plays a role in the discussion of jurists and legal philosophers. A thick veil covers it, a veil that he is determined to pierce in order to expose its presence in political and legal affairs and documents. According to rule-of-law liberalism, power resides in the legal system itself and not in any personal authority representing the state. Schmitt opposes this view from the very start.

When Schmitt reviews the currently held opinions on sovereignty he observes that its commonly accepted definition—"sovereignty is the highest underived power of domination"[6]—is valid but too abstract. This formulation leaves out the crucial issue of its concrete application, namely *who* decides in cases of extreme conflict, when public order and security (*le salut public*) are in jeopardy. For some interpreters this definition appears to have a certain affinity with Bodin's definition—*"la souveraineté est la puissance absolue et perpétuelle d'une République."*[7] This view is incorrect for it ignores the context of Bodin's definition. His views are determined by the struggle for supremacy between the prince and the estates. Should the prince's promises to the estates or the people abrogate his sovereignty? There is a natural obligation to fulfill one's promises, but that duty expires *"si la nécessité est urgente."*[8] In such cases everything reverts to the decision of the prince. According to Schmitt, the novelty of Bodin's view consists in his ability "to incorporate the decision into the concept of sovereignty."[9] And that decision can only be left in the hands of the one person who can effectively ensure the unity of the state—the monarch.

After Bodin, the natural-law theorists of the seventeenth century, particularly Hobbes and Pufendorf, also understand sovereignty in terms of who decides on the state of exception.[10] The question about sovereignty reduces to the question about its subject, about *who* decides. "Who is competent when there is no clear provision of competence,"[11] in other words, who decides the extreme case? Two related illustrations offered by Schmitt prove most revealing. First he considers the so-called monarchical principle. The context that leads to its original formulation in 1814 has to do with the question of who is competent to decide in cases when the juridical order does not settle the matter of competence. Then he examines Article 48 of the Weimar Constitution, which bestows on the *Reichspräsident* the faculty to decide on the exception. In granting the *Reichspräsident* this "unlimited absolute power,"[12] this article addresses the question of sovereignty precisely as Schmitt would define it. Sovereignty falls into the hands of the *Reichspräsident* for he is the one who decides on the exception. In fact, Schmitt explicitly associates Article 48 with Article 14 of the French Charte of June 4, 1814,[13] the document that institutes the monarchical principle during the Restoration period and brings the true notion of sovereignty back to life.[14]

Schmitt also notices that during the sixteenth and seventeenth centuries, a theology that embraces the philosophical conception of God as the sole architect of the universe determines the notion of sovereignty. This is what he refers to as "political theology." The modern prince is a transposition of the Cartesian God to the political world. Schmitt quotes from one of Descartes's letters to Mersenne: "*c'est Dieu qui a établi ces lois en nature ainsi qu'un roi établit les lois en son royaume.*"[15] Hobbes, despite his nominalism and his attachment to science and a mechanistic view of nature, reveals the same politico-theological conception. His political views are still tied to a decisionist and personalist view of politics. The Leviathan is the "colossal person" postulated as the "ultimate concrete deciding instance."[16]

Schmitt's conceptual and historical analyses, which tie sovereignty to the exception, bringing out its decisionist and personalist elements, lead conclusively to one result—only an absolute monarch can be the proper subject of sovereignty. With Rousseau things change substantially. According to Schmitt, his identification of the will of the sovereign with the general will means that "the decisionist and personalist element in the hitherto existing concept of sovereignty is lost."[17] Henceforth, the unity displayed by the people loses "this decisionist character,"[18] and no democratic arrangement will be able to claim genuine sovereignty. The "political metaphysics" of democracy cannot claim political theological status. In a democratic setting "the theistic and the deistic idea of God is unintelligible."[19] Democracy in America, as Tocqueville saw it, still maintained that the voice of the people is the voice of God. Today a political philosopher like Kelsen can only "conceive of democracy as the expression of a relativist and impersonal scientism."[20] Political theology has become unthinkable within a democratic context.

In 1922, his memory still fresh with the revolutionary events in Germany, Schmitt evokes the counterrevolutionary thought of Juan Donoso Cortés. Donoso realizes in 1848 that "the epoch of royalism is over. There is no royalism any more, because there are no more kings."[21] In view of this exhaustion and extinction of legitimacy, Donoso advocates dictatorship. Hobbes arrives at a similar result, from similar decisionist premises—*auctoritas, non veritas, facit legem.* Laws are essentially commands. They are based on a decision concerning the interest of the state, and the state's foremost interest is that a decision be made. In *Die Diktatur*, Schmitt writes: "the decision on which a law is based is, normatively speaking, created out of nothingness."[22] But Hobbes does not go this far. Caught within a rationalist outlook, Hobbes understands the power of the sovereign to rest on a more or less tacit agreement of the people. Only Maistre is able to shake off that rationalist residue and radically negate the sovereignty of the people.[23]

Schmitt agrees with Maistre and Donoso Cortés that absolute monarchs are the proper subjects of sovereignty. Both in *Die Diktatur* and in *Politische Theologie* he dismisses the people as a legitimate and fitting subject of sovereignty. He does not fully perceive that democracy and the notion that sustains it, namely popular sovereignty, diverge substantially from liberalism, the slayer of sovereignty. Like his Catholic counterrevolutionary mentors, Schmitt sees no possible compromise with liberalism. Inspired by their counterrevolutionary conservatism, Schmitt contemplates but one alternative in 1922—a sovereign dictatorship as an effective surrogate for the monarchical principle.[24]

II

Schmitt's *Verfassungslehre* does not directly discuss the notion of sovereignty, even though its thoroughly systematic argument presupposes it. The reason why Schmitt needs to circumvent its discussion is brought forth in the preface to that work, dated December 1927. In it he distinguishes between the political element of a constitution and its properly liberal element, i.e., the principle of the rule of law. The constitutional theory of liberalism, the theory that determines the spirit of the Weimar Constitution and absorbs Schmitt's attention in this work, tries to skirt the political element as such, which is essentially related to sovereignty. The ideal liberal constitution is defined exclusively in terms of the rule of law; its aim is strictly to confine the political prerogatives claimed by the state. As Schmitt admits, the whole endeavor of a liberal constitution aims at marking off a sanctuary for individual freedom and disavowing the political disposition of the state. Sovereignty, an essentially political notion, therefore, ought not be given any recognition in a liberal constitution.

Despite the overtly liberal framework of the Weimar Constitution, Schmitt's political antennae have no difficulty in finding the traces of sovereignty in its makeup. The constitution did not descend from heaven ready-made, but owed its existence to a decision of the German people. The genesis of a constitution is the locus where sovereignty is manifested with greater clarity. Weimar liberalism was not self-sufficient and self-generated, but presupposed a political decision in its favor. Sovereignty could not be ascribed to a legal system itself. In 1919, a sovereign people had decided to confirm its national unity and define the mode of its political existence by means of a constitution. This was the absolute decision on which stood a now relativized positive constitution. Schmitt saw here an opening to reintroduce the theme of sovereignty. The idea of absolute monarchy, as the sole subject of sovereignty, had perished in 1918, but absolute democracy, supported by the sovereign *pouvoir constituant* of the people, had replaced it.

In his *Verfassungslehre*, Schmitt appears to have modified his initial views on liberalism and democracy. First, it was easy to expose the view held by liberals that politics and sovereignty had been decisively expelled from human affairs. In fact, a compromise had been struck between the ideals sponsored by liberals and the political decisions needed to make those ideals effective. The Weimar Constitution was a case in point. Schmitt, in his *Verfassungslehre*, wanted to prove that Weimar liberalism was in fact an instance of such a compromise. Second, Schmitt saw the need to modify the personalist and hard decisionist conception of sovereignty he held earlier in his *Politische Theologie*. Influenced by the views of the Catholic counterrevolution, he had envisaged absolute monarchy as the only possible embodiment of sovereignty. In 1923, with the publication of his *Parlamentarismus*, he came to realize that democracy was a political form of government that could also serve as a vehicle for sovereignty.[25] The notion of democracy did not include liberal relativism and the liberal distaste for the political. This meant a shift in his conception of sovereignty and a weakening of its personalist and hard decisionist aspects.[26]

These two considerations ease the way for a political reading of the Weimar Constitution. Alongside its liberal elements Schmitt now incorporates a political dimension. It is this rearticulation of liberal and political elements that determines the argumentative structure of the *Verfassungslehre*. An expanded view of sovereignty permits the concurrent adoption of the liberal rule of law. Schmitt shifts from an intransigent adherence to the conservative revolutionary themes he shared with Maistre and Donoso Cortés to a more flexible posture. He sees now the need to adopt an entente with liberalism. This implies a shift toward acceptance of a conservative reading of liberalism, a reading that does not reject sovereignty offhand, whether it be expressed monarchically or democratically.

The mistake of rule-of-law liberalism lies in its outright denial of sovereignty. But sovereignty, never fully repressed, always finds channels for its manifestation. "What has suffered the most under this fiction and this method of avoidance is the concept of sovereignty. In practice, apocryphal acts of sovereignty are exercised, which are characteristically performed by non-sovereign state officials or bodies who, occasionally and with tacit tolerance, make sovereign decisions."[27] The exercise of apocryphal acts of sovereignty described by Schmitt takes place at the margins of normal constitutional life. It manifests the marginal presence assigned to the notion of sovereignty in the *Verfassungslehre*. As he himself acknowledges, a discussion of sovereignty belongs formally to the "theory of sovereignty" (*Lehre von der Souveränität*) or a "general theory of the state,"[28] not to constitutional theory. In spite of this methodological demarcation of fields that excludes a consideration of sovereignty from constitutional theory, Schmitt finds a way to reintroduce it at the very core of the *Verfassungslehre*. Without explicit acknowledgment, he employs the notion of constituent power (*pouvoir constituant* or *verfassungsgebende Gewalt*) as its surrogate.

Constituent power functions as a legal notion and falls within the range of interest of public law. It does not immediately bring the political to mind, but it adequately supplants the notion of sovereignty. As Schmitt's exposition unfolds, it becomes clear that constituent power is indeed a political notion. Sovereignty *qua* constituent power comes into view most clearly at the moment when a constitution is generated. A constitution does not just fall from heaven ready-made. Its existence is dependent on concrete historical circumstances. Most importantly, it is subservient to the contingent political decisions which bring it to life. The notion of constituent power represents sovereignty as a concrete manifestation of the will. It is the best way to bring both monarchy and democracy under one generic notion. But, as was indicated above, the condition for Schmitt's employment of the notion of constituent power as a surrogate for sovereignty, is a shift in his conception of the latter. Hard decisionism and personalism meant that only monarchs could be genuine subjects of sovereignty. It is inconceivable to think that Schmitt would grant his allegiance to the views of Maistre, Bonald, and Donoso Cortés and, at the same time, favor the sovereignty to the people. But this is precisely what he does in his *Verfassungslehre*, which marks his shift away from hard decisionism and personalism, toward a new conception of sovereignty.

III

I will now train my attention on what Schmitt has to say about the notion of constituent power in his *Verfassungslehre*. My aim is to demonstrate that the acceptance of this notion certifies the presence of sovereignty in this treatise. According to Schmitt, sovereignty becomes visible only during exceptional circumstances. Its visibility rises to prominence when a constitution is destroyed and another is born. In these circumstances, sovereignty shows up under the guise of constituent power. A central portion of his *Verfassungslehre*, therefore, explores the genesis of the Weimar Constitution. Its aim is to leave the notion of sovereignty exposed.

The genesis of the German constitution of August 11, 1919, the Weimar Constitution, is the political and existential key to Schmitt's constitutional theory. He observes how the destruction of the German constitution of 1871 is attended by the abrogation of the *pouvoir constituant* that sustained it, that is, the constituent power of the monarch. According to Schmitt, this coincides with the revolutionary genesis of the new constitution, now animated by the constituent power of the German people. Schmitt's account of this constitutional genesis is guided by a basic principle: "within each political unity there can be only one subject of constituent power."[29] In his historical study of Germany's constitutional development, Schmitt brings to light and identifies this truly unique political subject. He thus distances himself from liberal constitutionalism which relegates the question concerning the subject of constituent power to the sidelines together with the question of sovereignty. This does not solve the issue but only postpones what Schmitt foresees as an unavoidable decision. During the German Revolution of 1918, and during situations of similar conflictive and critical nature, this question resurfaces, forcibly surpassing the dilatory compromises that had veiled it. According to Schmitt, a constitution "is based either on the monarchical or on the democratic principle."[30] Any attempt to avoid this political alternative by means of normativist fictions—the "sovereignty of the constitution," for instance—will miss "the fundamental political question concerning constituent power."[31]

During the revolutionary events of 1918, the German people assumed, according to Schmitt, the exercise of constituent power. This was manifested by the democratic election of a National Assembly commissioned to write a new constitution. This action by the German people implied the destruction of the German constitution of 1871 and the abrogation of the *pouvoir constituant* of the monarch. It is this transition from monarchical to democratic legitimacy and the reconstruction of this fundamental event that feeds and determines in large measure the historical matrix of Schmitt's political and juridical thought. In what follows I will examine Schmitt's account of the genesis of the Weimar Constitution. I will then analyze certain aspects of the notion of constituent power that show its kinship with sovereignty.

The genesis of the Weimar Constitution has to be understood in the context of Germany's constitutional monarchy and the revolution that abrogates it in November 1918. Schmitt differs from jurists like Laband, Jellinek, and Kelsen, who emphasized the constitutional aspects of Germany's constitutional monarchy, and relativized its political, in this case monarchical, aspects. They denied the possibility of identifying and designating a subject of state sovereignty. In accord with normativism, they considered that sovereignty rested abstractly on the constitution itself. Schmitt notes how the monarchical principle has been watered down by constitutionalist thinking. Monarchs are not perceived as subjects of their own will. The will of the state dissolves into parliamentary chatter. But in monarchical Germany, and here Schmitt follows Friedrich Julius Stahl's interpretation, "the constitutional monarch still retained real power, his personal will was still meaningful and could not be traced back to Parliament."[32] Under the influence of functionalist liberalism it was possible theoretically to avoid the issue of sovereignty and constituent power. But in practice, Schmitt writes, "it was possible to observe, in cases of conflict, who was the subject of state power and the representative of political unity able to decide: the monarch."[33] According to Schmitt, the German constitutional monarchy that survived until 1918 left the constituent power in the hands of the monarch.

After defeat in World War I and the kaiser's abdication, the social democrats proclaimed the Republic and on November 10, 1918, they formed a provisional government, exercised by a Council of the People's Commissars. This council summoned an Assembly of Representatives, representing the councils of workers and soldiers. This assembly decided to convoke a Constituent National Assembly, elected democratically on February 6, 1919. Those councils constituted only a provisional government. As Schmitt notes, "in every revolution a [provisional] government is formed until a new decision concerning the subject of constituent power is reached."[34] Subsequently, the councils of workers and soldiers transferred their power to this Constituent National Assembly which assumed the exercise of constituent power. Germany adopted then for the first time, observes Schmitt, the democratic doctrine of the constituent power of the people. He also notes how prewar liberal constitutionalism, "seen as a method of formalist evasion of the constituent power of the monarch,"[35] was incapable of registering this fact.

The Constituent National Assembly, which first met in Weimar on February 6, 1919, formulated the content of the political decision of the German people by means of constitutional proposals which would define its exercise. It was not, according to Schmitt, the subject of constituent power but merely its agent. While it exercised its commission, it had no legal or constitutional limitations. This is, according to Schmitt, the mark of a dictatorship. "The special circumstances of a Constituent Assembly which meets after the previous constitutional laws have been abolished may be more properly designated as a sovereign dictatorship."[36] No other limitations can determine it other than those that it imposes on itself. It does not have competencies or a limited range of attributions, and therefore cannot be interpreted as a commissarial dictatorship limited by preexisting legislation. Such an assembly is a sovereign dictatorship, but *qua* dictatorship it conducts its business only by mandate. It is not the sovereign itself, "but it always acts in its name and commissioned by the people, which at any moment may cancel the authority of its commissars by means of a political act."[37] The promulgation of the Weimar Constitution on August 19, 1919, ended the sovereign dictatorship of the German Constituent National Assembly.

The task embraced by Schmitt was to bring to light the political element that hid behind the thick normativist veil spread over the Weimar Constitution by liberalism. Schmitt knew that cases of conflict and constitutional emergencies would force the recognition of the real subject of state power, the real representative of political unity. It was in such situations that the notion of constituent power would expose the fundamental political dilemma: democratic or monarchical sovereignty.

This is the historical context of Schmitt's decision to bring up and employ the notion of constituent power. Schmitt defines it as "the political will whose power or authority is capable of adopting the concrete global decision on the mode and form of political existence."[38] This definition reveals Schmitt's rejection of juridical normativism, taken to formalist extremes by neo-Kantians like Kelsen. The grounds of a constitution are existential. A constitution can only rest on a concrete sovereign will and not on an abstract norm. In no way is the constituent will exhausted within the positive constitution itself. The sovereign constituent will, configured juridically as constituent power, continues to exist outside and above the constitution. A unified and indivisible existential dimension grounds the other powers of the state and it cannot be assimilated by or coordinated with them.

IV

The discussion in the *Verfassungslehre* on the subject of *pouvoir constituant* and its activity confirms its close conceptual kinship with sovereignty. Whether its subject be the monarch, the people, or a strong group within the state,[39] constituent power stands "outside and above" the constitution.[40] This is a feature it shares with sovereignty. Again, the activity of constituent power, which at one point Schmitt describes as a generating source, a *natura naturans*, approximates it to sovereignty.

Shifting away from what he had maintained in his *Politische Theologie*, Schmitt, in his *Verfassungslehre*, designates the people as a legitimate subject of constituent power and rejects the monarchical conception that legitimized the German constitution of 1871. It is after all the decision of the people that gave birth to the Weimar Constitution. In 1919 Germany had come to terms with the French Revolution and Sieyès's conception of the people as the subject of constituent power. Sieyès had lifted that notion above and beyond positive juridical forms. In agreement with this view, Schmitt underscores the foundational nature of constituent activity. Constituent power *qua* sovereign transcends the constitution; the manner of its activity cannot be prescribed constitutionally. Only when the decision of a sovereign people has been expressed may one regulate its formulation and execution.

At a certain point, Sieyès had tried to bestow on constituent power a metaphysical character. As *natura naturans*, constituent power was to remain in a state of nature. From this matrix ever new forms were bound to arise. Accordingly, constituent power was the ultimate ungenerated source of all forms, the unformed (*formlos*) form of all forms. Schmitt, however, disengages this metaphysical interpretation from constitutional theory proper. That interpretation, he admits, belongs to political theology. I see here an attempt on the part of Schmitt to distance himself from his earlier view which subsumed constitutional discussions under politico-theological considerations.

After considering the issue of the subject of constituent power, Schmitt analyzes its activity. Constituent power, like sovereign power, precedes and rises *legibus solutus* above all positive constitutional normativity. Its activity escapes constitutional bounds, just as any measure transcends what is measured by it. In the case of sovereign monarchs, their activity could include the unilateral granting of constitutional charters. At times, prudence dictated that monarchs reach agreements with the representatives of special interests. But this did not imply a renunciation of their sovereignty. In democratic polities, the people exercises its constituent power by means of any manifestation which conveys its express will. According to Schmitt, the people as such is not a firm and organized entity, and not endowed *prima facie* with permanent authority. Even if its power and plastic energy cannot be extinguished and may embody an infinite variety of forms, the people is not an organized subject of decision. This is the reason for its weakness and may explain why its actual will may be falsified.

Constituent activity persists autonomously and independently from any positive constitutional legislation. This is an indication of sovereignty. Constituent power cannot be destroyed, changed, or altered in any way; it perseveres as the extra-constitutional ground of constitutions and constitutional laws. It is not exhausted by its exercise and "retains the ability to persevere in its existence."[41] The positive constitution, as an accident supported by constituent power, may be born, suffer alterations, and eventually die, but alongside and above it the *pouvoir constituant* continues to exist.

Two radical situations envisaged by Schmitt confirm the tie between constituent power and sovereignty. In the first place, it is possible that a constitution may be destroyed (*Verfassungsvernichtung*). During revolutionary situations, not only the constitution and the organs of constitutional legislation, but also the species of constituent power may be destroyed.[42] Schmitt considers the case of the German constitution of 1871, which was in effect destroyed by the 1918 Revolution. In a case like this, the destruction affects the constitution and the specific form attained by the constituent power that sustains it. One should stress that it is not the constituent power itself that perishes. In no case, not even in the most extreme political situation, may the substance of power, i.e., constituent power itself, be destroyed. What happened in Germany was that one subject of constituent power was replaced by another subject: the constituent power of the people substituted that of the monarch. Second, Schmitt refers to the abrogation of a constitution (*Verfassungsbeseitigung*). In this case a constitution is rescinded but there is no destruction of the *pouvoir constituant* that sustained it. A constitution, which rises from an act of *pouvoir constituant* derives from it and does not itself bear within it "the continuity of the political unity."[43] The latter task falls on the *pouvoir constituant*, the ultimate foundation of a constitution.

Destruction and abrogation of a constitution, the two most drastic manifestations of constituent power, confirm its conceptual kinship with the notion of sovereignty. In his *Verfassungslehre*, Schmitt is willing to concede what he earlier rejected in his *Politische Theologie*, namely democracy, and not only monarchy, as an expression of political absolutism. This, however, should not be regarded as proof of his democratic conversion. On the contrary, faced with a democratic revolution that was willing to appeal to the constituent power of the people, Schmitt attempts to disarm it by acknowledging and revitalizing an old adversary—the liberal ideal of the rule of law. Schmitt's *Verfassungslehre* is a careful balancing act, one which tries to offset opposed principles. The liberal rule-of-law component ought to neutralize the political democratic component and vice versa.

The recognition of the democratic political form and its constituent power has a price which Schmitt is eager to exact—the reintroduction of the theme of sovereignty as a legitimate theme for constitutional discussion. He now feels that he too can point out, without misgivings, what he calls "apocryphal acts of sovereignty." These sovereign actions set in motion the activity of constituent power in the daily ordeal of constitutional business. They take place, for instance, when particular constitutional norms are violated. Of themselves, such violations do not imply the destruction or suppression of the constitution as a whole. On the contrary, such cases confirm constitutional validity. According to Schmitt, particular constitutional norms are violated in order to safeguard the substance of a constitution. Those violations are only "measures"[44] and not constitutional norms. They are justified by particular exceptional and abnormal transitory situations. What these situations demonstrate is the "superiority of the existential over mere normativity."[45] They force the recognition of sovereignty. Sovereignty manifests itself when the legal order is violated. According to Schmitt, the sovereign is whoever has the faculty to violate, and thus relativize, the legal order as a whole. An absolute form of government, monarchical or democratic, implies a sovereign prince or sovereign people who stand *legibus solutus*, above the law. By contrast, the purpose of the liberal ideal is to subject the power of the state to the rule of law and expel sovereignty from its domain. For Schmitt, this ideal of absolute normativity constitutes a tenuous fiction. The political and the state cannot be simply erased by legal fabrications and methods of avoidance.

Acts of sovereignty will inevitably occur. But "these acts of inevitable sovereignty"[46] are better justified when they are seen as grounded on the constituent power of the people.

One should note that Schmitt's aversion to democracy is not superseded by his recognition of democratic sovereignty in the *Verfassungslehre*. On the contrary, he intends to make sure that once in power democracy can be more easily restrained than enhanced.[47] Thus, like Sieyès, he tied the doctrine of the *pouvoir constituant* of the people to the antidemocratic principle of representation.[48] According to Sieyès, the sovereignty of the people was to be delegated to their elected representatives, who in turn were not to act as popular commissars or agents. Rejection of an imperative mandate allowed the assembled representatives to assume, with autonomy and independence, what Sieyès considered to be the ultimate expression of sovereignty—the exercise of constituent power. In Hobbesian fashion, Sieyès fused sovereignty and representation together, but with a difference. The people, acknowledged Sieyès, never leave the state of nature. The delegation of sovereignty was only temporary and could legitimately be reclaimed at any time. This was supported by his metaphysical conception of the *pouvoir constituant* as an inexhaustible *natura naturans*. By contrast, Schmitt, in his *Verfassungslehre*, distinguishes the "positive doctrine" from the "metaphysics" of *pouvoir constituant*. The latter belongs to the "doctrine of political theology,"[49] which ascertains a "completely systematic and methodical analogy" with Spinoza's view on the relation between *natura naturans* and *natura naturata*.[50] Conscious of the radical weapons that a political theological conception of sovereignty can place at one's disposal, Schmitt denies these weapons to democracy. In his *Verfassungslehre*, he comes to accept and recognizes the *pouvoir constituant* of the people only because he has found a way to disarm it.

Notes

This essay was originally a paper read at a session of the 17th IVR World Congress held in Bologna in 1995. This was facilitated by a travel grant from Wilfrid Laurier University. For comments and suggestions I owe thanks to Heiner Bielefeldt, John McCormick, and William Scheuerman. I am particularly indebted to David Dyzenhaus for his commentaries and editorial help.

1 Carl Schmitt, *Politische Theologie. Vier Kapitel zur Lehre von der Souveränität* (Munich and Leipzig: Duncker & Humblot, 1922), at 20.

2 Ibid., at 20. See Ernst-Wolfgang Böckenförde, "Der Begriff des Politischen

als Schlüssel zum Staatsrechtlichen Werk Carl Schmitts," in Helmut Quaritsch, ed., *Complexio Oppositorum. Über Carl Schmitt* (Berlin: Duncker & Humblot, 1988), at 287.

3 Ibid., at 83. See Carl Schmitt, *Die Diktatur. Von den Anfängen des modernen Souveränitätsgedankens bis zum proletarischen Klassenkampf* (Munich and Leipzig: Duncker & Humblot, 1928), at 23.

4 See Renato Cristi, "Carl Schmitt on Liberalism, Democracy and Catholicism," *History of Political Thought* 14 (1993): 281, at 282–300.

5 Carl Schmitt, *Verfassungslehre* (Berlin: Duncker & Humblot, 1965), at 244.

6 Supra n. 1, at 12.

7 Ibid., at 13.

8 Ibid., at 14.

9 Ibid.

10 Ibid., at 15. Schmitt refers the matter to what he had written earlier on the state of exception. See *Die Diktatur*, supra n. 3, at 22–24.

11 Ibid., at 16. In *Die Diktatur*, Schmitt takes Hobbes and Pufendorf to be supporters of "scientific natural law [*wissenschaftliche Naturrecht*]" and opponents of the "natural law of justice [*Gerechtigkeitsnaturrecht*]" tradition. For them the issue is not the content of a decision, but only that a decision be effectively made; the real question is *who* adjudicates and *who* has the power to decide. See *Die Diktatur*, supra n. 3, at 21–24.

12 Ibid., at 18.

13 In his *Politische Theologie*, supra n. 1, at 18, Schmitt refers to "the Charte of 1815." This is obviously a misprint. In *Die Diktatur*, supra n. 3, at 193, he correctly identifies it as the Charte of 1814 and transcribes its Article 14: "*Le Roi est le chef suprême de l'état, il commande les forces de terre et mer, déclare la guerre . . . et fait les règlements et ordonnances nécessaires pour l'exécution des lois et la sûreté de l'état.*"

14 Erich Kaufmann maintains that the monarchical principle, defined as "*l'autorité préexistant du roi, supérieur et antérieur à l'acte constitutionnel,*" was first introduced by the Charte of 1814. See Erich Kaufmann, *Studien zur Staatslehre des monarchischen Prinzipes* (Leipzig: Oscar Brandstetter, 1906), at 38.

15 Supra n. 1, at 61.

16 Ibid., at 61.

17 Ibid., at 62.

18 Ibid.

19 Ibid., at 62–63.

20 Ibid., at 63.

21 Ibid., at 65–66.

22 *Die Diktatur*, supra n. 3, at 23.

23 Ibid.

24 In *Die Diktatur*, Schmitt develops the notion of sovereign dictatorship

based on the traditional role played by Roman commissarial dictators. While their function was the preservation of the constitutional order, the aim of a sovereign dictator is the elimination of "the whole existing order" and the generation of a new constitution, one thought to be the true constitution. "An appeal is thus made to the constitution that will be enacted, not to the one that actually exists" (ibid., at 137). This abrogation of the existing order translates into the adoption of a revolutionary stance whereby sovereign dictators place themselves above the constitution. It would appear that this is a purely political move, completely "devoid of juridical value" (ibid., at 137). But, according to Schmitt, what lies above and beyond a constitutional system is not purely a *Machtfrage*. A sovereign dictator appeals to a power that even if not constituted ought to be seen as the "foundation" of a constitution. "This is the meaning of the *pouvoir constituant*" (ibid., at 137) which allows one to transpose the limits of a legal system without crossing over the limits of the juridical. Schmitt's sovereign dictator borrows from the juridical status that attaches to commissarial dictators. Contrary to McCormick, who claims that the aim of *Die Diktatur* is to argue for the functional nature of temporary dictatorship, it seems to me that Schmitt here promotes the notion of sovereign dictatorship by upholding its juridical value. See John P. McCormick, "The Dilemmas of Dictatorship: Carl Schmitt and Constitutional Emergency Powers," in this volume.

25 I discuss this issue in "Carl Schmitt on Liberalism, Democracy and Catholicism," supra n. 4.

26 Schmitt's constant preference for a strong state was not challenged by this acceptance of monarchy *and* democracy as legitimate forms of government. In his *Verfassungslehre*, supra n. 5, at 236, he recognizes that democracy may be stronger and more decisive than monarchy.

27 *Verfassungslehre*, supra n. 5, at xii.

28 Ibid., at xii.

29 Ibid., at 53.

30 Ibid., at 54.

31 Ibid.

32 Ibid., at 289. According to Kaufmann, the monarchical principle is the pivotal concept of Friedrich Julius Stahl's political philosophy. See *Studien zur Staatslehre des monarchischen Prinzipes*, supra n. 14, at 80.

33 Ibid., at 56.

34 Ibid., at 58.

35 Ibid., at 57.

36 Ibid., at 59. See Pasquale Pasquino, "Die Lehre vom 'pouvoir constituant' bei Emmanuel Sieyès und Carl Schmitt," in Helmut Quaritsch, ed., *Complexio Oppositorum. Über Carl Schmitt* (Berlin: Duncker & Humblot, 1988), at 379.

37 Ibid., at 60.

38 Ibid., at 75.

39 Schmitt conceives of a third possible subject of constituent power, different from the monarch and the people. A minority may also be a subject of constituent power, and a state where this happens "has an aristocratic or oligarchic form of government" (ibid., at 81). Schmitt is not thinking of a quantitative or electoral minority. Such a minority, or political party or faction, cannot be a subject of constituent power. Only a "firm organization" (ibid., at 81) may be in the position of generating a constitution by means of its constituent power. Schmitt visualizes a circle of powerful families, as was the case in the Middle Ages, or a corporate order, such as the Soviets in the Soviet Union or the fiasco in Italy. He does not allude to a nation's armed forces, but surely they fit this scheme of things. At the same time, Schmitt admits that the theoretical construction that attributes constituent power to a minority "is not yet clear." An ambiguity encumbers the notion of a minority or an aristocratic group *qua* subject of constituent power. In cases like this, "there is no definitive renunciation to invoking the will of the people, for whose true and unfalsified expression one ought first to create the preconditions" (ibid., at 82). One should also say that to contemplate the possibility of this third kind of constituent power, implies, on the part of Schmitt, an exploration of the putschist possibilities of revolutionary conservatism. See Renato Cristi, "La noción de Poder constituyente en Carl Schmitt y la génesis de la Constitución chilena de 1980," *Revista Chilena de Derecho* 24 (1993): 229.

40 Ibid., at 242.

41 Ibid., at 92.

42 Ibid., at 94.

43 Ibid., at 93.

44 Ibid., at 107.

45 Ibid.

46 Ibid., at 108.

47 See Stefan Breuer, "Nationalstaat und pouvoir constituant bei Sieyès und Carl Schmitt," *Archiv für Rechts- und Sozialphilosophie* 70 (1984): 510.

48 Supra n. 5, at 80. See Jean-François Kervégan, *Hegel, Carl Schmitt. Le politique entre spéculation et positivité* (Paris: Presses Universitaires de France, 1992), at 306.

49 Ibid.

50 *Die Diktatur*, supra n. 3, at 142.

The 1933 "Break" in Carl Schmitt's Theory

Ingeborg Maus

New Introductory Comments

The following article begins by engaging in a debate with the literature on Carl Schmitt, a literature whose most obvious feature is its age. Nevertheless, the comprehensive engagement with Carl Schmitt's work which has appeared in the meantime has not in every respect advanced our knowledge in the area discussed in this article, because its attention is chiefly focused on other matters. But that in itself indicates a problem.

Biographies rich in detail, neglecting nothing in large archival holdings which are now accessible, have worked through hitherto unknown facts about Schmitt's development and his later entanglement in the Nazi system. Overall, interest in Schmitt's writings is today greatly on the rise. However, the more recent reception of Schmitt is characterized by its neglect of his main works which are in legal theory. The ever potential difference between the self-understanding of the author and the objective intention of his work is hardly acknowledged in the biographical reductionism, so that one believes that one can find the "key" to Schmitt's work in his diary entries, his emphatic profession of Catholicism, and his opinions on actual politics. In this fashion, Schmitt's theory is either reduced to an option based on political theology or understood as a whole in terms of his relationship to National Socialism. Both biographical interpretations treat him as an exotic exceptional case. Even the newer research which is oriented to Schmitt's works often misses the central content of his theory in limiting its focus mainly to the pamphlets with which he reached a wider public — for example, *The Concept of the Political, Political Theology*, and his critique of parliamentarism. It is, however, this limitation to the superficially "political" writings that has the effect of depoliticizing the topic.

It obscures the continuities which persist in legal theory beyond time-bound circumstances and hinders an appreciation of the ambivalences of *contemporary* legal theory and practice. This selective reception of Carl Schmitt also ensures that the already severely limited capacity to learn by dealing with the National Socialist past is left untouched.

What then is the continuity in legal theory and practice which helps to explain the actual though very equivocal topicality of Carl Schmitt? In his main theoretical works, Schmitt found the cause of the functional problems of modern parliaments in the necessary adaptation of state activity and the legal structure to the changed economic conditions of the twentieth century. The state's engagement in permanent economic crisis management requires possibilities for intervention which are situation-bound and oriented to single cases. And that brings the state into conflict with its bond to "standing" and general laws—that is, the output of parliament. Schmitt reacted to this accurately diagnosed tension between the traditional legal formalism of the nineteenth century and the function of the state in the twentieth by polemically playing his highly indeterminate concepts of law and constitution against the positive (statute) law and against the written content of constitutions. Since, according to Schmitt, all law, even though statutorily enacted, is constituted only in the concrete situation of application, he founded a legal theory that serves the economic conditions of activity of every modern state as well as the more specific needs of a political system of terror. This theory offers the political system the legitimation for permitting the content of the law to be defined in each single case by all the branches of the state, including the judiciary. And thus is first implemented the absolute discretion and discrimination of individuals and groups in accordance with the political situation, something altogether typical of the National Socialist system. This fundamental ambivalence of Schmitt's legal theory is what more than anything else makes it understandable that it could make headway in the Weimar Republic as well as in the National Socialist system and that it was from the outset, despite changing fashions of its reception, also the secret dominant legal theory of the Federal Republic, particularly of the Constitutional Court.

This idea of a dynamic and deformalized law for which Schmitt gave a theoretical foundation is today what we have in practice in all spheres of the law. At present, constitutional courts, especially that of the Federal Republic, use methods of interpretation in all spheres which permit them to determine the content of the constitution in accordance with the pending individual case. At the same time as they adapt constitutions to the dynamic legal structure which is suited to administrative activity oriented to single cases, they rob the written constitutions of the very function for which the bourgeoisie of the eighteenth century went to the barricades. The constitution is no longer the normative standard by which citizens can measure the conformity of state conduct to the constitution. On the contrary, it serves to empower and legitimate the state apparatus in programming itself. Even the courts which review administrative action have increasingly lost their grip on the positive legal criteria for such review, and the decisions of the ordinary courts, especially in civil cases, can hardly be predicted. The deformalization of law is today even entrenched in legal norms themselves. For example, environmental law typically contains the legislature's declarations of purpose and delegates every detail to the application process of the law. As a result, in the actual negotiations between the administrative agency and the industry which is burdening the environment, industry's ability to make threats in regard to choice of location and job creation gives it the upper hand on the declared purposes of the law.

This deformalization of law brings wholly into question the subjection of the state apparatus to democratically produced law, and thereby the functional requirements of parliamentary systems. Political systems, on the other hand, which concede a large sphere to judicial development of the law also change their character because of the deformalization of law. The calculability of the rule of law, which was guaranteed in the context of the classical precedential culture, is eroded in the degree to which the "princely judge" of the Free Law Theory, but also of Legal Realism or of the Critical Legal Studies Movement, takes center stage.[1] It is eroded even when a situation-bound application of law is desired in order to compensate for conservative legislation. Increasingly a method of solving problems is accepted which treats the structural conditions of control set by democracy and the rule of law as irrelevant.

In view of these general tendencies, it follows that when Carl Schmitt (as increasingly happens) is cited approvingly for his well-known authoritarian options, this means more an intensification than a qualitative difference. The strong state as guarantor of an economy liberated from all social responsibilities is again in demand. Forgotten are the facts about the most extreme implementation of this correlation in National Socialism, which were recorded in the OMGUS (Office of Military Government for Germany) reports by an American occupying power by no means hostile to capitalism.[2] Conversely, the priority of all problems stemming from the globalization of the economy over those of the institutionalization of democracy and the rule of law is so widely recognized that, adopting wholly Schmitt's perspective, the complexity of, and demands on time by, democratic procedures appear more as impediments. And since 1989[3] one even finds doubt cast on the main prize for which authoritarian state socialism was fought—the democratic control of political power.

Introduction

An interpretation of Carl Schmitt's theory[4] which assumed a complete turnaround in its intentions after 1933 would gain Schmitt's own approval. In 1958 he emphasized that "[m]y conceptions of constitutional law are . . . not an *ex post* function of retrospectives from later, structurally different situations, which have only arisen from the collapse of Weimar legality."[5] So Schmitt himself denies any continuity in this thinking before and after 1933, suggesting that his theory had always been a simple reflection of the constitutional reality of both Weimar and National Socialism, free of any expression of his personal preferences or position. He puts forward the absolute situational conditionality of his theories to exonerate himself, with the consequence that responsibility for those theories comes to lie abstractly in the situation itself.

Schmitt claims to have "never participated" in the "talk about the state of emergency" since he believed that in the time immediately preceding January 30, 1933, the "legal possibilities" of the Weimar Constitution "had by no means been exhausted."[6] But from the outset Schmitt had surrendered the substance of the Weimar Constitution (as well as its concept of legality, a term mentioned not merely in passing here) by relying on the postulate of legitimacy in order to reinterpret the constitutional order in accordance with the dictates of a presidential dictatorship. The difference between the kind of system he was propagating and the openly criminal system of National Socialism—in relation to which he later accommodated himself—may be counted in Schmitt's favor. But more important is the agreement in social functions of the two political systems which Schmitt seems to have considered as the only alternatives to Weimar in 1933. This correspondence is expressed with unusual clarity in Schmitt's theory.

It is the continuity of the social function of this political theory that underlies and ultimately survives all the situation-specific modifications of Schmitt's juristic constructs. Precisely because this social agenda realized itself to some extent in 1933, the continuity of Schmitt's position becomes clear in the transition from Schmitt's at first negative and then affirmative relationship to National Socialism.

Hasso Hofmann correctly describes Schmitt's work as neither an unproblematic unity, nor as a conglomerate of unrelated positions, but as characterized by steady and uninterrupted development.[7] Nevertheless, Hofmann seeks the underlying logic of this development almost exclusively in Schmitt's juristic constructs. By undertaking an immanent exposition of Schmitt's juristic constructs and by assuming that the driving forces behind their modification were "merely legal-theoretical reasons,"[8] Hofmann's interpretation disregards the true core of Schmitt's theory and contributes to its depoliticization. Building on von Krockow's comments to the same effect,[9] Hofmann correctly states that it is impossible to uncover the underlying intention of Schmitt's work by systematically looking at it as a homogeneous, ahistorical entity[10] or by understanding it as constituting a premature choice in favor of National Socialism.[11] Nor can we grasp its core by working out the contradictions between its pre-1933 and post-1933 phases, whereby the charge of ruthless opportunism is likely to be raised.[12] The first interpretation exaggerates the continuity of Schmitt's theory by trying to find such continuity within Schmitt's juristic constructs; the second interpretation robs Schmitt's theory of any coherence whatsoever.

Although Hofmann then promises to deliver a historical presentation of Carl Schmitt's theory, he understands history exclusively as the history of Schmitt's thinking. Hofmann disqualifies references to the reality of social history as merely biographical in character.[13] He appropriates Schmitt's "conceptual-sociological" method and undertakes a search for the "metaphysical formula" of Schmitt's theory and its "irreducible basic positions." By doing this and by understanding Schmitt's theory as "part of a development which transcends individual fate" which "ought to be called tragic,"[14] Hofmann approaches Schmitt's own self-understanding, even though this may be contrary to his intentions. Admittedly, Hofmann does not simply deduce Schmitt's developmental phases from the logic of a series of concrete "situations." Instead, he reflects on the situational dependency of Schmitt's thinking "in general." But even if it is true, as in Hofmann's account, that this situational dependency results purely from the discrepancy between normativity (*Normativität*) and disturbed normalcy (*gestörte Normalität*), it is still the case that Hofmann makes Schmitt's work into a simple—and the only possible—consequence of disturbed normalcy.

In what follows, a demonstration of the uniform social function of

Schmitt's theory in its apparently contradictory juristic arguments before and after 1933 will be attempted. These contradictory arguments
include Schmitt's insistence until the end of the Weimar Republic on
the postulate of the generality of law, while later he approved of the
individual measures (*Massnahmegesetze*) of the Nazi government, and
the fact that at a certain point in time Schmitt's decisionistic theoretical phase was followed by a "theory of concrete order" (*konkretes
Ordnungsdenken*), a set of constructions related to a special modification of the pluralism of the Weimar system.

I

Schmitt's deliberations in the Weimar period strictly distinguished between a rational concept of law and a voluntaristic concept of measures.
In an early piece from his normative phase, however, both *ratio* and
voluntas are united in the concept of law.[15] At this point, though, the
rationality of law does not yet refer to its general applicability, but rather
to the realization of a supra-empirical "reasonable" norm. At the same
time, the voluntaristic character of law results from its concrete realization through governmental lawmaking (*staatliche Rechtssetzung*) as
such,[16] which gives every law a moment of "indifference in relation to
its content" (*inhaltliche Indifferenz*).[17] While the normative component
of law is rendered exempt from the material demands which merely
"empirical" individuals raise in relation to the state, it is precisely the
empirical-decisionistic moment of law that also serves to enforce the
law effectively against individual claims; without regard to whether
the content of a law is right, especially in this situation, "it has to be
taken into account that the weak, first and foremost, need and want to
know where they stand."[18] Both moments of this concept of law thus
rescue the "supra-personal dignity of the state" from an interpretation
of it as a mere "institution for security" (*Sekuritätsanstalt*) or "welfare
organization" (*Wohlfahrtseinrichtung*).[19] In particular, the accentuation
of law's decisionistic moment[20] is directed against the realization of
concrete social demands and claims, which already are characterized so
as to suggest traces of the Hobbesian version of the conflict between
narrow-minded egoism and raw instincts. This decisionistic moment is
then emphasized in Schmitt's subsequent argumentation to the extent
that popular social demands are formulated more intensely and gain
an ever more impressive organizational expression, and as the inclusion of reformist Social Democracy into the pluralistic Weimar system

seems to constitute nothing less than the challenge of "civil war" to a bewildered bourgeoisie.[21] Ultimately, this process culminates in an absolute claim in favor of purely instrumental-rational individual measures (*zweckrationale Massnahmen*). So only during times of crisis does the Hobbesian formula Schmitt permanently cites hold true: *auctoritas non veritas facit legem.*

Nevertheless, Schmitt does not abandon the normative component of his original concept of law. Instead, it reappears in modified form. At first, the fact that after 1918 the Reichstag not only participated in lawmaking, but monopolized it, corresponded to Schmitt's distribution of the two moments of law to two different institutional bodies: the *ratio* of the law now refers to the law's generality with regard to the legislature; the moment of *voluntas* is reserved for the executive which decides on measures. In the strict distinction between a liberal-constitutional (*rechtsstaatliche*) and a political concept of law in the 1928 *Verfassungslehre*[22] (which has often been misunderstood as an affirmative description of the Weimar constitutional system), the basic function of this distribution is already anticipated. While in Schmitt's 1914 *Der Wert des Staates und die Bedeutung des Einzelnen* the decisionistic element essential to the realization of law was interpreted as an "act of sovereign decision-making,"[23] now the demand he makes on parliament to limit itself to the liberal-constitutional concept of law (which no longer refers merely to the equality of application, but also to an equality of content) reveals itself as a polemical move against the dreaded "sovereignty of parliament." Weimar legal positivism unconditionally endorsed the increasing expansion of merely formal laws and thereby a considerable increase in the authority of a legislature no longer controlled exclusively by the bourgeoisie; in contrast, Schmitt displaces this thoroughly "political" concept of law, one which circumscribes the measure, to the "center" of state sovereignty, which manifests itself as such in political conflicts: the executive. It is the executive which during a crisis then enforces the "moment of indifference in relation to the content" of law when the ratio or rightness of law cannot be determined.

The affinity of an executive acting in a purely decisionistic and instrumental-rational fashion to the state of emergency reveals what type of government Schmitt's theory unambiguously endorses in this phase—especially in light of Schmitt's description of the Weimar situation as an "economic-financial state of emergency."[24] This type of state corresponds to the principle that Schmitt projects upon the absolutist state seen as capable of bringing civil war to a close, "a state of the executive and the government," exclusively aimed at achieving a maximal degree of effectiveness; he describes it as a state that "produces public order and security."[25] What we have here is a state ruling by means of individual measures and legitimating itself through a permanent state of emergency: the perfect emergency regime.

Thus, it is hardly contradictory that Schmitt called for the Weimar parliament to respect the principle of the generality of law. The formal rationality of law, which was beneficial to the bourgeois interests of an individualistic competitive capitalism,[26] was already modified during the Weimar period. The increasing concentration of economic power reduced the importance of general laws, which had presumed a situation with approximately equal economic competitors. In correspondence to these changed economic conditions, measures that made individual regulations possible in the face of individual monopolies became more common.[27] Similarly, the pluralistic differentiation of those addressed by the law eliminated the preconditions for the abstract generality of law. The entanglement of state and economy and the growing tendency toward state intervention in the economy necessitated the firm organization of societal demands on the state. The heterogeneity of group demands was reflected in the specialization of legislative content. The same process, which Max Weber had analyzed before World War I in his discussion of the changing nature of legal and administrative practice, was repeated here on the level of lawmaking itself. At least insofar as it possessed progressive traits, the Free Law School (*Freirechtslehre*) had permitted the recognition of the material demands for social justice by underprivileged groups against a merely formal rationality of law. At the same time, however, this conception of law had made it less predictable.[28] Now, material demands for justice penetrated legislation itself and critically modified the laws. The absolute character of the formal concept of law ("the law is anything that a parliament has passed"), which Schmitt caricatures, was an attempt to take changed social and economic conditions into consideration. This trend did not surrender the predictability of law because individual measures were not simply put at the discretion of the administration or monopolized in the hands of the executive; instead, measures were still undertaken in the form of parliamentary law. This becomes obvious when considering the fact that formally equal law makes unequal addressees of the law more unequal, rather than equal; as a consequence, a differentiation of content becomes necessary. The rationality of law in Weimar manifested itself in the fact that Weimar legislation benefited societal groups that had previously been underprivileged. Thus, the legal system of the Weimar period achieved a high degree of rationality; it became "rational : . . in an eminently social sense, as well."[29]

In the face of a situation in which Schmitt himself insists on the necessity of individual measures, he demands that parliament limit itself to general laws in the sense that the postulate of equality contained in Article 109 of the Weimar Constitution is not only binding on the judiciary and the administration, but also on the legislature; equal application of the law no longer suffices. (It is not accidental that the necessity of this self-limitation is discussed by Schmitt with reference to the possibility of expropriation measures.)[30] More is at stake here than a repetition of Laband's derogation of formal law, which Hermann Heller characterized as exhibiting a tendency toward crypto-absolutism.[31] Schmitt wants to halt the ongoing tendency toward the rationalization of the content of law and limit the power of parliament, whose composition no longer guarantees bourgeois privileges. Schmitt prefers to hand over the guarantee of these privileges to an executive that monopolizes the authority to issue individual measures. Precisely those statements in "Legality and Legitimacy," which Schmitt claimed were an urgent plea to preserve the liberal constitutional state (which is admittedly true in Schmitt's sense of the concept, since he wants to preserve nothing but the liberal-constitutional core of the Weimar Constitution, i.e., the "protection of liberty and property" at the expense of other parts of the constitution)[32] culminate in the following prognosis: "In practice, however, the lack of distinction between law and measure is probably realized on the level of the measure. The administrative state, which manifests itself in the practice of measures, is more akin and closer in character to a "dictator" than to a parliament separated from the executive, which is charged with making general, predetermined and limited norms."[33]

So Schmitt is only able to deduce the obsolescence of the "legislative state" from the modern necessity of state intervention in the economy by reducing parliament to a maker of norms with general content. The intention is obviously to eliminate "socialist-unionist pluralism,"[34] which can only realize its demands against industry with the help of legal safeguards. So, especially during periods of state economic intervention, the legislative state appears inopportune from the perspective of "industry." Measures taken by an executive that is no longer democratically controlled are now supposed to grant protection from what Schmitt himself in a more recent formulation calls the "functionalization of property through immanent social duties."[35] A cynical form of bourgeois thinking about the limits of state activity is no longer directed against the executive, the "state" that used to be separate from society, but instead against parliament. The autonomy of society in a narrow sense, i.e., of those societal groups which identify with the state, is now threatened by previously underprivileged social groups. Therefore, this autonomy can only be guaranteed by a strong state.

That Schmitt fights in the name of a bourgeois-liberal demand against the bourgeois-liberal institution of parliament hence does not derive from a personal attempt to camouflage his intentions. Instead, it is an expression of a dialectic inherent in liberalism itself. In particular, it is the insistence on the fundamental bourgeois institution of the ownership of the means of production, which used to be protected equally through the generality of law as well as through the supremacy of parliament, that now compels the abandonment of parliament to the extent that its composition and function are transformed. In Schmitt's anachronistic revival of the generality of law, which is played off against the increased significance of legal measures, an operation familiar from Schmitt's general criticism of parliamentary systems repeats itself: by insisting on the "completely mouldy" intellectual foundations of parliamentary systems in the face of altered political and social conditions, the elimination of parliament is propagated in the very name of its fundamental principles. In this social context, it is not the growing significance of the measure itself that indicates the moment at which one of the groups competing in a pluralist-parliamentary system has monopolized the previously relatively "neutral" state for its own aims, and thereby emerges as the winner from the social "civil war." Instead, it is the transformation of the authority to take measures from the legislature to an executive that is no longer democratically controlled, and the modification of this authority into an exclusive competence, which marks the emergence of the monopolization of state power by one social group.

The group that did manage to identify with the state was already described as "typical capitalists" in Schmitt's 1914 publication. There he writes: "the capitalist, who does not care about his personal needs, instead cares deeply about the augmentation of his capital, becomes the servant of a cause, a civil servant (!)"[36] Consequently, he alone is adequate to the "value structure" that the state embodies. The abstraction from real societal interests that is asked of all merely "empirical" individuals therefore does not apply to capitalist interests. This is true because the asceticism heteronomously imposed upon all other societal groups seems an expression of autonomy to the capitalist. He has stylized himself into a "civil servant" by self-abnegation for the cause of augmenting capital, for grand and impressive moneymaking.[37] Thereby the capitalist has already achieved what later became legally binding in the fascist program, according to which "any economic activity" is "the holding of a public office."[38]

II

By the time the "pure state of measures" had established itself in 1933, Schmitt's insistence on the "fundamental distinction in a constitutional state" between general law and a decisionistic measure had fulfilled its function. This makes the thesis of a radical break in his theory all the more strange: "that in the national totalitarian state [*völkischer Totalstaat*] decisionistic thinking is replaced by a theory of concrete order means only that Carl Schmitt in 1933 ceases to be oriented principally towards the phenomenon of the state of emergency."[39] Not even Schmitt himself understood the conditions after 1933 as a "normal situation." Indeed, he never abandoned the "dialectical" legitimation of dictatorship that he developed in 1921: law must be negated in order to be realized, and situation-specific measures are necessary in order to create a "normal" state of affairs in the first place.[40] The National Socialist dictatorship was so dependent on its legitimation by reference to a state of emergency[41] that it was not concerned with "rushing to normalize itself."[42] The political function of the new theory is evident in the fact that Schmitt's early decisionistic thinking continues to underlie his "theory of concrete order": the completely irrational contents of a concrete, substantial order of the German *Volk* can only be determined in a decisionistic fashion.[43] Schmitt develops this new theory by referring to Maurice Hauriou's theory of institutions, by first describing it as institutionalist and then as a theory of concrete order. It serves to prove that pure decisionistic measures are necessities objectively resulting from the substantial "structure" of the German *Volk*.

Marcuse's thesis about the totalitarian theory of the state can be illustrated by examining this phase of Schmitt's theory. Marcuse holds that the totalitarian theory of the state disguises its true position in the battle by criticizing the liberal *Weltanschauung* while leaving the fundamental economic and social structure of liberalism untouched. In this interpretation, fascist theory only represents an ideological adaptation to the objective transition from individualistic competitive to modern monopoly capitalism.[44] Schmitt's own comments about this subject are clear enough. He approvingly cites von Beckerath's thesis that "with the increasing concentration of economic and political power in a few hands, the ideology of the majority will disintegrate"[45] and—referring to another author, this time Friedrich Naumann[46]—he emphasizes that he is only sketching out the consequences (here, for his theory of international law) of an "industrial-organizational" "process of growth," "through which the individualistic stage of capitalism is overcome."[47] The consequence for Schmitt's concept of law is the total dissolution of law. Law, which is no longer appropriate for the monopolistic structure of the economy, is overwhelmed by "inevitable" and "indispensable" vague legal clauses (*Generalklausel*).[48] Schmitt himself emphasizes that vague legal clauses make possible concrete answers to "concrete" situations, i.e., to take measures. Vague legal clauses, such as "in good faith" and "good morals," no longer refer to an individualistic bourgeois commercial order. Moreover, they change "the entire legal system without necessitating changes in a single 'positive' law."[49] They change it in the sense that a publication by Heinrich Lange[50]—a work commended by Schmitt—suggests: "The *clausula rebus sic stantibus* that liberalism presumed dead has rightfully reappeared openly or indirectly" and puts each positive law under its proviso.[51] The "dynamization" of law, in accordance with the imperatives of the monopolization of economic life, means that every rule is subjected to the dictates of the concrete situation. It can barely be distinguished from Schmitt's theory before 1933: Schmitt's theory of concrete order reveals itself to be thinking in terms of concrete measures. Thus, decisionistic thinking can be described as the juristic theory and the theory of concrete order as the juristic ideology of the authoritarian state.[52]

No less does the theory of concrete order fulfill the function of forcibly pacifying social antagonisms. In this, a peculiarity of Schmitt's adaptation of the inherently ambiguous Free Law Theory (*Freirechtstheorie*), which he had already undertaken in 1914, repeats itself. In his adaptation, Schmitt plays "reasonable" predictability off against the merely formal predictability of law, thereby placing positive law in question from "above," from the perspective of a supra-empirical norm, and not from "below," from the perspective of popular social demands. He did this just in case the positive law came to express welfare and social security related demands. An expression of this was Schmitt's attempt to emphasize—in juxtaposition to the proponents of the Free Law School—that at stake is a question "not of a jurisprudence of 'facts,' but one of norms."[53] After 1933 this basic structure is preserved in order to perform the same social function, though the norm is now replaced by the command of the *führer*,[54] enforced authoritatively from "above." The command of the *führer* functionalizes positive law and degrades the judge to an enforcer not of the law, but of the executive, which has now become absolute.

Schmitt's theory of concrete order refers directly to a society attempting to bring about an artificial restoration of a system of estates (*ständische Gliederungen*). When Schmitt comments that on January 30, 1933, "Hegel died,"[55] he is only saying that Hegel's construction of the "state of civil servants" has already had its day, since in the meantime a new social group has established itself as the class of "civil servants" loyal to the state. At the same time, Schmitt celebrates as "great and German beyond his time" the fact that Hegel does not accept the bipartite schema based on a contrast between state and society, and that he conceives of the corporations as a transitional apparatus situated between them. In Schmitt's theory of concrete order, the state appears as "the institution of institutions, in whose order a multitude of other self-contained institutions find shelter and order."[56] It appears that the dreaded pluralistic groups described so unsympathetically in Schmitt's theory of the Weimar period emerge once again here, but they are now modified in a manner consistent with a new set of realities, which turn the original purpose of their organization into its antithesis. When Schmitt now says that "[i]n a *Volk* divided into estates [*ständisch gegliedertes Volk*], there is always a majority of orders, the respective jurisdiction [*Standesgerichtbarkeit*] for which—'as many benches as there are estates'—has to take shape from within itself,"[57] the intention of this sentence only becomes clear in light of his earlier polemic against the "false exaggerations" of the social guarantees of the fundamental rights section of the Weimar Constitution. These social guarantees made any demand against the state a judicial matter, and thereby transformed the constitutional order into an "instrument of private egoism."[58] The new "jurisdiction of estates" (*Standesgerichtbarkeit*) is clearly not an institution for enforcing the rights of social groups, as Schmitt once feared might come about if a system of constitutional judicial review, with expanded standing, were to be established. According to Schmitt's theory of concrete order, the satisfaction of social needs is no longer guaranteed by legally enforceable legal rights, but instead by arbitrary measures, administrative acts of mercy which acknowledge the good behavior of those subject to their power.

Schmitt himself interpreted the doctrine of "institutional guarantees,"[59] which he first formulated in 1928 and then further developed in 1931, as a starting point for his theory of concrete order. In this doctrine, the intended derogation of pluralist organizations, which were still geared toward the protection of individual interests, in favor of "estate-like" groups independent of the individuals assigned to them, becomes clearly visible. After 1933, what Schmitt had previously emphasized in respect to the very limited number of institutional guarantees found in the Weimar Constitution, is seen as having general validity: "the granting of subjective rights is *subordinate* to the guaranty of the institution and must serve it. Consequently, the institutional point of view, and not the individualist-egoistic interest of the subjective rights-holder, is decisive" (emphasis in original). A more recent representative of institutional theory takes such a strict distinction between objective right and subjective entitlement as a reason not to count Schmitt within the ranks of institutionalist theorists at all.[60] However, Schmitt is only voicing with cynical clarity here what constitutes the true agenda of institutionalist legal theory—even, in contradiction to its self-understanding in Hauriou's theory:[61] make every subjective right vanish in the face of objective right.

Schmitt was justified in seeing a contradiction in the attempt to integrate institutional guarantees into a liberal constitution based on general and equal liberties. This contradiction need not necessarily culminate in the transition of a classical liberal constitutional system into an estate-based restoration. In making the guaranteed institutions independent not of the individual but of the state, especially insofar as institutional guarantees were extended to labor unions and employers' associations,[62] the outlines of an alternative system might take shape: a "sovereignty-less" system of economic democracy (*Wirtschaftsdemokratie*). It was precisely this system, opposed by Schmitt, which he saw Weimar pluralism as approximating. For him, the colonization of the state by society here reduced "its constitution to the sentence '*pacta sunt servanda*' "[63] and could only be transformed into a state that autonomously shapes society by eliminating freedom of contract. So it is quite consistent when Schmitt comments that the new National Socialist legal system systematically introduces binding arbitration (which had been the exception in the Weimar system): "the wage scale *contract* is replaced by the wage scale *order*; industrialist, employees, and workers are management and personnel of an enterprise that work *together* . . . in order to further the aims of the enterprise."[64]

The attempt at an estate-based restoration during a phase of societal development, in which the isolation of the state from society is the very precondition for the successful transposition of societal interests into political decisions enforced with the help of the state, hardly leads to a revival of the feudalistic identity of state and society. Instead, the opposite is true: insofar as we understand by society those groups that were *not* able to identify with the state, such restorative aspirations lead to a radicalized division between state and society. By once again annulling the distinction between public and private law, the unhampered ability of the state to interfere with individuals' freedom to do what they want is secured; however, at that juncture when societal groups no longer are directly represented by political groups, they are robbed of any political influence whatsoever. Schmitt reproduces the aspiration, found in the Hegelian theory of corporations, "to push the people back into the limitations of their private sphere."[65]

By failing to achieve the promised mediation between state and society, a sphere of the "purely political," heteronomously opposed to real social interests, is established in its stead. A metaphysics of the state is thereby given free reign. Nevertheless, one societal group is able to monopolize the sphere of the "purely political" for itself by allowing that its own organizational auxiliaries, alongside the organizational auxiliaries of other social groups, are shaped by and integrated into the state: economic power only takes an untrammeled form when freedom of contract has been eliminated, for this freedom ultimately benefits nonbourgeois social groups as well as the dominant group. Privileged economic power alone forces even that state which claims to have secured its supremacy over the economy, i.e., in the face of all organized economic associations (*Verbände*), to respect certain limits. Consequently, the state's interventionist measures "still find their limits, which are hard to define and dangerous to exceed, in economic rationality."[66] The expectations of industrialists who did not feel threatened by state economic intervention per se, but only by a system of state control that imposed "social obligations" on them, is hinted at in Schmitt's discussion of the state's growing power within the economy: the trend toward a "plan" is accepted, as long as the "rulers are planning" and the plan is not imposed.[67] In doing so, it is ensured that those who exercise a dominant role within the economy alone determine the course of the economy. The analogy to the juristic argument—those who are able to enforce the law should also be allowed to make it—nicely illustrates the economic context of Schmitt's decisionism.

In 1933, the bourgeoisie sacrificed its political existence in order to rescue its social existence.[68] It liquidated the liberal representative form of government when it no longer exclusively served bourgeois interests. Instead, the industrialists transferred pure and undivided political power into the hands of a radical group distinct from the bourgeoisie,[69] in order to be able to pursue nothing but its unhampered social and economic interests in the shadows of this radical group. These facts are formulated with great precision by Schmitt's "friend-foe" theory. By establishing a sphere of the "purely political," which is identical with the highest degree of intensity of conflict, a moment of liberal-bourgeois thinking about the limits of state power is preserved. Conflict, which originates in a specific social setting and possesses a specific content, here develops its *own immanent dynamic laws (Eigengesetzlichkeit)* precisely by becoming "political" and thus by disregarding the original content of its starting point.[70] Schmitt formulated a cynical version of this liberal-bourgeois thinking about the state even more precisely in a November 1932 speech before the *"Langnamverein,"*[71] the organized representatives of heavy industry. It is not only the occupation of the state by the economy that Schmitt criticizes there. He also criticizes the resulting politicization of the economy. He uses the term "economy" in an ambiguous way here: in the first case it refers merely to groups participating in the economic process which impose "social obligations" on other groups with the aid of the state; in the second case, however, Schmitt means the "economy" in a narrower sense, i.e., the industrialists. This ambiguous use of the term "economy" disguises Schmitt's main concern. State economic intervention only came to appear suspect to the extent that the "neutral" state of the Weimar period had not been reduced to the willing servant of industry, but had successfully guaranteed other societal organizations the opportunity to pursue their interests in opposition to the interests of industry.

Thus, Schmitt's concept of the political explicitly does not imply the "total usurpation" of all parts of society by the state and politics because of the "content-less" character of its conception of the political,[72] as one criticism of Schmitt's theory assumes. This criticism only serves to perpetuate Schmitt's own position. As Schmitt explicitly laments, it is precisely a state of affairs that "does not at all permit a sphere that is free of the state any more" [!] that is to be criticized.[73] On the contrary, the typically bourgeois acceptance of a strong state, by a bourgeoisie which has made "the political" its own special task, means that the Weimar "total state on the basis of weakness" is transformed into a "totalitarian state on the basis of strength," which aspires to protect the economic freedom of the privileged from state-backed popular social demands.

The "purely political," however, in reality took on a concrete form unintended by Schmitt. Von Beckerath's remark,[74] which Schmitt criticizes, to the effect that the fascism of the "first hour" was "a kind of *l'art pour l'art* in the political realm," is accurate to the extent that the original radical political movement of the middle classes in Italy and Germany[75] pursued a highly impractical political agenda. Even when the bourgeoisie ceded political power to these radical movements, they proved unable to pursue a coherent series of self-interested economic policies (*eine eigene Klassenpolitik*) in opposition to those interests that had the modern monopolistic structure of the economy on their side. The activism of a movement lacking any real direction could thus be used in a purely instrumental way by bourgeois interests.

Nevertheless, the political "l'art pour l'art" harnessed by the bourgeoisie actually did develop its own immanent dynamic. But this dynamic turned against the bourgeoisie—for instance, when an expansive foreign policy benefited heavy industry but harmed the export-oriented sector of industry, or when party organizations managed to gain the status of an autonomous political elite in opposition to all social interests.[76] The point in time at which a distinction that Schmitt made in 1937 became practically indistinguishable—when war was no longer only total "in the sense of the most extreme mobilization of power," but also in the sense of "total enmity,"[77]—occurred when the "neutral economy" was not only involved in the war in the sense of a profitable "mobilization of power" but also became integrated into the battle against the "enemy." This period also coincides roughly with Schmitt's own retreat into his inner emigration. This development is less revealing for understanding Schmitt's biography than it is for making sense of the underlying intention of his theory. It only reaffirms how during all of its phases, Schmitt's theory coincides with the interests of those parts of the bourgeoisie that did not autonomously bring fascism into existence in 1933, but that for a long time successfully used fascism for its own purposes, only to be cheated by it in the long run. The attempt to interpret Schmitt's theory as a sequence of abrupt discontinuities reveals a failure to perceive the continuity in real societal development before and after 1933.

Notes

This essay was translated by Anke Grosskopf and William E. Scheuerman. It first appeared in 1969, in one of the first issues of the left-wing German legal journal, *Kritische Justiz* (vol. 2), which emerged in the aftermath of the political upheavals of the mid-1960s. Although Professor Maus would likely alter some of its formulations today, the essay is being reprinted here as an exemplary expression of a rich tradition of engagement with the ideas of Carl Schmitt by scholars influenced by the Frankfurt School of critical theory. (The ideas of Franz L. Neumann and Herbert Marcuse play an important role in Maus's argument.) In addition, the piece offers a provocative analysis of the relationship between Schmitt's theorizing before and after the Nazi takeover—a topic that remains at the fore of contemporary debates about Schmitt in the English-speaking world. Maus considers what she describes as "the social function" of Schmitt's theory crucial to an understanding of this issue. (Translators' note.)

The author's new comments were translated by David Dyzenhaus.

1   The Free Law Movement reacted in Germany against the dominant stance of literal adherence to codified law. Its proponents emphasized the freedom of the judge to legislate interstitially. (Translator's note.)

2   The *Office of Military Government for Germany, United States*, conducted inquiries into the large banks and industrial concerns enmeshed with the National Socialist political center of power. Its reports concerned the formal and informal connections between the economy and politics in the National Socialist system and served as the preparation for the Nuremberg trials. (Translator's note.)

3   Professor Maus is referring here to the collapse of the systems of state socialism. (Translator's note.)

4   See Piet Tommissens' two bibliographies in H. Barion, E. Forsthoff, and W. Weber, eds., *Festschrift für Carl Schmitt zum 70. Geburtstag* (Berlin, 1959), at 273–330; and H. Barion, E. Böckenförde, E. Forsthoff, and W. Weber, eds., *Epirrhosis. Festgabe für Carl Schmitt*, vol. 2 (Berlin, 1968), at 739–78.

5   See Schmitt's retrospective comments on "Legalität und Legitimität," in C. Schmitt, *Verfassungsrechtliche Aufsätze aus den Jahren 1924-1954* (Berlin, 1958), at 350 (hereafter *Verfassungsrechtliche Aufsätze*).

6   Ibid.

7   H. Hofmann, *Legitimität gegen Legalität. Der Weg der politischen Philosophie Carl Schmitts* (Neuwied, Berlin, 1964) (hereafter *Legitimität gegen Legalität*).

8   For an explicit comment, see ibid., at 175.

9   C. G. von Krockow, *Die Entscheidung. Eine Untersuchung über Ernst Jünger, Carl Schmitt, Martin Heidegger* (Stuttgart, 1958), at 94, n. 3 (hereafter *Die Entscheidung*).

10 See P. Schneider, *Ausnahmezustand und Norm* (Stuttgart, 1957).

11 See J. Fijalkowski, *Die Wendung zum Führerstaat* (Opladen, 1958).

12 See the comments in *Legitimität gegen Legalität*, supra n. 7, at 7–9.

13 Ibid., at 11.

14 Ibid., and at 9.

15 C. Schmitt, *Der Wert des Staates und die Bedeutung des einzelnen* (Tübingen, 1914) (hereafter *Der Wert des Staates*). F. Neumann intensively revisited Schmitt's opposition in F. Neumann, "Der Funktionswandel des Gesetzes im Recht der bürgerlichen Gesellschaft," *Zeitschrift für Sozialforschung* 6, no. 3 (1937): 542, at 577 and passim (hereafter "Der Funktionswandel des Gesetzes").

16 Ibid., at 74–75.

17 Ibid., at 79f.

18 Ibid., at 81.

19 Ibid., at 85.

20 Ibid., at 84 and passim.

21 On the thesis that it was not revolutionary, but reformist Socialism which induced the bourgeoisie to cede its power to fascism, see O. Bauer, "Der Faschismus," in W. Abendroth, ed., *Faschismus und Kapitalismus* (Frankfurt, 1967), at 154 and passim.

22 C. Schmitt, *Verfassungslehre*, 3d ed. (Berlin, 1957), at 138–57.

23 *Der Wert des Staates*, supra n. 15, at 78.

24 C. Schmitt, *Der Hüter der Verfassung* (Tübingen, 1931), at 115–17.

25 C. Schmitt, "Die Wende zum totalen Staat," (1931) in C. Schmitt, *Positionen und Begriffe* (Hamburg, 1940), at 148.

26 M. Weber, *Wirtschaft und Gesellschaft*, vol. 1 (Cologne, 1964), at 624–26.

27 F. L. Neumann, "Der Funktionswandel des Gesetzes," supra n. 15, at 577 and passim.

28 *Wirtschaft und Gesellschaft*, supra n. 26, at 648–49.

29 See F. L. Neumann, "Der Funktionswandel des Gesetzes," supra n. 15, at 570 and 576.

30 C. Schmitt, *Unabhängigkeit der Richter, Gleichheit vor dem Gesetz und Gewährleistung des Eigentums nach der Weimarer Verfassung* (Berlin, 1926), at 18 (hereafter *Unabhängigkeit der Richter*).

31 H. Heller, "Der Begriff des Gesetzes in der Reichsverfassung" (1928), in *Gesammelte Schriften*, vol. 2 (Leiden, 1971).

32 C. Schmitt, "Legalität und Legitimität" (1932), in *Verfassungsrechtliche Aufsätze*, supra n. 5, at 331.

33 Ibid., at 335.

34 C. Schmitt, *Der Begriff des Politischen* (Berlin, 1963), at 119.

35 C. Schmitt, "Funktionalisierung des Eigentums durch immanente Sozialpflichtigkeiten," in *Verfassungsrechtliche Aufsätze*, supra n. 5, at 230.

36 *Der Wert des Staates*, supra n. 15, at 91.

37 Ibid., at 90–91.

38 E. von Beckerath, *Wesen und Werden des faschistischen Staates* (Berlin, 1927), at 99. This book is at the same time a treatise which conveys Schmitt's fascination with Italian fascism. See also Schmitt's review of it in *Positionen und Begriffe*, supra n. 25, at 109–11, and the preface to the second edition of C. Schmitt, *Die Diktatur* (Munich, 1928).

39 *Legitimität gegen Legalität*, supra n. 7, also at 179–80.

40 *Die Diktatur*, supra n. 38, at VIII–IX and passim.

41 See, for example, A. Thalheimer, "Über den Faschismus" in *Faschismus und Kapitalismus*, supra n. 21, at 33.

42 C. Schmitt, *Staat, Bewegung, Volk* (Hamburg, 1935; first ed. 1933), at 42.

43 *Die Entscheidung*, supra n. 9, at 96 and 103–4.

44 H. Marcuse, "Der Kampf gegen den Liberalismus in der totalen Staatsauffassung," in H. Marcuse, *Kultur und Gesellschaft I* (Frankfurt am Main, 1965) (hereafter "Der Kampf gegen den Liberalismus"), at 22–24.

45 *Wesen und Werden des faschistischen Staates*, supra n. 38.

46 F. Naumann, *Mitteleuropa* (Berlin, 1916).

47 C. Schmitt, *Völkerrechtliche Grossraumordnung mit Interventionsverbot für raumfremde Mächte* (Berlin/Leipzig/Vienna, 1941), at 4–5.

48 *Staat, Bewegung, Volk*, supra n. 42, at 43, and C. Schmitt, *Über die drei Arten des rechtswissenschaftlichen Denkens* (Hamburg, 1934) (hereafter *Über die drei Arten*), at 62.

49 *Über die drei Arten*, ibid., at 59.

50 H. Lange, *Liberalismus, Nationalismus und bürgerliches Recht* (Tübingen, 1933), at 17.

51 Hasso Hofmann also refers to this aspect of Schmitt, *Legitimität gegen Legalität*, supra n. 7, at 63.

52 "Der Funktionswandel des Gesetzes," supra n. 15, at 587.

53 *Der Wert des Staates*, supra n. 15, at 48, n. 4.

54 See, e.g., *Staat, Bewegung, Volk*, supra n. 42, at 44.

55 Ibid., at 32, also at 28.

56 *Über die drei Arten*, supra n. 48, at 57.

57 Ibid., at 63–64.

58 C. Schmitt, "Zehn Jahre Reichsverfassung" (1929) in *Verfassungsrechtliche Aufsätze*, supra n. 5, at 37 and 40.

59 *Verfassungslehre*, supra n. 22, at 170–72 and C. Schmitt, "Freiheitsrechte und institutionelle Garantien der Reichsverfassung" (1931), in *Verfassungsrechtliche Aufsätze*, supra n. 5, at 140–42; see the following citation there at 149.

60 P. Häberle, *Die Wesensgehaltsgarantie des Art. 19 Abs. 2 Grundgesetz* (Karlsruhe, 1962), at 92–94.

61 M. Hauriou, Die *Theorie der Institution*, R. Schnur, ed., (Berlin, 1965), esp. at 65.

62 *Verfassungsrechtliche Aufsätze*, supra n. 5, at 171.

63 C. Schmitt, "Das Problem der innerpolitischen Neutralität des Staates," (1930) in *Verfassungsrechtliche Aufsätze*, supra n. 5, at 55.

64 *Über die drei Arten*, supra n. 48, at 64; emphasis added.

65 J. Habermas, "Nachwort zur Ausgabe von Hegels politischen Schriften," in G. W. F. Hegel, *Politische Schriften* (Frankfurt am Main, 1966), esp. at 364 and 368; there the Marx quotation cited here can be found. See also H. Heller, *Europa und der Faschismus* (Berlin, Leipzig, 1929), at 123.

66 *Wesen und Werden des faschistischen Staates*, supra n. 38, at 139.

67 C. Schmitt, "Die Machtpositionen des modernen Staates" in *Verfassungsrechtliche Aufsätze*, supra n. 5, at 371. Cf. H. Freyer, *Herrschaft und Planung* (Hamburg, 1933), to whom Schmitt himself refers. In this work, the moment of control of the plan becomes absolute and the "plan" manifests itself as a socialist order of society.

68 "Über den Faschismus," in *Faschismus und Kapitalismus*, supra n. 21, at 19–21.

69 Translators' note: Maus is referring to the National Socialists here.

70 *Der Begriff des Politischen*, supra n. 34, at 39.

71 This speech was partially reprinted under the title "Weiterentwicklung des totalen Staates in Deutschland," in *Verfassungsrechtliche Aufsätze*, supra n. 5, at 185 ff.

72 W. Hennis, "Zum Problem der deutschen Staatsanschauung" (1959), in *Vierteljahresschrift für Zeitgeschichte*, vol. 7, at 23. The same misunderstanding can be found in "Der Kampf gegen den Liberalismus," supra n. 44, at 49, where the politicization discussed there naturally receives a different evaluation (esp. at 52) than in Hennis's writing.

73 *Verfassungsrechtliche Aufsätze*, supra n. 5, at 361.

74 See Schmitt's discussion of this author in *Positionen und Begriffe*, supra n. 25, at 110.

75 Translators' note: Maus again is referring to the Fascists and National Socialists here.

76 I. Fetscher, "Faschismus und Nationalismus. Zur Kritik des sowjetmarxistischen Faschismusbegriffs," *Politische Vierteljahresschrift* 3 (1962): at 59 and 62.

77 C. Schmitt, "Totaler Feind, totaler Krieg, totaler Staat," (1937) in *Positionen und Begriffe*, supra n. 25, at 235 ff.

The Dilemmas of Dictatorship

Carl Schmitt and Constitutional

Emergency Powers

John P. McCormick

Introduction

The first line of Carl Schmitt's *Political Theology* is perhaps the most famous sentence—certainly one of the most infamous—in German political theory: "Sovereign is he who decides on the exception" [*Souverän ist, wer über den Ausnahmezustand entscheidet*].[1] And yet the full significance of this famous sentence is often underestimated. I intend to focus on (1) its significance in the overall trajectory of Schmitt's Weimar work, and (2) its potential significance for contemporary constitutional theories of emergency powers.

I will examine Schmitt's first major theoretical engagement with the issue of emergency powers in *Die Diktatur* from 1921[2] and explain how his position, or at least his mode of presentation, changes in his second effort on this subject, *Political Theology*, published only a year later. In the earlier work, Schmitt describes the classical Roman institution of dictatorship as a theoretical-historical standard for emergency measures that preserve a constitutional order in a time of dire crisis. In classical dictatorship the political technology of emergency authority is consigned only to the temporary exceptional moment, and in this scheme the normal and rule-bound regular order is presented as substantively correct by Schmitt and worthy of restoration. However, in the latter work, *Political Theology*, the exceptional situation is that which calls for the emergence of a potentially all-powerful sovereign who not only must rescue a constitutional order from a particular political crisis but also must charismatically deliver it from its own constitutional procedures—procedures that Schmitt pejoratively deems technical and mechanical. The question I want to pose and answer is, Why does Schmitt in the span of a year change his orientation in one work where a temporary dictatorship is presented as an appropriate use of functional rationality, and where a rule-bound constitutional order is presented as something worth defending and restoring, to the position in the second work where an unlimitedly powerful sovereign is that which in time of crisis restores existential substance to constitutional orders that of necessity grow 'torpid' through 'mechanical repetition'?[3] I also ask whether there is anything useful in either Schmitt's earlier or later analysis, or indeed in the theoretical transformation from one to the other, for contemporary considerations on the issue of constitutional emergency powers. To this end, I focus on the intellectual history of liberal-constitutional emergency provisions, the relationship of popular sovereignty to such provisions, and the analytical difference between declaring an exceptional situation and acting to address it within such provisions.

Commissarial versus Sovereign Dictatorship

Schmitt takes up *Die Diktatur* in the context of the extensive use of emergency powers by the German Republic's first president, Friedrich Ebert, under Article 48 of the Weimar Constitution. Ebert used such measures against the forces that were besieging the republic on all sides in its early years: right-wing and Communist rebellion, as well as an overwhelming economic crisis. Thus Schmitt engages in a theoretical study of the institution of dictatorship to confront a series of urgent contemporary crises—yet he actually travels historically very far from contemporary conditions.[4]

In Schmitt's detailed account in *Die Diktatur*, the Roman dictator was appointed in a time of grave emergency to address the concrete specifications of that crisis and no other. The Roman Senate proclaimed an emergency: usually a foreign invasion, an insurrection, or a plague or famine. It then asked the consuls to appoint a dictator who could in fact be one of the two consuls themselves. The dictator had unlimited power in this task, acting unrestrained by norm or law, while being severely limited beyond the specific task in that he could not change or perpetually suspend the regular order. Instead he was compelled to return to it through the functional nature of his activity and the time limit placed on him. However, in the performance of his duty, the dictator knew no right or wrong but only expedience: according to Schmitt, for the dictator, "a procedure can be either false or true, in that this determination is self-contained by the fact that the measure taken is in a factually technical [*sachtechnische*] sense right, that is expedient" (*D*, 11). Normative or ethical notions of wrong and right, or legal or illegal, are not brought to bear in dictatorship, only that which is "in the factually technical [*sachtechnische*] sense harmful [to the regime], and thus false" (*D*, 12). The 'peculiarity' of dictatorship, according to Schmitt, lies in the fact that "all is justified that appears to be necessary for a concretely gained success" (*D*, xviii). The particular "concrete situation" [*Lage der Sache*] calls for the particular kinds of "tasks, powers, evaluations, empowerments, commissions and authorities" to be taken up by the dictator (*D*, xviii). The material specificities of a crisis—an immediate or initial end—generate the specific 'means' to be employed by the dictator, which cannot be determined a priori. On the other hand, the ultimate end is always understood, a situation of *status quo ante:*

> A dictatorship therefore that does not have the purpose of making itself superfluous is a random despotism. Achieving a concrete success however means intervening in the causal path of events with means whose correctness lies solely in their purposefulness and is exclusively dependent on a factual connection to the causal event itself. Dictatorship hence suspends that by which it is justified, the state of law, and imposes instead the rule of procedure interested exclusively in bringing about a concrete success. . . . [a return to] the state of law. (*D*, xvi)

Schmitt is at pains to argue in this early work that the functionally authoritarian quality of dictatorship is temporally bound and has as its sole aim the restoration of the previously standing legal order. But the misunderstanding of this has resulted in the contemporary disuse and abuse of the concept in the early twentieth century. According to Schmitt, the "bourgeois political literature" either ignores the concept altogether or treats it as a kind of slogan that it uses against its opponents (*D*, xi–xii). Schmitt is alarmed that the concept seems to be taken seriously only by the Communists with their famous doctrine of the "dictatorship of the proletariat" (*D*, xiii). The Communists have the concept partially right, according to Schmitt, for they recognize its purely technical and temporary characteristics: "The dictatorship of the proletariat is the technical means for the implementation of the transition to the Communists' final goal" (*D*, xiv). The "centralizing machine" and "domination-apparatus" of the state seized by the proletariat is not according to their ideology "definitive" for the Communists, but rather "transitional" (*D*, xiv).

Schmitt notes that one might then see the Communist theory of dictatorship as simply a modern incarnation of the classical institution: a negation of parliamentary democracy without formal democratic justification (since the Communists are often a minority) and a replacement of the personal dictator with a collective one (the party) (*D*, xiii). But this obscures the truly fundamental transformation of the essence of the classical concept: the Communist institution employs technical means to create a new situation, the classical institution employed them to restore a previously existing one. This difference has important ramifications for the question of just how limited a dictatorship can be if it is legitimated and bound by a future situation as opposed to if it is legitimated by a previously existing one.[5] This difference also lays the groundwork for the theoretical-historical distinction that governs the whole of *Die Diktatur:* the one between the traditional concept of "commissarial dictatorship," derived from the classical model, which is bound by allotted time, specified task, and the fact that it must restore a previously standing order, and "sovereign dictatorship," a historically modern phenomenon, which is unlimited in any way and may proceed to establish a completely new order.[6] I will return to these issues in greater detail below.

So, if the Communists partially understand the essence of dictatorship, liberals, to the extent that they pay attention to the concept at all, completely misapprehend it, according to Schmitt.[7] Liberals have completely forgotten its classical meaning and associate the idea and institution solely with the kind described by Schmitt as "sovereign" dictatorship: "a distinction is no longer maintained between dictatorship and Caesarism, and the essential determination of the concept is marginalized . . . the commissarial character of dictatorship" (*D*, xiii). Liberals deem a dictator to be any single individual ruling through a centralized government with little political constraint, often democratically acclaimed, and they equate dictatorship with authoritarianism, Caesarism, Bonapartism, military government, and even the Papacy (*D*, xiii).[8]

But by corrupting the notion of this important technique for dealing with emergencies and subsequently banishing it from constitutional concerns Schmitt suggests that liberal constitutionalism leaves itself especially susceptible to emergencies. Its blind faith in the technical apparatus of its standing constitutions and the scientistic view of the regularity of nature encourages liberalism to believe that it needs no technique for the extraordinary occurrence because the regular constitutional techniques are assumed to be appropriate to a nature free of the extraordinary. Classical dictatorship is a wholly technical phenomenon which restores that which is not wholly technical, the normal legally legitimated order. Schmitt intimates in *Diktatur* that liberal constitutionalism is in danger of rendering its normal legal order wholly technical and hence potentially illegitimate.

But in *Die Diktatur,* Schmitt gives no indication that this need *necessarily* continue to be the case for a constitutional regime or a *Rechtsstaat.* The Communist doctrine of dictatorship, on the other hand, completely changes the relationship of normal and exceptional situation, and hence communism inevitably and irreversibly transforms the nature of dictatorship. "From a revolutionary standpoint the whole [bourgeois] standing order is designated a dictatorship" and the Communists free themselves from the constraints of the rule of law associated with that standing order, as well as from the one implicit in the classical constitutional notion of dictatorship, because their "norm" is no longer "positive-constitutional" but rather "historical-political"; i.e., dictatorship is now dependent on a yet-to-be-realized historical *telos* rather than on a previously established constitutional order (*D*, xv). The Communists are "entitled" to overthrow the liberal state because the time is ripe, "but do not give up their own dictatorship because the time is not yet ripe" (*D*, xv). The Communist dictatorship is defined as the temporary negation, not of the past or the present, but of that which is to come: it is present absolute statism that supposedly brings about future absolute statelessness.

The Communist dictatorship represents, for Schmitt, the culmination of the modern historical trend toward totally unrestrained political action. In contrast to the—literally—conservative orientation of traditional politics wherein political activity is sanctioned by a previously existing good, according to Schmitt, the radical orientation of modern politics is driven by a fervor to bring about some future good, whose qualities are so vague as to justify unbounded means in the achievement of the end. For Schmitt, this is generated by the merging of the wholly technical activity of dictatorial action with a politics of normalcy in modern political theory and practice.

Niccolò Machiavelli, for instance, recognizes the specifically temporary technical-authoritarianism of dictatorship in the classical Roman sense and Schmitt himself initially adopts Machiavelli's formulation of the theory in the *Discorsi:*

Dictatorship was a wise invention of the Roman Republic. The dictator was an extraordinary Roman magistrate, who was introduced after the expulsion of the kings, so that a strong power would be available in time of peril. His power could not be curtailed by the authority of the consuls, the principle of collegiality, the veto of· the people's Tribune, or the provocation of the people. The dictator, who was appointed on petition of the Senate by the consuls, had the task of eliminating the perilous crisis, which is the reason for his appointment, such as the direction of a war effort or the suppression of a rebellion. . . . The dictator was appointed for six months, although it was customary for him to step down before the full duration of his tenure if he successfully executed his assigned commission. He was not bound by law and acted as a kind of king with unlimited authority over life and death. (*D*, 1–2)

Unlike the sovereign dictatorships of Caesar and Sulla, who used the office to change the constitutional order so as to further their own grasping at unlimited power, the classical notion was wholly commissarial (*D*, 3).

But Schmitt suggests that Machiavelli actually initiates the process of making the characteristics of dictatorship the very center of modern normal politics. In Schmitt's account, Machiavelli advocates the use of the political techniques of dictatorship in everyday politics. Dictatorship becomes one technique among many in a Machiavellian scheme dominated by technicity, and hence loses its essential extraordinary characteristic. Machiavelli's technicity regarding political practice, and his reputed agnosticism regarding the substantive worth of different regimes, subvert the notion of dictatorship as a technical exception of a nontechnical politics of normalcy, and reduces all of politics to mere technology. Thus despite the fact that Machiavelli never laid out a state theory, he is responsible for modern state theory's development out of the theory of dictatorship (*D*, 6–13).[9]

Subsequently, as the practical task of early modern state builders becomes the expansion of political power through the prosecution of boundary-defining external war and the suppression of internal religious civil war, the normatively unencumbered and technically disposed executive becomes the model of political practice. Civil war and foreign war, traditionally considered exceptional circumstances that might occasionally call for a dictator, become something else in the writings of state theorists such as Thomas Hobbes and Jean Bodin. In line with these historical transformations, Hobbes, who will later become Schmitt's intellectual hero, further inverts the relationship of a normal political situation and an exceptional one with his concept of the "natural condition" or the "state of nature."[10] Civil war becomes the ever-imminent normal state of affairs to which the sovereign state is the exceptional solution. Hobbes's sovereign state is hence a kind of dictatorship that has as its sole task guarding the ever-present exception. And because there is no sustained concept of stable political normalcy its authority cannot be a commissarial dictatorship. It is rather, appropriate to its name, a sovereign one (*D*, 22–25).

According to Schmitt, this process is radicalized as sovereignty becomes increasingly defined as *popular* sovereignty—as authority derives not from a specific and definite individual person like an absolute monarch but rather from an amorphous and differentiated populace. As a result, emergency action becomes more extreme as it is soon carried out by an elite whose actions are supposedly sanctioned by such popular sovereignty. Concomitantly there is a historical justification for the violent destruction of an old order and the creation of a new one out of nothing. Sovereign dictatorship becomes the power to perpetually suspend and change political order in the name of an inaccessible people and an eschatological notion of history. Schmitt's chief examples of this development are the writings of the French revolutionary theorists, such as Mably (*D*, 115–16) and especially Sieyès (*D*, 143–45), and more immediately the Bolsheviks.

Yet from the famous first sentence of *Political Theology* written only a year later it is clear that Schmitt has come to endorse something much closer to this latter kind of dictatorship: "Sovereign is the one who decides on the exception." He seems to celebrate the very merging of the normal and exceptional moments that in *Die Diktatur* he analyzed as politically pathological. He even encourages it with the ambiguous use of the preposition "on" [*über*], which belies the distinction that he himself acknowledges in the earlier book between, on the one hand, the body that *decides* that an exceptional situation exists—in the Roman case, the Senate through the consuls—and, on the other, the person that is appointed by them to *decide* what to do in the concrete particulars of the emergency—the dictator himself. The two separate decisions, one taking place in the moment of normalcy, the other in the moment of exception, are lumped together and yet hidden behind the ostensible directness of Schmitt's opening statement in *Political Theology*. Indeed, further on in the work Schmitt explicitly and deliberately conflates the two decisions: the sovereign "decides whether there is an extreme emergency *as well as* what must be done to eliminate it" (*PT,* 7, emphasis added).

There is also no attempt in *Political Theology* at prescribing what a priori time- or task-related limits might be imposed on a sovereign's action in the exceptional situation; Schmitt suggests in fact that this is potentially impossible:

> The exception, which is not codified in the existing legal order, can at best be characterized as a case of extreme peril, a danger to the existence of the state, or the like. But it cannot be circumscribed factually and made to conform to a preformed law.
>
> It is precisely the exception that makes relevant the subject of sovereignty, that is, the whole question of sovereignty. The precise details of an emergency cannot be anticipated, nor can one spell out what may take place in such a case, especially when it is truly a matter of an extreme emergency and how it is to be eliminated. The preconditions as well as the content of a jurisdictional competence in such a case must necessarily be unlimited. (*PT,* 6–7)

According to the commissarial notion of dictatorship, the dictator was free to do whatever was necessary in the particular exceptional moment to address a crisis precisely because the exception may never have been "foreseen in codified law." But the dictator was commissioned to do this by another institution, and he was bound as a "precondition" to return the government to that codified law. Schmitt occludes these crucial distinctions in the second more famous work on emergency powers and expands the unlimitedness of dictatorship by renouncing the very characteristics of the classical model he only recently admired *as well as* those of the liberal constitutionalism he consistently derides: "If measures undertaken in an exception could be circumscribed by mutual control, by imposing a time limit, or finally, as in the liberal constitutional procedure governing a state of siege, by enumerating extraordinary powers, the question of sovereignty would then be considered less significant . . ." (*PT,* 12). Indeed, his use of the terms sovereignty and sovereign implies some kind of lawmaking or lawgiving power that could change the previous order or even create a new one.

But Schmitt's attitude toward the normal order itself changes from *Die Diktatur* to *Political Theology.* Even though Schmitt chides the liberal political order in *Die Diktatur* for its infiltration by natural-scientific thinking, and its consequent blindness to both the possibility of the exception and to the potential necessity of resorting to the institution of the dictator on such an occasion, he never suggests that it would be impossible for that order to become aware in such a way. In fact, one of the ways in which the bulk of the book can be read is as an attempted corrective to this state of affairs: a call for the revival of the institution of a commissarial dictatorship to preserve a republican political order to which Schmitt does not seem all that opposed. But in *Political Theology* the normal liberal political order is presented as being so utterly corrupted by science and technology that it is actually *redeemed* by the exception and the sovereign dictatorial action for which it calls: "In the exception, the power of real life breaks through the crust of a mechanism that has become torpid by repetition" (*PT*, 15). In *Die Diktatur*, sovereignty is the bearer of the dangerous technicity and proto-authoritarianism that culminates with the Jacobins and the Communists and endangers any substantively worthy constitutional order; in *Political Theology*, sovereignty is that which is illegitimately surpressed by the mechanisms of constitutional orders such as the separation of powers: "the development and practice of the liberal constitutional state . . . attempts to repress the question of sovereignty by a division and mutual control of competences" (*PT*, 11).

What accounts for the shift in Schmitt's orientation? One explanation may be Schmitt's reception of Max Weber's theory of charisma. In fact, parts of *Political Theology* were to appear in a collection dedicated to Weber.[11] Does Schmitt make a theoretical-political move reminiscent of the great sociologist? As is well known, Weber shifted from a detached, wary, and even somewhat condescending analysis of charisma at the turn of the century to an endorsement of it as a solution to the mechanization brought on by bureaucratic politics. In parallel fashion, Schmitt moves from a cautious analysis of the rise of the concept of sovereignty in the reason of state literature in *Die Diktatur* to an endorsement of it as a solution to the Weimar predicament of constant crisis in *Political Theology*. The exception changes from a purely functional-political problem for a regime, to a kind of moment of divine intervention likened to a miracle (*PT*, 36); Schmitt remarks with satisfaction that "the exception confounds the unity and order of the rationalist scheme" (*PT*, 14).

Schmitt sees sovereignty as tied to the increasing technicization of politics in *Die Diktatur*, while he promotes it as the very solution to such technicization in *Political Theology*. Weber's category of charisma may hold the key here to Schmitt, because it is only as a charismatically imbued figure that the sovereign dictator can possibly be seen to deliver a constitutional regime from the danger of technicity.[12] In *Die Diktatur* Schmitt remarks that the concept of the political exception has not been 'systematically' treated and that he will do so himself elsewhere (*D*, xvii). In *Political Theology*, he offers not the promised systematic treatment of the concept but rather the mythologizing of it.

The difference between the two works is perhaps better explained by the following comparison:

—*Die Diktatur* (1921)
  exception: dangerous, not good; must be met with technical exactitude and temporal finitude by a defined quasi-charismatic commissarial dictator
  normal order: rule of law; normatively valued; worth restoring

—*Political Theology* (1922)
  exception: dangerous but good because an occasion for revivification; must be met by ambiguously sovereign dictator
  normal order: formally scientistic legality; abstract and lifeless; worth restoring but in need of reenlivening

The conclusion that one is compelled to draw from Schmitt's analysis in *Political Theology* is that a regime with institutional diversity, a constitutionally enumerated "division and mutual control of competences" (*PT*, 11), or what is more generally known as the separation of powers, is merely an overly mechanical construction that inevitably paralyzes a state in the face of an exception because it obscures who is sovereign, who must decide and act at that moment: "If such action is not subject to controls, if it is not hampered in some way by checks and balances, as is the case in a liberal constitution, then it is clear who the sovereign is. . . . All tendencies of modern constitutional development point towards eliminating the sovereign in this sense" (*PT*, 7). Fixation on the letter of the constitutional law to discern competence will either create a vacuum if no relevant competence is enumerated, or conflict should it not be clear.[13] Neither is of course a desirable state of affairs in the face of an emergency: "Who assumes authority concerning those matters for which there are no positive stipulations. . . ? In other words, Who is responsible for that for which competence has not been anticipated?" (*PT*, 10). According to Schmitt's formulation, in all cases of emergency it would seem necessary to have recourse to a unitary institution with a monopoly on decisions so that no such confusion or conflict occurs. Since the likelihood of such an occurrence is great (especially in the Weimar context), and since the same figure who acts upon the exception must first declare that it exists in Schmitt's scheme, it would seemingly be best to have such a person vigilant even during normal times. Thus, in violation of the main principles of classical dictatorship, normalcy and exception are collapsed, and ordinary rule of law is dangerously encroached on by exceptional absolutism.

The second possible explanation for Schmitt's transformation from *Die Diktatur* to *Political Theology* may be offered by the overall narrative thrust of *Die Diktatur* itself. Schmitt is distrustful of the general historical trend wherein the concepts of sovereignty—increasingly popular sovereignty—and emergency action are merged. As stated, for Schmitt this culminates in the abuses of the French and Russian revolutions. In Schmitt's view the revolutionary theorists advocate a sovereign dictatorship that destroys an old order and creates a new one *not* on the authority of a specific constitutional document or legal charge, but rather as the agent of a vague entity such as the 'people'. He writes in the earlier work: "While the commissarial dictatorship is authorized by a constituted organ and maintains a title in the standing constitution, the sovereign dictator is derived only *quoad execitium* and directly out of the formless *pouvoir constituant*" (D, 145).

In the conclusion of *Die Diktatur*, Schmitt returns to the issue of the Communists' use of the term dictatorship, for he clearly sees them as the heirs of the French revolutionaries: that is, a radical elite that will use violent means supposedly in step with world-historical processes and allegedly sanctioned by an anointed populace to which it can never really be held accountable. Schmitt writes:

> The concept of dictatorship . . . as taken up in the presentations of Marx and Engels was realized at first as only a generally requisite political slogan. . . . But the succeeding tradition . . . infused a clear conception of 1793 into the year 1848, and indeed not only as the sum of political experience and methods. As the concept developed in systematic relationship to the philosophy of the nineteenth century and in political relationship with the experience of world war a particular impression must remain. . . . Viewed from a general state theory, dictatorship by a proletariat, equated with the people, as the overcoming of an economic condition, in which the state 'dies out', presupposes a sovereign dictatorship, as it underlies the theory and practice of the National Convention. Engels, in his speech to the

Communist Union in March 1850, demanded that its practice be the same as 'March 1793'. That is also valid for the theory of the state that posits the transition to statelessness. (*D*, 205)

In other words, the dangerous spirit of France in 1793—a spirit of sovereign dictatorship in the name of a newly sovereign people, a spirit that culminates for Schmitt only in domestic terror and continental war—was radicalized in the revolutions of 1848, and is now embodied by the Soviet power to Germany's east and by the German revolutionary organizations who, at the very moment that Schmitt is writing *Die Diktatur*, were attempting to destroy or seize the German state.

Why does Schmitt conclude the book with this specter? What does his historical account of dictatorship offer such a situation? The tone of the conclusion differs significantly enough from that of the preface and the body of the work such that we can detect a subtle yet distinct change in strategy. Schmitt's preface seemed to suggest that his goal was (1) to make up for the scholarly deficiency in the 'bourgeois literature' on the subject of dictatorship; (2) to make it possible to deem the Communist use of the term 'sovereign', and hence somehow illegitimate, dictatorship; and furthermore (3) to offer a more legitimate, constitutional, commissarial alternative with which the new republic might address the various emergencies with which it was confronted.

But Schmitt intimates toward the close of *Die Diktatur* that perhaps what should confront the sovereign notion of dictatorship touted by domestic and foreign revolutionaries is not a notion of commissarial dictatorship at all, but perhaps a counter-theory of sovereign dictatorship. Since both absolutism and mass democracy arise out of the same historical movement, Schmitt suggests—gently and furtively— that perhaps a radicalized notion of sovereignty derived from absolute monarchy should engage the radicalized notion of sovereignty derived from the French Revolution:

> at least for the continental constitutional liberalism of the eighteenth and nineteenth centuries the historical value of absolute monarchy lies in the annihilation of the feudal and estatist powers and that through that it created a sovereignty in the modern sense of state unity. So is this realized unity the foundational presupposition of the revolutionary literature of the eighteenth century. The tendency to isolate the individual and to abolish each social group within the state and with that set the individual and the state directly across from one another was emphasized in both the

depiction of the theory of legal despotism and that of the social contract. . . . [According to Condorcet] we live today no more in time, in which there are within the state powerful groups and classes; the *puissante* associations have vanished. . . . In the years 1832 and 1848 — important dates for the development of the state of siege into a significant legal institution — the question was asked whether the political organization of the proletariat and their counter-effect did not in fact create a whole new political situation and with that create new state and legal concepts. (*D*, 203–4)

There are several possible conclusions to be drawn from this rather murky paragraph: Perhaps the conjunction of emergency powers and mass sociopolitical movements as embodied in the revolutionary moments of 1832 and 1848 ought not to be severed as they would be with a revival of the classical notion of commissarial emergency powers. Perhaps the return of powerful social groups threatening the state in the form of working-class movements ought to be met by a political response that is novel and yet somehow akin to the absolute monarchs' destruction of aristocratic and religious groups. Perhaps the populist Soviet state that can be directed to do almost anything by an all-powerful, unaccountable, historically legitimated elite, should be engaged by a similarly defined German state directed by a charismatically legitimated president. These are conclusions implicitly suggested, not explicitly argued, by the closing pages of *Die Diktatur*. Yet these pages serve as a signpost for his subsequent book, *Political Theology*, its infamous opening sentence and indeed the rest of his Weimar work. Gone from Schmitt's writings after *Die Diktatur* are the neo-Kantian attempts to keep his authoritarian tendencies within a rule-of-law framework that characterize his earlier writings and govern the moderating impulses of most of that book.[14]

In *Political Theology*, as described above, Schmitt espouses a neo-sovereignty embodied in the Reichspräsident, encumbered not by constitutional restraints but only by the ambiguous demands of the political exception. The president, as the personal embodiment of the popular will which cannot be procedurally ascertained in a time of crisis, has the authority to act — unconstitutionally or even anticonstitutionally — with all the force and legitimacy of that originary popular will.[15] Schmitt hence begins to champion the very fusing of popular sovereignty and emergency powers that he showed to be potentially abusive in *Die Diktatur*. Subsequently in his influential book *Parlia-*

mentarism, written the very next year, Schmitt, after purporting to show the illusory character of the *Reichstag*'s rivalry to the Reichspräsident, suggests that the only myth to counter-balance the Soviets' myth of a worldwide stateless and classless society is the myth of the nation.[16] And Schmitt spends much of his magnum opus from 1928, *Verfassungslehre*, building just such a conception of the nation into constitutional law, and providing the preeminent place within it for the Reichspräsident. Perhaps most dramatically, as Schmitt remarks regarding the Soviets in an essay appended to his notorious *Concept of the Political* in 1932: "We in Central Europe live under the eyes of the Russians. For a century their psychological gaze has seen through our great words and our institutions. Their vitality is strong enough to seize our knowledge and technology as weapons. Their prowess in rationalism and its opposite, as well as their potential for good and evil in orthodoxy, is overwhelming."[17] The strategy of formulating a neo-absolutist presidency that can fortify Germany in withstanding the Soviet threat becomes central to his Weimar work.[18]

But Schmitt would also continue to deal with emergency powers in Weimar. And while he had substantively abandoned the powerful notion of commissarial dictatorship that he revived in *Die Diktatur*, as we will see, he still tried to maintain the appearance of it in his writings.

Guardian or Usurper of the Constitution?

In the practical-political treatises that deal with emergency powers written after *Political Theology*—"Die Diktatur der Reichspräsident nach Art. 48 der Weimarer Verfassung" (The Dictatorship of the Reichspräsident according to Article 48 of the Weimar Constitution; 1924) *Der Hüter der Verfassung* (The Guardian of the Constitution; 1931), and *Legalität und Legitimität* (Legality and Legitimacy; 1932)—Schmitt continues to argue that only the Reichspräsident can defend the Weimar constitutional regime in a crisis.[19] However, it is not at first glance clear in these works whether the powers that Schmitt wishes to confer on the president are, according to the terms Schmitt developed in 1921, commissarial or sovereign. But the injection of the issues of charisma and sovereignty into his discussion strongly suggests the latter.

The "Article 48" piece of 1924 has made an accurate assessment of Schmitt's theory of emergency powers difficult because it was included in later editions of *Diktatur*, thus coloring the pre-*Political Theology* work with a post-*Political Theology* perspective. Many commentators have thus concluded that Schmitt had implied a sovereign type of dictatorship for the president's emergency powers from the start.[20] Yet even the essay written later is not so obviously an endorsement of sovereign dictatorship.[21] Schmitt declares that according to Article 48, dictatorial authority is only lent to the president (D2, 255), and argues for the scope of that authority to remain seemingly within a commissarial rubric: "The typical image of a rule-of-law regulation of the exceptional situation . . . presumes that the extraordinary authority as well as the content of that authority is circumscribed and delimited, as well as that a special control be established. Nevertheless with that a certain latitude [*Spielraum*] must remain to make possible the very purpose of the institution—energetic engagement—and to prevent the state and constitution from perishing in 'legality'" (D2, 255). Certainly the Roman dictatorship as Schmitt describes it in *Die Diktatur* fits just this description: legally prescribed time and task yet wide room for play within those established limits. And the dictatorship's very reason to be was in fact to suspend the legal constitution so as to restore it, rather than blindly maintain it and allow for its destruction. But somewhat less in the spirit of republican dictatorship, Schmitt does not want *too* extensive a limitation on the emergency powers of the president, because a constitution after all "is the organization of the state; and it decides what order is—what normal order is—and provides for the unity and security of the state. It is a dangerous abuse to use the constitution to delineate all possible affairs of the heart [*Herzensangelegenheiten*] as basic law and quasi-basic law" (D2, 243).

But Schmitt's descriptions of the source of the president's legitimacy in preserving the constitution in "Article 48" increasingly sound as though they were mandated *not* by the constitutional order itself but something like a sovereign will that is itself *prior* to that order: "The dictatorship of the *Reichspräsident* . . . is necessarily commissarial as a result of specific circumstances. . . . In as much as it is allowed to act so broadly, it operates—in fact, not in its legal establishment—as the residue of the sovereign dictatorship of the National Assembly" (D2, 241). Schmitt is thus coopting the revolutionary spirit of sovereignty in 1793 France *from* the revolutionary tradition itself and *for* his counter-theory of nationalist-authoritarian sovereignty by raising the issue of what might be done presently in the name of the 1919 National Assembly that established the Weimar Republic and its constitution.

At the conclusion of the essay, Schmitt recalls the framing of Article 48 at the Republic's constitutional founding: "In the Summer of 1919 when Article 48 came to be, one thing was clear: Germany found itself in a wholly abnormal crisis and therefore for the moment a one-time authority was necessary which made possible decisive action" (*D2*, 258–59).

Schmitt calls for similar "abnormal" and "decisive" action but attempts to allay the fears of those who might be concerned with the constitutional status of such action with his final sentence: "That would be no constitutional alteration" (*D2*, 259). In other words, he is supposedly not calling for constitution-abrogating action characteristic of sovereign dictatorship on the part of the president, but rather commissarial, constitution-preserving action. But of course his harkening back to the *crisis* in which the constitution was founded and to the preconstitutional constituting *decision* and not to the body of the constitution itself implies a repetition of a sovereign act of founding to save the constitution—one in which the constitution may in fact be changed as long as the preconstitutional will is not. This strategy of justifying presidential dictatorial action on the basis of the preconstitutional sovereign will of the people and not the principles embodied within the constitution itself becomes more pronounced after Schmitt formulates his constitutional theory in the 1928 book of that name, *Verfassungslehre*, along precisely these lines, and as he seeks a solution to the Weimar Republic's most severe crisis in his books published in the wake of devastating economic depression and widespread political unrest in the early 1930s, *Der Hüter der Verfassung* and *Legalität und Legitimität*.

Schmitt begins *Der Hüter der Verfassung* in much the same way that he began his book on dictatorship exactly ten years earlier. He blames nineteenth-century liberalism for bringing a crucial constitutional institution into ill repute and he draws on examples from classical Sparta and Rome to demonstrate the historical legitimacy of such a concept and authority. But whereas in *Die Diktatur* the example that Schmitt is attempting to revive is commissarial dictatorship, in *Der Hüter* it is the notion of a defender of the constitution (*HV*, 7–9), and indeed the merging of the two phenomena—emergency powers and the question of in what charismatic institution sovereignty lies—is again precisely his strategy.[22]

By consistently appealing to emergency circumstances Schmitt is able to sufficiently discredit the Weimar judiciary to keep it from playing any potential role in 'guarding' the constitution: the judiciary presupposes norms and a guardian of the constitution may need to act beyond norms (*HV*, 19), and moreover, since the judiciary acts *post factum*, it is always, "politically speaking, too late" (*HV*, 32–33). Schmitt does not fully engage the important question of whether in normal times the judiciary could be a guardian of the constitution through a practice of judicial review; he absolves himself from doing so by appealing to the "abnormal contemporary situation of Germany . . . of neither economic prosperity nor internal security" (*HV*, 13)—a claim repeated throughout the book to forswear the theoretical responsibility of confronting arguments that would weaken his position.

When raising the question of whether the necessary executive attention to the contemporary crisis is "dictatorial" (*HV*, 117) Schmitt still writes superficially as though it could in fact be performed according to commissarial principles: "strong attempts at remedy and counter-movement can only be undertaken *constitutionally* and *legally* through the *Reichspräsident*" (*HV*, 131). But the substance, limits, and justification of such remedies smack of what Schmitt had previously defined as constitutionally dangerous sovereign action. According to Schmitt, the socioeconomic fracturing of society caused by an uncontrolled pluralism have rendered parliament superfluous and threaten the very existence of the state: "The development toward an economic state was encountered by a simultaneous development of parliament into a stage [*Schauplatz*] for the pluralist system and thus in that lies the cause of the constitutional entanglement as well as the necessity for establishing a remedy and countermovement" (*HV*, 117). However, this particular situation that the president must address necessarily calls for activity that is substantially beyond commissarial action and restitution; it entails the wholesale redirecting of structural historical transformation on a macro-economic, social, and political scale.[23] This is a redirecting that could never be met in the time- and task-bound fashion of commissarial dictatorship, but that must rather be met by the constitution-amending action of a sovereign dictatorship. Does Schmitt expect that he can call for the wholesale reconstruction of the state-society relationship[24] and not be seen to simultaneously call for the wholesale reconstruction of the Weimar Constitution? As Hans Kelsen points out in his response to the book, Schmitt reduces the whole constitution to the emergency powers of Article 48.[25] This fact in combination with Schmitt's besmirching of the prestige of the other branches of government—judiciary and legislative—means that he can actually ignore the constitution without literally destroying it. As such he can claim ingenuously to promote a commissarial dictatorship of the president.

Moreover, in marginalizing the other branches of government in

Guardian, Schmitt cleverly removes any checks that could give the president's dictatorial actions any semblance of a substantively commissarial nature: Schmitt admits that a working *Reichstag* would be an appropriate check on presidential emergency powers (*HV,* 130–31). But since such a situation does not obtain he makes no effort to search for an alternative check. In fact, precisely because the president is plebiscitarily elected by the people there is no need for checks because the unity of the people's sovereign will is charismatically embodied within him and his emergency action is thus necessarily legitimate (*HV,* 116, 156–57).

Thus in *Der Hüter* Schmitt is a kind of prisoner of the very theoretical paradigm that he himself set out a decade earlier in *Die Diktatur.* Schmitt feels the need at least to attempt to cloak his proposed sovereign dictatorship in the garb of the commissarial one he described in the earlier work—a work which he suspiciously never mentions. There is no reference to the first edition of *Die Diktatur* despite the fact that he cites the post-*Political Theology* essay from 1924 on Article 48 that is included as an appendix in the second edition (*HV,* 130–31). He does not however neglect to recapitulate the key first sentence of *Political Theology:* "The exceptional situation . . . unveils the core of the state in its concrete singularity" (*HV,* 131). And accordingly he has continued the equation of sovereignty and emergency powers.

Yet despite the avoidance of *Die Diktatur,* his post–*Political Theology* merging of the concept of sovereignty with emergency powers is, as stated above, a response to the conclusions worked out in that book about the historical trajectory of popular sovereignty and state power. By the conclusion of *Der Hüter,* Schmitt has formulated a popularly legitimated sovereign dictatorship of the nation in the person of a charismatic German president, one who in essence mirrors the popularly legitimated sovereign dictatorship of the proletariat in the body of the Soviet Communist Party. Presumably it is against this latter external enemy and its domestic partisans that Schmitt's nation is ready to take action: The Weimar Constitution, concludes Schmitt,

> presupposes the entire German people as a unity which is immediately ready for action and not first mediated through social-group organization. It can express its will and at the decisive moment find its way back to unity and bring its influence to bear over and beyond pluralistic divisions. The constitution seeks especially to give the authority of the *Reichspräsident* the possibility of binding itself

immediately with the political total will of the German people and precisely thereby to act as guardian and protector of the unity and totality of the German people. (*HV,* 159)

In his book-length essay from the following year, *Legalität und Legitimität,* Schmitt would continue this line of argument such that it is almost impossible to recognize when he is discussing normal constitutional operations and when he is discussing emergency ones; all of the former have been subsumed in the latter. The oft-asserted existence of a tension within the Weimar Constitution that serves as the source for the title of the book—"plebiscitary legitimacy" versus "statutory legality" (*LL,* 312)—is to be resolved in favor of the former. The grounds for this lie in the historical necessity of a mass democratic moment, what Schmitt calls the "plebiscitary immediacy of the deciding people as legislator" (*LL,* 314). And he cites the intellectual originator of this historical moment, Jean-Jacques Rousseau and his "argument for immediate, plebiscitary, non-representative democracy" (*LL,* 314). The president as vessel for such immediacy takes on authority similar to that of the traditional "extraordinary legislator" who may act "against the law" (*LL,* 320). As we will see below, John Locke's notion of executive prerogative allows for political action that is explicitly against the law and yet is still true to the constitutional order; but a legislator such as the one Schmitt draws from Rousseau, as Schmitt himself explained in *Die Diktatur,* acts against the constitution and may in fact found a new one. According to the Schmitt of *Legalität und Legitimität,*

> in the person of the president the simple jurisprudential truth breaks through all normative fictions and obscurities: norms are only valid for normal situations and the presupposed normalcy of the situation is in a positive legal sense constitutive of their "validity." But the legislator of the normal situation is something different than the Action-Commissar of the abnormal crisis who restores the normal situation of "security and order." If one views him as a "legislator" and his measures as "statutes" then, despite all such equations, there remains a distinctiveness which brings it about that the "legislative measures" of the Action-Commissar, precisely because they are equated with "statutes," destroy the system of legality of the parliamentary statutory state. (*LL,* 321)[26]

Schmitt appears concerned that the distinction might be lost between law made under normal legislative circumstances and measures issued by executive decree during emergency ones. Schmitt's emphasis on the distinction might allay the fears of those who worry about the latter alternative becoming permanent. But Schmitt's categories would make it impossible to remove such a regime once in place by appeals to "normalcy." Thus it is *Schmitt's* equation of the normal and the exceptional that would intentionally destroy the parliamentary state.

In his 1958 introduction to *Legalität und Legitimität* in the collection in which it was ultimately included, Schmitt claimed that he had always—and particularly in that work—argued for commissarial dictatorial authority for the president, because that is all that was granted to the office by the Weimar Constitution (*LL*, at 260–61). As we can see, by 1932 Schmitt moved so far away from this position that the distinction between sovereign and commissarial dictatorship no longer had any meaning. In *Die Diktatur* he criticizes the Communists for underestimating and disparaging the importance of the normal political order at the expense of the exceptional one: "Whoever sees in the core of all law only [the possibility of its suspension] is not quite able himself to find an adequate concept of dictatorship because for him every legal order is only latent or intermittent dictatorship" (*D*, xvii). He thus aptly describes the Carl Schmitt of *Political Theology* and after, the one who would attain such infamy for his subsequent Weimar and post-Weimar career.[27] But is there anything to be culled from Schmitt's Weimar work on emergency powers that is relevant to an adequate contemporary theory of the subject?

Constitutional Emergency Powers

I have demonstrated above how Schmitt's book on emergency powers from 1921, *Die Diktatur*, is not in fact the blatant apology for executive absolutism that most interpreters have deemed it. For the most part, this book differs significantly from the works that would follow it—especially Schmitt's next effort, *Political Theology*—even if within *Die Diktatur* is found the germ of his subsequent transformation. Through this we can observe perhaps more clearly than before where, how, and even why a particularly brilliant Weimar conservative in fact became a Weimar fascist: to confront the malignant development of popular sovereignty as revolutionary dictatorship in Soviet Russia and state-threatening internal revolutionary groups, Schmitt resorts to a no less malignant definition of sovereignty as expressed in a nationalist presidential-dictatorship. His role in undermining the Weimar Constitution and his subsequent political affiliation need no comment here.[28] This is more or less consequential from the standpoint of the history of political thought, but one might still ask what can this authoritarian *Beserker*—to employ the term by which Schmitt would often refer to fanatics on the left—offer anyone remotely interested in constitutional democracy? I think that there are several important points to be drawn from Schmitt's Weimar work on emergency powers—particularly as they relate to the distinction between commissarial and sovereign dictatorships and to the infamous first sentence of *Political Theology* that explodes that very distinction:

a. Liberal constitutionalism has been insufficiently attentive to the idea of political exceptions;

b. The notion of sovereignty should be uncoupled from the institution of emergency powers in constitutions that have them; and

c. There ought to be a constitutional distinction between who decides and who acts in emergency situations.

Liberalism and the Decline of the Exception
According to Schmitt's account, as Enlightenment political thought falls increasingly under the thrall of modern natural science it comes to regard nature, and hence political nature, as more of a regular phenomenon. Consequently there is deemed less need for the discretionary and prudential powers, long conferred on judges and executives by traditional political theories, including Aristotelianism and scholasticism— discretion and prudence that found its extreme example in the case of classical dictatorship. As the functional necessity of such discretion apparently subsides in the Enlightenment, the normative assessment of it becomes increasingly negative, and such prudence becomes associated with arbitrariness and abuse of state power.[29]

However, Schmitt accuses liberalism of abandoning exceptional prudence far earlier than is actually the case. In *Political Theology*, Schmitt remarks that the exception was "incommensurable" with John Locke's theory of constitutionalism (*PT*, 13). Yet Locke's famous "Prerogative" power is actually the "last hurrah" of the notion of political prudence within liberalism:

'tis fit that the Laws themselves should in some Cases give way to the Executive Power . . . that as much as may be, all the Members of the Society are to be preserved . . . since many accidents may happen, wherein a strict and rigid observation of the law may do harm. . . . [I]t is impossible to foresee, and so by laws provide for, all Accidents and Necessities, that may concern the publick . . . therefore there is a latitude left to the Executive power, to do many things of choice, which the laws do not prescribe.[30]

Locke does then contradict Schmitt's interpretation, for he has a notion of acting above or against the law in times of unforeseen occurrences, that is compatible with—nay, is embedded within—his constitutionalism.

While it has become a kind of ritual for liberals to wave their copies of the *Second Treatise* (open to the passages on prerogative) when criticized for having an inadequate notion of exceptional circumstances and emergency powers, Schmitt's criticisms of liberalism after Locke are in fact quite legitimate. And his focus on the subsequent theory of the separation of powers, particularly in the form that Montesquieu made so influential, as somehow culpable in the mechanistic de-discretionizing of politics is on the mark.[31] As Bernard Manin observes, "One of Montesquieu's most important innovations was precisely to do away with any notion of a discretionary power in his definition of the three governmental functions."[32]

Liberalism's denial of the exception and avoidance of the discretionary activity that was traditionally sanctioned to deal with it, not only makes liberal regimes susceptible to emergencies but also leaves them vulnerable to alternatives like the one eventually put forth by Schmitt. As Manin describes it, "Once the notion of prerogative power was abandoned, no possibility of legitimately acting beside or against the law was left."[33] The only apparent recourse available in this milieu to political actors confronted with a political exception is to act *illegitimately* and hope to pass off such action as legitimate.[34] Lack of constitutionally facilitated emergency prerogative may also provide the opportunity to those like Schmitt who would use this particular liberal deficiency as a ruse to scrap the whole legal order. In this sense, Schmitt's deciding sovereign can be seen as the violent return of the prerogative repressed by scientistic liberalism.[35]

The simple fact that the supposed pinnacle of Enlightenment constitutional engineering, the United States Constitution, does not have a clearly enumerated provision for emergency situations is a powerful testament to liberalism's neglect of the political exception. It is this liberalism, particularly in its post-Kantian form, that Schmitt was most concerned to criticize for attempting to systematize all of political phenomena.[36]

Disengaging Sovereignty from Emergency Powers

Put most crudely, sovereignty concerns self-defined political entities that through noncoercive procedures, such as constitutional conventions, transfer a political will into a constitution that allows for further expression of that will through formally correct laws, and even change of that will through emendations to the constitution itself. Constitutional mechanisms such as parliamentary procedure or separation of powers are not meant to thwart, stymie, or retard the political will of the populace, but rather to insure that this will is not self-destructive through rash demands and abuse of numerical minorities.[37] An emergency provision should be seen as one such mechanism among many constitutional provisions. It therefore has no privileged link, neither direct nor exclusive, with the "original" political will—a link that Schmitt so dramatically asserts in *Political Theology*. Furthermore, in a constitution with a proper scheme for separating powers, no branch—whether explicitly responsible for emergency activity or not—has an independent claim on sovereignty. (But of course, the separation of powers as well as parliamentary deliberation and judicial review, are precisely the kinds of liberal principles that Schmitt works so hard to discredit and destroy in his political theory after 1921.) Using Schmitt against himself, the refreshingly technical quality of classical dictatorship should be brought to bear in considerations on modern emergency powers and not the substantively existential quality of sovereign dictatorship. As Schmitt demonstrates in *Die Diktatur*, the Roman Republic was not reduced to a mere technocracy by the highly technical deployment of emergency powers; nor would a modern liberal democracy be so reduced by uncoupling the notion of democratic 'substance' from executive emergency action.[38]

In short therefore, Schmitt's exclamation in *Political Theology* that "It is precisely the exception that makes relevant the subject of sovereignty, that is, the whole question of sovereignty" (*PT*, 6) is a patently false and, as he himself suggested in his previous book, a dangerous position. The exception does not reveal anything—except perhaps that eighteenth- and nineteenth-century liberals were politically naive about constitutional emergencies; and perhaps that constitutions and their framers are not omniscient. It offers a no more existentially profound truth than that. If the constitution's primary purpose is to establish an institution such as a presidency to exclusively embody the preconstitutional sovereign will in a time of crisis then the constitution is inviting its own disposability. The ultimate purpose of emergency powers, as Schmitt knew quite well, is a goal diametrically opposed to this one, that is, the prolonged endurance of a constitution.

Who Decides on the Exception? Who Acts on It?
Besides the sovereignty/exception dichotomy there is another distinction deliberately obfuscated by the first sentence of *Political Theology:* the previously mentioned ambiguity over the theoretical-political implications of the preposition "on" [*über*]. The genius of the classical notion of dictatorship that Schmitt reveals in 1921 and then conceals in 1922 is this: the normal institution that decides that an exceptional situation exists (for instance, the Roman Senate) itself chooses the one who acts to address that situation (for instance, the dictator through the consuls). This has the obvious practical advantage that a collegial body of numerous members, like the Senate, commissions a smaller body, such as the consuls, to appoint a single individual to more expediently deal with an emergency than could a multimembered body. But there are more subtle ramifications as well: for instance, the initiating institution cannot so readily declare an exception that it might in turn exploit into an occasion for the expansion of its own power, emergency authority now lying in the hands of another institution. Moreover, given how jealous political actors are of the boundaries of their own authority, the fact that the normal institution decides to give up its own power in the first place will probably insure that a real emergency exists. This technique also helps guarantee that an agent is chosen who is sufficiently trustworthy to give that power back. This external authorization on the execution of emergency powers works simultaneously as a kind of check on, and compensation for, the relinquisher of power who declares an emergency, as well as a potentially astute selection device for the executor on the exception. This is a technique neglected by even the more sophisticated formulations of emergency provisions in modern constitutions that is, however, worth reconsidering.[39]

None of the preceding is meant to suggest that constitutional emergency provisions will necessarily prevent the collapse of regimes in situations of crisis. Indeed we know from both the contemporary context of certain Latin American regimes and Schmitt's own context of Weimar Germany that emergency provisions can themselves serve on occasion as the pretense for *coups*. In societies where there is not firm civilian control of the military, constitutional emergency provisions often do more harm than good. Nor is the presentation above intended to imply that the institution of classical commissarial dictatorship ought to be revived and applied wholesale to contemporary constitutional concerns. Clearly, while the classical institution of dictatorship suspended the rule of law in a relatively unproblematic fashion, it did not have the now indispensable notion of rights with which to grapple. While the formula of suspending law only to reinstate it shortly more or less makes sense, it finds no corollary with the element of rights; it is far less convincing to argue that it is necessary to suspend or violate rights in order ultimately to uphold them. This is the kind of logic all too characteristic of the many modern 'sovereign' dictatorships that effectively eclipse the classical notion.

But certainly Schmitt's exposure of liberalism's metaphysical bias against constitutional contingency at least suggests a reconsideration of the relative prudence of constitutional emergency provisions in contemporary liberal democratic regimes. Also the potential abuse of the merging of emergency powers and popular sovereignty as both forewarned against and perpetuated by Schmitt deserves serious attention. And finally the precise mechanisms of better identifying and addressing an emergency situation is a necessity of contemporary constitution-making, particularly in places like the former Communist regimes of Eastern Europe.[40]

Conclusion

Schmitt argued that one could define the essence of a particular regime by specifically discerning what its emergency provisions negated: if the classical dictatorship negated the rule of law, then that was the essence of classical Roman politics, according to Schmitt. One might not wish to vouch for the analytical or metaphysical efficacy of this theoretical method in general. But I do think that by considering what Schmitt himself negates with the opening sentence of *Political Theology* and observing how that work repudiates much of what is perhaps valuable in the book published before it, we may learn something about the history, the potential necessity, and the better deployment of constitutional emergency powers.

As stated above, the contents of Schmitt's first book on emergency powers, *Die Diktatur*, are often conflated with those of an essay appended to it in 1924 as well as with the arguments of the more famous and more extremist treatise of 1922, *Political Theology.* I have demonstrated how the intuitive thrusts of *Die Diktatur* are in fact quite different than what has often been presented by commentators. I say 'intuitive thrust' because *Die Diktatur* is not necessarily a book of arguments but rather one of historical musings and suggestive moments. It is by no means an explicit argument for, or straightforward endorsement of, a liberalesque rule-of-law approach to emergency powers. But it is precisely the unargued explication of the history of emergency powers in *Die Diktatur* that allows certain potentially nonauthoritarian facets of that tradition to emerge—even if Schmitt himself violently repudiates those instances in his very next book, *Political Theology.* In the course of the article I have suggested that this transition from *Die Diktatur* to *Political Theology* indicates a shift from conservatism to fascism in Schmitt's theory. As he begins to sense the irresistibility and intensity of the leftist mass-democratic movements he describes in *Die Diktatur* Schmitt begins to formulate a rightist mass-democratic conception in *Political Theology.* Wary of the revolutionary fusing of popular sovereignty and emergency provisions in *Die Diktatur* Schmitt begins to endorse a reactionary fusing of the two in *Political Theology*— an endorsement announced by its dramatic first line.

I hope to have salvaged the useful examples of emergency powers in Schmitt's historical account in the earlier work from the weight of the polemical writings on emergency powers that came after and buried them; and perhaps offer them to a wider scholarly field of constitutional emergency provisions. In terms of the potentially generalizable themes from Schmitt's analyses, I have suggested that we take seriously Schmitt's characterization of liberalism as avoiding and repressing political exceptions. But in so doing I have proposed that we also follow Schmitt's initial impulse on not conflating popular sovereignty with emergency powers, and not collapsing the separation of deciding and acting on the exception. In other words, we should retain for heuristic purposes the distinction between commissarial and sovereign types of emergency action.

Notes

This essay was originally a paper presented at the 17th IVR World Congress, Bologna, June 16–21, 1995. For comments and criticisms on earlier drafts I thank Stephen Holmes, Ulrich K. Preuss and my panel coparticipants in

Bologna. However I am most deeply indebted to Bernard Manin from whom I have learned much about emergency powers in numerous conversations, from his lectures, and his work-in-progress on the subject. The Fulbright Commission supported this paper with a grant for a year of research at the Center for European Legal Policy, University of Bremen.

1 *Political Theology: Four Chapters on the Theory of Sovereignty* (1922), trans. G. Schwab (Cambridge, Mass.: MIT Press, 1986), at 5 (hereafter *PT*). German references to the work come from *Politische Theologie: Vier Kapitel zur Lehre von der Souveränität* (Munich: Duncker & Humblot, 1934), 11.

2 *Die Diktatur: Von den Anfängen des modernen Souveränitätsgedankens bis zum proletarischen Klassenkampf* (Berlin: Duncker & Humblot, 1989) (hereafter *D*).

3 *Politische Theologie*, supra n. 1, at 22.

4 See F. M. Watkins, *The Failure of Constitutional Emergency Powers under the German Republic* (Cambridge, Mass.: Harvard University Press, 1939), at chaps. 2 and 3, for an account of Ebert's use of Article 48 against the authoritarian Kapp Putsch of 1920, the Hitlerian Beer Hall *Putsch* of 1923, as well as against the many Communist insurrections between 1919 and 1923. On Ebert's use of the article in the economic sphere, see C. Rossiter, *Constitutional Dictatorship: Crisis Government in Modern Democracies* (Princeton, N.J.: Princeton University Press, 1948), at 41–43. On the context of the book, *Die Diktatur*, more specifically, see J. Bendersky, *Carl Schmitt: Theorist for the Reich* (Princeton, N.J.: Princeton University Press, 1983), at 30–31.

Under the rather broad powers provided for by Article 48, the directly elected Reichspräsident could compel, with armed force if required, an individual state or *Land* to comply with federal law (par. 1); and he could take "necessary measures" to restore or protect "public order and safety" by suspending constitutional rights and by recourse to armed force when public order was "disturbed or endangered" (par. 2). The limits to the president's emergency powers as enumerated within the article itself include the immediate informing of the general parliamentary body, the Reichstag, of any emergency action; the Reichstag's right of revoking such action (both, par. 3); and a statute to prescribe the exact details of the president's authority (par. 5); from without the article itself, the counter-signature of the chancellor of the parliamentary government was required for all presidential measures including those issued under Article 48 (Art. 50) and there existed a constitutional provision for impeachment (Art. 43). The president could bypass such restrictions by dissolving the Reichstag (Art. 28) or by colluding with the chancellor (and as an aside, the statute to circumscribe presidential emergency powers was never enacted). Social Democrat Ebert did not abuse the constitution in any of these ways during the Republic's early period of crisis, as did conservative Paul von Hindenburg in machination with successive right-wing chancellors (Brüning, von Papen, and von Schleicher), during the second and final period of crisis between 1929 and 1933. See K. D. Bracher, *Die Auflösung der Weimarer Republik: Eine Studie zum Problem des Machtverfalls in der Demokratie* (Düsseldorf: Droste, 1984); D. Peukert, *The Weimar Republic: The Crisis of Classical Modernity* (New York: Hill and Wang, 1987); A. Winkler, *Weimar: 1918–1933* (Munich: C. H. Beck, 1993); and H. Heiber, *The Weimar Republic*, trans. W. E. Yuill (Oxford: Blackwell, 1993). I will deal with Schmitt's writings on presidential emergency powers and complicity with the right-wing constitutional usurpers during this period in later sections of this paper.

5 Schmitt's onetime student, Otto Kirchheimer, criticizes the way that socialists wrongly define dictatorship and cites, problematically, *Die Diktatur* and *Politische Theologie* as equivalents (see "The Socialist and Bolshevik Theory of the State," [published 1928] in F. S. Burin and K. L. Shell, eds., *Politics, Law and Social Change: Selected Essays of Otto Kirchheimer* [New York: Columbia University Press, 1969], 6). He goes on to paraphrase Schmitt on the apparently commissarial yet actually sovereign nature of Bolshevik dictatorship, ibid., at 15. As faithful as Schmitt's leftist students often were to Schmitt's theory of dictatorship, their frequent equating of the arguments of *Die Diktatur* and *Politische Theologie* have done as much to obfuscate as to clarify the crucial issues involved (Kirchheimer repeats this equation in his essay from 1944, "In Quest of Sovereignty," ibid., 191). On the specifics of Schmitt's intellectual relationship to leftist legal scholars such as O. Kirchheimer and F. Neumann, see W. E. Scheuerman, *Between the Norm and the Exception: The Frankfurt School and the Rule of Law* (Cambridge, Mass.: MIT Press, 1994) (hereafter *Between the Norm and the Exception*).

6 On Schmitt's appropriation of the etymological-theoretical distinction from Jean Bodin, and for a general discussion of the thesis, see G. Schwab, *The Challenge of the Exception: An Introduction to the Political Ideas of Carl Schmitt between 1921 and 1936* (New York: Greenwood Press, 1989), at 30–31 (hereafter *The Challenge of the Exception*).

7 Interestingly, Schmitt's complaint from the 1920s is still relevant today, as the "bourgeois political literature" in English on dictatorship and emergency powers is paltry and outdated: besides the classics by Watkins and Rossiter, supra n. 4, see most recently J. E. Finn, *Constitutions in Crisis: Political Violence and the Rule of Law* (Oxford: Oxford University Press, 1991) and J. Lobel, "Emergency Powers and the Decline of Liberalism," 98 *Yale L.J.* 1989, 1385. It is still the Left that exhibits more interest in the concept of dictatorship. Two post-Marxists influenced by Schmitt who have written extensively on the subject are Paul Hirst and Norberto Bobbio. Schmitt's former student, leftist lawyer Franz Neumann, remarked in the 1950s: "Strange though it may seem, we do not possess any systematic study of dictatorship." He cites Schmitt's *Die Diktatur* but declares with no explanation that "his analysis is not acceptable" ("Notes on the Theory of Dictatorship"

[published 1954], in H. Marcuse, ed., *The Democratic and the Authoritarian State: Essays in Political and Legal Theory* (New York: The Free Press, 1957), at 233, 254, n. 1). As I will argue, this conclusion can only be drawn by conflating the respective analyses of *Die Diktatur* with *Political Theology*.

8 Schmitt distinguishes between dictatorship and military government, or the state of siege, in "Diktatur und Belagerungszustand: Eine staatsrechtliche Studie," *Zeitschrift für die gesamte Strafrechtswissenschaft* (1917): at 38. For an extensive discussion of the essay that may however too baldly read back into this early work Schmitt's later more extreme authoritarianism, see P. C. Caldwell, *Constitutional Theory in the Weimar Republic: Positivists, Anti-Positivists and the Democratic Welfare State* (Ph.D. diss., Department of History, Cornell University, August 1993) (hereafter *Constitutional Theory in the Weimar Republic*).

9 For an alternative account to the one offered by Schmitt of Machiavelli's conception of exceptional circumstances and the institutional means with which to deal with them, see J. P. McCormick, "Addressing the Political Exception: Machiavelli's Accidents and the Mixed Regime," *American Political Science Review* 87 (1993): 888.

10 On Schmitt's appropriation of Hobbes, see H. Münkler, "Carl Schmitt und Thomas Hobbes," *Neue Politische Literatur* 29 (1984); D. L. Dyzenhaus, "'Now the Machine Runs Itself': Carl Schmitt on Hobbes and Kelsen," 16 *Cardozo L. Rev.* 1994, 1; and J. P. McCormick, "Fear, Technology and the State: Carl Schmitt, Leo Strauss and the Revival of Hobbes in Weimar and National Socialist Germany," *Political Theory* 22 (1994): 619.

11 See G. Schwab, "Introduction," in *PT*, xv, n. 11.

12 On Schmitt and Weber, see W. Mommsen, *Max Weber and German Politics, 1890–1920*, trans. M. S. Steinberg (Chicago, Ill.: University of Chicago Press, 1984). For discussion of Schmitt and Weber that deals specifically with the relationship between dictatorship and charisma, see G. L. Ulmen, *Politische Mehrwert: Eine Studie über Max Weber und Carl Schmitt* (Weinheim: VCH Acta Humaniora, 1991), 390–400. Ulmen correctly points out that Weber, unlike Schmitt *always* associated dictatorship with charisma and hence as a kind of Caesarism, whereas Schmitt, at least in *Die Diktatur*, recognizes and emphasizes the purely functional nature of the classical notion of commissarial dictatorship. But as George Schwab observes, and as I will demonstrate more specifically below, Schmitt moves increasingly toward the charismatically imbued sovereign type of dictator after the publication of the work; see *The Challenge of the Exception*, supra n. 6, at 40, 44.

13 Schmitt discusses in great detail the supposed dangers of literal constitutional interpretation in C. Schmitt, *Verfassungslehre* (1928) (Berlin: Duncker & Humblot, 1989), at 26–27, 56, 110, 125, 146, 200.

14 On Schmitt's early neo-Kantianism generally, see J. Bendersky, *Carl Schmitt: Theorist for the Reich*, supra n. 4, at 8–11; and on his early theoretical

proximity to his later intellectual adversary, neo-Kantian H. Kelsen, see Caldwell, *Constitutional Theory in the Weimar Republic,* supra n. 8.

15 On the relationship between the French revolutionary theory of sovereignty and Schmitt's own, see S. Breuer, "Nationalstaat und pouvoir constituant bei Sieyès und Carl Schmitt," *Archiv für Rechts- und Sozialphilosophie.* 70 (1984); and P. Pasquino, "Die Lehre vom pouvoir constituant bei Abbé Sieyès und Carl Schmitt: Ein Beitrag zur Untersuchung der Grundlagen der modernen Demokratietheorie," in H. Quaritsch, ed., *Complexio Oppositorum: Über Carl Schmitt* (Berlin: Duncker & Humblot, 1988). On the contemporary ramifications of this conception of sovereignty, see U. K. Preuss, "The Politics of Constitution Making: Transforming Politics into Constitutions," *Law & Policy* 13 (1991); "Constitutional Powermaking for the New Polity: Some Deliberations on the Relations Between Constituent Power and the Constitution" 14 *Cardozo L. Rev.* 1993, 639, at 651–2; as well as the essays included in *Revolution, Fortschritt und Verfassung* (Frankfurt am Main: Fischer Verlag, 1994).

16 *The Crisis of Parliamentary Democracy,* trans. E. Kennedy (Cambridge, Mass.: MIT Press, 1985), at chap. 4 (hereafter *Parliamentarism*).

17 "The Age of Neutralizations and Depoliticizations (1929)," trans. M. Konzett & J. P. McCormick, *Telos* 96 (1993): 119, at 130.

18 In claiming that Schmitt is attempting to formulate a radical answer to the external threat of the Soviet Union and the internal one of working-class parties, I am in accord with R. Mehring, *Pathetisches Denken. Carl Schmitts Denkweg am Leitfaden Hegels: Katholische Grundstellung und antimarxistische Hegelstrategie* (Berlin: Duncker & Humblot, 1989), although I differ with him on the specifics of Schmitt's anti-Marxism as well as the playing out of his alternative Hegelian strategy.

19 "Die Diktatur des Reichspräsident nach Art. 48 der Weimarer Verfassung," (1924), appended to subsequent editions of *Die Diktatur* (hereafter *D2*); *Der Hüter der Verfassung* (Tübingen: Verlag von J. C. B. Mohr [Paul Siebeck], 1931) (hereafter *HV*); and *Legalität und Legitimität* (Munich: Duncker & Humblot, 1932) (hereafter *LL*, from the reprint in *Verfassungsrechtliche Aufsätze aus den Jahren 1924-1954: Materialien zu einer Verfassungslehre* [Berlin: Duncker & Humblot, 1958]).

20 Ernst Fraenkel, for instance, describes the whole book as an attempt to "exploit" Article 48; see *The Dual State: A Contribution to the Theory of Dictatorship* (1941), trans. E. A. Shils (New York: Octagon Books, 1969), at 213, n. 17. This does not prevent him from explicitly appropriating Schmitt's distinction between commissarial and sovereign dictatorship (at 213, n. 4). To his credit though, Fraenkel is more sensitive than Schmitt *ever* was to the fact that an emergency can very easily be used as an occasion for a *coup* (10). Another of Schmitt's leftist students, Otto Kirchheimer, reminds us that modern emergency powers are used more often than not to reinte-

grate the proletariat into the state order: see "Weimar—and What Then?" (1930), in *Politics, Law and Social Change*, supra n. 5, at 42. There is indeed vast historical precedence for this as it should be pointed out that despite the positive light in which I have presented the Roman institution of dictatorship, it was quite often used as a tool by the Roman Senate to keep the plebeians at bay.

21 There is little scholarly consensus on the exact moment of Schmitt's conversion to sovereign dictatorship: Renato Cristi, for instance, locates it already in the 1921 main text of *Die Diktatur*, while Stanley L. Paulson dates it even after the 1924 "Article 48" essay: R. Cristi, "Carl Schmitt on Sovereignty and Constituent Power," in this volume; and S. L. Paulson, "The Reich President and Weimar Constitutional Politics: Aspects of the Schmitt-Kelsen Dispute on the 'Guardian of the Constitution'" (paper presented at the annual meeting of the American Political Science Association, Chicago, August 31–September 3, 1995).

22 For a detailed account of this strategy, see I. Maus, *Bürgerliche Rechtstheorie und Faschismus: Zur sozialen Funktion und aktuellen Wirkung der Theorie Carl Schmitts* (Munich: C. H. Beck, 1980), at 127–31.

23 On the radically dynamic as opposed to statically conservative character of Schmitt's socioeconomic proposals, see ibid., at 109, 126.

24 On Schmitt's analysis of this relationship, see J. Cohen and A. Arato, *Civil Society and Political Theory* (Cambridge, Mass.: MIT Press, 1992).

25 H. Kelsen, "Wer soll der Hüter der Verfassung sein?" *Die Justiz* 6 (1930–31).

26 "Action-Commissar" (*Aktionskommissar*) is an allusion to the *Reichskommissar* who was the agent of the federal government, appointed in exceptional circumstances to govern over a particular territoriality within Germany, in place of the local authorities, who was answerable ultimately only to the *Reichspräsident*. Schmitt uses the term here because it evokes "commissarial" emergency action *in name* when *in fact* it was becoming increasingly a tool for the right-wing government's "sovereign" emergency action in the early 1930s.

27 In the autumn of that year Schmitt had a chance to put his theory of presidential dictatorship into practice before the High Court by justifying the German state's "emergency" seizure of Prussia's social-democratic *Land* government and appointment of a *Kommissar* to replace it earlier in July. For an excellent account of the historical events leading up to the state's *coup* and the theoretical-political stakes in the subsequent court hearing, see D. L. Dyzenhaus, *Legality and Legitimacy: Carl Schmitt, Hans Kelsen and Hermann Heller in Weimar* (Oxford: Oxford University Press, 1997).

28 On the subject of Schmitt's involvement with National Socialism, see B. Rüthers, *Carl Schmitt im Dritten Reich: Wissenschaft als Zeitgeist-Verstärkung?* (Munich: C. H. Beck Verlag, 1989).

29 Another of Schmitt's students, historian Reinhart Koselleck, traces the his-

torical decline of attention to the "contingent" in the Enlightenment in
Futures Past: On the Semantics of Historical Time (published 1979), trans.
K. Tribe (Cambridge, Mass.: MIT Press, 1985), at 119–25.

30 John Locke, "The Second Treatise on Government," chap. XIV, at par. 159,
lines 15–19, in P. Laslett, ed., *Two Treatises on Government* (Cambridge:
Cambridge University Press, 1988), at 375. Or as he defines it more suc-
cinctly later in the text: "Prerogative being nothing, but a Power in the
hands of the Prince to provide for the publick good, in such Cases, which
depending upon unforeseen and uncertain Occurrences, certain and un-
alterable Laws could not safely direct, whatsoever shall be done manifestly
for the good of the people" (chap. XIII, par. 158, lines 15–20, at 373).

31 See Baron de Charles de Secondat Montesquieu, *The Spirit of the Laws*,
trans. A. M. Cohler, B. C. Miller and H. S. Stone, eds., (Cambridge: Cambridge University Press, 1989), XI, 6.

32 B. Manin, "Checks, Balances, and Boundaries: The Separation of Powers in
the Constitutional Debate of 1787," in B. Fontana, ed., *The Invention of the
Modern Republic* (Cambridge: Cambridge University Press, 1994), 41, n. 51.

33 Ibid., at 41. Albert Dicey even went as far as to define the rule of law exclusively as the opposite, not only of "arbitrariness," but also "of prerogative,
or even of wide discretionary authority on the part of the government" (see
A. V. Dicey, *Introduction to the Study of the Law of the Constitution* [orig.
pub. 1915] [Indianapolis, Ind.: Liberty Classics, 1982], at 120). A more nuanced definition of the rule of law is offered by F. F. Gaus, "Public Reason
and the Rule of Law," in Ian Shapiro, ed., *The Rule of Law* (NOMOS XXXVI)
(New York: New York University Press, 1994).

34 Without recourse to specifically enumerated, constitutionally legitimated
emergency provisions to address a large-scale political rebellion in the
American Civil War, Abraham Lincoln was forced to stretch the traditional
means of suspending *habeas corpus* far beyond reasonable limits, putting
himself in the position of being called a tyrant in his sincere attempt to
preserve the republic. Constitutional enabling provisions would prevent a
legitimately acting executor from running the risk of compromising his or
her legitimacy at a time when it is most important. On these issues, see R. J.
Sharpe, *The Law of Habeas Corpus* (Oxford: Oxford University Press, 1991)
and M. E. Neely Jr., *The Fate of Liberty* (Oxford: Oxford University Press,
1991).

Another case in point from the American context is Franklin Roose-
velt's well-known and perhaps over-extended appeal to the "general welfare"
clause of the preamble of the U.S. Constitution as justification in dealing with the economic emergency of the Great Depression. A far-fetched
justification for emergency measures may in some respect compromise a
constitution at the very moment when it is most threatened, should the
appeal be successfully challenged as illegal and in fact illegitimate. The

respective successes of the two emergency actors in these two examples should not be taken at face value as proof of the efficacy of *not* having constitutional provisions—the political proficiency of the respective political leaders and the "prudence," allegedly characteristic of the American populace, surely cannot be counted on in all circumstances of crisis. Blind faith in the inevitable emergence of true statesmen and the acquiescence to them by an understanding people in times of crisis is as unreasonable and naive as is the complete trust in purely constitutional means of addressing political emergencies consistently and rightfully derided by *Realpolitikers*.

35 Indeed, the devious acumen of Schmitt's Weimar political strategy lies in the fact that he points out liberalism's theoretical deficiencies vis-à-vis the "exception" at the very historical moment when liberalism is grappling with the sociopolitical reality of the exceptional or situation-specific measures implemented by the twentieth-century welfare state in the German context. Schmitt intimates that his authoritarian interventionism is more appropriate to the historical reality of such exceptionalism than anything liberalism could ever offer. On Schmitt and the exceptionalism of welfare state law, see W. E. Scheuerman, *Between the Norm and the Exception*, supra n. 5.

36 After all, the framers of the United States Constitution of 1787 are perhaps the most famous practitioners of separation of powers and checks and balances. In the essays defending the constitution collected as *The Federalist Papers* (New York: Mentor, 1961), it is interesting to observe the contrast between the papers written by James Madison, on the one hand, the liberal technician who seeks to account for all possibilities by enumerating them or building them into the constitutional mechanism, and Alexander Hamilton, on the other, the proponent of political prerogative who seeks to keep open the possibility of exceptional circumstances. In his study of parliamentarism, Schmitt, not surprisingly, criticizes the Madisonian *Federalist Papers*, and praises the Hamiltonian ones (see *Parliamentarism*, supra n. 16, at 40, 45).

37 For a more fully elaborated argument of how such constitutional procedures do not hinder democratic expression but rather render it more articulate, see S. Holmes, "Precommitment and the Paradox of Democracy," in J. Elster and R. Slagstad, eds., *Constitutionalism and Democracy* (Cambridge: Cambridge University Press, 1988).

38 The U.S. Constitution seemingly identifies the document itself, and thereby the sovereign popular will manifested within it, with the institution of the president. In a way that it does not for any other representative of any other governmental branch, the constitution dictates the inaugural oath for the president and concludes it with the declaration that he or she will "preserve, protect and defend the Constitution of the United States" (Art. 2, sec. 1, par. 8). But this is certainly an attempt at an added precaution against the branch that is the most likely institutional threat to the constitution

rather than any substantively existential equating of the document to the office itself. Ironically, the Weimar Constitution contained an oath for the Reichspräsident that less explicitly identified the institution as a "guardian" of the constitution in the existential Schmittian sense than does the U.S. Constitution's oath (Weimar Article 42 requires only "observance" of the constitution by the president). The Basic Law of the German Federal Republic also enumerates an oath for its president (Art. 56), whose role is, however, more ceremonial than that of the American or the Weimar president.

The French Constitution of 1958 is perhaps a more problematic example of the relative identity of the executive to constitutionally expressed popular sovereignty because its definition of the presidency was clearly framed with the charismatic Charles de Gaulle in mind. Article 5 declares that the president "shall see that the constitution is observed, . . . shall ensure the proper functioning" of the government, and "the continuity of the state," as well as serve as, among other things, the "guarantor of national independence." But surely these clauses can be interpreted as statements regarding the *functional efficacy* of the president's performance of these duties rather than as pronouncements of his or her *personal identification* with the constitution, the government, the state, and the nation.

39 Article 16 of the French Constitution allows for the president's initiative in emergency circumstances after he or she first "officially consults" with representatives of the other governmental branches. The postwar German constitution—which does not have a specific article dealing with emergencies but rather disperses such provisions throughout the constitution (no doubt in reaction to the "fate" of the singular Article 48 in Weimar)—generally gives emergency initiative to the "Federal Government" or cabinet (and hence *de facto* to the chancellor whose office and person is seldom mentioned explicitly in these provisions) provided that there is either consultation with the *Bundestag* or the *Bundesrat,* or a power of revocation residing with either of those bodies (e.g., Art. 35: natural disasters—revocation by *Bundesrat;* Art. 37: federal coercion of individual *Länder* to comply with federal law—consent of *Bundesrat;* Art. 81, pars. 1 and 2: the so-called legislative emergency where the government in conjunction with the *Bundesrat* overrules the *Bundestag* on a law; Art. 87a, par. 4: use of armed forces against insurgents—revocation of *Bundestag* and *Bundesrat;* Art. 91, par. 2: appropriation of local police forces by the federal government—rescinding by *Bundesrat.* Only the complicated Art. 115a employs a clear-cut authorization: the "state of defence" is requested by chancellor, and then determined by *Bundestag* and *Bundesrat).* The general point is whether the determinate quality of an act of authorization by one body over another is superior to the vagueness inherent in a "consultation" between them. Also, it may be arguably more legitimate for one body to revoke the action of

another body if that first body commissioned or authorized the action rather than was merely a "consultant" in the emergency initiative.

40 Most of the new constitutional regimes of Central and Eastern Europe deal with emergency powers through the authorization method that, according to the criteria established here, may be judged superior to most Western efforts. The majority of these new constitutions call for parliamentary declaration on the crisis with subsequent executive action to address it (even if in certain cases the executive may request such authorization or even declare a state of emergency when the legislature is not in session, dependent on its subsequent approval). See the following constitutions and provisions: Bulgaria (Art. 84, par. 12; Art. 100, par. 5); Estonia (Arts. 129, 65, par. 14; Art. 78, par. 17); Hungary (Art. 19, par. 3, h, i; Art. 15, par. 4); Slovenia (Arts. 108, 92); and Serbia (Art. 83, par. 8). And even those constitutions that allow for a rather wide latitude for executive prerogative in emergencies, nevertheless put some serious checks in place: e.g., Latvia (Art. 62); Lithuania (Art. 84, par. 17); Romania (Art. 93); Slovakia (Art. 102, par. 1); and Poland (Art. 37, par. 1; Art. 46), which is the only regime to use the classical element of a time limit (three months, renewable). There are really only two extreme cases in the region: the Czech Republic, which has no emergency powers provision at all in the constitution, and Croatia whose own provision (Art. 101) is more expansive in its scope of presidential emergency power than was even Weimar's Article 48.

Revolutions and Constitutions

Hannah Arendt's Challenge to Carl Schmitt

William E. Scheuerman

No two names better recall the polarized character of political life in mid-century Europe than Carl Schmitt and Hannah Arendt. Like so many of his peers in the Weimar intelligentsia, Schmitt eagerly polemicized against the Weimar Republic and actively sought its destruction. In 1933 he sold his soul to the Nazis and soon became one of their most impressive intellectual apologists. In striking contrast, Arendt risked her life to help antifascists and fellow Jews struggling to escape Germany in the immediate aftermath of the Nazi takeover. Forced to join the ranks of the thousands of "stateless" persons stripped of their German citizenship by the new regime, she ultimately found her way to New York City and a stunning career as one of our century's most impressive critic of totalitarianism. While Schmitt would continue to seize every opportunity to belittle the achievements of liberal democracy, even after the establishment of the relatively robust German Federal Republic in 1949, Arendt refused to abandon her chosen *Heimat*, the United States, even in its darkest hours. For Arendt, Vietnam and Watergate offered indisputable proof that the republican legacy of the American founding demanded our critical loyalty, but hardly—as one can imagine Schmitt arguing—of the inevitability of senseless political violence and authoritarian government.

In light of Arendt's heroism and Schmitt's cowardice—how else are we to describe their political and intellectual choices in the 1930s and 1940s?—it might seem mean-spirited to identify argumentative similarities between Schmitt and Arendt. Yet if we are to shed fresh light on the difficult problem of the relationship between revolutionary politics and constitutional government, we clearly need to do precisely that. In myriad respects, Arendt's thinking constitutes a powerful corrective to Schmitt's worrisome brand of authoritarian decisionism. Arendt and Schmitt both emphasize the ways in which the spirit of the revolutionary moment inevitably haunts the political and legal institutions that it helped bring to birth. *Yet Arendt suggests that we need neither to accept Schmitt's vision of revolutionary politics as a mere exercise in arbitrary willfulness nor to accept the vision of dictatorship that logically follows from it.* An interpretation of Arendt that sees her as offering nothing but a "soft" brand of political existentialism, like that discernible in so many influential mid-century European thinkers, misconstrues core elements of her political theory.[1]

Nonetheless, I do think that Arendt's work is similar to Schmitt's in one crucial way. In their respective meditations on the question of the relationship between revolutionary politics and constitutional government, Arendt and Schmitt both rely on a similar, one-sided interpretation of the heritage of the French Revolution. For *both* Schmitt *and* Arendt, the French Revolution represents little more than a precursor to contemporary forms of mass-based authoritarian nationalism. Both authors offer a historically anachronistic interpretation of French revolutionary practice and theory in which they misleadingly situate the most ominous elements of twentieth-century political experience; both seek to identify an affinity between twentieth-century mass-based dictatorship and the heritage of the French Revolution. In contrast to Schmitt, however, Arendt distances herself from the French legacy by turning instead to the American founding to demonstrate the existence of an alternative. But her famous account of the founding of the American Republic suffers in part because the model of the French Revolution counterposed to it, like Schmitt's account, is too one-sided. Although Arendt suggests how we might begin to provide an answer to Schmitt's authoritarian constitutional theory, her own response to Schmitt ultimately remains incomplete.[2]

Why should we care if Arendt reproduces one of Carl Schmitt's characteristically truncated interpretations of the modern political experience? As Arendt noted in 1963, and as recent events in Eastern Europe again confirmed, ours has been "a century of revolutions."[3] If we are to realize an adequately democratic brand of constitutionalism in a political universe in which it remains far too underdeveloped, we need to do a better job of conceptualizing the relationship between revolution and constitutional government. Schmitt's brand of authoritarianism represents a blatant and even cynical betrayal of the best of the modern

revolutionary tradition. Yet Arendt's espousal of the American constitutional tradition, though obviously superior to Schmitt's position, also
represents a deeply enigmatic appropriation of the revolutionary legacy.

I

Evocative of contemporary advocates of a so-called new constitutionalism, Schmitt repeatedly argues that constitutionalism consists of more
than a set of restraints and limits to state authority.[4] Constitutionalism
certainly includes limiting or negative elements; the rule of law, and
its celebrated insistence on exercising governmental power by means
of calculable, predictable legal channels, is paradigmatic in this respect.
But unless we simultaneously focus on the political "decision" which
underlies the establishment of every operating constitutional system
and alone makes it possible, Schmitt insists that we cannot even begin
to make sense of the workings of the rule of law or any of a host of related negative restraints on state power. Even the most dogmatic classical liberal conception of constitutionalism necessarily presupposes the
existence of a functioning political entity in need of regulation or control. Even the most orthodox liberal implicitly assumes the existence of
a "positive decision," in favor of a particular form of constitutional government, which transcends the characteristically liberal obsession with
legal limitations on state authority. Although typically downplayed
by liberals, constitutionalism not only *limits* political power. Simultaneously, constitutionalism is realized and made possible by means of a
willful exercise of political power.[5]

How are we to make sense of this originating exercise of willful
power? For Schmitt, the fact that liberals have long tried to obscure
constitutionalism's dependence on an underlying "positive decision"
suggests that we need to turn precisely to that dramatic attempt to
found a new constitutional order, viz., the French Revolution, which
generated so much embarrassment for liberalism. For Schmitt, it is no
accident that liberals have long struggled with this legacy. The French
experience points to the Achilles' heel of liberal constitutional theory,
which is its failure to take the all-important concept of the constituent
power, the *pouvoir constituant*, seriously. In Schmitt's highly selective
reading of French revolutionary theory and practice, the French made
two genuinely pathbreaking discoveries. First, they envisioned the
existence of an unlimited and indivisible sovereign, the *pouvoir constituant*, or constitution-making power, described most clearly in Abbé

Sieyès's extremely influential *What is the Third Estate?* Second, they attributed the exercise of arbitrary, supralegal constituent power to the "nation," the sovereign *peuple:* a "people" conceived from the outset in an ethnically particularistic fashion. The French thus acknowledged the absolutely pivotal role in every constitutional system of the omnipotent, legally and normatively unregulated *Volk*, acting in accordance with "a pure decision not based on reason and discussion and not justifying itself . . . an absolute decision created out of nothingness."[6] For Schmitt, Sieyès, Rousseau, and the Jacobins ultimately represent precursors to his own idiosyncratic brand of political existentialism.

French theory and practice brilliantly capture, for Schmitt, the political verity that constitutionmaking always rests on the preexistence of an ethnically homogeneous nation, capable of differentiating itself from other peoples and, if necessary, waging battle against them.[7] The indivisibility and omnipotence of the *pouvoir constituant* can only be understood in this context. For Schmitt, the *pouvoir constituant* is more than a mere conceptual fiction. In a very concrete sense, the *Volk* is always "constituted" first and foremost by defining itself in opposition to a "foe," by gaining a capacity for violent action against challenges to its collective identity. Only if a political entity can then effectively guard itself against "the other, the stranger . . . existentially something different and alien, so that in the extreme case conflicts with him are possible," does the apparatus of "limited" constitutional government have an opportunity to survive in the first place.[8] In light of the constitution-making power's dependence on illiberal and violent instruments, it makes perfect sense to conceive of this power not only as the source of all law, but as unlimited by law. Especially in moments of life-threatening crises, when the identity of the homogeneous *Volk* is under attack, far more effective instruments of battle may need to be employed than those made available by existing legal and constitutional devices.

In contrast, the American Revolution *anticipates* some of the key concepts of modern constitutionalism. But it ultimately fails to formulate them with adequate precision. The *Federalist Papers* offers little more than meager details "about practical organizational questions," and American thought collapses the foundation of the social order and of a new constitutional order into one act. In contrast to the French, Schmitt thereby suggests, the Americans downplay the truth that constitution-making presupposes the existence of a unified, homogeneous *Volk* with a real capacity for willful action.[9] In failing adequately to acknowledge that every constitutional founding rests on an exercise of arbitrary power illegitimate from the perspective of the constitutional order which it intends to generate, the American experience reproduces liberal constitutionalism's conceptual blindspots.[10] Although the French Revolution generated a number of typically liberal demands for restraints on state power, the French never allowed their concessions to liberalism to impede their prescient insistence on the centrality of the exercise of a willful "decision," which alone makes constitutionalism possible.[11] Combined with its relative conceptual sophistication, it is precisely this element of political realism that made the French model politically efficacious, whereas the theoretically inchoate American Revolution vanished from the vision of most political actors on the world scene.

Although Schmitt argues that Sieyès's *pouvoir constituant* stems in part from the legacy of French Absolutism, he refuses to take this as evidence of its problematic nature. In France, the "heightening of state power, the more intense unity and indivisibility"[12] that resulted from the French people's historic battle with the forces of Absolutism, allowed the sovereign nation to preserve its authentic political character, namely an ability to distinguish effectively between friend and the existentially "different and alien" foe. Conversely, the fact that the American uprising *failed* to take place in the shadows of Absolutism probably contributed to its political immaturity and relatively limited impact. *Pace* modern liberalism, the survival of "absolutist" elements in French revolutionary thought hardly constitutes a flaw. On the contrary, it alone allows the resultant constitutional system to survive in an explosive and violent political universe, whose underlying dynamics inevitably conflict with the "normativistic" illusions of universalistic liberalism and its naive aspiration to eliminate the specter of violence from the political universe. Schmitt also posits that the omnipotence of the revolutionary *pouvoir constituant* stems from the fact that the "aftereffects of Christian theological conceptions of the constituent power [of an awesome] God were still vibrant and alive in the eighteenth century, despite the Enlightenment."[13] Yet, rather than suggesting the anachronistic character of absolutist power in a disenchanted moral and political universe in which nothing can be sacred, for Schmitt, this merely suggests the politically efficacious character of a religious past that has yet to come under the spell of modern relativism and nihilism.[14]

In Schmitt's creative gloss on French revolutionary theory, *no* legal procedure or institution can hope to contain or fully subsume the *pouvoir constituant*. The omnipotent founding popular sovereign gives expression to its unlimited "power by means of ever new forms, and generates new forms and organizations out of itself, but it never conclusively subordinates its political existence to a particular form."[15] The *pouvoir constituant* may choose to employ liberal constitutional and legal devices, but it also may legitimately opt to disregard them. As Sieyès allegedly taught us, "it suffices if the nation wills it."[16] By reducing constitutionalism to a set of negative restraints on political power, liberals thereby commit an additional sin of falsely suggesting that the resultant constitutional system, the *pouvoir constitué*, can successfully absorb the *pouvoir constituant*. In Schmitt's view, this view is incoherent. Not only does it disregard the crucial idea of the *inalienability* of the sovereign nation, but it wrongly implies the possibility of subjecting the unlimited and arbitrary *willfulness* of the *pouvoir constituant* to the mundane, everyday *lawfulness* of the *pouvoir constitué*, a manifest absurdity given the radically different underlying principles at hand here. Hoping to tame the *pouvoir constituant* by absorbing it into the everyday workings of constitutional government is akin to transforming fire into water, which trick, in Schmitt's view, amounts to nothing but the naive fantasy of liberal alchemists.

The vicious circle of constitutional founding (recall that an act of willful power, unregulated by the constitutional order that it aspires to establish, alone makes the constitutional order possible) inevitably continues to haunt the everyday realities of liberal democratic politics long after the act of foundation seems complete. For Schmitt, *the original unharnessed willfulness which alone made constitutional government a reality can never be extinguished.*[17] The unlimited, sovereign *Volk* "remains the real origin of all political events, the source of all power."[18] The all-powerful omnipotent subject of every liberal system, the people, continues to have a very real existence above and beyond the institutional complex of liberal constitutionalism. The *pouvoir constituant* remains a force to be reckoned with well after the revolution.

Yet because the people purportedly "can only engage in acts of acclamation, vote, say yes or no to questions" posed to them from above, Schmitt's insistence on the inalienability and continuing viability of the original *pouvoir constituant* hardly forces his theory to take a radically democratic direction.[19] Schmitt's argument here is as straightforward as it is problematic: the people "cannot counsel, deliberate, or discuss. It cannot govern or administer, nor can it posit norms; it can only sanction by its 'yes' the draft norms presented to it. Nor, above all, can it pose a question, but only answer by 'yes' or 'no' a question put to it."[20] Hence, the seemingly omnipotent *Volk* is destined to occupy a passive role in the actual day-to-day exercise of political decision making. Because the sovereign people are only capable of responding to simple questions, the actual exercise of power is best left to a powerful executive, outfitted with the authority to act outside legal and constitutional procedures that may stand in the way of the omnipotent will of the *pouvoir constituant* upon which his claim to power rests.

In short, an executive unfettered by traditional liberal legal devices, exercising awesome authority on the basis of an appeal to a particular *ethnos*, represents the best embodiment of the legacy of the French Revolution.

II

Alas, Schmitt's interpretation of the French Revolution says more about his own project than the eighteenth-century revolutionaries who wrote scathing attacks on the ancien régime, authored new constitutions, or struggled to make sense of the explosive dynamics of revolutionary politics. This is crucial to recognize for two reasons: (1) it robs Schmitt's preference for a plebiscitarian dictator of one of its most important theoretical supports; (2) Schmitt's mistakes help us identify the far less onerous—but nonetheless troublesome—failings of Hannah Arendt's analysis of the relationship between revolutionary politics and constitutionalism. I do not intend to provide another uncritical eulogy for the French Revolution; myths about the French Revolution surely have been far too widespread for too long.[21] But we need to offer a more subtle vision of its legacy than is found in either Schmitt or Arendt.

So where does Schmitt go wrong? No one could possibly deny that the legacy of Absolutism, dictatorship, and militant nationalism make up indispensable elements of the story of the French Revolution. Thus, Schmitt seems justified in focusing on these elements. Yet we need to distinguish between the theory and practice of the French Revolution. Simply to assume an underlying affinity between these events and the core of the theoretical legacy of the French Revolution represents sloppy intellectual and political history. Schmitt projects the most ominous facets of twentieth-century nationalism and mass-based authoritarianism back onto the complex theoretical legacy of the French Revolution.[22] In doing so, Schmitt leaves us with nothing more than a crude distortion of a set of ideas which still may have something important to teach us today. If we accept Schmitt's—and, as we will see, Arendt's—view of this legacy at face value, we may miss its lasting contributions.

For example, Sieyès's influential conception of the "nation" is remarkably free of the ethnicist qualities which Schmitt at least implicitly attributes to it. Sieyès defines the "nation" as nothing but "a body of associates living under *common* laws and represented by the same *legislative assembly*," and he argues that basic political and civil liberties rightly "belong to all."[23] Sieyès does claim that the French nobility stands outside the "nation," but this is only because it possesses special privileges and rights denied other groups and thus "does not belong to the common order, nor is it subjected to the common laws."[24] Once the nobility abandons its special privileges and subjects itself to the "common laws," there is nothing to prevent it from being reintegrated into the French nation. The nobility's exclusion from the nation is thus a temporary affair that can, and should be, altered. Indeed, *What is the Third Estate?* is filled with polemics against aristocratic writers, such as Boulainvilliers, who offered ethnicist arguments in order to defend the purportedly "Germanic" French aristocracy and its privileges vis-à-vis commoners, "the descendants of mere Gauls and Romans."[25] For Sieyès, "all races are mixed . . . the blood of the Franks (none the better for being pure) now mingles with the blood of the Gauls," thus we can "hope that one day will see the end of this long parricide which one class is proud to commit day after day against all the others."[26] There is no emphasis here whatsoever on the need for common ethnic roots in Sieyès's emphatically inclusionary and formalistic conception of nationhood. On the contrary, Sieyès's conception of citizenship is arguably more pluralistic than those institutionalized in most democratic constitutional systems today.

From the perspective of the most recent scholarship on the relationship of citizenship to nationhood, Schmitt's interpretation of the French experience crudely reduces the French Revolution's universalistic and implicitly cosmopolitan ideals of citizenship to a competing concept of the nation conceived of "as an organic cultural, linguistic, or racial community—as an irreducibly particular *Volksgemeinschaft*."[27] At least in part because of the influence of writers like Schmitt, this alternative view continues to have real influence in Central and Eastern Europe. But it has little to do with the intellectual legacy of the French Revolution. The short-lived Jacobin Constitution of 1793 sought to extend political rights to "every foreigner at least twenty-one years of age who has resided in France for a year and lives there by means of work or property, or has married a French woman, cares for a child or supports a senior citizen"—a far more generous standard for "naturalization" than found in any contemporary democracy. An August 1790 decree abolishing special regulations on foreigners, the *droit d'aubaine*, demanded that France "open its bosom to all the peoples of the earth, by inviting them to enjoy, under a free government, the sacred and inviolable rights of humanity." Likewise, the preamble to the 1791 Constitution announced that there would be "no privilege, no exception to the common law of all Frenchmen."[28] One can hardly imagine a greater distance between this view and Schmitt's own.[29]

Nor does the theory of the *pouvoir constituant* possess the existentialist pathos that Schmitt anachronistically attributes to it.[30] In his description of the "nation" as the rightful possessor of the constituent power, Sieyès comments that "[t]he nation is priori to everything. It is the source of everything. Its will is always legal; indeed it is the law itself."[31] Here Sieyès's rhetorical flourish should not be taken at face value, as the—oftentimes ignored—succeeding sentence in the most famous passage of *What is the Third Estate?* makes clear: "Prior to and above the nation, there is only natural law." In stark contrast to the unfettered arbitrariness of Schmitt's *pouvoir constituant*, the constituent power within Sieyès's theory, in fact, *is* limited by the imperatives of natural law. It is "everything" only in the sense that its legitimacy is greater than the *pouvoir constitué*, legal and political institutions created by the constitution-making power in accordance with a set of normative procedures and principles derived from Sieyès's rationalistic conception of natural law. Sieyès, the social contract theorist, speaks openly of the "sacred" right of property, and he argues in great detail that the "will of the nation" is legitimate only when it acts in accord with the "common security, the common liberty and, finally, the common welfare."[32] Thus, representative bodies are forbidden to undertake nongeneral legal acts, and they have no authority "to regulate the private affairs of individual citizens."[33] Only if an assembly representative of the *pouvoir constituant* respects such standards can it "justify in the name of reason and fair-play its claim to deliberate and vote for the whole nation without any exception whatsoever."[34]

This vision of the *pouvoir constituant* is clearly a long way off from Schmitt's *Volk*, acting according to "a pure decision not based on reason and discussion and not justifying itself." Because the constituent and constituted powers in Sieyès's theory share a similar normative

horizon—both rest on the principles of Sieyès's characteristically Enlightenment model of the social contract—he need not juxtapose the
pouvoir constituant and *pouvoir constitué* in as ominous a manner
as Schmitt does. Hence, we find no unbridgeable gap here between
a purportedly "normativistic" *pouvoir constitué* and a "decisionistic"
pouvoir constituant. Sieyès admittedly comments that an extraordinary
assembly of the nation "is not subjected to any [specific] procedure
whatsoever."[35] But this is no argument for a Schmittian exercise of
arbitrary power. Rather, Sieyès simply understands that a diversity
of conceivable procedures and institutions are compatible with his
underlying normative vision. A people may rightfully choose a set of
procedures for extraordinary sessions of the *pouvoir constituant* unlike
those embodied in ordinary lawmaking devices—a practice, by the way,
that even today has much to be said in its favor.[36] Whereas the *pouvoir
constituant* in Schmitt's theory is reduced to a quasi-mythical source of
legitimacy for powerful leaders able to manipulate and mobilize mass
sentiment, Sieyès readily points to concrete institutional forms which a
polity can legitimately employ in order to make the "nation" a real force
in political affairs: most importantly, the people should never abandon
the authority to elect extraordinary representative bodies, nor should
existing legislative bodies be denied the right to call such bodies into
existence "just as litigants are always allowed to appeal to the courts."[37]
Although one assuredly can dispute the practical merits of such proposals, one thing is indisputable. In dramatic contrast to Schmitt, Sieyès
offers an argument with genuinely liberal and democratic credentials.

Schmitt's attempt to usurp the humane elements of the French Revolution's legacy is one of continental political thought's truly amazing
sleights of hand. We would do well not to fall for it.

III

Hannah Arendt, in at least one crucial respect, does fall for it. For her
as for Schmitt, the intellectual legacy of the French Revolution merely
reproduces the most heinous features of Absolutism, particularly its
vision of an indivisible, omnipotent, and legally unlimited sovereign.
"What else did even Sieyès do but simply put the sovereignty of the
nation into the place which had been vacated by the sovereign king."[38]
Sieyès's theory of the *pouvoir constituant* is essential for understanding
the critical failing that ultimately undermined his countrymen's quest
for stable republican order: "Both power and law were anchored in the

nation, or rather in the will of the nation, which itself remained outside and above all governments and all laws."[39] Arendt considers this catastrophic, in part because the French simultaneously conceived of power as a superhuman force, "the result of the accumulated violence of a multitude outside all bonds and all political organization."[40] Hence, constitutional and legal forms were rendered dependent on nothing but the transient "will" of political majorities, the mere quicksand of a "subjective state of mind."[41] In Schmitt's terminology: the French Revolution burdened its political successors with a *decisionistic* concept of law.

Again like Schmitt, Arendt believes that the French ultimately failed to escape the paradoxes of the vicious circle of foundational politics. She accepts Schmitt's view that modern mass-based dictatorship legitimately lays claim to the French revolutionary heritage: the formless "national will could be manipulated and imposed upon whenever someone was willing to take the burden or the glory of dictatorship upon himself. Napoleon Bonaparte was only the first in a long series of national statesmen who, to the applause of the whole nation, could declare 'I am the *pouvoir constituant'*."[42] The polity's foundational sin, the act of arbitrary force that made it possible in the first place, thus continues to haunt governments wherever they have been significantly influenced by the French experience. Yet, whereas Schmitt seems relatively unconcerned by the practical dangers of the French attempt to found legal forms on a purely subjective exercise of willful power, Arendt interprets the French constellation as a poisonous recipe for permanent revolution, for repeated attempts to dismantle legal and constitutional forms in the name of any of a diversity of political and social groups likely to claim the awesome power of the *pouvoir constituant*. In Arendt's sober reading of modern European history, the instability of constitutional government provides evidence enough of the unambiguously disastrous character of the theoretical and practical legacy of the French Revolution.

Arendt also accepts Schmitt's claim that the *pouvoir constituant* anticipates the most disturbing facets of modern nationalism. Even Sieyès, whom Arendt describes as "one of the least sentimental and most sober figures of the Revolution," is a prophet "of national revolutions or revolutionary nationalism, of nationalism speaking the language of revolution or of revolutions arousing the masses with nationalist slogans."[43] Indeed, revolutionary conceptions of "the rights of man" were flawed from the outset. They rested on the dubious idea of national sovereignty, which meant in practical terms that rights were destined to be discarded as soon as they conflicted with the arbitrary dictates of irrationalist nationalist ideology.[44] Rousseau's theory is proto-nationalistic as well, for "Rousseau's concept of the general will presupposed and relied upon the unifying power of the common national enemy."[45] As Schmitt had similarly argued, Rousseau's antipluralistic conception of *le peuple* places substantial weight on its capacity for resolute, potentially violent action in the face of external foes.

Rousseau looms even larger in Arendt's selective account of the French story than in Schmitt's, in part because of Arendt's view of the relatively unambiguous character of Rousseau's relationship to Jacobinism and its modern-day totalitarian successors. While Schmitt rightly acknowledges the contradictory character of Rousseau's thought and is reluctantly forced to identify its liberal elements, Arendt occasionally reduces Rousseau to little more than a forerunner of Hitler or Stalin. The reader is repeatedly confronted with imaginative attempts to demonstrate an "elective affinity" between the horrors of modern mass-based politics and Rousseau's complex political theory. In the process, Arendt badly misrepresents crucial components of Rousseau's thinking.

For example, Arendt simply takes Rousseau's claim at face value that the general will, like Sieyès's *pouvoir constituant*, is altogether *unbound* and *absolute*. Thus, Arendt believes that we can ignore Rousseau's own adamant insistence in his crucial discussion of "The Limits of Sovereign Power," that political power is only legitimate when exercised in accordance with the ideal of the rule of law.[46] Nor, it seems, do we need to take Rousseau's detailed description of the proper *presuppositions* of legitimate republican government—modest size, and a substantial degree of social and economic equality, for example—very seriously. For Rousseau, such preconditions represent pivotal limitations on the absoluteness of the general will. Because Rousseau believed that the sovereign "never has a right to burden one subject more than another,"[47] he clearly hoped to *minimize* the scope of legislative activity. But for Arendt, Rousseau contributed to modern totalitarianism's destruction of the private sphere by trying to complement the idea of an external foe with the concept of an "internal" enemy existing "within the breast of each citizen, namely, in his particular will and interest."[48] Allegedly, it is here that we can identify the conceptual roots of the French Revolutionaries' most terrifying character flaw, their frightful, and ultimately disastrous, obsession with unmasking hypocrisy. For Arendt, the tremendous political resonance of Rousseau's conceptual framework stems from precisely this element: the struggle to unmask and discredit the hypocrisy of the rich and powerful is bound to gain overriding significance whenever revolution occurs in a situation of abject poverty, which tends to give the abstractions of Rousseau's theory an "obvious plausibility."[49] Thus, if we are to make sense of the fascination exerted by the French Revolution on so many political actors in so many different parts of the world, we need to recognize its correspondence to the dictates of a political universe in which the poor and underprivileged have suddenly been "brought out of the darkness of their misery" and onto the political scene for the first time in human history.[50] Whenever the "social question" is raised, at least *some* version of Rousseauism is likely to appear on the revolutionary stage as well.

Arendt also offers a terribly one-sided interpretation of Rousseau's discussion of sovereignty. When Rousseau famously criticizes "the conjuring tricks of our political theorists" who "make of the sovereign a fantastic creature composed of bits and pieces," he is criticizing predemocratic conceptions of "divided sovereignty," in which distinct governmental bodies are simply distributed among distinct estates.[51] *Pace* Arendt, he is *not* perpetuating Absolutism's quest to centralize governmental institutions. For Rousseau as for Locke, the "unity" and "indivisibility" of the "people" constitute an important contrast to premodern visions of the political community as consisting of differentiated and unequal status groups. Arendt conflates the Enlightenment defense of a unified, indivisible popular "sovereign" with an argument against a separation of powers within the decision-making apparatus and, thus, a *differentiation* or *division* of authority among *institutional* instances, which both Locke and Rousseau clearly endorse. For both Locke and Rousseau, "[p]opular sovereignty is the actual or potential force that unifies the state which, for convenience, divides its functions."[52] Arendt's claim that Rousseau sought the awesome centralization of *institutional* power evident in the worst moments of the French Revolution rests on a failure to make an elementary conceptual distinction: one can insist on the unity and indivisibility of the democratic "people" *without* demanding the centralization of political authority into the hands of a tiny group of decision makers.

What lesson does Arendt draw from her fiction? Whereas Schmitt clearly delights in the presumed irrationalism of the French experience, Arendt thinks that we can do better. Thus, she turns to the example of the American Constitution in order to show how we might finally liberate ourselves from the vicious circle of foundational politics. In her account, the Americans avoid all the miserable mistakes committed by their French brothers and sisters. "[T]he greatest American innovation in politics as such was the consistent abolition of sovereignty within the body politic of the republic. . . ."[53] The Americans offer an authentically pluralistic vision of the citizenship; they point the way to an alternative conception of power which moves well beyond the French romanticization of the unharnessed will. The fiction of the unbridled *pouvoir constituant* could never gain a following among the colonists given the everyday "working reality" of colonial self-government, an experience of "the *organized* multitude whose power was exerted *in accordance with laws and limited by them.*"[54] Free of abject poverty, the Americans are spared the specter of Rousseau's proto-totalitarian theory. Montesquieu proves to be a far more significant—and, for Arendt, unambiguously beneficial—influence on the founding fathers. Most important perhaps, the Americans "were never even tempted to derive law and power from the same origin. The seat of power to them was the people, but the source of law was to become the Constitution, a written document, an endurable objective thing . . . never a subjective state of mind."[55] In contradistinction to the French, the Americans avoid the perils of legal decisionism. The curious American worship of the Constitution represents the most obvious manifestation of the durability and perpetuity that the Americans, unlike the French, managed to attribute to constitutional forms, chiefly because they rightly refused to rest constitutional government on an ever-changing act of willfulness.

Although Arendt admits that the founders themselves may have been no more than faintly aware of the world-historical significance of their discovery, they purportedly discovered a path beyond the vicious circle of foundational politics. For Arendt, "[w]hat saves the act of beginning from its own arbitrariness is that it carries its own principle within itself," namely the vision of a shared political life based on "common deliberation and on the strength of mutual pledges."[56] Even though the American Revolution represents a novel political experience, and notwithstanding the fact that "[i]t is the very nature of a beginning to carry with itself a measure of complete arbitrariness,"[57] the Americans effectively harness this arbitrariness by subjecting it to a set of (implicitly normative) principles that contrast dramatically with the willfulness and violence of the French experience. For Arendt, the very *ethos* of the foundation of the American Republic presupposes the ideal of a "mutual contract by which people bind themselves together in order to form a community . . . based on reciprocity," an implicit model of political life resting on the "binding and promising, combining and covenanting" that alone can provide real substance to the struggle for mutuality and self-respect in an ever-changing and profoundly unpredictable world.[58] By avoiding the unharnessed arbitrariness and brutality of the French experience, the American revolutionaries set out on a path beyond the incestuous cycle of decisionism and dictatorship. "The way the beginner starts whatever he intends to do lays down the law of action for those who have joined him in order to partake in the enterprise and to bring about its accomplishment."[59] Because those who "began" the United States did so in a manner compatible with a defensible vision of republican political principles, the Americans may be able to succeed in preserving a polity that continues to preserve those principles. No foundational "original sin" haunts the American Republic. Hence, Americans need not fear the retribution that inevitably follows in the wake of such sins.

At least in the United States, *some* elements of the original revolutionary spirit continue to survive in the everyday operations of constitutional government: American constitutionalism has yet to extinguish the revolutionary flame.[60] Like Schmitt, Arendt thinks that the revolutionary tradition demonstrates the truncated quality of traditional liberal conceptions of "limited" constitutionalism. For her, the American case shows that a "positive" political element can make up an indispensable feature of a successful constitutional system. Constitutional government can *perpetuate* the most noble qualities of the revolution. In Arendt's alternative to Schmitt's account, however, the political element preserved by the American Republic consists of a readiness for common deliberation and self-enabling forms of political exchange and action, based on mutuality and reciprocity. It is light years away from Schmitt's monological will, acting in accordance with "a pure decision not based on reason and discussion and not justifying itself . . . an absolute decision created out of nothingness."[61]

IV

Although Arendt's attempted resolution to the vicious circle of foundational politics remains praiseworthy, her problematic view of the French experience ultimately generates a corresponding enigmatic view of the American experience. Unfortunately, Arendt simply complements the fiction of the unambiguously ("bad") French Revolution with a myth of the ("good") American Revolution. We certainly should applaud the gist of Arendt's implicit response to Schmitt. But precisely because Arendt shares too many of Schmitt's assumptions about the modern revolutionary experience, her response to Schmitt is incomplete.

Many commentators have rightly criticized the selective character of Arendt's portrayal of the American founding. But few point to the most basic source of this failing: because Arendt's story of the French Revolution is flawed, her attempt to construct an *inverted* portrait of the French experience, by means of a fanciful retelling of the American founding, necessarily succumbs to the same tendentiousness. Although obsessed with the horrors of the abject poverty of revolutionary France, the barbarism of American slavery receives passing notice in Arendt's discussion.[62] Notwithstanding Arendt's emphasis on the pluralism of American conceptions of citizenship, as a matter of fact, that pluralism is the product of a long—and by no means complete—series of political struggles; we need only recall the Supreme Court's infamous Dred Scott ruling, let alone the terrible truth that most African Americans were still denied their basic political rights even at the time of the publication of *On Revolution*. The French are roundly criticized for raising "the social question," yet it is pivotal for understanding the American founding as well.[63] The dreaded concept of the *pouvoir constituant* was hardly as alien to the American founders as Arendt would prefer to have us believe.[64] Hamilton and Madison even acknowledged, as Bruce Ackerman perceptively comments, "that the People best express themselves through episodic and anomalous 'conventions,' and not through regular sessions of ordinary legislatures."[65] The analytical distance here vis-à-vis French revolutionary theory is far less dramatic than Arendt ever seems to recognize.

But let me focus on one blind spot in Arendt's account; her uncritical assessment of the American conception of the separation of powers continues to have real significance today. Arendt's failing here should concern us because it potentially supports an excessively self-satisfied vision of the fundaments of the American Republic. Combined with an instinctive hostility to the ("bad") French revolutionary legacy, this self-satisfaction risks contributing to the political parochialism and intellectual ethnocentrism so widespread in the United States today. It would be truly tragic if the most important influence on American political culture of a thinker as learned and cosmopolitan as Arendt turned out to be nothing but a reinforcement of precisely those conformist trends that rightly worried her so much.

Arendt's flattering view of Montesquieu's place in the formation of the American conception of the separation of powers reproduces the ills of her complementary discussion of Rousseau's influence on the French. After describing Montesquieu's conception of the separation of powers, Arendt can barely restrain herself: "How well this part of Montesquieu's teaching was understood in the days of the foundation of the republic!"[66] Her enthusiasm here is only matched by her evident distaste for Rousseau in her closely related account of the French Revolution. I hope Arendt exaggerates Montesquieu's influence, because, if she *is* right, it suggests that the American polity is burdened by premodern institutional vestiges potentially incompatible with modern democratic ideals. Montesquieu criticized Absolutist claims to sovereignty in order to defend a *traditional* ideal of "divided sovereignty" in which separate institutional instances represent distinct social groups. In his own quest to preserve the privileges of the aristocracy, Montesquieu "related the three [governmental] powers to social groups. To him the monarch, who was to have the executive power, represented social interests different from those of the legislature; the legislature, in turn composed of two houses, was to represent the aristocracy and the bourgeoisie respectfully; while the judiciary, being '*en quelque facon nulle,*' was to represent everybody."[67] In contrast to Locke and Rousseau, Montesquieu is no defender of typically modern, universalistic conceptions of human equality and liberty, and thus he is no advocate of a characteristically modern conception of *popular sovereignty*, like that found in many competing Enlightenment theories. Montesquieu's theory is eclectic: civic republican elements coexist uneasily alongside a defense of the privileges of the nobility. It should hardly come as a surprise that his political influence was often greatest among conservatives and even reactionaries.[68] His is surely a powerful criticism of the concept of sovereignty, but nonetheless a critique written from the perspective of a theorist who often seems to aspire to preserve crucial features of a "moderate" monarchy based on "mixed constitutionalism." If Arendt is correct in seeing Montesquieu's influence on the early Republic as decisive, we will need to examine the possibility that the American conception of the separation of powers reproduces Montesquieu's decidedly antidemocratic biases.[69] This possibility does not seem to have worried the "republican" Arendt. But those of us less hostile than the republican Arendt to the achievements of modern representative democracy should be concerned.[70]

From this perspective, Arendt's equally uncritical view of the American Supreme Court takes on fresh significance. One would never know from Arendt's stylized account that the proposed Supreme Court was one of the most controversial innovations sought by the Federalists. Notwithstanding her explicit emphasis on the "mutual deliberation" of the American founding, the voices of those critical of Arendt's own institutional preferences, the Anti-Federalists, are sadly missing from her account.[71] Purportedly modeled on the Senate of classical Rome, Arendt believes that the Supreme Court continues to provide the American Republic with the *authority* missing from legal and constitutional forms in other democracies. Here Arendt's argument rests in part on an etymological observation: "For *auctoritas*, whose etymological root is *augere*, to augment and increase, depended upon the vitality of the spirit of foundation, by virtue of which it was possible to augment, to increase and enlarge, the foundations as they had been laid down by the ancestors."[72] The authority of the Supreme Court stems from its capacity for simultaneously conserving and augmenting the Constitution, the most concrete achievement of the original act of foundation, as seen in the Court's never finished task of interpreting and reinterpreting the Constitution. It both protects and builds on the achievements of the original act of foundation, and thus helps provide for precisely that measure of permanence and stability so rare elsewhere. For Arendt, the Supreme Court derives its special status from the fact that it exercises "a kind of continuous constitution-making, for the Supreme Court is indeed, in Woodrow Wilson's phrase, 'a kind of Constitutional Assembly in continuous session.'"[73]

Unfortunately, this view of the American Supreme Court raises as many questions as it purports to answer. It seems to conflict with Arendt's earlier conception of authority, as formulated in the crucial "What is Authority?" Whereas *On Revolution* implies that the ongoing "constitutional conversation" of the Supreme Court represents an augmentation of the "mutual deliberation" basic to the act of founding itself, the earlier essay bluntly asserts that "[a]uthority . . . is incompatible with persuasion, which presupposes equality and works through a process of argumentation. Where arguments are used, authority is left in abeyance. Against the egalitarian order of persuasion stands the authoritarian [or authority-based] order, which is always hierarchical."[74] It is difficult to imagine what status such a conception of authority can rightfully possess in a modern, disenchanted democratic polity: particularly in a democracy, only argumentation and discursive "persuasion" can legitimately justify the exercise of state power. Any attempt to hide the decision-making apparatus—and the American Supreme Court surely engages in extensive forms of legislative action—from the scrutiny of critical publics constitutes an attempt to reassert traditional forms of political domination. Arendt's remarks notwithstanding, the pervasive blind worship of the Constitution and the Supreme Court in American political culture represents, at best, an ambiguous political good.[75]

Even if we ignore Arendt's curious comments in "What is Authority?" and instead emphasize the argument of *On Revolution*, an additional dilemma immediately presents itself. Let us accept the need for an institution that demonstrates the interrelated character of the experiences of foundation, augmentation, and conservation. Let us also presuppose that "a kind of Constitutional Assembly in continuous session" is essential to the guarantee of continuity and perpetuity in an unstable and unpredictable political universe. Does Arendt's uncritical portrait of the American Supreme Court in *On Revolution* automatically follow from these observations? Might there not be alternative, potentially superior institutional embodiments of this normative aspiration? My worries here are twofold. First, Arendt's view glosses over the more troublesome (and idiosyncratic) elements of the American constitutional court, such as the fact that Supreme Court justices have life tenure. In short, it discourages a serious discussion of the merits of alternative models of judicial review. Second, Arendt's fascination with the "novelty and uniqueness" of the American Supreme Court ultimately prevents her from engaging in an adequate analysis of alternative institutional devices suited to the task of constitutional "augmentation." Admittedly, Arendt *acknowledges* what seems to me to be central to any discussion of this issue, namely amendment procedures which purportedly allow "the people" to reenact the role of constitutional founder, but she fails to offer an adequate account of the place of constitutional amendment because of her peculiar obsession with the Supreme Court and its Roman origins.[76] Elsewhere in *On Revolution*, Arendt powerfully criticizes continental European legal traditions that reduce constitution-making to nothing but the monopoly of a narrow group of politically distant, technical legal experts.[77] But how exactly is the American Supreme Court different in this respect? Although the "blind worship" of homegrown institutions in the United States has effectively closed the eyes of even the keenest American observers of political affairs to this fact, an American-type Supreme Court represented a historical anomaly until quite recently. Nor does the record of the American Supreme Court reveal any more inherent virtue than that of any competing institutional site. Then why assume that a tiny group of judges, indirectly elected and then outfitted with awesome legislative power, represents a satisfactory embodiment of the noble aspiration to preserve and build on the heroic acts of the founding generation?

Hannah Arendt never provides an adequate answer to this question. Like so many citizens of her adopted homeland, she succumbs to her own peculiar "blind worship" of the American constitutional tradition.

V

Let me underline the most important, perhaps counterintuitive, lesson of this essay. Hannah Arendt's inadequately critical portrayal of crucial facets of the American constitutional legacy is intimately related to Carl Schmitt's hostile view of liberal constitutionalism. In her attempt to retell the story of modern constitutionalism, Arendt turns Schmitt on his head. But she does so without questioning a set of deeply problematic common assumptions about the nature of the French Revolution and its legacy for modern constitutionalism. Arendt rightly tries to escape the confines of Schmitt's intellectual universe by defending the Americans against their French peers. Because she accepts a problematic "Schmittian" gloss on the French experience, her view of the American experience proves equally misleading. Furthermore, this interpretation inadvertently contributes to the widespread tendency to engage in a form of "blind worship" of the most enigmatic elements of the American revolutionary heritage. In light of growing evidence that so many of our political and constitutional mechanisms are badly in need of reform, Arendt's analysis seems particularly worrisome.[78]

In the final analysis, Arendt seems to believe that the ills of Schmitt's legal decisionism can be effectively combatted by means of an awesome American-style Supreme Court outfitted with unprecedented judicial powers. The legal insecurity and arbitrariness countenanced by Carl Schmitt and his ilk can be avoided by establishing a group of juridical experts empowered with authority both to conserve and augment the work of the constitutional framers. But what if the obscure Anti-Federalist Brutus was right when he described the American Supreme Court as "invested with such immense powers, and yet placed in a situation so little responsible?" Surely, constitutional checks on the American Supreme Court, despite its impressive powers, remain minimal. But this would seem to bode poorly for Arendt's claim that the Americans undertook a "consistent abolition of sovereignty within the body politics." Hasn't the Supreme Court on occasion come close to taking over the role of an indisputable "final arbiter," in part because of the American framers' failure to develop even the most modest set of checks on the Court and its members? Moreover, the annals of American constitutional jurisprudence hardly represent a paragon of legal regularity and predictability. Whatever its other merits, a Supreme Court as envisaged by Hannah Arendt hardly seems to constitute the ideal antipode to the ills of legal decisionism. How much constitutional jurisprudence has entailed highly "creative" readings of a text whose broad language remains, for better or worse, so indeterminate?

If we finally are to succeed in responding to Schmitt's authoritarian constitutional theory, we will need to do more than answer Schmitt's deceptive vision of the French revolutionary experience with an equally partial eulogy for the American founders. Indeed, we may even need to consider the possibility of institutional devices unknown to the American Founders and to one of their most idiosyncratic modern-day students, Hannah Arendt. In the aftermath of the horrors of totalitarianism, the unfinished task of democratic constitutionalism demands nothing less.

Notes

I would like to thank David Dyzenhaus and Iris Young for their written comments on an earlier draft, as well as Seyla Benhabib and Ingeborg Maus for words of encouragement and, of course, criticism.

1 Richard Wolin and Martin Jay have offered suggestive analyses of Arendt's alleged existentialism in Richard Wolin, *Labyrinths: Explorations in the Critical History of Ideas* (Amherst: University of Massachusetts Press, 1996), at 162–74; Martin Jay, *Permanent Exiles: Essays on the Intellectual Migration from Germany to America* (New York: Columbia University Press, 1986), at 237–56. But I believe that Maurizio Passerin d'Entreves effectively answers arguments of this sort in his fine *The Political Philosophy of Hannah Arendt* (New York: Routledge, 1994), at 85–90.

2 Arendt seems to have been familiar with the basic outlines of Schmitt's political and legal thought, as numerous references to Schmitt in her writings demonstrate. Although I have found no specific reference to the 1928 *Verfassungslehre* (Munich: Duncker & Humblot, 1928), where Schmitt offers the most lucid account of his constitutional theory, she may well have been aware of its core claims. One of Arendt's friends, the émigré Waldemar Gurian, was a former student of Schmitt's who devoted significant energy to developing a critique of his former teacher's legal thought. Although it is best to avoid speculation on such matters, I find it difficult to avoid imagining that Gurian and Arendt discussed Schmitt and his ideas, particularly

in light of Schmitt's complicity in the horrors of Nazism. Hannah Arendt, "Waldemar Gurian: 1903–1954," in Hannah Arendt, *Men in Dark Times* (New York: Harcourt Brace Jovanovich, 1983), 251.

3 Hannah Arendt, *On Revolution* (New York: Penguin, 1963), at 18.

4 Stephen Elkin and Karol Soltan, eds., *A New Constitutionalism: Designing Political Institutions for a Good Society* (Chicago: University of Chicago Press, 1993).

5 Schmitt, supra n. 2, at xii, 40–41. All translations are my own. For Schmitt, Kelsen's vision of the legal order as based on nothing but a "basic norm," from which the entire legal structure is produced, represents the best contemporary example of liberalism's failure to acknowledge the existence of a foundational sovereign will at the basis of every legal system. For a discussion of Schmitt's constitutional theory and its relationship to Kelsen, see William E. Scheuerman, "Carl Schmitt's Critique of Liberal Constitutionalism," *Review of Politics* 58 (1996): 299.

6 Carl Schmitt, *Political Theology: Four Chapters on the Concept of Sovereignty* (Cambridge, Mass.: MIT Press, 1985), at 66.

7 Schmitt writes that "[a] people (*Volk*) must already exist as a political unity if it is to become the subject of constitution-making power." He then praises Sieyès's preference for the term "nation" in favor of "people," arguing that it better captures the idea of a *Volk* "capable of political action," in contrast to those political entities not fully coherent in ethnic or cultural terms (*"nur eine irgendwie ethnisch oder kulturell zusammengehörige . . . Verbindung von Menschen"*). Schmitt, supra n. 2, at 61 and 79. Schmitt also identifies the French Revolution as the birthplace of "national democracy" and comments that the presupposition of this type of democracy is "national democracy" and comments that the presupposition of this type of democracy is "national homogeneity," ibid., at 231. Although Schmitt does leave open the possibility that national homogeneity may take distinct forms, I believe that most evidence suggests, as Ulrich Preuss notes, that Schmitt tended to favor an "ethnicist" form in which the *ethos* is substituted for the *demos;* das *Volk* is conceived as an "ethnic and cultural oneness," with a "capacity to realize its otherness in relation both to other people and the liberal-universalist category of mankind." Ulrich Preuss, "Constitutional Powermaking for the New Polity: Some Deliberations on the Relations Between the Constituent Power and the Constitution," 14 *Cardozo L. Rev.* 1993, 639, at 650.

8 Carl Schmitt, *The Concept of the Political*, trans. George Schwab (New Brunswick, N.J.: Rutgers University Press, 1976), at 27.

9 Schmitt's comments on the American case are scattered and unsystematic. Nonetheless, his argument seems to take the following form: the concept of a social contract, to the extent that "one considers this construction at all necessary," makes "political unity" possible in the first place. In turn, only a *Volk* possessing the quality of "political unity" is capable of con-

sciously exercising its will in a coherent manner, thus "deciding" in favor of a particular constitutional system. By conflating these two moments, the Americans risk obscuring this point. The Americans, therefore, ignore the importance of homogeneity as a precondition of constitution-making. Schmitt, supra n. 2, at 61, 78–79.

10 In Arendt's words: "those who get together to constitute a new government are themselves unconstitutional, that is, they have no authority to do what they set out to achieve. The vicious circle in legislating is present not in ordinary lawmaking, but in laying down the fundamental law . . . which, from then on, is supposed to incarnate the 'higher law' from which all laws ultimately derive their authority." Supra n. 3, at 184.

11 Schmitt, supra n. 2, at 51.

12 Ibid., at 51.

13 Ibid., at 78.

14 The target here, once again, is Kelsen, who accepted Weber's vision of modernity as disenchanted and sought to justify a fallibilistic conception of liberal democracy appropriate to the morally "relativistic" dictates of modernity. Hans Kelsen, *Vom Wesen und Wert der Demokratie* (Tübingen: J. C. B. Mohr, 1929).

15 Schmitt, supra n. 2, at 79; see also Carl Schmitt, *Die Diktatur* (Munich: Duncker & Humblot, 1922), at 140–52, where Schmitt summarizes the *pouvoir constituant*.

16 Schmitt, supra n. 2, at 79.

17 This claim has a number of striking similarities to contemporary French post-structuralist conceptions of constitution-making. For a defense of the view that constitutional government rests on and perpetuates an unavoidably arbitrary exercise of power, see Bonnie Honig, "Declarations of Independence: Arendt and Derrida on the Problem of Founding a Republic," *American Political Science Review* 85 (1991): 97. For a response, see Seyla Benhabib, "Democracy and Difference: Reflections on the Metapolitics of Lyotard & Derrida," *Journal of Political Philosophy* 2 (1994): 1.

18 Schmitt, supra n. 2, at 79.

19 Ibid., at 315.

20 Carl Schmitt, *Legalität und Legitimität* (Munich: Duncker & Humblot, 1932), at 93.

21 Notwithstanding his oftentimes caricatured interpretations of French revolutionary political thought, this is the important insight of Francois Furet, *Interpreting the French Revolution* (Cambridge: Cambridge University Press, 1981).

22 Ingeborg Maus has forcefully criticized interpretations of the French experience that mistakenly interpret it in light of the barbarism of mid-century European politics. My remarks here have been inspired by Maus, in more ways than I can begin to acknowledge. For a succinct summary of her

response to contemporary caricatures of French revolutionary political ideals, see Ingeborg Maus, "'Volk' und 'Nation' im Denken der Aufklärung," *Blätter für deutsche und internationale Politik* 39 (1994): 602. Maus is correct to emphasize that too many interpretations of this experience conflate French revolutionary thought and practice, in part because such conflations serve antidemocratic political causes. Along these lines, Rogers Brubaker argues that we need to distinguish between the "conspicuously cosmopolitan" character of French revolutionary ideology and the xenophobia apparent in the revolution's waning days, "a product of war and factional struggle, which engendered a climate of extreme suspicion of the internal enemies that might knowingly or unknowingly be in the service of external enemies." Rogers Brubaker, *Citizenship and Nationhood in France and Germany* (Cambridge: Harvard University Press, 1992), at 45–46.

23 Emmanuel Joseph Sieyès, *What is the Third Estate?*, trans. M. Blondel (New York: Pall Mall, 1963), at 58–59.

24 Ibid., at 58.

25 Ibid., at 60. Furet also underplays this absolutely crucial point. Sieyès simply contradicts Furet's claim that the French conceived of the nation as a "homogeneous" body in which "the multiplicity of individuals and of private interests is immediately cancelled out. . . ." Supra n. 21, at 33, 44. Far more reliable here is the little-known monograph by Murray Forsyth, *Reason and Revolution: The Political Thought of the Abbe Sieyès* (New York: Holmes & Meier, 1987), at 71.

26 Supra n. 23, at 60.

27 Brubaker, supra n. 22, at 1.

28 Ibid., at 45.

29 Of course, one might respond to this argument by referring to Rousseau, whom Schmitt considers to be an influence on some features of Jacobin practice as well as a precursor to his own vision of a homogeneous *Volk*. Schmitt, supra n. 2, at 229–30. But two immediate responses are possible here. First, even if we accept this reading of Rousseau as a prophet of a nationally homogeneous democracy, substantial historical research suggests that his relationship to French revolutionary practice is extremely complicated. We simply cannot uncritically accept the view, stated recently by Furet as well, that Rousseau's "political thought set up well in advance the conceptual framework of what was to become Jacobinism. . . ." Supra n. 21, at 31. For a more balanced treatment of this issue, see Joan McDonald, *Rousseau and the French Revolution* (London: University of London Press, 1965) and Iring Fetscher, *Rousseaus Politische Philosophie* (Frankfurt: Suhrkamp, 1973). Second, Rousseau's vision of a homogeneous community is more complex than this view suggests. He clearly shows a preference for simple, small-scale, economically underdeveloped, and culturally homogeneous political communities (most famously, Corsica). But his is generally a

backwards-looking, even nostalgic view. He does not seem to believe that homogeneity of this type can be produced or manufactured. To suggest that Rousseau's ideal is analogous to the homogenizing tendencies of the large-scale modern nation-state or, for that matter, totalitarian attempts to *create* a national *folk community*, is probably anachronistic.

30 In a similar vein, see Stefan Breuer, "Nationalstaat und pouvoir constituant bei Sieyès und Carl Schmitt," *Archiv für Rechts- und Sozialphilosophie* 70 (1984): 495. In other words, Schmitt is wrong when he claims that Sieyès's theory already represents an attempt to transcend Enlightenment rationalism. *Die Diktatur*, supra n. 15, at 142.

31 Supra n. 23, at 124.

32 Supra n. 23, at 156–57, 183. We might recall Sieyès's influence on the Declaration of the Rights of Man, and his view that "the object of every social union, and consequently of every political constitution, can be nothing other than to guarantee, to serve, and to extend the rights of man living in society." Cited in Forsyth, whose discussion here is essential for understanding Sieyès's radical brand of liberalism, in supra n. 25, at 109. Sieyès is far closer to Locke than commentators acknowledge. Sieyès's theory of the *pouvoir constituant* bears a striking resemblance to Locke's view that power rightfully reverts to the hands of the people as a whole when government steps beyond the bounds of the principles and procedures outlined in Locke's rationalistic, natural law-based model of the social contract. The fact that Locke believes that sovereignty then belongs to the (noninstitutionalized) "people" (conceived, by the way, as an inalienable and indivisible entity), and *not* to existing legal and constitutional devices, hardly makes him a "totalitarian" anymore than it should Sieyès.

33 Supra n. 23, at 152.

34 Ibid., at 152.

35 Ibid., at 132.

36 One ill of too much of contemporary constitution-making is that the constituent power is left in the hands of ordinary legislative channels, which means in practical terms that parliamentary representatives and the interest groups they represent are left to determine the fate of fundamental constitutional issues. For a good discussion of the dangers of this approach in eastern Europe, see Andrew Arato, "Dilemmas Resulting from the Power to Create Constitutions in Eastern Europe" 14 *Cardozo L. Rev.* 1993, 661, and Bruce Ackerman, *The Future of the Liberal Revolution* (New Haven: Yale University Press, 1992).

37 Supra n. 23, at 137.

38 Supra n. 3, at 156.

39 Ibid., at 163.

40 Ibid., at 181. For a critique of this view of power, see Hannah Arendt, *On Violence* (New York: Harcourt Brace Jovanovich, 1970).

41 Supra n. 3, at 157, 163.

42 Ibid., at 163.

43 Ibid., at 75, 158.

44 Hannah Arendt, *The Origins of Totalitarianism* (New York: Harcourt Brace Jovanovich, 1979), at 230–31. There is only a "contradiction" between the idea of universal human rights and the nation-state if, like Schmitt and Arendt, we deemphasize the cosmopolitan character of early revolutionary conceptions of the "nation." To the extent that revolutionary theorists aspired for a "universal" republic, or at least an international federation of republics, there is *no* contradiction here.

Although she more clearly acknowledges the cosmopolitan character of revolutionary French conceptions of citizenship, Julia Kristeva far too uncritically accepts Arendt's argument on this point: "Hannah Arendt is right in thinking that the national legacy served as guarantee for Nazi criminality." Julia Kristeva, *Strangers to Ourselves*, trans. Leon S. Roudiez (New York: Columbia University Press, 1991), at 151.

45 Supra n. 3, at 77.

46 It is important to note that Rousseau's claim in Book 2, chapter 4, that "the general will, to be truly such, must be general in its objects as well as in its essence . . . that it loses its natural rectitude when directed toward any individual and determinate object . . ." would be incompatible with a *vast* array of legislative acts today, many of which are "individual" and situation-specific in scope. Authors who emphasize Rousseau's "totalitarian" side repeatedly ignore this rather inconvenient fact. Jean-Jacques Rousseau, *The Social Contract*, in Frederick Watkins, ed., *Political Writings*, trans. Frederick Watkins (Madison: University of Wisconsin Press, 1986), 32.

47 Ibid., at 31.

48 Supra n. 3, at 78.

49 Ibid., at 94.

50 Ibid.

51 Supra n. 46, at 27. For a refreshingly clear-headed account of this issue, see Ingeborg Maus, *Zur Aufklärung der Demokratietheorie* (Frankfurt: Suhrkamp, 1992). For a provocative recent attempt to defend traditional conceptions of sovereignty, see Blandine Kriegel, *The State and the Rule of Law*, trans. Marc A. LePain and Jeffrey C. Cohen (Princeton, N.J.: Princeton University Press, 1995).

52 Franz Neumann, *The Democratic and Authoritarian State* (New York: Free Press, 1964), at 136.

53 Supra n. 3, at 153.

54 Ibid., at 166; my emphasis.

55 Ibid., at 157.

56 Ibid., at 212–13. Arendt does not deny the religious overtones of early American political thought. She rightly concedes that many attempts to resolve

the vicious circle of foundational politics in the American Revolution ultimately depend on traditional religious ideas. Yet while Schmitt, as I noted
above, praises the fact that French revolutionary theory remained under
the sway of traditional religious notions, Arendt believes that the American
Founders at least *anticipate* a solution to the vicious circle of foundational
politics that requires no religious grounding. In other words, they point to a
conception of legitimate constitutional government suitable to the dictates
of a disenchanted moral and political universe.

57 Ibid., at 206.

58 Ibid., at 170, 175. Clearly, much more is involved in Arendt's notion than
the mere "language game" described by Honig in her defense of Derrida's
(quite Schmittian) critique of Arendt. Honig, supra n. 17. Unfortunately, I
cannot discuss the complexities of Arendt's republican vision of action and
deliberation in adequate depth here. To understand this vision, see Hannah
Arendt, *The Human Condition* (Chicago: University of Chicago Press, 1958),
at 175–247.

59 Supra n. 3, at 212–13.

60 The increasing significance of the "social question" and the closely related
Europeanization of American politics, however, pose an omnipresent threat
to this possibility in Arendt's view.

61 Supra n. 6, at 66.

62 It simply does not suffice to assert that "[s]lavery was no more part of the
social question for Europeans than it was for Americans" at the end of the
eighteenth century, particularly in light of the important role played by
debates over slavery in the French Revolution. Supra n. 3, at 71–72.

63 For a similar criticism, see Sheldon Wolin, "Hannah Arendt: Democracy and
the Political" *Salmagundi* 60 (1983): 3.

64 In *Federalist Papers*, no. 40, Madison defends the manifest illegalities of the
constitutional convention by noting that "in all great changes of established
governments forms ought to give way to substance; that a rigid adherence in
such cases to the former would render nominal and nugatory the transcendent and precious right of the people to 'abolish or alter their governments
as to them shall seem most likely to effect their safety and happiness' . . .
it is . . . essential that such changes be instituted by some *informal and
unauthorized propositions*, made by some patriotic and respectable citizen
or number of citizens." Clinton Rossiter, ed., *The Federalist Papers* (New
York: Penguin, 1961), at 252–53. An excellent discussion of this point is
provided by Akhil Reed Amar, "Popular Sovereignty and Constitutional
Amendment," in Sanford Levinson, ed., *Responding to Imperfection: The
Theory and Practice of Constitutional Amendment* (Princeton: Princeton
University Press, 1995), at 89–116.

65 Bruce A. Ackerman, "Neo-Federalism?" in Jon Elster and Rune Slagstad,

eds., *Constitutionalism and Democracy* (New York: Cambridge University Press, 1988), 153 at 163.

66 Supra n. 3, at 164.

67 Supra n. 52, at 137.

68 In particular, Arendt would have done well to recall that "Jefferson apparently did not think too highly of Montesquieu's version of the separation [of powers] doctrine." Ibid., at 139.

69 For an extremely provocative recent discussion of this possibility, see Maus, supra n. 51, at 227–46.

70 For a thoughtful analysis and critique of Arendt's ideas about modern representative democracy, see George Kateb, *Hannah Arendt: Politics, Conscience, Evil* (Totowa, N.J.: Rowman & Allanheld, 1983), at 115–48.

71 For example, the Anti-Federalist "Brutus" asked "whether the world ever saw, in any period of it, a court of justice invested with such immense powers, and yet placed in a situation so little responsible . . . There is no power above them, to control any of their decisions. There is no authority that can remove them, and cannot be controlled by the laws of the legislature. In short, they are independent of the people, of the legislature, and of every power under heaven. Men placed in this situation will generally soon feel themselves independent of heaven itself." Herbert J. Storing, ed., *The Anti-Federalist* (Chicago: University of Chicago Press, 1985), at 183.

72 Supra n. 3, at 201.

73 Ibid., at 200.

74 Hannah Arendt, "What is Authority," in Hannah Arendt, *Between Past and Future: Eight Exercises in Political Thought*, enl. (New York: Penguin, 1961), at 93.

75 "The great measure of success the American founders could book for themselves, the simple fact that their revolution succeeded where all others were to fail . . . was decided the very moment when the Constitution began to be 'worshiped', even though it had hardly begun to operate." Supra n. 3, at 198–99. I suspect that this "blindness" has contributed to the many instances when those who claimed the mantle of American constitutionalism—McCarthy, for example—were able to dismantle basic civil liberties.

76 Supra n. 3, at 200, 228. For an excellent discussion of the controversies concerning constitutional amendment procedures, see Levinson, supra n. 64. I do not mean to deny Bruce Ackerman's recent claim that we need to provide adequate space for "normal" or "ordinary" politics in which questions of constitutional significance no longer possess primacy. In fact, I believe that Ackerman's vision of a "dualist democracy" has much to be said in its defense. My question here simply concerns the appropriate *institutionalization* of this model. Very much in the shadow of Arendt, Ackerman believes that when the Supreme Court declares a statute unconstitutional, it is

simply "signaling to the mass of private citizens . . . that something special is happening in the halls of power; that their would-be representatives are attempting to legislate in ways that few political movements . . . have done with credibility," in short, with the fact that "ordinary" legislators are now trying to break with a rough consensus achieved during a previous period in which "the people" made use of the track of "higher-lawmaking." But even Ackerman admits that this view still leaves unanswered the question of "[w]hat prevents [the Supreme Court] from misusing its constitutional authority to further one or another factional interest rather than to interpret the meaning of the past constitutional achievements of the . . . People?" Why, in other words, need we assume that an American-style Supreme Court provides the most effective instrument for institutionalizing and preserving the achievements of "higher lawmaking." Supra n. 65, at 172, 192. See also Bruce Ackerman, *We the People*, vol. 1 (Cambridge: Harvard University Press, 1991).

77 Supra n. 3, at 144.

78 Daniel Lazare, *The Frozen Republic* (New York: Harcourt Brace Jovanovich, 1996). My hunch is that academics will ignore *Village Voice* journalist Lazare's muckraking book, because of its breezy style and, at times, populistic assumptions. Nonetheless, Lazare does a fine job of explaining why so many of the idiosyncrasies of American constitutionalism can be linked to growing political alienation.

Carl Schmitt's Internal Critique
of Liberal Constitutionalism

Verfassungslehre as a Response to the Weimar State Crisis

Jeffrey Seitzer

Introduction

In one of his most famous dicta, the German legal and political theorist Carl Schmitt proclaimed it "obvious" that "all political concepts, images, and terms have a polemical meaning," because "[t]hey are focused on a specific conflict and are bound to a concrete situation."[1] Taking Schmitt at his word, I argue that one must read Schmitt's masterpiece of comparative law from the Weimar period, *Verfassungslehre*,[2] as a response to the Weimar state crisis. Schmitt's conceptual approach in *Verfassungslehre* aims to create a form of constitutional theory capable of compensating for structural defects of the Weimar state. Reading *Verfassungslehre* in this way also reveals that Schmitt does not present his constitutional theory as an alternative to liberal constitutionalism, but rather Schmitt's comparative history of constitutionalism in *Verfassungslehre* locates his decisionism at the very core of the liberal constitutional tradition.

The initially surprising fact that Schmitt develops his decidedly illiberal constitutional theory through an internal critique of liberal constitutionalism does not mean that Schmitt accepted liberal principles at a more profound level. Schmitt's systematic reconstruction of the liberal constitutional tradition, we shall see, was a tactical maneuver, indeed a quite brilliant one, the purpose of which was to enhance central state power, not revive liberal institutions.[3]

My aim in examining the design and execution of *Verfassungslehre* is to make clear the true character of Schmitt's challenge to liberal constitutionalism. For, as in the Hollywood thriller *When a Stranger Calls*, it is necessary to warn liberal constitutionalists that Schmitt is calling from inside the house. The pressing need for such a clarification is illustrated by the fact that Schmitt's constitutional theory is in vogue in Central and Eastern Europe.[4] Ulrich Preuss is right, therefore, that "[w]e cannot exclude the possibility that the constitutions being devised in Central and Eastern Europe . . . will fall prey to a . . . reinterpretation" "similar" to Schmitt's interpretation of the Weimar Constitution.[5] Laying bare the true nature of Schmitt's *Verfassungslehre*, I argue, is the best means of heading off any such possible missteps, for it prevents Schmitt's advocacy of a strong, independent state from drawing added persuasiveness from an association with liberal constitutionalism.

The argument proceeds in three steps. First, prominent continuities in Schmitt's approach to the Weimar state crisis, when compared with important features of the work of the French Syndicalist Georges Sorel, suggest the motivation for Schmitt's internal critique of the liberal constitutional tradition. Second, a confluence of changes in law, politics, and society over the nineteenth and twentieth centuries compel Schmitt to alter the prevailing understanding of the role of legal theory in politics. And, finally, a systematic reconstruction of liberal constitutional history provides the foundation for Schmitt's theoretical response to the Weimar state crisis.

Schmitt's Critique of Liberal Constitutionalism: Problem-Oriented History or History as Myth

Schmitt's continuing hold on the imagination of theorists across the political spectrum is partly due to the rhetorical brilliance of his writings. Schmitt's gift for conceptual formulations that are simultaneously lucid and suggestive, along with an at times surprising caginess about his own intentions, combine to frustrate efforts at easy ideological categorization. The ineffectiveness of such standard scholarly labor-saving devices complicates the task of interpreting Schmitt.

Rather than relying on biographical accounts or engaging in esoteric textual readings,[6] I focus on what might be termed objective patterns in Schmitt's writings. More specifically, I consider continuities in Schmitt's approach to the Weimar state crisis in reference to structural similarities between the historical methodology of Schmitt and the French Syndicalist Georges Sorel, who was more candid about his intentions than Schmitt was. This brief comparison suggests Schmitt's motivation for casting his comparative history of liberal constitutionalism as an internal critique.[7]

It is often suggested that Schmitt's narrative of decline in *The Crisis*

of Parliamentary Democracy[8] is a myth in Sorel's sense, the purpose
of which is to discredit parliamentary government. A comparison with
Sorel also illuminates Schmitt's positive response to the problems of the
Republic. Of particular interest is Sorel's approach to history, which he
terms "diremption."[9] The central feature of diremption is the deliberate
effort to isolate features of ideas, institutions, events, or developments
from their respective contexts. By abstracting away from contextual
factors which limit the usefulness of an idea or institution in resolving a
particular practical problem, diremption enhances the capacity of an object to serve as a rallying point for political action, because it heightens
the perceived opposition between alternatives. With a zero-sum view of
the world, one is far more likely to struggle to the bitter end. For otherwise one might be tempted to compromise for short-term gain, which
steadily drains ideas, movements, and institutions of their vibrancy.[10]

Schmitt's approach to developing guiding principles throughout the
Weimar period, including *Verfassungslehre*, is structurally quite similar
to Sorel's method of diremption. The last section focuses on Schmitt's
historical methodology in *Verfassungslehre*. In this section, I illustrate
this feature of Schmitt's approach in reference to his interpretation of
Hobbes in earlier works,[11] because this reveals a continuity in Schmitt's
approach, which, in turn, sheds important light on his motivation in
Verfassungslehre.

Central to Hobbes is the natural equality of individuals, which means
individuals cannot alienate their natural liberty without their consent.
This has important consequences for constitutionmaking. Most importantly, it invalidates the type of constitutions formed from contracts
between rulers and the estates. In these "agreements," monarchs concede or grant certain rights and privileges to the estates, retaining many
for themselves, but the government remains independent of the people.
That is not to say that the people could not exert influence on the
government; quite the contrary, these agreements resulted from power
struggles between the people, represented in estates, and monarchs.
Rather, this means that the government does not owe its very existence
to the people. Under this new conception, the people form a contract
among themselves, establishing or "commissioning" governments to
protect their natural rights. The government is not independent of the
people, and its exercise of authority is legitimate only to the extent that
it fulfils its commissions.

The act of constitutionmaking, according to Hobbes, is legitimate to
the extent that it ensures norms, the validity of which are independent

of the act itself. The problem is that while Hobbes insisted on the primacy of the natural rights of the individual, he did not envision effective institutional mechanisms for ensuring these rights against sovereign authority. Schmitt defined the entire enterprise of constitutionalism in reference to this ambiguity.

By stressing what he considered the "personalistic" core of the *Leviathan*, Schmitt attempted a startling reversal. There is an important ambiguity in the *Leviathan* regarding the ground of legitimacy of laws as commands. Is the legitimacy of law rooted in the purpose for which commands are issued, or is it merely the act of issuing them? Schmitt collapsed this tension in favor of the latter. The fundamental question for Hobbes, in Schmitt's reading, is not "what" is decided, but rather "who decides."[12] This shifts the focus from the purpose for which order is established and maintained to the act itself of establishing and maintaining order, effectively stripping Hobbes's command theory of law, admittedly ambiguous, of any normative content.

There are theoretical reasons for Hobbes's failure to develop effective institutional restraints on the exercise of sovereign authority. The natural equality of the individual, based on the universal possession of reason which can discern the natural law, limits sovereignty and locates it in the people, and the indivisible character of sovereignty ensures that the sovereign would not act against itself.

The contextual and polemical reasons for this omission, however, are more important. Hobbes must be understood in reference to the struggle against traditional authority. In seventeenth-century England, the individual was caught in the cross fire between rival powers. In response, Hobbes sought to centralize authority and make its legitimacy contingent on the protection of the individual.

This also explains Hobbes's reliance on reason as a restraint on sovereign power. The religious wars of the seventeenth century were fueled by superstition and prejudice. Hobbes sought to counter this by insisting on the capacity of reason to provide a workable basis for a peaceful order. Hobbes, of course, never claimed that a thoroughly rational politics would ever obtain; in fact, he conceded that abuses would continue. But his emphasis on the clarifying, conciliatory power of reason was meant to dampen and modify the natural passions which fueled and, in turn, were aggravated by superstition and prejudice.[13] Hobbes, ever attentive to the complexity of human motivation, knew that one does not bolster confidence in reason by stressing its deficiencies.

Leo Strauss agrees with Schmitt that any fundamental critique of liberalism must begin with Hobbes. But Schmitt does not engage Hobbes in a thoroughgoing manner, according to Strauss, for Schmitt ignores the essential civilizing core of the *Leviathan*.[14] Strauss argues that Schmitt's misreading of Hobbes is traceable to his concern with the moral per se in that it constitutes a "polemic" against "entertainment," one, moreover, which rejects "civilization" for the sake of moral "seriousness."[15]

This is very probably true. Generally, though, Schmitt, unlike Sorel, was quite cagey regarding his underlying intentions. It is exceedingly difficult, therefore, to prove that Schmitt deliberately misread Hobbes. Indeed, he may have simply been wrong. Nonetheless, the extraordinary one-sidedness of Schmitt's interpretation of Hobbes harmonizes so well with his argument concerning the centrality of "decision" in constitutionalism considered in the last section that it suggests strongly that this was a deliberate move on his part. Again, this begs the question, why not simply reject liberal constitutionalism outright and assert the independent legitimacy of decisionism, much as Sorel insisted on the superiority of socialism over capitalism?

Sorel was initially drawn to the Syndicalist movement because he thought its rich associational life provided the basis for a complete break with the Third Republic. The vibrancy of these institutions, for him, was traceable to the great inspirational power of Marxist historiography, which reduced history to a final struggle between the proletariat and the bourgeoisie that the former was destined to win. The workers' movement, in other words, had a distinct advantage over Christianity in that it still had a doctrine of eschatology which could inspire great acts of resistance. The problem was this eschatology was threatened by its very source. Because orthodox Marxism insisted that the socialist revolution would result inevitably from the "iron law of necessity," it obscured the fact that a successful socialist revolution would require decisive human action. Sorel's myth of the general strike was meant to reinvigorate the Marxist view of history. By actively configuring historical materials to stress the desperate need for and potential efficacy of heroic action, one could enhance the motivational power of Marx's idea of class struggle. Whether that which sparked heroic action was true or not is irrelevant, if it is successful. For Sorel, in other words, history was strictly a tool useful in sparking radical social change.

Much in the way the Marxist view of history draws enormous power as a motivational force from its reduction of history to an epic struggle between the proletariat and the bourgeoisie, I suggest that Schmitt believed his theory of constitutionmaking as decision can take on added strength by being portrayed as a defense of Western constitutionalism. This is not to say, of course, that Schmitt was actually a liberal, either in classic or then contemporary terms. Schmitt clearly sympathized with the counterrevolutionary rejection of liberalism. But Schmitt believed it was necessary to work with "existing materials," and in his time this meant first the democratic ideal. The counterrevolutionaries, however, were uncompromisingly antidemocratic, so their vision of social order found little resonance in an era dominated by the democratic ideal.[16] The great challenge, in Schmitt's view, was to redefine the democratic ideal such that it enhanced rather than eroded the social order.

The unavoidable necessity of working with existing materials also meant that one must operate within the Weimar Constitution. The Weimar Constitution was a complicated compromise of competing visions of social order. Schmitt redefines the democratic components of the constitution such that the ordinary political process is not the primary institutional means of expressing political aspirations. Schmitt also subordinates what he considers the liberal components of the constitution to the democratic portion as he defines it.

I diverge from critics like Ulrich Preuss, however, on the issue of how Schmitt effects these changes. Schmitt executes these displacements through a systematic reconstruction of the liberal constitutional tradition, particularly of the American and French Revolutions, which Preuss rightly identifies as seminal events in this tradition. In this sense, Schmitt's interpretation does not put the Weimar Constitution in tension with its primary sources, the American and French Revolutions, as Preuss claims.[17] On the contrary, Schmitt's manipulation of comparative history brings his interpretation of the Weimar Constitution into harmony with these sources by redefining their respective places in the Western constitutional tradition.[18]

Like Sorel, therefore, Schmitt uses history as a tool. Once recalibrated through his manipulation of comparative history, the liberal constitutional tradition provides an effective response to the Weimar state crisis as *he* understood it. Before examining Schmitt's reconfiguration of the liberal constitutional tradition, I must elaborate on his understanding of the Weimar state crisis.

Turning Things Around: Making Legal Theory Serve the State

By stressing the need to read Schmitt in general and *Verfassungslehre* in particular in reference to Schmitt's understanding of the unique problems of Germany, I do not deny that Schmitt believed Germany was caught up in larger Western developments.[19] A full appreciation of Schmitt's project in *Verfassungslehre,* however, requires seeing how closely tailored Schmitt's approach is to his view of the German context. In this section, I examine Schmitt's understanding of the peculiar convergence of material and spiritual factors in nineteenth- and early-twentieth-century Germany, which, in his view, compel a fundamental change in the role of legal theory in politics.[20]

Schmitt's analysis of German law and politics in *Verfassungslehre* follows a long scholarly tradition stressing the divergence of German political development from that of much of the rest of Europe and North America.[21] A leitmotif in this style of historiography is his emphasis on the fact that German legal and political reform in the nineteenth century proceeded at different paces. Prussia's devastating defeat by Napoleon in 1806 sparked the so-called revolution from above. Liberal bureaucrats, in other words, introduced important reforms which promoted legal unity and introduced a significant degree of civil freedom. On a political level, however, little had changed; the state retained an essentially absolutist character.[22]

The failure of the Revolution of 1848 brought with it important changes. After declining to accept the throne from the Frankfurt Parliament in 1849, the Prussian monarch finally promulgated a constitution which gave constitutional status to many of the progressive civil law changes achieved by the *Allgemeines Landesrecht* (ALR), the General Law of Prussia. Though relatively progressive, the "imposed" Prussian Constitution of 1850, modeled after the liberal Belgian Constitution of 1831, constituted a booby prize of sorts for those who favored a unified, liberal constitutional state under the aborted Paulskirche Constitution.[23]

The founding of the German Reich in 1871, of course, did not constitute the complete victory of what we today consider modern constitutionalism. At the time, though, it was widely seen as fulfilling important goals, most particularly providing the aspiration for German political unity with concrete form. Moreover, Bismarck's Reich Constitution satisfied many of the demands of liberals who were most insistent on constitutional reform, but it did so without undercutting entirely the social position of many traditionally powerful groups.[24]

Speaking in the broadest possible terms, therefore, during much of the Reich period, but particularly between 1870 and 1890, it was not necessary to reconcile traditionally powerful groups to the existing system, because the complex constitutional compromise gave them an important stake in the system. Relatedly, in contrast to the previous half century, the efforts of reformers were primarily directed at solidifying and extending the current system.

Of more immediate relevance for our purposes, these conditions also made possible a shift in emphasis in legal scholarship from continuity to discontinuity, in Schmitt's view. For the previous half century, legal scholarship compensated for the considerable confusion regarding sources of law due to the highly fragmented legal character of the German Confederation. They did so, for example, through historical studies which discerned a national spirit behind the seemingly fragmented, often contradictory sources of the law.[25] The establishment of the Reich provided Germany with a concrete political framework for national aspirations. Of course, the Reich legal system was itself a composite of the legal systems of the various Länder. Still, there was a common framework, through which one could achieve genuine legal unity. Most legal professionals directed their attention to the task of achieving this legal unity through the promulgation of a Civil Code and the establishment of a unified federal court system.[26]

Under these conditions, Schmitt argues, legal scholarship could afford to become decidedly ahistorical. Because Bismarck's complex constitutional compromise provided a minimum degree of legal and political unity, it was no longer necessary for legal theorists to compensate for a lack of unity through elaborate historical and philosophical constructs. This is reflected in the fact that the dominant form of legal theory in the Reich period, legal positivism, bolstered the existing system by identifying legal legitimacy with strict adherence to formal procedural mechanisms for the establishment and execution of laws.

Schmitt opposed legal positivism because it ignored the fact that law is rooted in larger cultural, political, social, and economic contexts.[27] In the Reich period, according to Schmitt, legal positivists were safely able to efface the distinction between constitutional and ordinary law, because the conservative state Prussia had a hammerlock on the constitutional system. It had enough votes in the Bundesrat, for instance, to veto any proposed constitutional changes. The structure of the system, in other words, provided an effective, though unacknowledged, substitute for a substantive distinction between constitutional and ordinary law.[28] In this sense, the "feeling of political and social security" of the Reich period allowed legal theorists to enjoy a comforting abstractness, according to Schmitt.[29]

Schmitt insists that legal theory could not retain the same detachment from reality under the unique conditions of the Weimar Republic. Due to its highly democratic character as well as its difficult domestic and international position, the Weimar system is much less successful at containing social conflict than its predecessor. In Weimar, competing groups, *Weltanschauungsparteien*, seek to utilize the democratic system first to solidify their position relative to that of their opponents by lending constitutional status to their view of proper human association and second to eliminate their opponents altogether.[30]

Schmitt believes that various features of the Weimar Constitution facilitate this potentially debilitating ideological conflict. Most important is the constitution's ambiguity in regard to the overall purpose of the system.[31] Recalling the ill-fated Paulskirche Constitution, the promulgation of which was delayed by debate over rights provisions, the principal drafter of the Weimar Constitution, Hugo Preuss, advocated focusing on the basic organizational framework of government. With the organizational framework of government securely established, Preuss believed, the more divisive question of type of system, liberal-capitalist or democratic-socialist for example, could have been addressed.[32] Friedrich Naumann, a prominent Christian social theorist and politician, believed that the collapse of the imperial system offered the opportunity to establish a new type of system combining features of the capitalist West and socialist East.[33] The Second Principal Part of the Weimar Constitution, containing as it did a wide array of rights provisions, traditional political and civil rights as well as economic and social ones, reflected Naumann's vision.[34] Schmitt believed that the rights provisions of the Weimar Constitution reflected the fact that the constitution did not represent a "genuine" compromise and, as such, made a bad situation much worse.[35] By lending apparent constitutional status to a wide array of often contradictory claims for governmental action, the rights provisions, in his view, encouraged competing groups to seek special treatment, exacerbating rather than moderating the social tensions which cause political instability.[36]

Under these circumstances, Schmitt claims, it is necessary to discern behind the confusing mass of seemingly contradictory provisions a solid core which provides meaning to the document as a whole and would not be subject to amendment. This substantive component would be the standard by which all particular disputes are resolved. Moreover, by removing important principles from the divisive competition among political parties, it would provide a stable pole around which defense of the constitutional order could revolve.[37]

The legal positivists are not able to achieve this aim, Schmitt claims, because they insist on following the letter of the law. The law, however, offers little guidance. The text of the Weimar Constitution, for example, does not distinguish among different provisions, indicating which are primary and how conflicts about them are resolvable. The legal positivist response to such a problem is merely to refuse to address it. Take, for example, the position of Gerhard Anschütz on the constitutional crisis over the military budget in Prussia during the 1860s: "[W]hen the highest state organs cannot agree on a budget, 'there is not only a gap in the law, that is, in the text of the constitution, but moreover in law as a whole, which can in no way be filled by juristic conceptual operations. Here is where public law stops'; the question of how to proceed in lieu of a budget law is not a legal question."[38]

Legal positivism's insistence on strict adherence to the letter of the law is also problematic, according to Schmitt, because in some senses the law is too explicit. The Weimar Constitution is clear, for example, in regard to constitutional amendments, requiring only a two-thirds majority vote of Parliament. This simplified amendment procedure creates the impression that all constitutional provisions are of equal status, since every provision is subject to the same simple amendment procedure. This is clearly absurd, in Schmitt's view, because it implies, for example, that the principles established in Article 1 of the Weimar Constitution, that the German Reich is a "Republic" and that "all state authority stems from the people," are subject to amendment in the same way as obviously less fundamental provisions, such as the protection of the "well-earned rights of civil servants" under Article 129.[39] For Schmitt, this lends credence to the view that the Weimar Constitution itself is merely provisional by bolstering the claim that the entire system could be transformed through simple amendment procedures. Schmitt believed this renders meaningless the distinction between constitutional and ordinary law.[40]

If the constitutional order is to be preserved, Schmitt argues, it is necessary to determine which elements of the Weimar system are truly fundamental. We have seen that the text of the Weimar Constitution provides little guidance in this regard. Another alternative is to examine the materials pertaining to the drafting of the Weimar Constitution. Schmitt, however, rejects this alternative as well. For Americans, this neglect of "the intent of the framers" is quite striking, but it is not surprising in view of the German legal tradition.

In the interpretation and application of law, Germans stress "objective" over "subjective" factors.[41] For the most part, for example, Germans are not concerned with what Americans term the "intent of the framers," since this involves subjective states of mind of particular persons. Instead, they attempt to place particular laws within larger wholes. During the Reich period, for example, the legal positivists positioned laws within an allegedly complete and coherent system of concepts.[42] Earlier in the nineteenth century, the theorists of the Historical Law School associated with Friedrich Carl von Savigny believed that the diverse and apparently ever-changing customs and practices of a people were more than contingent responses to the political and social environment. For Savigny and his followers, rather, these customs and practices were indications of a *Volksgeist*, a composite greater than the sum of its parts. These apparently discrete instances, in other words, are merely different manifestations of an underlying continuity, and, as such, they have an "objective" status, because they are abstracted from the discrete actions and specific intentions of particular individuals and groups.[43]

When Schmitt occasionally turned to the drafting history of particular provisions to resolve interpretive questions, however, this analysis was clearly subordinate to determination of the larger purpose of the constitution in general.[44] But this rank ordering of interpretive canons does not mean that Schmitt was committed to traditional modes of interpretation. On the contrary, Schmitt seeks to recast the way in which history is deemed relevant to law.

The theorists of the Historical Law School and those of the German Idealist tradition stemming from Kant but especially Hegel disagreed about the ultimate ground of history. The Historical Law School saw the unique *Volksgeist* of a people as the ground of history, whereas the German Idealists stressed the "idea," or "world spirit." Savigny and his followers insisted that national experiences are incommensurable. Hegel's focus on the idea, by contrast, tends to obscure the essential differences among cultures. Nonetheless, both the Historical Law School and the German Idealists believed that history is characterized by an underlying continuity.[45]

Schmitt, by contrast, believed history is characterized by discontinuity, so it is problematical to assume continuity on any level. The greatest offenders in this regard, according to Schmitt, are Enlightenment thinkers, who confuse the apparent repetitiveness of phenomena with permanence. That similar actions are taken over extended periods of time does not mean these actions are identical, nor that they will necessarily recur under similar circumstances. There is always an element of contingency in human affairs, but this is obscured in the drive to achieve universal principles through the exaggeration of similarity.

To the extent one can speak of continuity, according to Schmitt, it is only in reference to human action or decision, the conscious, deliberate effort to take up principles and apply them to particular circumstances. The principles themselves can claim no validity outside such efforts. That they emerge in some form in different contexts and are successfully applied there does not indicate that they are generally applicable. The surface similarity between different contexts might suggest their potential usefulness at a particular point, but it is only after they are successfully applied that one can say they were applicable.[46]

The problem with legal positivism is not that it fails to recognize the contingency of norms, but rather that it does not come to terms with the institutional implications of this fact.[47] In the Reich, more specifically, the structure of the system made the contingency of norms a nonissue. The political system of the Weimar Republic, by contrast, gives full vent to fundamental political differences, and the result is general state paralysis. Rather than automatically according legitimacy to the outcomes of a deeply flawed political process, as does legal positivism, legal theory should develop guiding principles which compensate for important defects in state structure. In other words, whereas during the Reich an independent state provided a safe haven for legal theory, in the interwar period legal theory must create a "theoretical space" for a beleaguered state apparatus.

Schmitt's understanding of constitutionmaking as decision is carefully tailored to this purpose. By grounding legitimacy in founding moments with few, if any, concrete reference points,[48] Schmitt's decisionism renders inviolate the commitment to core principles, while at the same time it gives the state extraordinary freedom of action in ensuring these principles.[49] In Schmitt's view, therefore, legal theory itself becomes a form of political action in that the legal theorist defines the relevant points of continuity/discontinuity and similarity/difference such that the founding moment becomes an effective response to the Weimar state crisis. It remains to be seen how Schmitt elaborates his state-friendly constitutional theory through a reconstruction of Western constitutional history.

Putting Humpty Back Together Again: Creating a State-Friendly Constitutional Theory

The Weimar Constitution, Schmitt argues, "conforms thoroughly" to the type of constitution, the *bürgerlicher Rechtsstaat*, which gained classic expression in the rounds of constitutionmaking surrounding the American and French Revolutions.[50] The defining feature of this type of constitution is the guarantee of the separation of powers and certain basic rights.[51] But it is mistaken, in Schmitt's view, to identify this type of constitution with constitutionalism per se.[52] For the legitimacy of these constitutions, as well as that of the Weimar Constitution, rests on the sovereign power of the people to give itself a constitution, regardless of its particular form.[53]

This is Schmitt's famous distinction between the political (democratic) and *rechtsstaatlich* (liberal) elements of the Weimar Constitution.[54] Critics are right to point out that this distinction enables Schmitt to preserve the form of limited government at the expense of its substance. What is underappreciated among commentators is the significance of the fact that Schmitt develops this distinction through a systematic reconstruction of the classic American and especially French efforts at constitutionmaking. That this reconstruction effectively redefines the liberal constitutional tradition becomes evident only when Schmitt's comparative history of constitutionmaking is examined in reference to the larger history of Western constitutionalism.[55]

According to Schmitt, early constitutional struggles, such as that which led to the Magna Carta, involved groups which, to the extent they defined themselves at all, did so in contradistinction to other groups vying for control of the same territory. The nobility, "freemen," seek to wrest concessions from the monarch, for example. The results of these struggles are "agreements," "contracts," which aim to guarantee the relative positions of the contracting parties. These agreements are not, however, "constitutions" in the modern sense, according to Schmitt, because the actors involved do not act consciously as a unit in order to define themselves "politically."

The Glorious Revolution marks the beginning of constitutional law in the modern sense, according to Schmitt. By that time, all relevant social groups, including the king, are "represented" in Parliament. This relatively inclusive representation reflected a common identity which enabled the English to act as a unity. The agreement with William of Orange, for example, did not "constitute" this common identity; rather, the agreement with William "presupposed" this unity.[56]

This notion of preexisting unity has both spiritual and material components. It is the product of historical development understood in existential terms. There is no necessary development toward a common identity, the achievement of which constitutes an end phase of sorts, because this depends on circumstances which vary considerably between contexts, as well as on decisive human action.

Schmitt argues, for example, that the relatively high degree of centralization in France at the time of the Revolution distinguishes French constitutionmaking from that of the Americans less in an institutional than in a spiritual sense. Americans compensated for the splintered character of their political system by sending representatives to a "constitutional convention." The crucial difference is that the French have a common identity, forged over many centuries and which came to full flowering in the absolutist era. The centralizing efforts of the French monarchs broke down the great multiplicity of local bonds, so that increasingly the French identified with the central state. America, by contrast, has a long tradition of local self-government, a legacy of its truly unique development as English colonies, which solidified these local attachments. At the time of the Revolution, for example, Americans saw themselves first as members of particular colonies, second as citizens of a country.

Because of this common identity, the French were able to act in a way not possible for Americans. In fact, in Schmitt's view, the round of constitutionmaking inspired by the French Revolution is truly the first instance of a people reaching a "decision" regarding their "political existence" as a whole. During the Glorious Revolution, the English people through Parliament acted as a unity, but the revolution involved a rearrangement, more or less, of an existing system, the sanctioning of a series of developments which occurred over an extended period of time. The French, by contrast, consciously made a radical break with their past, and, on the basis of their common identity, chose a new political form. The great French insight, Schmitt argues, is seeing the act of establishing a constitution as itself "constitutive." In other words, the authority of the people acting in its collective capacity is unrestrained by any norms prior to the act itself. In fact, it is the act of will itself which establishes norms.[57]

The next closest instance was the American Revolution. But here again, Schmitt argues, only an institutional restructuring took place. The Americans anticipated this notion of a people consciously adopting a new political form, and yet they were unable to act on it, because they were preoccupied with finding an institutional framework to accommodate their various political identities. The Americans had to "constitute" their identity through the act of constitutionmaking itself, whereas the French were able to "presuppose" this identity.[58] The Americans, in other words, were stuck at some sort of preparatory stage, unable to grasp the great opportunity offered by their own Revolution.

Schmitt identifies an important aspect of the French tradition. The French are not defined by their constitutions in the way that Americans are by the American Constitution. The French state was formed before the Revolution, and it is in an important, though ill-defined or perhaps even undefinable way, independent of particular forms of government. Certain institutional loci of French national identity exist—the centralized bureaucracy for example—and French national identity has undergone some changes, most notably through the Revolution itself. Nonetheless, it is preexisting, independent.[59]

It is quite understandable that Schmitt oriented his attempt at a "systematic" comparative constitutional theory toward the "classic French constitutions."[60] The aborted Paulskirche Constitution of 1849 marked the apex of American influence on German law before the founding of the Federal Republic.[61] Otherwise, German legal institutions and legal theory were heavily influenced by the French model.

The problem, however, is that Schmitt defines constitutionmaking not merely in reference to the French model, which he rightly argues occupies a central place in the Western constitutional tradition, and one of special relevance for civil law countries like Germany.[62] Rather, Schmitt defines Western constitutionmaking exclusively in reference to the most radical strand within the French tradition.[63] His reading of the Western constitutional tradition, in other words, is doubly one-sided. In this, Schmitt makes good on his claim that "[t]he rule proves nothing; the exception proves everything: [the exception] confirms not only the rule but also its existence, which derives only from the exception."[64]

Schmitt correctly stresses the central role of Sieyès, who embodies perhaps better than anyone the ambiguities of the Revolution, as well as the importance to revolutionary thought of Sieyès's concept of a radical break with the past. Schmitt, however, ignores the great tensions in Sieyès's thought as well as those between it and various other strands of revolutionary thought. Relatedly, he severs the concept of radical break from its historical context, overlooking the pressing practical problems to which it was a response and which serve as a potential limit on its scope. Sieyès links will with representation and identifies the national will with that of the National Assembly first in order to discredit the traditional system of representation, which tended to bolster traditional authority for the very reason it was more democratic: imperative mandates reinforced provincialism. Sieyès links will with representation also in order to justify the activity of the National Assembly, which was already a going concern. As the National Assembly became tyrannical, however, Sieyès hedged and sought to limit its authority in a variety of ways.[65]

The blizzard of French constitutions in the first generation after the Revolution effaced the distinction between the form and substance of constitutions. Nonetheless, the French accepted, at least initially, something similar to the American understanding of a normative constitution, as evidenced by articles 2 and especially 16 of the *Declaration of the Rights of Man and Citizen*, a fact which Schmitt himself acknowledges.[66] The legal status of the *Declaration* is a matter of some dispute,[67] but it is not the case that the French reject the notion of norms anterior to constitutions. Even in the late nineteenth century, when leading constitutional theorists turned from natural rights as conceived in the social contract tradition, they still believed that the lawgiver was bound in some essential way, and this under a constitution, famous for its brevity, which established only the bare framework of government and provided amendment procedures only marginally more demanding than those for ordinary legislation.[68] The principal problem in the French tradition has been finding the proper institutional means through which such norms could gain expression.[69] Schmitt's focus on Sieyès's idea of a radical break with the past obscures this important connection between the French and American traditions.

One must always guard against interpretations which deny the plurality and ambiguity of rich, complex traditions.[70] Still, it is not too much of a stretch to claim that the American and French Revolutions form the epicenter of what we today consider modern liberal constitutionalism. More specifically, the seminal instances of constitutionmaking surrounding these revolutions gave classic expression to the core liberal commitment to limited government in service of individual liberty. How one understands individual liberty changes over time. In fact, commentators are right to point out an important difference in this regard between the American and French Revolutions themselves.[71] But central to these revolutions and the traditions of constitutional theory and practice they inspired, including the Weimar Constitution itself, is the idea that the legitimacy of constitutions is intimately bound up with the protection of individual liberty, however one understands this concept.

By systematically obscuring this important commonality between the American and French constitutional traditions, Schmitt does more than deny their rich diversity. Rather, he slips his theory of decisionism into the very core of the liberal constitutional tradition.[72] More specifically, in arguing that the central lesson of these classic instances of liberal constitutionmaking, particularly that stemming from the French Revolution, is the idea that the legitimacy of constitutions depends on a sovereign decision of the people, and not whether the resulting constitution protects individual liberty, Schmitt effectively shifts the theoretical epicenter of the liberal constitution tradition. In this sense, Schmitt does not develop a theoretical antipode to the liberal constitutional tradition so much as transform it from the inside out such that it serves as a theoretical foundation for his illiberal constitutional theory.

Conclusion

Schmitt's account of the Weimar Constitution calls to mind a bag of party favors. There is something for everyone, for example, in the extensive, though internally contradictory, Catalogue of Rights. The rich variety of German aspirations is also reflected in the Republic's complex, though mostly dysfunctional, political system.

For Schmitt, however, one must evaluate constitutions not by whether they give expression to the full range of societal aspirations. The important consideration is whether and to what extent constitutions establish clear guiding principles and institutional mechanisms well-suited for achieving these principles in practice. In specific regard to the Weimar Constitution, Schmitt believed that unless a solid core could be formed from its mélange of competing principles and institutional forms, the constitution would fall victim to its own complexity.

Schmitt's solution to this difficulty was a substantive understanding of the constitution. Schmitt argues that certain provisions of the constitution represent fundamental decisions of the German people. As such, these provisions form the axis of the entire system and are thus not subject to change, even through a constitutional amendment. Only a new act of constitutionmaking can bring about a fundamentally different form of political and social ordering.

In abstract terms, Schmitt's substantive vision of constitutions has considerable merit. In the postwar period, for example, numerous states have also lent constitutional status to a wide range of constitutional rights. Distinguishing among constitutional provisions according to their relative fundamentality provides a potentially useful way of mediating the inevitable tensions among competing constitutional claims.

We have seen, however, that one misunderstands Schmitt if one reads his works apart from their immediate context. Schmitt's substantive constitutional theory was designed to compensate for the structural defects of the Weimar state, not mediate the inevitable conflicts among competing groups in a complex, rapidly changing society. And, for this purpose, Schmitt's theory of constitutionmaking as decision provided the theoretical foundation for presidential government subject to few, if any, practical limitations. In the end, Schmitt preserved the guiding principles and the basic organizational structure of the system only by draining them of any substance, making his constitutional theory the constitutional politics equivalent of a neutron bomb which destroys life but leaves untouched the structures that house it.

This peculiar disjunction between form and substance in Schmitt's constitutional theory is understandably the cause of much distress among commentators. My analysis echoes many of the concerns of Schmitt's critics, but I place these criticisms of Schmitt on firmer footing by advancing a novel claim.

I argue that Schmitt's argumentative strategy in *Verfassungslehre* is far more complicated than generally recognized. As many claim, Schmitt redefines the democratic ideal, in order to circumvent the ordinary political process which he considers fundamentally flawed. It is also true that Schmitt subordinates what he terms the liberal part of the constitution, its extensive civil and political rights, to the democratic portion as he defines it, thus effectively subverting the liberal commitment to genuinely limited government. I demonstrate, however, that Schmitt does so not by discrediting liberal constitutionalism. Rather, through his brilliant manipulation of comparative history, Schmitt reconfigures the liberal constitutional history such that his theory of constitutionmaking as decision forms its core.

This is not to say that in *Verfassungslehre* Schmitt suddenly develops a soft spot for liberalism. Schmitt's understanding of the institutional implications of the radical contingency of norms under the unique conditions of the Weimar Republic induces him to seize the opportunity offered by important ambiguities in liberal constitutional history to craft an especially state-friendly constitutional theory. For Schmitt, in other words, legal theory becomes a form of political action in that it deliberately defines the relevant points of continuity and discontinuity within German history as well as between German and Western histories such that the resulting constitutional theory displaces a deeply flawed political process. Relatedly, Schmitt cast his defense of the Republic in terms of the liberal constitutional tradition, because it might lend added legitimacy to his project, thereby helping to ensure that it might "inspire confidence," to speak with Schmitt.

As many commentators have pointed out, the principal problem with Schmitt's comparative-historical approach is that his understanding of the Weimar state crisis led him to unfairly discount the admittedly already limited range of moderate institutional solutions to the Republic's problems. Nonetheless, Schmitt was right to insist that constitutional theorists must look beyond philosophical and doctrinal issues to the structural features of states, if they are to engage effectively the pressing problems of constitutional democracy. Schmitt, in other words, was heading in the right direction, but he made several very important wrong turns. Liberal constitutionalists, however, can learn from Schmitt's mistakes to develop a comparative-historical approach to constitutional theory which focuses more narrowly on developing moderate institutional solutions to concrete problems. My investigation of Schmitt's *Verfassungslehre* is meant as a first step in this direction.

Notes

I am grateful to Olivier Beaud, Hartwin Bungert, David Dyzenhaus, Gary Herrigel, Stephen Holmes, Oliver Lepsius, Bernard Manin, John McCormick, George Schwab, and Janet Smith for helpful advice and encouragement as well as to the German Academic Exchange Service for a grant to complete some of the research for this essay at the Max Planck Institute for European Legal History in Frankfurt am Main, Germany.

1 Carl Schmitt, *The Concept of the Political*, trans. George Schwab (Chicago: The University of Chicago Press, 1996), at 30 (hereafter *Concept of the Political*).

2 Carl Schmitt, *Verfassungslehre*, 7th ed. (Berlin: Duncker & Humblot, 1989) (hereafter *Verfassungslehre*).

3 A focus on Schmitt's methodology distinguishes my analysis from more narrowly philosophical treatments. Compare in this regard the famous claim by Leo Strauss that Schmitt's critique of liberalism is "in the horizon of liberalism." See, for example, *Concept of the Political*, supra n. 1, at 107.

4 András Sajó, for example, claims that "for Hungarians, the natural interpretation of power is based on 'decisionism'" and that "the dissatisfaction of the power elite" in Hungary "is derived from Carl Schmitt's interpretation of power." See Irena Grudzíska-Gross, ed., *Constitutionalism in East Central Europe* (Bratislava: Czecho-Slovak Committee of the European Cultural Foundation, 1994), at 56ff.

5 See "Constitutional Powermaking for the New Polity: Some Reflections on the Relations between Constituent Power and the Constitution," in Michel Rosenfeld, ed., *Constitutionalism, Identity, Difference, and Legitimacy: Theoretical Perspectives* (Durham, N.C.: Duke University Press, 1994), at 153.

6 Joseph W. Bendersky, *Carl Schmitt: Theorist for the Reich* (Princeton: Princeton University Press, 1983) and Günther Meuter, *Der Katechon: Zu Carl Schmitts fundamentalistischer Kritik der Zeit* (Berlin: Duncker & Humblot, 1994) offer examples of biographical and esoteric approaches, respectively. For a thoughtful analysis of the potential of the esoteric approach pioneered by Leo Strauss, see Olivier Beaud, "L'art d'écrire chez un juriste: Carl Schmitt," in Carlos-Miguel Herrera, ed., *Le Droit, le Politique: autour de Max Weber, Hans Kelsen, Carl Schmitt* (Paris: Éditions L'Harmattan, 1995).

7 In many respects, my analysis in this section echoes much recent scholarship on Schmitt's relation to Sorel. My treatment differs in that I argue that parallels between Sorel and Schmitt suggest why Schmitt cast *Verfassungslehre* in the form of an internal critique of liberal constitutionalism. The conventional view, by contrast, stresses Sorel's influence in Schmitt's efforts to discredit liberal institutions.

8 Carl Schmitt, *The Crisis of Parliamentary Democracy*, trans. Ellen Kennedy (Cambridge, Mass.: MIT Press, 1988).

9 See George Sorel, *Reflections on Violence*, trans. E. Hulme and J. Roth (London: Collier Books, 1950), at 259 and 263–64 for Sorel's description of his method. According to the translators, diremption is Sorel's coinage.

10 This is illustrated by Sorel's analysis of the struggle between the Catholic Church and the French state, for example. In the struggle with secular authority, according to Sorel, the church was forced to surrender control of ever more extensive portions of the social order. This is neither surprising, nor disturbing, since secular authority was better suited to execute many essential tasks. The problem, in Sorel's view, was that the church acquiesced on the truly important moral/religious issues, mistakenly seeking to preserve its position in secular society by compromising its stewardship of moral and religious truth, which is the true basis of its authority. There are many good reasons for cooperation with secular authority, according to Sorel. Such cooperation is especially important for the masses, for whom a degree of "economic-juridical uniformity" guaranteed by secular authority is beneficial. But compromises on these larger questions eroded the church's

authority. In the long run, this did much more to undermine the position of the church within society than would have its steadfast refusal to compromise its principles. Ibid., at 253–73.

11 On Schmitt's relation to Hobbes, see Helmut Rumpf, *Carl Schmitt und Thomas Hobbes: Ideelle Beziehungen und aktuelle Bedeutung mit einer Abhandlung über: Die Frühschriften Carl Schmitts* (Berlin: Duncker & Humblot, 1972) and John P. McCormick, "Fear, Technology, and the State: Carl Schmitt, Leo Strauss, and the Revival of Hobbes in Weimar and National Socialist Germany," *Political Theory* 22 (1994): 619.

12 See *Political Theology: Four Chapters on the Concept of Sovereignty*, trans. George Schwab (Cambridge, Mass.: MIT Press, 1985), at 33–35 (hereafter *Political Theology*).

13 For an excellent treatment of Hobbes's effort to counter the destructive power of irrational beliefs, see Stephen Holmes, *Passions and Constraint: On the Theory of Liberal Democracy* (Chicago: The University of Chicago Press, 1995), at 69–99.

14 On the complex relationship between Schmitt and Strauss as well as important changes in their respective interpretations of Hobbes in the interwar period, see McCormick, "Fear, Technology, and the State," supra n. 11.

15 *Concept of the Political*, supra n. 1, at 100–101.

16 This explains the peculiar book report quality of Schmitt's treatment of the counterrevolutionaries in the final chapter of *Political Theology*, supra n. 12, at 5. Schmitt opened the chapter by recounting in a sympathetic tone the counterrevolutionary "recognition that their times needed a decision." Since much of Schmitt's work in the Weimar period, but especially *Political Theology* itself, is devoted to showing the necessity of decision in his time, this leads one to expect Schmitt to conclude the work with an argument for the continued relevance of the counterrevolutionary vision of social order. Instead, he merely reviewed their rejection of liberalism and advocacy of hierarchical authority without taking a stand on it. The closest Schmitt comes to this, in fact, is his claim that Donoso Cortes's characterization of the bourgeoisie as the "discussing class" is "not the last word on Continental liberalism in its entirety, but it is certainly a most striking observation"; *Political Theology*, at 62–63.

17 See Preuss, "Constitutional Powermaking for the New Polity," supra n. 5, at 153.

18 Reinhard Mehring rightly stresses the connection between Schmitt's "sociology of concepts" in *Political Theology* and the conceptual framework of *Verfassungslehre*. Schmitt deems it necessary to resolve oppositions between conflicting principles and to produce harmony between reigning principles and the institutional structure of states. But Mehring mistakenly argues that in *Verfassungslehre* Schmitt seeks to produce the necessary harmony by discrediting and replacing liberalism. See Mehring, "Carl Schmitts

Lehre von der Auflösung des Liberalismus: Das Sinngefüge der 'Verfassungslehre' als historisches Urteil," *Zeitschrift für Politik* 200 38 (1991): at 214.

Given Schmitt's understanding of the radical contingency of norms, there is no principled reason why the liberal tradition cannot be simply transformed such that the necessary harmony is secured, if this seems the most effective means to this end. Schmitt's only concern is whether his reconstruction of liberal constitutionalism is able "to inspire confidence" and spark action in defense of the Republic as *he* has interpreted it.

19 For an overview of Schmitt's understanding of world history, see John P. McCormick, "Introduction to Schmitt's 'The Age of Neutralizations and Depoliticizations," *Telos* 96 (1993): 119. This topic is handled more extensively in G. L. Ulmen, *Politische Mehrwert: Eine Studie über Max Weber und Carl Schmitt* (Weinheim: VCH Acta humaniora, 1991).

20 I have stressed the need to properly contextualize Schmitt's works, because Schmitt tailors his approach to respond to particular problems. This is not to say that one cannot read Schmitt's works in reference to one another, only that one must remain aware of the important differences between them. With this in mind, I suggest Schmitt's underappreciated essay, *Hugo Preuss: Sein Staatsbegriff und seine Stellung in der deutschen Staatslehre* (Tübingen: J. C. B. Mohr [Paul Siebeck], 1930) as a companion volume to *Verfassungslehre*. For reading the two essays together shows that *Verfassungslehre* is an attempt to reconstitute the unified science of the state on different grounds than the nineteenth-century version. For an excellent overview of traditional German state theory, see Rupert Emerson, *State and Sovereignty in Modern Germany* (New Haven, Conn.: Yale University Press, 1928; Westport, Conn.: Hyperion Press, 1979), at 1–46.

21 Generations of scholars have devoted themselves to explaining Germany's belated transition to a full-fledged liberal democracy. See, for example, Thorstein Veblen, *Imperial Germany and the Industrial Revolution* (New Brunswick, N.J.: Transaction Publishers, 1966); Helmut Plessner, *Die verspätete Nation: Über die politische Verführbarkeit bürgerlichen Geistes* (Stuttgart: Kohlhammer, 1974); Friedrich Meinecke, *The German Catastrophe: Reflections and Recollections* (Boston: Beacon Press, 1950); Leonard Krieger, *The German Idea of Freedom: History of a Political Tradition* (Boston: Beacon Press, 1957); Ralf Dahrendorf, *Society and Democracy in Germany* (Garden City, N.Y.: Doubleday & Company; Anchor Books, 1968); and David Blackbourn and Geoff Eley, *The Peculiarities of German History: Bourgeois Society and Politics in Nineteenth-Century Germany* (Oxford: Oxford University Press, 1984).

Schmitt's emphasis on the peculiarities of German federalism and Bismarck's brilliant political leadership echoes Weber's famous argument to this effect. See esp. "Parliament and Government in a Reconstructed Germany: A Contribution to the Political Critique of Officialdom and Party Politics," in Guenther Roth and Claus Wittich, eds., *Economy and Society: An Outline of Interpretive Sociology* (Berkeley: University of California Press, 1978).

Unless otherwise indicated, my analysis in this section draws from Schmitt's treatment of parliament (*Verfassungslehre*, supra n. 2, at 303–59), particularly his discussion of constitutionalism in the Reich (*Verfassungslehre*, at 330–38).

22 The best work on the Prussian reform movement, particularly the relation of political and legal reform, remains Reinhart Koselleck, *Preussen zwischen Reform und Revolution: Allgemeines Landrecht, Verwaltung und soziale Bewegung von 1791 bis 1848*. 3d ed. (Munich: Deutscher Taschenbuch Verlag, 1989).

23 For a thorough analysis of the tumultuous events surrounding the "imposed" Prussian Constitution of 1850 and the legal and political changes it effected, see Ernst Rudolf Huber, *Deutsche Verfassungsgeschichte seit 1789*, vol. 3 (Stuttgart: Verlag W. Kohlhammer, 1960), at 35–128. An overview is offered in Dieter Grimm, *Deutsche Verfassungsgeschichte, 1776-1866: Vom Beginn des modernen Verfassungsstaats bis zur Auflösung des Deutschen Bundes* (Frankfurt am Main: Suhrkamp Verlag, 1988), at 175–217.

24 Blackbourn and Eley, supra n. 21, provide an excellent treatment of the failed "bourgeois revolution" during the Reich period. Though they underestimate the significance for German political development of the failure to institute full political reform in the nineteenth century, they are right that legal reform at the Reich level provided liberals with many of their demands. Also, many of the individual Länder constitutions protected an extensive array of civil liberties, compensating somewhat for the absence of constitutional rights under the Reich Constitution. See Gertrude Luebbe-Wolff, "Safeguards of Civil and Constitutional Rights—The Debate on the Role of the Reichsgericht," in Hermann Wellenreuther, ed., *German and American Constitutional Thought: Contexts, Interaction, and Historical Realities* (New York: St. Martin's Press, 1990).

25 This is clear, for example, in Savigny's understanding of the role of the legal profession in German politics. See Carl Friedrich Savigny, *Of the Vocation of Our Age for Legislation and Jurisprudence* (London: Littlewood, 1975), where he praises Roman jurists for cultivating a system of customary law with the necessary scope and elasticity for a complex, rapidly changing society. For an excellent discussion of the importance for nineteenth-century German politics of the efforts of Savigny and his followers to promote the Roman Law, see James Q. Whitman, *The Legacy of Roman Law in the German Romantic Era* (Princeton: Princeton University Press, 1990).

26 On the complicated politics surrounding the drafting and promulgation of the Civil Code, see Michael John, *Politics and the Law in Late Nineteenth-*

Century Germany: The Origins of the Civil Code (Oxford: Oxford University Press, 1989).

27 Walter Ott, *Der Rechtspositivismus. Kritische Würdigung auf der Grundlage eines juristischen Pragmatismus*, 2d ed. (Berlin: Duncker & Humblot, 1992), at 32–116, offers a good overview of the diverse strains of legal positivism in Germany. On the basic issues and positions in the debate over legal positivism in the Weimar Republic, see Helga Wendenburg, *Die Debatte um die Verfassungsgerichtsbarkeit und der Methodenstreit der Staatsrechtslehre in der Weimarer Republik* (Göttingen: Verlag Otto Schwartz, 1984).

Legal positivism is the dead horse of German legal theory. For useful correctives, see Ingeborg Maus, *Rechtstheorie und politische Theorie im Industriekapitalismus* (Munich: Wilhelm Fink Verlag, 1986), at 205–26; Peter Caldwell, "Legal Positivism and Weimar Democracy," *American Journal of Jurisprudence* 39 (1994): 273; and Horst Dreier, *Rechtslehre, Staatssoziologie und Demokratietheorie bei Hans Kelsen* (Baden-Baden: Nomos Verlag, 1990). Maus offers a nuanced understanding of legal positivism, Caldwell disputes the oft-repeated charge that legal positivism is politically naive, and Dreier supplies an impressive reinterpretation of the unfairly maligned Hans Kelsen.

28 For an overview of the complex constitutional structure of the Reich, see Gordon A. Craig, *Germany, 1866–1945* (Oxford: Oxford University Press, 1978), at 38–60.

29 *Verfassungslehre*, supra n. 2, at ix.

30 This view is presented throughout Schmitt's works from this period. Drawing on Schmitt's contemporary Richard Thoma, Caldwell, "Legal Positivism and Weimar Democracy," supra n. 27, at 297–98, rightly points out that "Schmitt's invocations of a tyrannical two-thirds majority . . . were absurd in a period when a simple majority in the Reichstag was almost impossible to reach."

31 *Verfassungslehre*, supra n. 2, at 28–36.

32 Preuss also sought to build and maintain bridges between warring social factions. Though his preference was for a Western-style parliamentary democracy, Preuss was favorably impressed by the fact that at the "decisive moment" the Social Democrats opted for "political democracy" rather than "dictatorship." This bodes well for the future, according to Preuss, as it indicates that the bourgeoisie and the socialists can work together. But it should not lead one to believe that the class struggle is over, nor that there are not real differences between the classes. Formal equality alone is not enough, in his view. The new Republic, rather, must infuse formal legal equality with the "social spirit." See Hugo Preuss, *Staat, Recht und Freiheit: aus 40 Jahren deutscher Politik und Geschichte* (Hildesheim: Georg Olms Verlagsbuchhandlung, 1964), at 421–28, esp. at 428.

Despite his stature as a legal theorist in the Reich period and his important role in the early part of the Weimar Republic, Preuss has not received much scholarly attention. On Preuss's political theory, see Detlef Lehnert, "Hugo Preuss als moderner Klassiker einer kritischen Theorie der 'verfassten' Politik. Vom Souveränitätsproblem zum demokratischen Pluralismus," *Politische Vierteljahresschrift* 33 (1992): 33.

33 On Naumann's role in the early Republic, particularly his position on the Basic Rights, see Peter Theiner, *Sozialer Liberalismus und deutsche Weltpolitik: Friedrich Naumann im Wilhelmischen Deutschland (1860-1919)* (Baden-Baden: Nomos Verlag, 1983), at 283-304, esp. at 292-94.

34 The economic and social rights lent constitutional status to the extensive social legislation of the Reich. In practical terms, therefore, the inclusion of these rights represented mostly an only symbolic change from the previous era, though not an altogether insignificant one. On the Basic Rights in the politics of the era, see Detlev Peukert, *Die Weimarer Republik: Krisenjahre der klassischen Moderne* (Frankfurt am Main: Suhrkamp Verlag, 1987), at 137-47.

35 *Verfassungslehre*, supra n. 2, at 157-82, esp. at 181-82.

36 Of course, class conflict was a major factor in the unstable politics of the era, but it is difficult to say whether the Basic Rights provisions further exacerbated already tense social relations. For example, civil servants insisted their salaries not be curbed and unions objected to increases in unemployment contributions for workers. These disputes contributed to the governability problems of the Republic. But both of these groups no doubt would have agitated for their cause even absent constitutional provisions supporting their claims. On social conflict in the Weimar Republic with a view to the Basic Rights, see Peukert, *Die Weimarer Republik*, supra n. 34, at 132-47.

37 See *Verfassungslehre*, supra n. 2, at 20-36, esp. at 24-25. Schmitt's aim in removing issues from political contestation in the usual way was not the liberal one of moderating political conflict for the sake of the democratic process generally. It was, rather, to enhance central state power. For an excellent analysis of the liberal insight regarding the removal of contentious issues from everyday political struggle, see Holmes, *Passions and Constraint*, supra n. 13, at 202-35.

38 Quoted in *Verfassungslehre*, supra n. 2, at 332.

39 Though the civil service was a traditional preserve of the bourgeoisie and was an important component of the independent state Schmitt envisioned, Schmitt rejected the claim based on Article 129 that the salaries of civil servants could not be reduced. Besides noting that this provision was meant to ensure merely the retention of then serving civil servants at the inception of the Weimar Republic, Schmitt points out how such a subjective right contributes to the worsening financial condition of the Republic. See *Verfassungsrechtliche Aufsätze aus den Jahren 1924-1954: Materialien zu einer Verfassungslehre*, 3d ed. (Berlin: Duncker & Humblot, 1958), at 174-79.

40 *Verfassungslehre*, supra n. 2, at 99–112. Schmitt's insistence on the primacy of the constitution as a whole over its particular parts was quite novel at the time. "In Schmitt's *Verfassungslehre*," according to a recent French commentator, "one finds for the first time a systematization of this thesis of a substantive limitation on the power of amendment." See Olivier Beaud, *La Puissance de l'État* (Paris: Presses Universitaires de France, 1994), at 340.

I examine the problems in state structure which induce Schmitt to embrace the concept of superconstitutionality, and I show how Schmitt elaborates his "systematization" through a comparative history of constitution-making. A more complete study would examine in full Schmitt's relation to French constitutional theory in the Third Republic, particularly to that of Maurice Hauriou.

41 The classic statement of this tendency is Robert V. Mohl, *Staatsrecht, Völkerrecht und Politik*, vol. 1 (Berlin: Tübingen, 1860), at 96–143. An excellent contemporary treatment in reference to constitutional law is Konrad Hesse, *Grundzüge des Verfassungsrechts der Bundesrepublik Deutschland*, 18th ed. (Heidelberg: C. F. Müller Juristischer Verlag, 1991), at 19–32.

42 For an excellent overview of legal theory in the Reich period, see Emerson, *State and Sovereignty in Modern Germany*, supra n. 20, at 47–91.

43 A useful introduction in English to Savigny's view of history and of the state is the famous lecture *Of the Vocation of our Age*. For an introduction to his method, see *Anleitung zu einem eigenen Studium der Jurisprudenz* (Stuttgart: K. F. Koehler Verlag, 1951). Regarding Savigny's "idealism," see Joachim Rückert, *Idealismus, Jurisprudenz und Politik bei Friedrich Carl von Savigny* (Ebelsbach: Verlag Rolf Gremer, 1984). For an interesting discussion of theoretical problems with the Historical School approach, see Ernst-Wolfgang Böckenförde, "Die Historische Rechtsschule und das Problem der Geschichtlichkeit des Rechts," in *Staat, Gesellschaft, Freiheit: Studien zur Staatstheorie und zum Verfassungsrecht* (Frankfurt am Main: Suhrkamp Taschenbuch Verlag, 1976), at 9–41.

Savigny does not come on Schmitt's radar screen until late in World War Two (1943–44). Ulmen, *Politische Mehrwert*, supra n. 19, at 74–86, provides a thorough discussion of Schmitt's treatment of Savigny.

44 In an appendix to his book on dictatorship, for example, Schmitt draws on the intent of the framers to resolve a tension between the first and second clauses of the Weimar Constitution's infamous Article 48. Schmitt stresses, however, that the intent of the framers has no independent normative validity—the drafting history is not examined for its own sake, in other words. Rather, it "demonstrates the dominant sentiment of the Weimar national convention that Germany is in an abnormal situation." See *Die Diktatur: Von den Anfängen des modernen Souveränitätsgedankens bis zum proletarischen Klassenkampf*, 5th ed. (Berlin: Duncker & Humblot, 1989), at 233

(hereafter *Diktatur*). It is this "general awareness" which provides the "rationale" for the clauses in question.

45 Carl J. Friedrich provides a useful comparison of Hegel and the Historical Law School on this point. See *The Philosophy of Law in Historical Perspective* (Chicago: The University of Chicago Press, 1963), at 131–42.

46 See, for example, Schmitt's view of the implications of the radical contingency of norms for existing understandings of constitutions in *Verfassungslehre*, supra n. 2, at 44–91, esp. at 87–91.

47 Kelsen's understanding of democracy, for example, is premised on this recognition. See esp. *Vom Wesen und Wert der Demokratie*, 2d ed. (Aalen: Scienta Verlag, 1981).

Though Schmitt expressed disdain for Kelsen, there are important parallels between his theory of decisionism and Kelsen's value relativism, as many commentators have pointed out. For a recent reworking of this claim in reference to Schmitt's critique of liberal constitutionalism, see William Scheuerman, "Carl Schmitt's Critique of Liberal Constitutionalism," *Review of Politics* 58 (1996): 299.

Kelsen is arguably the most misunderstood legal theorist of the twentieth century. Kelsen's relativism was far from naive about the nature of power. The Pure Theory of Law seeks the depoliticization of legal scholarship, but not of law, which Kelsen considers inseparable from politics. And his emphasis on formalism seeks to derail the tendency to use legal scholarship for ideological purposes.

For an excellent example of Kelsen's efforts to hinder the politicization of legal scholarship, see his dismantling of Rudolf Smend's theory of integration: *Der Staat als Integration: Eine Prinzipielle Auseinandersetzung* (Vienna: Verlag von Julius Springer, 1930). A good introduction to Kelsen's view of the relation of law and politics is "Was ist die Reine Rechtslehre?" in Hans Klecatsky, René Marcic, and Herbert Schambeck, eds. *Die Wiener Rechtstheoretische Schule: Schriften von Hans Kelsen, Adolf Merkl, Alfred Verdross* (Vienna: Europa Verlag, 1968).

48 Bruce Ackerman's understanding of dualist democracy is structurally quite similar to Schmitt's decisionism both in terms of their respective views of a sovereign people asserting its will in founding moments as well as in their insistence on a qualitative distinction between the founding moment and ordinary politics. An important difference between them is that Schmitt, but not Ackerman, accepts the concept of an unconstitutional constitutional amendment. See *We the People: Foundations* (Cambridge, Mass.: Harvard University Press, 1991), at 3–33 for Ackerman's elaboration of dualist democracy.

49 The peculiar abstractness of Schmitt's understanding of founding moments is illustrated by his claim that there is an underlying continuity between

Bismarck's Reich and the Weimar Republic. In 1870 the Germans obviously attained a "national" identity, according to Schmitt. Less obviously, he argues, they recognized but did not act on the democratic principle. They established the Reichstag, for example, as a limited means of expressing the democratic will of the people, but they still adhered to the monarchical principle in regard to constitutionmaking. With the discrediting of the monarchical principle, the Germans adopted the democratic principle to its fullest extent, that is, in regard to constitutionmaking as well. On the surface, this is a fundamental change, Schmitt argues, but it obscures the fact that the Germans merely sought to "renew" not eliminate the "Reich" (*Verfassungslehre*, supra n. 2, at 46–60).

Schmitt is referring here to the Republic's official title "the German Reich." According to the principal drafter of the Weimar Constitution, Hugo Preuss, the retention of the designation German Reich aimed merely at placating potential rightist opponents and signified nothing in regard to the source of governmental authority or its particular form. See Hugo Preuss, *Staat, Recht, Freiheit*, supra n. 32.

50 *Verfassungslehre*, supra n. 2, at xi.

51 Ibid., at 38–40.

52 Ibid., at 36–38.

53 Ibid., at 49–51.

54 Ibid., at 23–25.

55 *Verfassungslehre* revolves around Schmitt's distinction between the political and *rechtsstaatliche* components of the constitution; see, for example, ibid., at 40–41. This is because this distinction permits Schmitt to subordinate the ordinary political process to energetic presidential government. Schmitt's theory of constitutionmaking as decision provides the theoretical foundation for this distinction, and Schmitt develops this theory through a comparative history of constitutionmaking, so it is necessary to examine this feature of his argument, if one is to fully understand *Verfassungslehre*.

Most treatments of Schmitt, however, do this to only a very limited degree. Scheuerman rightly stresses, for example, the importance of Schmitt's reinterpretation of Sieyès, but he wrongly argues that according to Schmitt "liberal democratic jurisprudence *implicitly* recognizes the existence of an omnipotent, inalienable, and indivisible founding subject, the *pouvoir constituant.*" See Scheuerman, "Carl Schmitt's Critique of Liberal Constitutionalism," supra n. 47, at 309. Reading Schmitt's reinterpretation of Sieyès in reference to Western constitutional history, rather than focusing narrowly on Schmitt's treatment of early modern liberal theory and the legal positivism of Hans Kelsen, as does Scheuerman, demonstrates that for Schmitt this recognition is not "implicit." In Schmitt's account, rather, a peculiar strand of Sieyès's thought comes to define liberal constitutionmaking.

56 *Verfassungslehre*, supra n. 2, at 46–47.

57 Ibid., at 76–80, esp. at 78.

58 Ibid.

59 For an excellent brief comparison of the American and Continental understandings of the state and an analysis of the implications of these understandings for constitutionalism in the United States and Europe, see Gerhard Casper, "Changing Concepts of Constitutionalism: 18th to 20th Century," 1989 *Supreme Court Review*, 311.

60 *Verfassungslehre*, supra n. 2, at xi.

61 On the American influence on German constitutional development, see Helmut Steinberger, *200 Jahre amerikanische Bundesverfassung: Zu Einflüssen des amerikanischen Verfassungsrechts auf die deutsche Verfassungsentwicklung* (Berlin: Walter de Gruyter, 1987).

62 John Henry Merryman, *The Civil Law Tradition: An Introduction to the Legal Systems of Western Europe and Latin America* (Stanford, Calif.: Stanford University Press, 1985) provides a concise introduction to the civil law tradition and how it differs from its common-law counterpart.

63 For an overview of the complex strands in the French constitutional tradition, see Alec Stone, *The Birth of Judicial Politics in France: The Constitutional Council in Comparative Perspective* (New York: Oxford University Press, 1992), at 23–45.

64 *Political Theology*, supra n. 12, at 15.

65 Kenneth Baker provides an excellent discussion of Sieyès's role in the French Revolution. See "Sieyès," in François Furet and Mona Ozouf, eds., *A Critical Dictionary of the French Revolution* (Cambridge, Mass.: Harvard University Press, 1989), at 313–23.

Stefan Breuer also examines Schmitt's appropriation of Sieyès. We agree that Schmitt radicalizes Sieyès's understanding of constituent power by failing to properly contextualize Sieyès's writings and political activity. But whereas Breuer's treatment focuses on social relations, my analysis stresses the immediate political context and Sieyès's place in the French constitutional tradition. See "Nationalstaat und pouvoir constituant bei Sieyès und Carl Schmitt," *Archiv für Rechts- und Sozialphilosophie* 70 (1984): 495.

66 Article 2 reads: "The aim of every political association is the preservation of the natural and imprescriptible rights of man. These rights are liberty, property, security, and resistance to oppression." Article 16 reads: "A society in which the guarantee of rights is not secured, or the separation of powers not clearly established, has no constitution." See "The Declaration of the Rights of Man and of the Citizen," in Kenneth Baker, ed., *The Old Regime and the French Revolution* (Chicago: University of Chicago Press, 1987), at 237–39.

Schmitt recognizes the importance of the concept of normative constitution for the French and American efforts at constitutionmaking (*Verfassungslehre*, supra n. 2, at 38–39), but he sees the concept of a normative constitution as merely another in a number of attempts to portray political aims as constitutionalism per se. Nonetheless, he believes that these revolutions reveal the nature of the constitutionmaking power, though in different ways.

The normative understanding of a constitution associated with the American and French Revolutions differs from the understanding of a constitution as "a unified, closed system of the highest and most fundamental norms" Schmitt attributes to early liberals and Hans Kelsen. For Schmitt's treatment of the latter, see *Verfassungslehre*, at 7–9.

67 See, for example, Jörg-Detlef Kühne, "Die französische Menschen- und Bürgerrechtserklärung im Rechtsvergleich mit den Vereinigten Staaten und Deutschland," *Jahrbuch des Öffentlichen Rechts der Gegenwart* 39 (1990): 1; and Loïc Philip, "La protection des droits fondamentaux en France," *Jahrbuch des Öffentlichen Rechts der Gegenwart* 38 (1989): 116.

68 On this crucial period in French constitutional history, see François Geny, *Science et Technique en droit privé positif, Seconde Partie: Elaboration Scientifique du Droit Positif (L'irreductible "droit naturel")* (Paris: Societe anonyme du Recueil Sirey, 1927), esp. sections 130–32.

Schmitt's great French contemporary Leon Duguit provides an especially interesting contrast in this regard. Schmitt's reading of the French understanding of the nation and its importance for constitutionmaking echoes Duguit's in important respects. Moreover, both Schmitt and Duguit stress the need to break from outdated concepts. Interestingly, though, Schmitt applies the concepts of the nation and a radical break with the past to problems in the interwar period, whereas Duguit argues for an alternate understanding of the state centering on the notion of "public service." See Leon Duguit, *Law in the Modern State* (New York: B.W. Huebsch, 1919), esp. at 1–66.

69 This concern was reflected in the debate in France over the appropriateness of American-style judicial review early in this century. See esp. Raymond Carré de Malberg, *La Loi, expression de la volonté générale* (Paris: Economica, 1984); and Eduoard Lambert, *Le gouvernement des juges et la lutte contre la législation sociale aux États-Unis: L'expérience américaine du controle judiciare de la constitutionalité des lois* (Paris: Marcel Giard, 1921). On the importance of this controversy for French constitutionalism generally, see Stone, *The Birth of Judicial Politics in France*, supra n. 63, at 33–40.

70 For a particularly eloquent statement of the need for vigilance on this score, see David Tracy, *Plurality and Ambiguity: Hermeneutics, Religion, Hope* (Chicago: University of Chicago Press, 1994).

71 The classic treatment of this issue remains Hannah Arendt, *On Revolution* (London: Penguin Books, 1973).

For a thoughtful recent treatment on the novel challenge to liberal constitutionmaking stemming from an understandable concern with social justice, see Ulrich K. Preuss, "Patterns of Constitutional Evolution and Change in Eastern Europe," in Joachim Jens Hesse and Nevil Johnson, eds., *Constitutional Policy and Change in Europe* (Oxford: Oxford University

Press, 1995). Preuss's treatment is also noteworthy for his interesting argument regarding the implications of particular understandings of constituent power for the structure of government.

72 In this regard, Ackerman and Schmitt arrive at a common destination via different routes. By refusing to read the American constitutional tradition through the distorting lens of dangerous foreign theorists, such as Locke, Hume, and Kant, Ackerman gives pride of place to what he considers the most distinctive American contribution to political theory, more specifically, Ackerman's rather Schmittian notion of Dualist Democracy. See Ackerman, *We the People*, supra n. 48, at 3.

Notes on Contributors

Heiner Bielefeldt (Diploma in Theology, Tübingen; Dr. Phil., Tübingen, 1990) is a research fellow in the Centre for Interdisciplinary Research into Multi-Ethnic Conflicts in the University of Bielefeld. He is the author of *Neuzeitliches Freiheitsrecht und politische Gerechtigkeit.*

Ronald Beiner is Professor of Political Science at the University of Toronto. His recent books include *What's the Matter with Liberalism?* (1992) and *Philosophy in a Time of Lost Spirit: Essays on Contemporary Theory* (1997). He has also edited *Theorizing Citizenship* (1995) and *Theorizing Nationalism* (forthcoming).

Ernst-Wolfgang Böckenförde (Dr. Iur., Dr. Phil., Dr. Iur. H.C., Basel, 1987) is Professor Emeritus of public law, constitutional history, and legal theory at the University of Freiburg (Germany). From 1983 until 1996 he was a judge of the Federal Constitutional Court in Germany. He is the author of several books.

David Dyzenhaus (B.A., LL.B., Witwatersrand; D.Phil., Oxford, 1988) is Professor of Law and Philosophy at the University of Toronto. He is the author of *Hard Cases in Wicked Legal Systems* and *Legality and Legitimacy: Carl Schmitt, Hans Kelsen, and Hermann Heller in Weimar.*

Robert Howse (B.A., LL.B., Toronto; LL.M., Harvard, 1990) is Associate Professor of Law and Associate Director, Centre for the Study of State and Market, University of Toronto. He has translated and provided a commentary of Alexandre Kojeve's *Esquisse d'une phenomenologie due droit* (coauthored with Bryan-Paul Frost; 1998).

Ellen Kennedy (B.A., Trinity College; Ph.D., London School of Economics, 1977) is Associate Professor of Political Science at the University of Pennsylvania. She is the translator of Carl Schmitt's *The Crisis of Parliamentary Democracy.*

Dominique Leydet (B.A., McGill; M.A., Paris IV; Doctorat, École des Hautes Études en Sciences Sociales, 1990) is Associate Professor of Philosophy at Université du Québec à Montréal.

314 *Contributors*

John P. McCormick (B.A., Queens College, CUNY; M.A., Ph.D., Chicago, 1995) is Assistant Professor of Political Science at Yale University. He is the author of *Carl Schmitt's Critique of Liberalism: Against Politics as Technology* (1997).

Ingeborg Maus (Dr. Phil., Frankfurt am Main; habilitation Frankfurt am Main, 1980) is Professor of Political Science and Political Philosophy at the University of Frankfurt am Main. Her third book, *Zur Aufklärung der Demokratietheorie, Rechts- und demokratietheoretische Überlegungen im Anschluss an Kant,* was published in 1992.

Reinhard Mehring (M.A., Dr. Phil., Freiburg, 1988) holds a research position in the Institute for Philosophy at the Humboldt University (Berlin). He is the author of *Heideggers Überlieferungsgeschick, Carl Schmitt zur Einführung.*

Chantal Mouffe (Licence en Philosophie, Louvain; M.A. Essex, 1974) is Senior Research Fellow at the Centre for the Study of Democracy at the University of Westminster in London. She is coauthor with Ernesto Laclau of *Hegemony and Socialist Strategy. Towards a Radical Democratic Politics* and the author of *The Return of the Political.*

William E. Scheuerman (B.A., Yale; Ph.D., Harvard, 1993) is Assistant Professor of Political Science at the University of Pittsburgh. He is the author of *Between the Norm and the Exception: The Frankfurt School and the Rule of Law,* and editor of *The Rule of Law Under Siege.*

Jeffrey Seitzer (B.A., M.A., Nebraska-Lincoln; Ph.D., Chicago, 1993) is Visiting Assistant Professor of Political Science at Indiana University Northwest. He is the author of *Constitutional Democracy and the State: An Institutional Approach to Comparative Constitutionalism* (forthcoming).

Index

Library of Congress

Cataloging-in-Publication Data

Law as politics : Carl Schmitt's critique
of liberalism / edited by David
Dyzenhaus ; foreword by Ronald Beiner.

p.   cm.

Articles previously published in the
Canadian journal of law and
jurisprudence.   Includes index.

ISBN 0-8223-2227-7 (cloth : alk. paper).
— ISBN 0-8223-2244-7 (pbk. : alk. paper)

1. Schmitt, Carl, 1888–

2. Liberalism.   I. Dyzenhaus, David.

JC263.S34L38   1998

320'.092—dc21   98-13618   CIP